Muah!

The Sound of a Kiss Goodbye

The Final Writings of Sheryll O'Brien

Book One

November 2021 – May 2022

This is my story; pieces of my life, and my final journey. Every word, thought, or emotion came from my heart unless otherwise credited.

ISBN 978-1-939351-49-4

Sheryll O'Brien

About the Woman … I like things a certain way. I function well when I travel between a sturdy set of guardrails. That in no way should imply that I don't bang against the rails from time to time and it certainly doesn't mean that I haven't veered onto 'roads less traveled'. It simply means that I like being on a charted course for the long haul — but I truly love the unexpected exit ramps, the ones that deposit you on dimly lit, bumpy roads of uncertainty.

The Charted Course … I'm a child of the '50s. I was raised to accept and appreciate things that I'd been given. I wasn't raised to imagine things I could achieve. That's perfectly okay because every wonderful thing in my life came out of thin air. There was no charted course for my employment years other than to put myself in the position to grow, to recognize opportunity, and to do the 'ask' even though rejection was the likely outcome. There was no stated plan for marriage and children other than I was open to the wonders of both. There was no Sheryll O'Brien Road Atlas because I had no idea where I was headed. I only knew I'd been set on a road with endless miles of broken white lines between a set of guardrails — ones that had been erected around me.

The Chosen Course … The life I've lived with my husband, Tim, and our daughters, Hannah and Jessica, is testament that coming back from the 'road less traveled' and claiming safety between guardrails can be a very good thing. I willingly, happily, lovingly traveled a most wonderful road with my family. That's not to say it was without twists and turns, and potholes and detours, and reasons to pull off to the side for aid and assessment. It simply means that we took our seats, planned our course, buckled up, and enjoyed the ride.

The Charitable Course ... The life I lived as a storyteller needed a bit of charity, sacrifice by those who love me. Having lived within the guardrails for sixty years, I knew I needed to veer off course — way off course. I needed to travel along dimly lit, bumpy roads of uncertainty and I needed to do it with my family along for the ride — my ride. I readily admit that I could not have pushed-in on my lifelong dream of putting 'pen to paper' without family and friends who offered encouragement, when a raised-hairy-brow-of-judgment was the easier call.

The Chastened Course ... The road I travel now allows no choice, no real companionship, no chance of veering off course. It is a long and arduous journey between rigidly set guardrails. The restraints of this course have inflicted suffering but, more to the point, it has allowed me the opportunity to accept the journey and be open to what awaits me on the ultimate 'road less traveled'.

A note from my publisher ...

Sheryll. My dear friend Sheryll.

In some ways it seems like yesterday when I got a call from your editor, my friend Andria, asking me if I was interested in working with a new author she had as a client. She said you were one of her favorite clients, and a very talented writer, so how could I not be interested. Within just a few days of that call, you and I chatted for the first time and I was certain I'd made the right decision.

I started on the first book, and was instantly drawn to your writing style. As time went on and we started pushing through book after book, and communicating more and more, we both relaxed and went from a professional relationship to a newly forming friendship.

It now seems like we've known each other forever. We have so many things in common, including our personalities! I recently saw a small sign that I thought was perfect for us; Sassy, Classy, and a little bit Smart-Assy! We have our spiritual side, and we have our sassy side. We can be content with a silent sharing of space with those we care about, or we can love being surrounded by a constant buzz of chatter, laughter, and fun.

Although we have never shared space, we have spent the last couple of years communicating almost daily about one thing or another. During that time our friendship has grown and has become a truly treasured thing. I want the world to know you as I do, and I hope this book can help make that happen.

It doesn't matter that we've never met, my life has been immeasurably enriched having you as a part of it. And I will love you always, my friend!

Love and hugs,
Nancy Pendleton

Dear Reader …

The decision to journal about the days between my diagnosis and death was more akin to an internal demand. Out of the blue, I found myself with a finite amount of time that needed to be filled, and an infinite number of feelings that needed a place to land. I began writing my blog in November, 2021. It took on the form of the many journals I wrote throughout my life — a rambling of thoughts — a pouring out of memories and musings.

Muah! The Sound of a Kiss Goodbye is my story; but it is so much more than that. These pages hold wonderful and wacky childhood memories, and tidbits that turned into treasured traditions, and tales that remind me of the full, rich life I've lived — one that is ending far too soon for my liking — one that I am honored to share with you.

~ Sheryll

1. Just Keep Dancing ...

I've had my pushes against death and dying; a cervical fracture (in my twenties), a major surgery when I was six months pregnant (in my thirties), a daylong surgery to remove an acoustic neuroma that buddied up to my brainstem (in my forties), and a bout of breast cancer (in my fifties). My battle with the head tumor was big, scary, and left me with life-changing things to deal with, hearing loss in my left ear, some facial paralysis, never-ending vertigo, and a sense of vulnerability to which I was very unaccustomed. My skirmish with cancer, however, was short and to the point. I had a tumor removed, had the sentinel nodes checked, did the radiation, and the oral chemo/hormonal drug for five years. And then in October, 2017, I was sent on my way to imagine the worst was behind me. I really haven't thought much about breast cancer and never really considered myself a survivor, maybe because I never really thought I was going to succumb to the disease in the first place. Sure, I was scared when I received the initial diagnosis, and before surgery, and during the first radiation treatment, and during the hospitalization for cellulitis and radiation burns, but I never really had that pit in my stomach, I never thought I wouldn't survive the experience.

I think part of the reason was because the professionals who deal with breast cancer know their shit. They know it because there are so many women, too many women, who get the diagnosis and need to get on with it. I remember remarking to my husband, Tim, the man I tongue-in-cheek refer to as Mr. Wonderful, that I got the diagnosis and was immediately put onto the breast cancer conveyor belt: *"We'll do an ultrasound, and a needle biopsy, then there will be surgery, and radiation, and perhaps chemotherapy — all you need to do is show up."* Perhaps that efficiency, coupled with my showing up for the breast cancer two-step and being sent off with the welcomed pronouncement, *"That's it. You're five years out. You are a survivor, so off you go, now,"* were at the core of my belief that the worst was behind me. Those words lulled me into a state of stupid. Well, that state of ignorance was bliss and it is now over. I now know breast cancer is forever. I now know the crappy cells of this insidious disease are stealth muthafuckers. When you least expect it, they will drag your ass into another dance through Hell.

Sadly, my dance card has been filled with a partner, metastatic breast cancer of the bones. I do not want to go for another dance with this disease. Sadly, it doesn't matter what I want. What does matter is this disease has claimed me as its partner by taking residence in my bones. Lots of bones. Important bones: my skull, my cervical, thoracic, and lumbar spine, and in my pelvis, and in my hips, and in my femurs, and in my knees, and for shits and giggles it's in a few of my ribs.

As I write this, I do not know if my organs are already part of my new cancer dance. While I wait to see what two-step I'm doing, I'll hang out with family and friends, and then I will reluctantly move across the dance floor. God, I hope the dance of choice is a soft, slow waltz.

2. *It Doesn't Matter ...*

> *Cancer doesn't matter.*
> *It is the final chapter of my life,*
> *but it is not the important part of my story.*
>
> *~ Sheryll O'Brien*

I woke this morning replaying the words I heard yesterday, *"You have incurable metastatic breast cancer."* Really hard words to hear, nearly impossible to process. I have decided the diagnosis doesn't matter because it is a beautiful crisp fall day with red, orange, and yellow leaves in all their autumnal glory — of course the beauties are all over my yard and driveway, but that is Tim's issue to deal with.

It doesn't matter ... because I spent time with Mr. Wonderful having our morning coffee, sipping in silence, each thinking about the things going on in our lives, but not wanting to spoil the moments we love so much with the clang of cancer talk.

It doesn't matter ... because my darling granddaughter knocked on our front door ready for breakfast at MammyGram's and Gee's house, oblivious to the hard news that she will soon hear.

It doesn't matter ... because I had a really good night's sleep, the first in weeks — of course it was delivered courtesy of a pain pill and a Xanax, but whatever.

It doesn't matter ... because I have wonderful family and friends who have been reaching out with love and support and sending hugs from afar.

It doesn't matter ... because I have the most wonderful primary care physician who is a skilled clinician, but more importantly a kind, decent man who

I know has lost sleep over my condition and will bravely and compassionately walk the last steps of my life with me — allowing me to lean against him when the path gets rough.

It doesn't matter … because I have two sisters-in-law, Kathy and Eileen, who share their medical knowledge with me with kindness and with complete honesty and who tell me often that they love me, and I know they do.

It doesn't matter … because my best friend, Donna Eaton, is up day and night and at the ready for any call that I need to make, and I make them.

It doesn't matter … because my mother, Shirley, my brother, Donnie, and my sister, Marjorie, the people who have been with me on every step of my life's journey, are still walking with me, slump-shouldered with the weight of sadness, but they trudge along.

It doesn't matter … because our little family tribe has grown with welcome additions, a wonderful sister-in-law and adorable babies for my niece and her tree-climbing, worthy man.

It doesn't matter … because Tim's family, all 973 of them (just kidding) are thinking of me and praying with me — of course they are doing it at Breens lifting a pint, as it should be.

It doesn't matter … because my husband, Tim, and daughters, Hannah and Jessica, are holding me up when I need it, hugging me tighter because I need it, and comforting me with the knowledge that I will live on in their thoughts and hearts.

I have decided that cancer doesn't matter. It is the final part of my story, but it is so not among the important parts of my story. Those are about the love I gave and received every day, and will continue to share when I'm gone. So, my hope now is to greet every day with the same joy I felt this morning when I woke. And end each day with appreciation that I lived to see it.

3. Being Angry at God ...

Someone asked me if I am mad at God. To be perfectly honest, the question caught me off guard. It never occurred to me that that was an option. For the record, I am not mad at God. I don't think He got up one day and said, *"Hmmmmm, I'm gonna screw with Sheryll O'Brien and I'm gonna screw with her big time."* Maybe it's because I don't think God is a punishing higher being.

I believe He ... is benevolent and isn't likely to want pain and suffering for His children.

I believe He ... the creator of the wonders of this universe, couldn't possibly be responsible for unleashing this cancer crap on me.

I believe He ... has way bigger and better things to be doing with His time.

I believe He ... gave His loved ones the splendor of nature in all its glory so we could enjoy it and He probably hopes to Hell we will protect it.

I believe He ... gave us the capacity to love one another and He's probably waiting for us to get our shit together and reach beyond ourselves with compassion for our neighbors, or the strangers who could be friends, if we allowed it.

I believe He ... knows I am facing challenges and I pray that He hears my request – that I am given no more than I can handle. If that ends up being a handful of months, or perhaps a year, then so be it.

I believe He ... supports my decision to not torture myself when I'm told there is no more hope.

I believe He … does not want me to suffer.

I guess what I'm saying is this, I will take the hand of God and trust that He will help me find my way through this mess, that He will hold me in His mercy because He accepts my faith in Him. And I believe my God is grateful that I chose to follow Him through my life and now toward my death. God is good. God is great. And I love Him.

4. Maybe It's Just Me …

Like everyone who walks this earth, I have been on the receiving end of other people's bad news. Hearing about a friend's mom or dad who were doing the slow shuffle toward death, the adult child who lost their battle with addiction, the young mother who just got through the terrible twos with her babe and won't live to see the child's first day of kindergarten.

Tragic news hits me like a sucker punch; it knocks the breath free and when breathable air returns, I manage to say something. Hopefully, it is the right thing, the understanding thing, the supportive thing; and then I walk away because I can.

I always tell the suffering to, "Give me a call if you need anything, please … no really … anything … just ask." I mean those words, and hope I deliver them with sincerity, but I rarely get the call. In retrospect, I wish I'd made the calls, but I didn't. It wasn't because I didn't think and worry and feel sadness, it was because I didn't want to intrude. I didn't want to be a bother; I didn't want to remind them they were dealing with crap, if by chance they had managed to put the crap aside for a few minutes. Let's face it, there is no putting a bad diagnosis aside. It is in your face, night and day. I'm not advocating that people drag their asses through someone else's nightmare, but I am suggesting that a conversation about the little somethings in life can amount to big somethings to someone needing to put a pause on their shit fest.

If I am called to witness a painful journey, I am going to be fully present. I am going to make the calls to a family member or a friend who is facing a challenge. And if the person on the other end isn't interested in taking my call, then I am going to try again some other day. And when the day comes that I need to make a condolence call, I'll know the path will have been laid with heartfelt concern. I guess this is a call to my friends and family, please make the calls and tell me about the wonders of your life, and listen to the wonders of mine. Because they are still happening.

5. Mr. Wonderful ...

My husband, Tim, is a gentleman, in every sense of the word. Do not confuse his kind ways and soft heart with the idea that he is a weak man. Tim's strength is quiet and it is at the ready when it is needed most.

First, a little background on Mr. and Mrs. O'Brien. Tim and I first met in high school, though we never really traveled in the same group of friends. We got somewhat close during our senior year when he asked me, cajoled me, and ultimately convinced me to run for Senior Class Vice President. As soon as I said 'yes' he put me front and center and did all of the behind the scenes work to get me elected; he talked up my intelligence, and my popularity, and my school spirit – you know, the stuff that mattered in a candidate for such an esteemed position.

On the day of the candidates' speeches, I took to the stage wearing the shortest dress I had, and sporting waves in my long hair courtesy of a new-fangled thing called a curling iron, and batting eyelashes coated with a couple swipes of mascara. I used my feminine wiles to get the male vote which resulted in a landslide win. Go ahead and judge me. It was the '70s and I was straddling the line between feminism and hot-chick-ism. And on that day, I clearly succumbed to the power of curves in all the right places, and legs to die for.

Years later, at our ten-year reunion, I saw Tim for the first time since graduation. He was recently back from Texas and he was all Yee-Haw grown up and hot and sexy in his Wranglers and white button-down shirt with the sleeves cuffed back to his elbows, standing lean-to against a wall holding a beer. I was lassoed and we started a *thing* that night – a *fling*, most people figured. The assumption that our dalliance would be a hit and run experience was perfectly reasonable. Tim and I are polar opposites in so many little ways: I am bawdy and bold, he is somewhat reserved; I'm the talker, he uses words sparingly; I'm the yeller, he's the head-shaker; I'm the comedienne, he's my audience; I push in, he leans in; I'm the risk taker, he's the soft place to land.

And thank God he is … Mr. Wonderful helped me land safely after hearing the news. He stiffened his spine, wrapped his arm, and let me lean all-in. As we are moving toward the end of our relationship, Mr. Wonderful is showing the kind of strength I need most. He is holding my hand tightly as we march to appointments for this and that, none of which will change anything. He is shouldering my need to talk in the middle of the night. He is wiping away as many tears from his cheeks as I am from my own. He is preparing for the day when he needs to let me go. So, when all is said and done, my gentleman husband will stand tall and show those in his life how truly strong he is. It's something I've known all along.

6. The Name Game ...

> *We don't own the children we bring into this world.*
>
> *They are not extensions of who we are.*
> *They are not a do-over for our lives.*
> *They are here to write their story.*
>
> *Our blessing is getting to watch it unfold.*
>
> *~ Sheryll O'Brien*

Hannah - I fell in love with the name when I was a young girl reading every *Nancy Drew* mystery I could get my hands on. For those who don't know, Nancy Drew was a precocious, buttinsky kid who solved mysteries. Part of Nancy's backstory was that she was raised by her busy lawyer-father and a housekeeper-nanny named Hannah. It wasn't until I was in my late teens that I learned my maternal grandmother's middle name was Hannah. She hated the name and flipped a nut when she learned I planned to use that name for my way-in-the-future, firstborn daughter. I think she would have been pleased had she lived to meet my baby girl.

As soon as Tim and I learned our baby bundle would be of the pink variety, we began calling her Hannah Leigh. Then, a funny thing happened, our daughter was born on Tim's grandmother's 100th birthday. Tim never met his nana, but suggested we incorporate her name somehow. A lovely thought, so we named our firstborn, Hannah-Leigh Elizabeth O'Brien. Pleased as punch I was when Tim's mother came to meet her newest grandchild. "Our daughter's name is Hannah-Leigh Elizabeth," I beamed, "Elizabeth in honor of your mother," I gushed. Within seconds I went from happy new mom to potential star on an episode of *She Snapped.* Apparently, the 100-year-old deceased woman's name was Ellen. I sent eye-daggers my mate's way then laughed my ass off when he rightly said, *"We're lucky her name isn't Hannah Nana."*

Jessica - Tim and I were worlds apart on naming our second daughter. There were way too many names that we loved. We'd chosen Haley, but Tim's brother Joey and his wife Traci named their daughter Kaleigh, so we abandoned that name for obvious rhyming reasons. Tim's top choice became Jessica though I am the Shakespeare reader in the family, and The Bard is credited with penning the name in *The Merchant of Venice.* Kathleen became my top choice because I find it lyrical, and I always imagine little Kathleens to be a bit on the mischievous side of life.

Anyway, Tim and I became desperate and foolhardy. We each wrote our top three choices on a piece of paper, dragged our near-two-year-old daughter, Hannah, into the fray, read her the names, and had her choose one from his list and one from my list. Within seconds our soon-to-be bundle was named, Jessica Kathleen Belle O'Brien. Hannah decided she needed to be in on the name game and insisted the Disney character's name be part of her new sister's moniker. So, there you have it. The O'Brien Name Game in all its glory. Thanks be to God our two-year-old didn't choose Maleficent.

7. Another New Pain ...

Like every married couple, Tim and I divvied up things that needed to be done. He does the yardwork because he loves it, except for the part where he hasn't been able to grow more than a 100 blades of grass in 35 years, but that's a very long and very painful story in Mr. Wonderful's life, so I'll let him do the complaining if he so chooses.

While he's outside tending his gardens and doing his fair amount of cursing, the kind that wouldn't offend any flora or fauna, I'm usually inside doing the housework: tidying stacks of things that never find a home, and doing dishes, and the vacuuming, and the dusting (sometimes with a blow dryer), and the blah, blah, blah, and the cooking. I love to cook. I'm not a culinary queen by any stretch of the imagination, but I can put together some really good meals. Almost in the blink of an eye, everything has changed. There won't be as much divvying of duties. For me, there won't be much of anything.

The other day, I met with an oncologist for the first time since my metastatic breast cancer diagnosis. After a very brief introduction, she said there was nothing she could do — that the cancer was too advanced and too aggressive. She went on to say my death would be, *"Excruciatingly painful, but there might be a pill that might lessen the pain, and there might be a pill that could slow the bone deterioration, but an orthopedic oncologist would have to make that determination."*

Breathe in. Breathe out.

The unimpassioned physician continued with, *"There is another immediate concern, your L-1 vertebrae is completely affected and there is potential for nerve damage. Oh, and you have several rib fractures. My suggestion is that you limit your walking and all other activity until you see the ortho-oncologist."* The 'suggestion' became an insistence that I use a wheelchair to get from the doctor's office to the lab and to the parking garage.

"Are you kidding me?" I hissed at Tim. "A wheelchair? Already? When people see me they're going to think I'm sick."

"You are sick," he said, all ashen-faced.

The wheelchair thing came at the end of what was a sledgehammer appointment. The oncologist's words banged the fuck out of my head as Tim wheeled me here and there and there, *"Incurable. Terminal. Nothing can be done."* Oh, and let's not forget this, *"Dying of bone cancer is an excruciatingly painful death."*

On some level, on every level, I could have gone without knowing that. I certainly could do without the constant clang of those words in my head. Really, what am I supposed to do now that I know what my future holds? Knowing that my death is imminent is bad enough. Knowing I will suffer during my last days on earth is excruciatingly painful!

The suddenness of all this has left me wondering, "How on God's green earth could I be working at my computer hours each day, and buzzing here and there doing the housework, the tidying, and dishes, and vacuuming, and dusting, and blah, blah, blah, without knowing I was on the cancer death march? How is it that a simple blood abnormality on an annual physical on October 18th could reveal, less than one month later, that I am filled with cancer from my skull to my knees?

Ever since the diagnosis, I've been asked, *"Haven't you been in pain?"* The retrospective answer is, "Yes, I've been in constant pain in my lower back, and I've had intermittent stabs and jabs of pain in my legs, mostly the thighs, and some persistent pain in my rib area," but I am 63 years old, and I sit at my desk upwards of 15 hours a day writing, researching, editing, and proofing my work. Ergo, I have aches and pains.

And furthermore ... My friends and siblings have aches and pains and my friends and siblings are in their 60s, the age when aches and pains begin to settle. I would venture a guess that a heating pad and a couple extra OTCs are the standard remedy for the onset of age-related ouches here and there. And I would venture to guess no one thinks they have total body bone cancer when an, "Ouch," escapes their lips. It never crossed my mind. I have to tell you, ever since I learned I have to limit my movements and stay at home until the ortho part of this is figured out, I have a whole new pain. And it's in my ass.

8. A Cry in the Night ...

> *Sometimes whispers for help get lost in the clang of fear.*
>
> *~ Sheryll O'Brien*

A cancer diagnosis is tough. Hearing the disease is throughout your entire body and there is nothing that can be done is: shocking, sickening, terrifying, saddening, maddening, numbing — go ahead and pick one of these, or all of these, or find your own words to imagine how you might feel. I felt them all, and I feel them all over and over and over, again. Within a matter of weeks, I went from complete ignorance that I was even sick to discussions about hospice.

One month ago, I wrote the first few chapters of a new book in a new series I was particularly excited about. I'd sent my publisher the chapters and received an enthusiastic thumbs up, so I thought about the major elements of the story, started writing it, then let my characters take me on a journey. I was off to a very good start, which meant I was putting in long hours at my desk writing, and longer hours in my recliner researching locations for the story. I was experiencing aches and pains from sitting and discussed them in passing with Nancy who was experiencing a bout of lower back pain of her own. Thankfully, her pain is from the aging process, mine, not so much.

Now that I know I have terminal cancer, the pains I am feeling are in my head and in my heart. From sunup to sundown, I am thinking about what this disease is doing to me and to my loved ones. My grown daughters are easily brought to tears when they give me a kiss and head out the door or when they see me after a long day away. My girls do not want to lose their mother, the woman who is always at the ready with advice (solicited or not), and who is at the ready with the healing hug that can only be found in a mom's embrace — their mom's embrace.

The sadness of leaving my life, my very simple life, is absolute torture. It is a very heavy burden to carry on an already weakening skeleton. I generally save my tears for the still of night when I am alone, although I had a rather long emotional break when talking with my sister-in-law, Kathy, the other day. The former nurse retired to a wonderful life that she so rightly deserves after putting in countless days tending to the physical and emotional needs of patients. Then, in the blink of an eye, she was pulled back into the thick of it by the wife of her brother who is in need of explanations of what is said at doctor's appointments. I know how hard it is for her to do the clinician's dance with someone she cares deeply about, and I hurt inside for her.

And then there is my other sister-in-law, Eileen, the deeply spiritual woman and skilled nurse who has spent decades working with hospice patients. Imagine my good fortune that she has broached the reality of my future with empathy and surety that I will be well cared for. I don't know how either of these women do what they do, but I am eternally grateful they are walking this road with me. There's not much else any of us can do about any of this. So, I'll save my emotional breaking for the still of the night.

9. Cups of Tea ...

As of today, Tim and I have been married 35 years, 5 months and 1 day. That equates to 12,926 days give or take a few missed Leap Years. That also means that on 12,926 evenings, Mr. Wonderful has asked me if I'd like a cup of tea and a couple Figgie cookies when he makes his nightly Lipton. For 12,926 nights I have replied, "No thanks," and on plenty of nights I've snipped, "I don't want a cup of tea! Why do you keep asking me?" Mr. Wonderful calmly replied, *"Because you might want one, tonight."* I suppose that could be true, but come on. So, for way too many nights I've said, "Nope, but I'll have a Figgie cookie with you.

For those who don't know, Tim and I live in Massachusetts, the Bay State, the home of Plymouth Rock where the Pilgrims landed, and Fenway Park where my beloved team finally broke the Curse of the Bambino in 2004, and Boston Common, the oldest city park in the United States. Massachusetts is home to the first ever zip code 01001, and the first ever subway, and where the Tabby is the official state cat, and where it is illegal to put tomatoes into New England Clam Chowder. I never knew there were laws on the books about tomatoes in chowder, although I wholeheartedly support this piece of legislation.

My scenic state is home to beautiful seaside and island destinations: Cape Cod, Nantucket, Martha's Vineyard, and the North Shore. It is home to wacky-quacky, wacky-barky, and wacky-witchy attractions, like: the Boston Duck Boat sightseeing tour; or the Boston Harbor Cruise Day for Dogs; or the Salem Witch Museum where you can revisit the hysteria of 1692 by touring the dungeon where women were imprisoned by a bunch of lunatics who missed some important stuff during the trials. Did it not occur to those living in Salem that a witch might have had the ability to free herself from chains, or levitate above the reach of murderous madmen, or perhaps cast a spell for torrential rainfall before being burned in town square? I digress, but really, come on.

Getting back to the wonders of Massachusetts, we have some of the finest colleges and universities in the world. These higher institutions of learning have educated countless individuals who went on to make significant contributions to science and technology, music and entertainment, and things of note, big and small.

Massachusetts is a beautiful, exciting, and lovely place to live and to visit. I am proud to be a Bay Stater, proud of the state's historical significance and grateful for its beauty and wonder. Still, in my humble opinion, the greatest claim of Massachusetts is the Fig Newton cookie. The ones my husband offers me every night with a cup of tea which I consistently decline. The cookies, however, I gladly accept.

10. Hope Floats …

> *Beginnings are scary. Endings are usually sad.*
> *It's what's in the middle that counts.*
> *So, when you find yourself at the beginning,*
> *just give hope a chance to float up.*
> *It will.*
>
> ~ Steven Rogers, Hope Floats: The Screenplay.

My family is facing a beginning. A world without me in it. It dawned on me in the wee hours this morning that this event in my life will be far worse for them.

My mother will be losing a child … Sure, I'm in my sixties, but I am her child, nonetheless. I'm the one who has pushed all of her buttons over the years, and the one who has brought her to fits of laughter in nearly every one of our conversations.

My older brother and younger sister will be losing the kid in the middle … The one who marched to her own beat, was really good at keeping secrets, and who felt fortunate to have clowns to the left and jokers to the right.

My husband will be losing one half of the bickering couple … Good Lord, we've bickered, but we never really had huge fights, we had huge laughs. I could bring that man to tears with my antics. When he moves through the grieving process, the one I assume will be an emotional torture trip, I hope he will remember the laughter because there was so much of it in our lives.

My daughters will be losing their mother … Their impending pain and loneliness hurts me to my core because that is where they live — in the center of my heart and soul. I love my two girls and would give anything to stay with them. I hope the women in my life, my sister and sisters-in-law, and my friends and my girls' friends will reach out and help them find a place for their grief as they find their way back to happiness. Please find your way back to happiness.

Sadly, my darling granddaughter will be losing her MammyGrams … This loss will hit her hard. I have had the blessing of being with her every day of her life, imparting little nuggets of wisdom, and writing silly poems and songs, and yelling the word, 'monkey' for absolutely no reason. I know she will wish things were different, and she will hurt as she tries to understand why they are not. And I know she will miss me dearly and I ache in ways that are almost too much to bear. I pray that those I leave behind will remind Hadley that she can find me in the place she touched me most — in her heart.

11. Time …

When does the quantity and quality of time become the focus of your life?
When you're running out of it.

~Sheryll O'Brien

As God is my witness this happened. A few weeks before my doctor got my funky blood results that started him down the path of finding out what might be going on inside me, my daughter, Jessica, and I were hanging out, just shooting the breeze. Out of the blue I asked, “Would you want to know the date and time you were going to die?” She blurted an emphatic, *“Absolutely not.”* She asked me the same question, I blurted an emphatic, “Absolutely yes.”

We debated the pros and cons of our choices, each of us making a salient point here and there, but neither of us denting the other’s strongly-held position. Jessica’s be all and end all was that knowing the date and time would be like having a death sentence hanging over her head. My position was that since death is the only certainty about life, we should know when it’s coming. Now that I am nearing death, I am even more committed to my position. Knowing my end is near, but not knowing exactly when it will arrive is driving me nuts. Suddenly, I am struggling with the concept of time. I find myself looking at the clock way more than I used to. I find myself counting seconds to see how close I get to the change of the digital numbers on the cable box.

The measurement of time, the quantity of it, the quality of it, and how to best fill it is driving me crazy, most especially, the heavy weight of time that falls in the middle of the night. I no longer know what the hell to do during the hours of darkness. I used to fill them with writing, or researching, or editing my newest novel. There will be no new novel, so I can’t escape into the pages of a book I should be writing.

So, out with Plan A and in with Plan B. I have filled some of the time writing blogs, but this exercise occasionally pushes my emotional buttons, so at best, it kills a bit of time here and there. As many of you know, I write mysteries. I love mysteries, but not this mystery. I don't like being the main character in a book that could be titled, *How Much Time Does She Have Left?* (Shit, I wish I'd thought of that title when I was writing novels). I digress. I do that a lot. You'll see. Back to my dilemma, the question of how much time I have leaves me not knowing how much living and loving I can squeeze in.

I don't know ... how many morning cups of coffee I'll enjoy with, or offers of tea I'll refuse from Mr. Wonderful, or how many loving embraces I'll get from my girls, or off to school waves I'll get from my granddaughter.

I don't know ... how many more visits my 86-year-old mother can make to my house when I should be traveling to hers.

I don't know ... how many more heart-emoji texts my sister, Marjorie, will send, or how many more phone calls from Georgia my brother, Don, and sister-in-law, Denise will make, or how many 'thinking of you' texts I'll receive from my niece, Nicole, or from relatives and friends before my time runs out.

I don't know ... how many unfinished things I'll leave my wonderful publishing team to handle on my behalf. I already know I won't be sending my editor, Andria Flores, the woman I refer to as The Warden, any new manuscripts because I won't be writing any more stories. I already know that much of my remaining work will fall onto the shoulders of my publisher, Nancy Pendleton, a bold Texan whom I refer to as The Goddess because who else could put 23 books of mine into publication in little more than a year's time? I already know that Jessica Champion, gatherer of information and presenter of dreams and visions whom

I refer to as The Guru will be handling my website and social media pages.

I don't know ... how long they will work on my behalf, but I am beyond pleased and comforted knowing these women will continue our work until it comes to its eventual conclusion.

I don't know ... how much time I have left, but I do know this, my remaining time will be spent doing the most important things in my life. Loving the people who have enriched it and helped make it memorable.

12. Firsts and Lasts ...

> *Thank you God, for being with me*
> *through my challenges.*
> *I will share them and bear them because*
> *we both know I can.*
>
> *~ Sheryll*

This blog is a mashup of things — things I have never done before — things I may never do again.

Thanksgiving ... This was most likely my last and it was very different from all others. I saw an orthopedic oncologist early the previous week. After he did a head to toe analysis of where the cancer is and where it has done the most damage, he insisted I leave his office using a walker, and that I use it every time I move about, and then suggested I not move about. "Limit yourself to bathroom trips, and don't go outside, unless it's to a doctor's appointment or for a diagnostic scan." Trust me on this point, I would much rather have left my home for a turkey dinner than for a recent bone biopsy, but maybe that's just me. In a future blog, I'll tell you about that shit show.

Snowfall ... The first snowfall of each winter season is a big deal in New England. Most often it is a flurry here and there and doesn't amount to much of anything (except for Halloween a few years ago when we got a blizzard, but that's a story for another time). Anyway, the first snowfall came in the afternoon the other day. The annual event is always greeted by me with a squeal of delight. This year, my squeal was followed by an uncontrollable push of tears. For each snowflake that fluttered past my window, a big, fat teardrop began its journey from my eye, down my cheek, and onto my chest. "My last-first snowfall," I blurted to my husband. He patted my shoulder as he walked past me, trying to hide his tear-filled eyes, "Don't worry, you'll be cursing the snow in no time at all," he reminded.

Priests ... A priest came to the house the other day — it sounds like the beginning of a joke — it certainly felt like one. A little background, Tim was raised Catholic and I was raised Protestant. Our children were baptized in the Catholic church and attended Catholic high school. That decision was part of our religious plan for them from the get-go. Tim and I didn't have a get-go on our religious plan. We spent the early years of our marriage visiting churches, looking for the right fit for each of our religious needs. Sadly, we never really found our religious home. No big deal for our daily lives, but a bit problematic now that I need a spiritual leader on my current journey.

My bestie, Donna, solved my problem with one phone call to her priest, a dude she's been raving about for years. The other day she showed up with the man in tow, the man I need, the man I could have benefitted from knowing my whole life. The laidback priest took a seat in my husband's favored mission chair although he might have been equally comfortable in a bean bag tossed on the floor, or swinging from a hammock in the backyard while listening to a little Van Morrison or Joan Baez. Father Dude became part of the scene. He didn't arrive with expectation, or vie for the leadership role. Honestly, his vibe was that we were just hanging out together. He wanted to know about me, sure, but offered no Plan A or Plan B on how to accomplish that. He just sat back and let me tell him what I wanted to tell him. In other words, the man of ministry knew we'd find our way.

In retrospect, I can honestly say the only thing that set the cleric apart from any other dude I've invited into my home was the black and white collar he wore. This priest was as easy a conversationalist as I am, but he was way better at listening, part of his training, I suppose. He was open to discussing the differences between Catholicism and Protestantism, and more importantly, the Christianity that binds the two. He skillfully guided me around a tiny complaint I expressed in the God department. "The only thing I have prayed for since the beginning of this ordeal, is that God won't give me more than I can handle. Sometimes, I think He might be missing my prayer," I said in a near-whisper.

My visiting holy man wanted examples. I gave him a rundown. "I've sort of been getting one blow after another: you have metastatic breast cancer; it's in your bones; it's full body bone cancer; it is terminal; your femur and L-1 are your biggest concerns; dying of bone cancer is excruciatingly painful; there may be a pill that can help with the amount of pain you have getting from here to hospice; you'll need to have a bone biopsy to see if you're eligible for the pill; the biopsy can be painful; you should meet with hospice in the near future; you should begin planning a funeral; and, and, and. All of this happening in the span of a few weeks. It's sort of been a lot, and it feels like it's more than I can handle, sometimes."

Mr. Priestman let me work it through for myself. I filled the slightly uncomfortable silence with, "But, I guess I'm handling it because my friends and family tell me they can't believe how strong I am, or how important it is for me and for others that I'm blogging about this, or how in awe they are that I'm still enjoying life." Father Dude smiled. I fell asleep that night without saying my prayers, a pain pill and a Xanax are to blame. If I had spent time with God that night, I would have thanked him for sending this priest my way because I know that with him by my side, I will be better able to handle whatever comes my way. Had I chit-chatted with God I would have told him, I have faith that He will bless me with a journey I can handle.

13. Tough Choices ...

When an oncologist starts an appointment by saying, *"You have terminal cancer,"* the automatic reaction is that you wait for the word, "BUT." At least that's what I did. In my case, the BUT preceded news that there was nothing that could be done, that I was going to die — best case scenario, I might have six months. There was, however, a two pill glimmer-of-hope. Neither pill would lengthen my life, but one pill *might* help with the quality of it by decreasing the pain I would experience getting from here to hospice, the other pill *might* help strengthen the bones not already weakened by the cancer-nibbling mouse that's taken residence inside, and has been feasting on the hip bone that's connected to the thigh bone that's connected to the knee bone — you get the gist.

In order to find out if I was a candidate for either pill, I would need to undergo a bone biopsy. I initially declined the procedure because the pills wouldn't lengthen the amount of time I have left, and because a bone biopsy is an unpleasant experience. After some pushback from the oncologist that I was being hasty, and the enticing suggestion that I might be in less pain getting from here to the morphine of hospice, I acquiesced. I had the bone biopsy.

In retrospect, that was the wrong decision, not because I learned I wasn't a candidate for the pills, but rather because I learned I was. A little background. When Mr. Wonderful and I feared my illness might be terminal he asked me what I wanted. My response was quick and concise. "To enjoy the Christmas season, to finish as much of my work as I can, maybe start a blog about this, and when appropriate, speak with hospice." The next part of my answer was delivered through sobs. "If I have terminal cancer, I am not going to wage a fight that I won't win. I am not going to torture myself or drag our seven-year-old granddaughter through a shit fest. I am going to enjoy the time that I have."

I have to tell you, thinking I might have less pain while spending that time was very enticing. So, I had the bone biopsy. The news that I was a candidate for the pills was delivered on December 1st and met with a huge sigh because I wasn't going to be in "excruciating pain" for months. Then I learned some things that made that moment in time very painful. In order to get either pill, I would need to: have a consult with a radiologist, undergo an MRI or some other body scan, and have 10 consecutive radiation treatments on my femur and L-1.

The treatments wouldn't change anything, but they *might* help with pain.

While those medical procedures were being done, the oncologist would need to get approval for the drug, and Tim and I would have to figure out a payment plan. Why? Because one of the drugs costs **$12,000 per month**. NOT A TYPO and not something we were previously told. By the way, the pill that costs more than my first car is the pill that's intended to improve the quality of my life. I zoned out of the conversation and later learned from Tim that a portion of the cost would be paid through insurance and the rest could be paid through a personal loan. We never learned the cost of the second drug because I popped a Xanax and Tim suffered a minor stroke — one that left him temporarily deaf.

When we swung back into the doctor's monologue, we learned that taking the pills would require biweekly trips to the hospital's lab for bloodwork. Apparently, each drug can cause life-threatening situations, hence the frequent blood-letting mandate. RECAP: radiology consult + body scan + 10 radiation trips + biweekly labs = 14 appointments before Christmas — the season I really wanted and needed to enjoy.

An important thing to remember ... I was told by an orthopedic oncologist that the cancer in one of my thighs had deteriorated the bone to such a degree that it is structurally unstable and that my L-1 is an even more serious situation AND I was not allowed to leave the ortho's office without purchasing a walker AND I was told to limit my movement AND I was banned from the upstairs in my home AND I ate Thanksgiving dinner on my recliner AND I watched our Christmas tree being decorated AND I make as few bathroom trips as possible.

Two weeks later, I was being told that in order to get the super-de-duper drugs prescribed for a better quality of life, I would have to leave my home a minimum of 14 times, thereby jeopardizing myself with trips for treatments and scans that will not lengthen my life. In fact, the trips could shorten my life if for instance, I fell on the way to the car, or if a person fell on me in the hospital lobby — could happen — did happen — on the day of my bone biopsy, but that is a story for another day.

An important thing to note … The potential side effects of the super-de-duper drugs would require a separate blog to list them all, and I will, at some point in time. If bad luck was on my side and I encountered any of the side effects, I could very likely be hospitalized and/or die from whatever befalls me. A review of my recent run of shit luck helped clear things up. "It's time we go back to Plan A," I told my husband who was scrounging the car seat cushions for loose change to help pay the $12,000 monthly pill cost.

"What was Plan A, again?" he mumbled.

"I am not going to wage a fight I won't win. I am not going to torture myself or drag our seven-year-old granddaughter through a shit fest. I am going to enjoy the time that I have." We discussed our day and the options with our daughters who nodded their agreement through tear-filled eyes then went separate ways to deal with the newest reality. Mr. Wonderful went to the kitchen, put on the teakettle, and offered me a cup. This time, I accepted.

14. Pill Pusher ...

When Tim and I learned I was in deep shit, we had a sit-down with Hannah and Jessica. We told them what we knew, and they asked things they needed to know. Hannah, the daughter of mine who shuffles to a very rhythmic beat, wanted to know about comfort and care: recliners that had lifting capabilities to help me get up, and pain management options, and nursing services, and whether insurance helped defray costs of things. Jessica, the daughter of mine who marches to a very rat-a-tat-tat beat, had rat-a-tat-tat thoughts about those things, but she quickly honed in on the steady beat of: When? She needed to know if I had been given a timeframe. Was there some sort of death clock we should be watching? Were we told when — exactly? Keep in mind, Jessica is the daughter who absolutely did not want to know about dates of death when I casually brought up the subject months ago. Her tune changed and she got stuck on a loop: "*When? How long? When? ... When? How long? When ...*" she sobbed. I raised a quizzical brow and pushed all-the-way-in. "I thought you didn't want to know about death dates." *"I don't want to know MY death date, but yours..."* She caught herself mid-sentence, turned all guilty-faced, and then fell into the fit of laughter her mother, father, and sister had already begun.

When we gathered ourselves, we rehashed my position on the subject of knowing when. I found my position had changed a tiny bit. Instead of wanting to know when, I wanted and needed assurances that I'd have this Christmas season. I wanted and needed to know that I'd enjoy it and perhaps be feeling as good as I'd been feeling — of course taking pain and anxiety pills were definitely part of the feeling good part of life.

To be perfectly honest, I had absolutely no idea how effective the pain pill/anxiety pill combo was, until I slept through one of my regularly scheduled pill popping events and the pain got ahead of me. Going without a dose of Tramadol let me know that I'm experiencing a lot more pain, deeper and more prolonged stabs and jabs of pain than I was a few weeks ago. I'd still been feeling discomfort, but I definitely wasn't feeling all of the pain. The realization of how much cancer crap was going on inside me was really painful, physically and mentally.

The medication mishap really knocked Mr. Wonderful for a loop. Every jab and jolt of pain in my leg, or hip, or rib cage, registered on his face and turned my medicine-manager into a hovering-husband. *"Maybe if you raise — lower — raise — your recliner. Maybe if I put a towel, a pillow, a soft blanket under your leg. Maybe if you sit further up or lie flat or sort of get between the two."* I pushed this button and that button on the motorized recliner to no avail. He grabbed the pill bottle and read the instructions hoping the label would miraculously change. On occasion he muttered, *"One tablet every six hours, as needed for pain."* After several minutes he conceded, *"Okay, it's 3 PM, you just took one, so that should kick in and you can take another at 9."* He watched my flinches, and expressed his frustration with some rapid-fire cussing when the pill didn't kick in quickly enough, *"Son-of-a-bitch. I should have woken you. What the fuck was I thinking letting you rest?"*

I bet he was thinking I needed the rest.

First, some background ... I am the swearer in the family. I find the F-bomb to be very useful, and so long as little ears are out of range, I feel free to launch. I am well aware that there are people who wouldn't use the

F-word if their mouths were full of Fs, and I respect that, but come on, there are times when that word just fits. Tim, on the other hand, manages to muddle through life with infrequent bomb-dropping (unless sparse blades of grass are involved, then all bets are off). Though infrequent, his mouthful of Fs have been dropped on his barren lawn.

On the missing pill day, Mr. Wonderful lobbed his bomb then sat close by my side, groaned with my every stab or jab, then made a managerial decision. He handed me a pain pill at 7 PM. *"Here take this. It's close enough to 9, and I can't take the pain any longer."* As soon as I swallowed the pill, we sighed our relief. And when the stabs and jabs were masked by the wonders of Tramadol, I yawned and started watching a Hallmark movie. Tim stood near my carnival-chair, ran his hand across my head, kissed me and promised, *"I'll be back at 1 AM with your next dose."* Gotta love him. I do.

15. Blessings ...

> *Take time to appreciate the big blessings in life.*
> *As for the small blessings, there's really no such thing.*
>
> *~ Sheryll O'Brien*

Big blessing. I learned about my cancer. Granted I found out a bit late in the game, but whatever. Happily, I was put on notice that I am on my final journey. For those who know me well, you know that my receiving this little tidbit of information is for the best. After all, I am a planner, an organizer, a doer. I manage my life to the nanosecond, and to varying degrees, I manage the lives of those around me. I make lists for everything; I even make lists reminding myself that I have lists. So, I imagine I would have been really pissed if I found myself dead one day leaving behind a basket of unfolded towels, or a half-written novel, or a half-eaten Ben & Jerry's in the freezer. I'm quite sure God knows about my obsessive-compulsive disorder, and I suspect it weighed heavily into His decision to give me fair warning about my impending demise. I don't question for one single second that He has the patience of a saint, probably has it in spades, but still, I think He figured a little preemptive work was in order. I imagine it this way: He's sitting in his office dictating to a previously deceased stenographer.

Dear Sheryll,

You are cordially invited Home at a date to be determined. Use this gift of time wisely. Get your things in order and enjoy the pint of Truffle Kerfuffle in the freezer. BTW, no R.S.V.P. required, and please arrive on your best behavior and with your mouth shut!

Love, God

Not likely I know, but it could happen. I'm referring to the 'shut mouth' part, BTW. Since I was given a preemptive warning about my death, I went about tending to things that would have resulted in a fitful eternal rest had they been left undone. As it turns out, most are so mundane.

If I'd died suddenly … I wouldn't have had the opportunity to personally hand off the bills to Tim, and to set him straight, "No, I don't write checks anymore. I pay over the phone or online. Good Lord, drag your ass to the future, cause it's here." And I wouldn't have had time to hand off the tax prep work I do every year, or had time to review our Last Will and Testament, or find my birth certificate, or our marriage license, or all of the other documents he will need to prove I was me, and he was my significant everything.

If I'd died suddenly ... I wouldn't have had the opportunity to choose cremation, and insist that I don't want a wake or a funeral, that I want a gathering at a funeral parlor where people can come and hang out and offer support to my loved ones, and listen to the cool priest present my case for eternal life in Heaven. I sure do hope Father Dude is tight with the Big Guy, and hasn't done anything to piss Him off.

If I'd died suddenly ... I wouldn't have had the opportunity to write a book for Hadley, to put a lifetime of grandmotherly advice between the covers of a 75 page book. Then again, I wouldn't have had gut-wrenching time to grieve the things that I won't be here to share with her. And to ache in places I didn't know existed. It breaks my heart that she will be profoundly sad when she no longer finds her MammyGrams' wide-open arms ready for the hug she'll need — the hug only I can give, but won't be here to give.

Even though this time is hard, I am grateful when I see the sun come up over the McTigue's house, as I have for the past 30+ years. And when I hear Hadley's knock upon my door for her daily breakfast trip, and her announcements, *"It's Mashup Monday,"* (hash and applesauce), *"It's Toast Tuesday,"* (one slice of peanut butter and one slice of cinnamon), *"It's Wacky Wednesday,"* (whatever her heart desires), *"It's Eclectic Thursday,"* (peanut butter crackers, fruit salad, and a cookie), *"It's Fancy Friday,"* (scrambled cheesy-egg and a side of bacon). My having time to really enjoy the things that could have slipped by without my appreciating them is the truest blessing of all.

16. Life Passing Before Me ...

We've all heard about the phenomenon of a person's life passing before them as they leave this earth. I haven't gotten that far yet, and I can't say for certain if and how it all goes down, but I've imagined it this way:

Death scene ...

The end is nearing. I'm reclining in a chair or a bed and a big-ass screen lowers from above. Orchestrated music begins in surround-sound, and the face of God fills the screen, much like the MGM lion, or the Paramount mountain, or the globe of Universal Studios does at the beginning of the movies we've all watched over the years.

A slow crawl of credits inches along the bottom, maybe with my name and birth date and other pertinent pieces of information. Hopefully not my Social Security number, cause you know, we're supposed to keep that 9-digit number secret. An exercise in futility if you ask me, since every damned bank, school, hospital, insurance company, municipal agency, and pizza delivery dude makes you fork over the digits before you can open an account, register for a class, wait in an ER, get utilities into your home, or a policy to insure the digs in case some catastrophic event sends you into the night looking for the pizza delivery dude who has your Social Security number and your pepper and pepperoni.

Holy crap, I totally digress. I'm leaving the tirade cause it's sort of how my mind is working now, and I sort of find it funny.

Anyway, back to the movie reel … It might happen that way, but recent events have me thinking my 'end of life phenomenon' won't be a splashy cinematic event, in fact, I think I'm already experiencing the phenomenon and it is so without fanfare. If I am correct, my movie reel has been chopped into little segments that would be announced at the Academy Awards like this, *"And the winner in the Dribs and Drabs category ……. Sheryll O'Brien."* Truthfully, I should win that category. Why? Because my life isn't about a few big events here and there, it's about a collection of wonderful dribs and drabs.

Example #1 … For the past few weeks, I've been receiving calls, emails, and text messages; some with emojis I didn't know existed, and some with emojis that caused confusion on my part. "A thumbs up on my terminal cancer announcement? Is that a good thing or a bad thing," I asked Jessica.

"It's a supportive thing," she laughed.

"If you say so," I grumbled.

Other communiques were on the short and sweet side of things. *"Hi, Sheryll. Hope all is well."*

"As well as can be expected," I've heard myself grumble.

Other messages went immediately into the 'brain teaser' category. *"Hey, do you remember that time we did this or that?"* Apparently, most of the 'this or that' events in the earlier days of my adult life were done after copious amounts of celebrants were consumed, so no, I don't remember, but I bet 'this and that' was fun.

Some emails are full-on rambles of things the sender wants me to know before I go. I read every word and end up happy to learn about the full lives of people I knew once upon a time. Surprisingly, one quick dispatch reminded me that I still have that _______ I borrowed, and could it be returned before I go? For the record, it *was* returned. But, if I'm wrong, the jackass owner can pry the _______ from my cold, dead hands, or take it up with the widower who will be living alone at my former address on a date to be determined. Oops. That rant feels a bit iffy in the karma category. Still, I'm going to give myself a pass on this one because I've been really good in thought and deed lately. I'm not trying to pull the wool over God's eyes because let's face it, He already knows all about me. Still, I figure it can't hurt to do a little cleaning and sprucing up before I make my appearance. As for the little snit-fit I just had, I hope He accepts that it very well could have been the result of my skull cancer.

Example #2 … My mailbox has seen way more activity lately with people sending cards — not Get Well cards because, well, you know, but rather Thinking of You cards. It's nice that people take the time to send along a Hallmark message, or one they've penned themselves and slipped into a pink, purple, blue, green, or yellow envelope meant to bring a bit of cheer. I did an experiment the other day, I left the envelopes unopened to see if just having them in the house brought joy. I stared at the pretty rainbow of 4 x 6 paper enclosures with pretty scripted return addresses announcing who the card was from (sort of diminished the 'surprise' element, but whatever). My hypothesis bore out what I suspected, the colors and the names made me happy, the messages inside brought a plethora of emotion, mostly smiles, but a few tears, for sure. I especially enjoy the Kraft brown envelopes and matching note cards that have been coming with regularity from my editor. Andria has taken to sending me cards with quotes from my books, and then penning something sweet or sassy about the line I wrote. A truly fabulous thing to do and to receive.

Anyway, I've decided the calls, emails, and cards are part of the dribs and drabs life-passing phenomenon of Sheryll O'Brien. Over the past few weeks, I've heard from people I haven't seen in years. People I have missed and thought of on many, many occasions, but went on missing because the push of life got in the way of reaching out. Happily, the push of death, my death, has them reaching out. One of those individuals is someone I wouldn't have wanted to leave this earth without hearing from — an end-of-life blessing, for sure. I probably got her Irish up by mentioning this, but hearing from her means the world to me, so I figure she'll give me a pass.

Example #3 ... My favorite life passing experience fills my heart with joy. My daughters have taken it upon themselves to spend time with their mom — quality time. On occasion, we have filled the hours with chit-chat, and other times with movies, the kind that begin with the roar of a lion, or the majesty of a mountain, or the spin of a globe. Hannah and I, or Jessica and I, have kicked back and watched one of MY favorite movies: *You've Got Mail, Six Days Seven Nights, White Christmas, The Big Chill, Out of Africa*, the list goes on and on. These are the movies I've suggested we watch together over the years, only to have received an eye-roll and a counter suggestion that we watch something from this millennium.

Example #4 ... I suspect my loved ones have been picking and choosing things that might show up at my 'going away' party — the one I won't be attending.

Example #5 ... My home has been filled with the sound of MY music. This isn't unusual because I listen to music all of the time. What is unusual is that the Bose system in the kitchen will suddenly start and one of my favorite tunes will fill the air: *Into the Mystic, Helpless, Don't Let Me Down, Turn the Page, Innamorata*. Those were yesterday's selections courtesy of the people who can and do bring music to my life. I smile because I know one of my loved ones is thinking of me and sending a tune that reminds me of some part of my past.

See — dribs and drabs. That is how my life is passing before me and it is wonderful. I take solace during these difficult days that my loved ones are joining me on the journey of my life. They are listening to voicemails, reading emails and notes, watching MY movies, smiling wide at the things their mom saved from their childhoods, and filling the air with the sounds that make ME happy. There still may be a movie starring Yours Truly at the end of my life. If so, I expect it will be wonderful. It has to be because I have lived a truly wonderful life.

17. Worst Weekend of My Life ...

> *Strength comes from a quiet place.*
> *So, when you need it most, be still and let it find you.*
>
> *~ Sheryll O'Brien*

Last Friday kicked off a banner weekend of information gathering, option weighing, decision making and unmaking and remaking. It ended with heart wrenching grief.

At noon, Mr. Wonderful opened our front door and welcomed in two women. The Women of Hospice I'd labeled them when we learned they'd be coming. I had a nanosecond to nonchalantly size them up before introductions were made. The Women of Hospice were nothing like the images I had conjured up in my mind, angels of mercy wearing white Grim Reaper garb, magically materializing in my home. These end-of-life-professionals were young, probably in their early thirties, and very pleasant.

My social worker was dressed the way my daughters dress for work, business casual, slacks and sweater, and she was wearing a kick-ass pair of ankle boots. She knew how to 'talk the talk' of death and dying. She handled the uncomfortable topic by striking the perfect balance of I'm sorry that this is the way it is, but this is the way it is. Then she assured me that they can help with all of my end-of-life choices and challenges. And I totally believed she was committed to doing that — for me — a complete stranger.

My nurse case manager was dressed the way nurses dress for work, comfy pants and matching top with the ubiquitous stethoscope slung casually around her neck. While she removed this and that from her carryall, I silently questioned why she chose to do this type of work. Why would she spend her days helping people die? Let's face it, she is of the caregiving profession. And people who join the nursing ranks usually spend their days helping people heal or live through some critical situation, and yet here was a lovely young woman, all fresh-faced and scrubbed clean, preparing to help me die. I didn't come up with a good answer, but I know I have good fortune that these women are leading my hospice team.

Now for the inside of the room recap. Let's have some fun with it. Tim and I board a plane, nope, we board a Learjet and find The Women of Hospice in the cockpit. They go through their pre-flight checklist, confirm takeoff with flight control, and announce, *"Lift off."* We're flying at 36,000 feet, when the social worker goes on autopilot with an overview of what hospice is and what it is not. She delivers a perfectly paced and informative presentation; one I suspect she's done often — once too often in my opinion. In a nutshell, my words, not hers, hospice care prioritizes comfort and quality of life for terminally ill patients by reducing pain and suffering.

Listening to the possible and probable scenarios of how I might progress from hanging out in my comfy recliner to climbing onto my future deathbed increased my emotional pain and suffering immediately, and sufficiently. I found myself checking the clock to calculate the time before my next Xanax. There was a bit too much time left for my liking.

Some background on what I thought about the process of dying … I would join hospice. I would lose my right to make decisions about my life. I would get sicker. I would climb onto a hospital deathbed when I was told to. I would lose my dignity. I would get morphined up by interloping strangers. I would slip away. I admit I'd already given considerable thought to what pieces of furniture would have to be moved to accommodate a bed in my living room, thereby converting it to my dying room.

Those who know me know that I like the way I have my living room arranged and they won't be surprised that I angst over the looming changes. I admit I've spent considerably less time thinking about who would care for me whilst I was in suspended animation upon my deathbed. Okay, I gave it some thought, but doing so caused heart palpitations, so I quickly moved on to other things, like blogging and gift buying. (Don't tell Mr. Wonderful, but I went a bit overboard with

Christmas gifts. With or without a hospital bed in our living room, we will be hard pressed to get all of the 'last gifts I'll ever buy' into our 14 x 18 foot room).

I digress ... Back to the point of this blog. The social worker, cockpit pilot began our descent toward Earth whilst offering options. If I choose to do the whole home death routine, there would be daily visits from my hospice team, but that would leave 23 hours each day to consider. If I didn't want my husband and daughters to do the bulk of my health care work — I do not, thank you very much — then other agencies would need to come in. It was 'suggested' that given the state of my bones, trained health care workers should be hired and they usually work an eight-hour shift at a hefty hourly wage. I let Tim do the calculating because I suck at math and because I had another question, "So, if I wanted to stay here until I get really bad, could I then go to a super-de-duper assisted dying facility?"

"Assisted living facility," the nurse corrected.

"Potato. Po-tah-to," I grumbled. Anyway, the answer to my question was, *"Yes .... but."* I hate that kind of answer on a good day, this was not a good day.

The Women of Hospice tag-teamed on this topic of discussion. *"There are facilities. Most accept patients prior to the transitioning phase."* I wasn't ready to hear about this phase. The other professional read the room, eased in and continued on.

"Where you can go is very much dependent on what facility has an open bed. Every facility will give you care and comfort, but because Covid is on the rise again, you might find that visitors are restricted or prohibited from the facility."

"So, I could die alone?" I croaked/choked the words.

"Yes."

I felt my heart constrict and my head threaten to blow. "If I have a stroke right now," I addressed my nurse, "will you attempt to save me?"

"Yes."

"Shit." I looked at Mr. Wonderful and wondered if he was stroking out. I addressed my nurse, "If he has a stroke, save him, cause, you know." After about two hours, I'd had about all I could handle. I think I said some sort of goodbye pleasantries, accepted the shiny laminated stuffed-to-the-brim pocket folder of information, reached for the Xanax I so desperately needed, and went into some blank state.

Hannah, Jessica and Hadley came for dinner and after we'd eaten, we played a Christmas game we enjoy. We put A-Z letters into a brown paper bag and took turns drawing a letter. Then we set about naming some Christmas-related thing that corresponds with that letter. (BTW, if you ever play and get the letter U, use the word unwrap). Anyway, after the second game, I sat my sweet granddaughter down and told her the news. The hopeful look on her face that she might have misheard, the tears that filled her eyes and ran like rain when she realized she hadn't, and the hug that lasted an eternity broke my heart. I'm sure the pain of it all will last an eternity, for Hadley. Oh how I wish I could hug her pain away.

18. My Bestie and My Doctor ...

The first person I called when I got the news about a high alk phos was my bestie, Donna Eaton, a former phlebotomist who starts every medical sentence with, *"That's not my field, but ..."* and then always manages to 'talk the talk' on any part of the anatomy.

Her first question that day was, *"The alkaline phosphatase, how high are we talking?"* My first answer was a ramble of non-specifics, "Not sure exactly, but the one I had for my 2019 annual physical showed an alk phos that was within normal range, I didn't have a physical last year because of Covid, and now it's over 600, I think. Maybe."

She immediately started a game of Trivial Pursuit: The Anatomy Edition with questions about blood counts, and enzymes, and functions of this and that, none of which I could answer. *"You need to get better at asking questions and getting information,"* she suggested calmly, but pointedly.

"Yeah, I know. I suck at absorbing all that medical crap. But I'll have the super-de-duper blood test results in a few days so that should help."

"What super-de-duper blood test?"

"I don't know what it's called, but the test focuses on the alk phos. I guess it looks for three areas of concern—"

She cut me off. *"Liver, bones, and intestines."*

"Yeup." And just like that, Donna had three wedges of pie for her Trivial Pursuit game piece while mine was still empty and sitting shell-shocked in a corner. A little background on my bestie. Donna shoots straight from the hip, offers immediate triage to the truth wounds she inflicts, slaps on a dressing to stem the flow of vital fluids, then kisses the boo-boo. Her frankness is oddly refreshing, even if you're the one bleeding out from one of her direct hits — like this one.

"Sheryll, with your history, the concern is metastatic breast cancer that's spread to the bone or liver, maybe somewhere else."

"And?"

"This is gonna suck, but I love you."

She didn't need to ask her next question because she knows I avoid medical-research like the plague, but she asked anyway. *"Are you gonna research this?"*

"Nope."

"I am. Gotta go."

A few days later, I called Donna with the super-de-duper alk phos blood work results, "82% bone, 18% liver, 0% intestines."

This time, she didn't need a whole bunch of specifics, and she had only one question, *"You're scheduled for a bone scan, right?"*

"Yeup." This time I followed up with a big-ass question of my own. "The 82% bone reading, that's pretty conclusive about what's happening?"

"Yes."

"And?"

"This is gonna be bad, but I love you."

The other person who knew how bad a situation I was in was my PCP, the man I refer to as Dr. Wonderful. He broached the possibility of metastatic breast cancer when he told me about the elevated alk phos. He made sure I didn't leave his office without getting the super-de-duper blood test. He scheduled an immediate bone scan, a procedure I really did not want to have because of a big-ass problem I have with claustrophobia. He stressed the necessity of the procedure and talked me off the ledge with an offer of Xanax. He didn't need to ask me twice.

He delivered ***the news*** — a death sentence really — with clarity and sympathy. Then he gave me his personal cell phone number. *"In case you need to talk, day or night."* I haven't called him, but he has called me, often enough for me to know that he cares about *me*, not only as his patient, but as a person. I am very fortunate to have Dr. Wonderful handling my care.

There are many others who have jumped in and offered knowledge, support, and love, and I appreciate them all in so many ways. But, at the end of the day, my bestie and my doctor are the main characters in this chapter of my life. As for the day-to-day with Donna, things have changed dramatically.

Texts from September

Me: Reading anything interesting?
Donna: OMG you are a twisted bitch. I didn't think you could get darker than the stuff that happens in *Her Scream*, but *Stay Safe* is really disturbing. I need to go watch Mary Poppins or something wholesome so my brain can destress for the night.

Texts from October

Donna: Just finished *Ashore on Stony Beach*. Send the next one.
Me: I need to write it.
Donna: Then write it, bitch. You really left me hanging.

Texts from November

Donna: Almost texted you in the middle of the night to tell you how much I'm loving *Adrift on Stony Beach* and then I remembered you might be asleep — you never used to sleep. This cancer shit really sucks.
Me: Yeup.

Texts from December

Donna: What are you doing?
Me: Reading my DNR forms for hospice. What are you doing?
Donna: Writing your eulogy.

Me: How the hell did this shit happen?
Donna: Haven't a clue, but I love you.
Me: Good to know. By the way, is the eulogy funny?
Donna: What do you think?
Me: That I should have asked someone else to write it.
Donna: Too late.
Me: For a lot of things.
Donna: I know, but I love you.

I know Donna loves me, and I know how hard all of this is for my bestie. To quote her from when this nightmare began. "This is gonna suck."

It does.

A note from Donna Eaton ...

Sheryll's blogs share intimate details of her journey with terminal cancer. She does an excellent job of addressing a topic that is not only painful but difficult to discuss. She introduces you to people near and dear to her and takes you on an emotional roller coaster that life has become for all of us.

I highly recommend Sherylll's blogs to anyone struggling with or who knows someone struggling with a terminal diagnosis. I would characterize her blogs as thoughtful, thorough and intensely honest. You will experience a wide range of emotions: gentleness, love, concern, sadness, humor and spirituality. By going through her more difficult times, it brought perspective to my own life.

Anyone who reads Sheryll's words will have insight that likely differs from mine. Her blogs are a gift from an amazingly strong woman. I will never be ready to say goodbye to her or her bits of courage and wisdom.

19. Not More Than I Can Handle ...

I used to think He has way more important things in His day to day than to micromanage the comings and goings of Sheryll O'Brien, but I've changed my tune a bit. In fact, I think God has been in lock step with me this entire time. Why? Let's take a look.

I could not handle ... leaving Tim and our girls without letters that needed to be written.

I could not handle ... leaving my mom, brother, and sister without conversations they needed as much as I did.

I could not handle ... leaving Hadley without a care package of things that will fill her time and remind her of me.

I could not handle ... traveling this road without the care and support of my doctor, my hospice team, my sisters-in-law, and my bestie.

I could not handle ... leaving my work unfinished or thanking the women who put me and my books front and center with polish and panache.

I could not handle ... leaving this life before meeting Father Dude. If I had, I would have missed the unspoken assurances that God was hearing my prayer and He was answering it, and that I'd find that truth along the way.

I know these things now. I know them because I am handling every bit of this journey, and along the way, I am being blessed with enough time to enjoy this season with the people I cherish most in the world. With God by my side there is nothing I can't handle. God is Good. God is Great. And I love Him.

20. Twelve Days Before Christmas — the first six days ...

Monday, December 13th

Today was a really tough day. It followed a really tough weekend. I started the weekend by meeting with hospice, and then telling Hadley that her MammyGrams is sick and is going to die.

The news was delivered as gently as possible, but the reality of the situation is harsh, to say the least. I forced myself and the adults around me to put the sadness aside and to do the Christmas activities that I'd planned weeks ago, the ones that have become part of our holiday season. Saturday was spent with Tim hanging our staircase garland. It's always the last piece to our decorating festivities. After that, he headed next door for the decorating of Hannah's and Hadley's tree. I watched one event, and heard about the other. Sunday was spent having a big breakfast together and making this year's snow globes. The theme for the wintry 2021 keepsakes was woodland animals, chosen by Hadley because most everything we do is centered around that little girl.

When I woke this morning, I was exhausted from holding my emotions in, and had a bit of an emotional break when everyone went off to work or to school. I allowed myself one box of tissues, and when they were sopped through, I moved beyond the choppy breaths that come at the end of a good cry, and tuned into a Hallmark Christmas movie, the one where a lawyer goes from stomping on her dance instructor's feet one week to performing the perfect waltz on a massive stage in front of a packed audience the next week. I know what you're thinking because I thought the same thing — Fat Chance, but it *could* happen. Right? I mean miracles happen — especially at Christmas. I would love a Christmas miracle. Just sayin.

Tuesday, December 14th

I finished my final readthrough of *Awake on Stony Beach* and sent it off to my publisher then slipped into some sort of funk and spent long blocks of time staring at a wall and drumming my fingers on the arm of my recliner. Whenever Tim came downstairs to check on me he asked, *"What are you doing?"* I pulled a long sigh, "I'm waiting to die," was my response. My only response. Each declaration received a different reaction from Mr. Wonderful: he sat across the room and tried to catch my eye, he offered to light the Christmas tree, he patted my head and kissed it, the kind of kiss that lingers with meaning. On the last of his trips he offered me a cup of tea. The offer wasn't received well and the Figgies were declined. A rarity for sure.

Wednesday, December 15th

I woke in the same predicament — I have a terminal illness, but I woke with a different perspective. I called Donna and told her about the previous day, and after she asked about the health and well-being of Tim she told me it was about time I let the depression breakthrough and wallow in it. I know she is right, but honestly, I'm afraid of going there. I'm afraid that I won't be able to pull myself back, so when the funk pushes hard against me I push back — way back. And for the most part, I've had great success.

Thursday, December 16th

I woke with a really sore arm from my Covid shot, but considering the pain I've been in lately, I laughed at the hot, bumpy area, and took my morning Tramadol. And Voilà! Thank you very much. I had a very productive day writing blogs. I bugged the crap out of

Guru Jessica, my website designer and social media manager because I had a very productive day writing blogs. She might have freaked out behind the scenes when my emails came rapid fire, but she attended to my requests with patience and perfection. The experience reminded me how much I enjoy working with her, and how much I'm going to miss her. Though we've never met, and despite our 30+ year age difference, we've become very good friends.

On a completely unrelated note, my appetite has been hit or miss lately — mostly miss, so when I told Mr. Wonderful I was craving a chicken and mashed potato dinner, he grabbed a precooked rotisserie chicken from Shaws, sliced the pieces paper-thin, whipped a few spuds, covered my portion with gravy, and put a dollop of cranberry sauce on the side. By the time dinner was served, I'd lost my appetite. I forced myself to eat some of it because he made it for me, but I handed back a nearly-full plate. My concerned husband said nothing, though his eyes said something. An hour or so later he offered me a cup of tea and handed off 3 Figgie cookies which I ate like a champ.

Friday, December 17th

I met with my hospice nurse and my social worker at noon. By 2 PM, I'd signed the following forms: Do Not Resuscitate, Do Not Intubate, and Do Not Transport to a Hospital. Essentially, I, Sheryll O'Brien, admitted defeat to an illness. That's because I wasn't given a fair chance at fighting this beast. There wasn't a battle planned or waged, or a skirmish here or there because the enemy's attack was full-on and a direct blow.

Those who know me know I'm a fighter. I show up for battle, any kind of battle, certainly medical battles. I've had my skull opened for a daylong brain surgery, and then reopened to stem brain fluid leakage,

I've done the step by step of breast cancer, and did a few other unrelated surgeries here and there because there was a reason and/or a chance. This time, the only thing I could do was admit defeat. That was symbolically done by my signing forms that removed any question of whether or not anyone should try to help me live. This process was hard. And when it was done, it was time for a Xanax — thank God.

Saturday, December 18th

I woke to a crappy weather day. It was overcast early in the morning, and by noon a bit of sleet had moved in. It was just enough to make things slick outside. The conditions underfoot and on roads didn't affect me because I wasn't planning a trip out, in fact my last trip out of my home was December 1st. That was the day I went to the oncologist's office and put a kibosh on a $12,000 monthly pipe dream. Now that I'm swaddled in the blanket of hospice, I don't expect to make another trip out until I make the *final* trip out.

I'm okay with staying in. I am very comfortable in my home, with all of the things I've selected over the years, the ones that turned 183 Wildwood into the place we lived our lives and made our memories. It's where I happily made mud pies with Jessica, and tossed a softball with Hannah during my enjoyable stint as a stay-at-home mom. It's where I set up shop when I began writing grants for non-profit organizations. It's where I set a formal office for my writing career, the one I dreamt about for decades. And it's where I took lead opposite Tim in our very own production of the Bickersons of Wildwood. Mostly, it's where I found my greatest fulfillment as the wife of Mr. Wonderful.

I watched my man leave a few minutes ago with Hannah, Hadley, my sister, and my mother to go see Santa travel the quaint streets of Auburn perched high on a firetruck — God only knows why, but there you have it. Since I can no longer venture out or be left alone in my home, Jessica stayed with me. As soon as the group left she asked if I wanted company, then nodded and smiled when I said no. *"Call if you need anything, Mom,"* she said as she climbed the stairs I no longer go near, the ones with the pretty banister all twined with garland. Garland I used to hang — garland I watched being hung.

21. Twelve Days Before Christmas — the last six days ...

Sunday, December 19th

A little background. Mr. Wonderful and I have answered our morning alarm at 5:15 AM for our entire marriage. We used to do a quick jog downstairs to plug in the pre-built percolator, set about doing this and that while it moaned and groaned, and gargled and gurgled our Chase and Sanborn brew, then parked our asses in the living room and just chilled together before anyone woke and sought us out.

We are still doing our morning routine, although he's the one jogging downstairs. I'm already there waiting in my super-de-duper recliner, the one my fabulous sister bought me. The beautiful buff-colored leather contraption is very much like a carnival ride for the chairbound. The seat part goes up and down, the lower section lifts to all levels, and the back can recline fully or raise the head and shoulder area to any comfort level. My extra-deluxe model has a built-in heater to help soothe this or that bit of pain here and there. I appreciate Marjorie's generosity and think of her whenever I kick back and am warmed all around. It's very much like she's there giving a big hug — the kind I shy away from now out of fear I might crumble.

Anyway, on this particular morning ... I missed coffee with Mr. Wonderful because I had a very painful Saturday evening which caused Tim to place his first ever call to the 24/7 hospice nurse — who consulted a physician — who upped my Tramadol to handle the stabs and jabs. Unfortunately, the extra meds knocked me into a semi-comatose state from which I could not escape until mid-morning.

When my eyes finally slit open, I sucked down a big-ass mug of coffee and got on with my half-day. I wrote some blogs, enjoyed a ham and cheese omelet (some of it), spent some wonderful time listening to Hadley tell me where Bernadette, her Elf on the Shelf, was hiding this morning (in a hanging planter), and after she laughed at the sleeping habits of winter pixies, she went mouth-first into an extended ramble on the topic of IF and WHEN she might hear from the North Pole. She's been waiting as patiently as any seven-year-old to find out if she made the Good Girl List. I assured her she was a shoo-in, but she was emphatic that she needed proof.

After that back-and-forth, Hadley wanted to play some sort of guessing game that she made up using a plastic egg carton full of plastic animal figurines. Game Rules: *"Close your eyes, MammyGrams, take a figurine, feel it and guess what it is."* Unfair Advantage: I had absolutely no idea what part of the Animal Kingdom we were dealing with, unlike she who loaded up the egg carton and knew full well. Needless to say, I totally sucked at this game, but I had quite the time listening to her laugh when I suggested the cat I chose might have been a water buffalo. We finished the game,

12 to 0, and off she went to brag about her victory and tell her mom about the feline/bovine incident.

I wound down for the night by watching a Hallmark movie. That evening's 'drama' was about a group of former high school friends who return home for the memorial service of their favorite teacher. These young professionals abandoned their jobs and their lives and flew in from all over to share their grief. I was more than impressed with their commitment to the man and it made me wonder who might attend my memorial service. I was immediately reminded of classmates who passed before me, the ones whose names are etched in my memory because they were really good people who died way too early. I hope I get to see them in Heaven. Perhaps it'll be a chance meeting at the grocery store like it used to be when they were here on earth, or perhaps a more pre-planned event will be announced over Heaven's surround-sound speaker system: *"South High School, Class of '75, a welcoming gathering for Sheryll O'Brien is now taking place in Aisle 7."* God I hope Aisle 7 is the freezer aisle. You can bet your ass I'll be reaching for a pint of Truffle Kerfuffle as soon as we catch up on our lives and afterlives.

Monday, December 20th

The Good Girl List arrived! I heard Hadley's voice announcing the long-awaited event as she sprinted from her house next door to ours clutching tight to the scrolled paper announcement Bernadette delivered from the North Pole. *"... And she was hiding in the Christmas tree. And she had it in her hands. And I'm on the Good Girl List. And Santa will be coming!"* the adorable kid breathlessly announced before bounding back out the door proclaiming, *"I need to get dressed for school, then I'll be back for Mashup Monday breakfast!* Mr. Wonderful and I basked in the glow of youthful exuberance. I thanked the good Lord I was here to witness it and I branded it to memory.

Speaking of memory ... This happened and it broke my heart, nope, it shattered it into a million pieces. Nancy, my publisher, emailed me as she has 22 times before saying she was at the pre-publication stage where she needed the front matter for my book, *Alva*, and also the book jacket blurb. I got busy writing the dedication and the acknowledgements and deciding this and that about all the stuff that comes after the front cover and before the book actually begins.

And then this happened ... I opened a new document page so I could write the blurb for *Alva* — the last book I will ever publish — the 17th book in my Pulling Threads series — the saga I have been crafting over the course of three years. From the start, I've put characters who I've come to love like family into perilous situations, saving those whom I adore and offing those I deemed unworthy. Oh, the power! Anyway, *Alva* was crafted with two goals in mind: push the central story to its conclusion and take my readers down memory lane by reintroducing character-specific storylines meant to tug at a few heartstrings. Anyone who's picked up a book in a store or library and flipped to the back cover to read the blurb knows how important those 100 or so words are. The intent is to turn a potential-reader into a real-reader and hopefully a hooked-reader. My job as the author is to write a compelling reason why people should invest their valuable time reading a 90,000 word tome written by Sheryll O'Brien. After a couple of hours staring at a blank page I broke. I began sobbing and before long I was in a full-blown panic attack, shaking uncontrollably and gasping for air.

Tim heard me from upstairs and came running. *"What's wrong?"*

"I can't remember."

"What? You can't remember what?"

"*Alva*. I can't remember what the story is about."

Silence. "I wrote the damned book and I can't remember the damned book! I have a vague idea about what my characters did, but I can't drill down to the STORY." Silence. "My final story and I can't remember it. I can't write the blurb." Hysterics.

Some backstory … Mr. Wonderful and I have mentioned, in passing, my memory lapses and increased confusion over the course of, I can't say exactly because I forget how long, but for weeks, I guess. Until 'The Alva Incident', the things I've forgotten haven't had much relevance or maybe they have and I can't remember. But this memory lapse — this big-ass black hole of nothingness inside my head terrified me and then it unhinged me.

When I gathered myself enough … I wrote Nancy an email asking that she or Andria craft the blurb and send it to me to read. I explained in one sentence the situation. She simply replied, *"No problem, girlfriend. I'm here for whatever you need."* I know the situation broke her heart. And like I said before, it shattered mine.

Tuesday December 21st

My hospice nurse came today. Two weeks ago, I dreaded the notion of opening my door to The Women of Hospice, strangers who were going to take me hostage in my living room and stand guard until Death came calling. I was set straight on that point during our first chit-chat. According to my hospice tag team, my nurse would 'visit' as many times a week as needed. She would do a physical and ask some questions and, based on the 'show and tell' portion of the visit, she would decide what I needed, provide what was needed, and decide when to return.

On this trip to Wildwood, Nurse M got the *"How are you feeling"* and the *"have you noticed any changes"* part taken care of lickety-split then got to the other reason she was there, a review of the Comfort Kit, a plastic pouch that contains little bottles of narcotics that I'm assuming could get me arrested and put behind bars if I was caught walking the streets with them. Since I'm no longer allowed to walk to the kitchen, I doubt I'll be running into a cop, but just having the 'stuff' in the house caused a sweat. The 'stuff' of course is morphine, my soon-to-be drug of choice.

Nurse M started her overview of what was inside the kit. I paid attention as she pulled this and that bottle and syringe from the bag. Mr. Wonderful, in comparison, honed in like an eagle readying for a dive of knowledge. He inched to the edge of his seat, leaned his forearms onto his legs, and stretched his talons or cracked his knuckles. In all honesty, I'm still not sure what took place in those few seconds, but it was intense.

Time for a little backstory ... Tim is a question-asker. No matter the subject, Tim is at the ready with a question, and then another, and then another. He likes to drill down into the minutiae and find out every little thing about every little thing. I, on the other hand, am the one in the room screaming, "It's wall-to-wall carpet, so yes it goes from one damned wall to the other and yes it goes on the floor!" So when Nurse M said she'd be giving a tutorial on the Comfort Kit, I knew I'd be needing a morphine drip that afternoon. After Tim's third question about quantum physics conversions from milliliters to milligrams or some shit neither he nor I know anything about, I decided to call in reinforcements. "Hannah, get your ass over here now!"

"Why?"

"The hospice nurse is showing your father how to syringe morphine and he's asking questions."

"On my way!"

Just having her in the room slowed my heart rate and helped with my breathing. My daughter became my human form of morphine. Nurse M sighed mightily at the confident person I put in charge of my controlled substances and that person's name is Hannah. When Nurse M backed off our driveway, my daughter and I took bets on whether the healthcare provider calls in sick on her next scheduled visitation day.

<u>Wednesday, December 22nd</u>

I had an awesome day! The increased Tramadol did the trick and, aside from causing an extra nap or two, I felt really good. I didn't feel like writing so I spent some time watching the Hallmark channel, and by watching, I mean to say that I stared at the screen and let my eyes glaze over. My television set is permanently tuned to the feel-good channel because I just don't have the mental capacity to handle upsetting shows like Sesame Street anymore. I guess you can say I've become a devotee of the 24/7, October-January Christmas fest on Hallmark. It's not that bad, really. The actors and actresses are easy on the eye and the storylines are easy to follow, much easier than guessing the Number of the Day with Count von Count.

Later that afternoon, I spent a good amount of time chit-chatting with my mother and it was wonderful. Our conversations have been on the short side lately and I've missed our 'other' talks, the gabfests that usually ended with the poor old woman gasping for air because of something I said that tickled her funny bone.

On this particular day, Mom was busy getting ready for the invasion of Confederate troops on Union soil. My brother, Don, and his lovely wife, Denise, were coming from Georgia to share my last Christmas, and they were staying with my mother and sister at the hermetically-sealed, modified-Cape the women share in Auburn. Instead of preparing a musket or two, Mom was arming the fortress with Lysol wipes, antiseptic squirt bottles, and boxes of disposable masks. God bless the woman. She's been in an emotional kerfuffle since she heard about her middle-child's medical crisis, and now the sanitized abode she'd locked herself into two years ago was being breached. The concern of course is Covid — the damned menace of eighty-six-year old women, and those hoping to see their sixty-fourth birthday.

I slipped into a momentary fog where I envisioned poor Don and Denise being forced to enter a pop-up structure on Mom's front lawn for a quick decontamination shower, much like the ones forced on Meryl Streep in the movie Silkwood, and donning full hazmat suits before being allowed inside the Auburn residence or anywhere near me. Mom and I didn't discuss any of that during our call, we stuck to the drama-free topic of meatballs and sauce simmering on her stovetop *"Do you think you could eat some? I could send some over."*

"I'd love some, Mom."

"Good, oh that's good, Sheryll Anne. Someone can pick them up mid-afternoon."

I wasn't sure at that time whether I'd be able to eat them, but I wanted them here just in case. As you know, I'm not eating a whole lot these days and what I am eating is usually found on the bland side of a menu card. I've noticed my clothes are a bit baggier and certain parts of me are sagging and dragging a bit more lately. "I'm losing weight," I declared one day. "Finally, a diet that works," I scoffed. Tim laughed, shook his head, and went about doing this and that.

I had a bout of nausea late afternoon and worried that I wouldn't be able to tolerate the sauce and balls, but by 7 PM nausea edged out and hunger eased in and I ate a good bit of the dinner my Mom sent me. It tasted like I knew it would and it made me cry because it tasted like I knew it would. Comfort food — Mom's comfort food.

Thursday, December 23rd

Nurse Ratched was right on time for my appointment. My hospice nurse, the one with a great sense of humor, got quite the kick out of my calling her that. It'll be a one-time thing because she is far too kind to suggest otherwise, even playfully. I consider myself fortunate to have her as part of my life, no matter how close to the end she entered it. Nurse M did her chit-chat and observation schtick, then nodded her head and smiled at my declaration. "I'm feeling good, really good, yesterday and today I've been pain free." When she removed her stethoscope from around her neck and started packing her things I asked the two questions I ask each time she comes. "I'm going to get Christmas and my birthday and New Year's, right?"

She smiled wide. The happy expression was hidden behind her mask, but the crinkle of a few lines around her eyes gave away her show of happiness. *"Barring any catastrophic event, based on today's exam I'd say you will be having those days and I hope they are wonderful."*

My husband and I exchanged glances of joy. And then I asked the second question. "Do you think I'm looking at a two, maybe three month time-frame?"

She prefaced her answer as she always does about offering no guarantees, but she didn't laugh out loud in incredulity either. Mr. Wonderful and I did the whole glance of joy, once again.

Late afternoon, Hadley visited and immediately filled our home with the jubilant sounds of a kid at Christmas. When it was time for her to travel off to her father's home for an overnight stay and exchange of gifts, she wrapped her arms tight and held on for quite some time then bounded out the door for Round One of giving and receiving.

Early evening, Hannah and Jessica joined Tim and me in the living room, the one filled from end to end with gifts he lugged from the basement. Mr. and Mrs. Wonderful relaxed into the moment with our girls, each of us knowing it marked the beginning of our last Christmastime together. We shared an almost sacred bit of silence near our lighted tree and sort of just looked at one another — taking mental snapshots, I suppose. "I have something special for each of you." They sighed heavily knowing there were tears in their immediate future. After I presented my daughters with pieces of my jewelry, there were tears all around.

Friday, December 24th

I woke Christmas Eve morning with no pain, no nausea, and no fatigue. Tim joined me downstairs and opened the front door so we could watch the beauty of a light snowfall. He lit the tree and kissed my head on his way to the kitchen to plug in the percolator. After handing off my mug, he sat in his mission chair, as he has countless times before, and stared at me, as he has so often in recent weeks. After many minutes I broke the silence, "I've had three back-to-back wonderful days. Honestly, Tim, I can't remember when

I've felt better. Do you think this is one of those rally things hospice patients get?"

His response was immediate. *"Nope. I think it's the power of prayer. I think everyone who loves you is praying that you get to enjoy this holiday season and God is hearing their prayers."* My tears were immediate. "And He answered them."

God is good. God is great. And I love Him. I love my family and friends, too. And I pray that you all have a Merry Christmas and a happy and healthy New Year.

22. Christmas ...

> *When I kissed him goodbye, I whispered, "See you on the flip side, Donnie."*
>
> *~ Sheryll*

I've had some really great Christmas mornings in my very-soon-to-be 64 years. Of particular note was the year I turned eight, that was the year Santa left a really cool bike parked adjacent to the Christmas tree with my name written on the hanging tag.

My cool bike was a 'girl's bike'. It had metal structural elements that angled away from important girly bits, a semi-banana-shaped seat of white, a bright white basket affixed to the handlebars, royal blue and white streamers hanging from bright white handlebar grips, and white-walled tires. It was beautiful and it was given to me in the dead of a Massachusetts winter. I ached to hop on that baby and ride it around the Columbus Park neighborhood, but the best I could do was ride it from one end of the 10x10 foot kitchen to the other end and wait for spring. My sigh of disappointment could have been heard at the North Pole when I was told to put it onto the enclosed front porch and wait for good weather.

An awesome Christmas surprise … A little before noon, my father took the bike out through the front door, carried it past four-foot-high snow banks and put it onto Hobson Avenue. *"Get your coat and go for a ride,"* he said upon return. I flew out past him, learning pretty quick why my bike was outside, the temps that Christmas morning were in the 50s and the streets were snow-free. *"Stay on Hobson Avenue,"* he said as he closed the front door.

"No problem," and off I went. I stayed on our dead-end street that had minimal traffic on most days, and on that Christmas afternoon it had no traffic. It was my street. I rode my new bike all afternoon, stopping occasionally to puff warm air onto really cold hands beginning to freeze into the shape of handlebar grips as the temps began to plummet. I was a bit peeved when dusk arrived and a bit sad when I lugged my brand-new bike into the house and saw white-walled tires all splattered with winter yuck. I grabbed a rag and wiped her down, parked her into a corner and bounded inside the warm abode. I walked the few steps to the living room, adjusted the rabbit ears on the television and thawed my ass while waiting for Harvey Leonard to predict the weather for the next day. As soon as I heard temps wouldn't get higher than the teens, I slumped a bit knowing I was back to the springtime waiting game.

I grabbed a piece of ribbon candy from a pretty glass bowl and bit into the glass-shard-shit, threw half of it back into the bowl, and wondered why the torture treats always ended up at our house, and why I always bit one. As soon as the tiny slices to the roof of my mouth stopped bleeding, I smiled wide at my good fortune of that Christmas day — the one when I could ride free like the wind because Santa brought me a bike and an unseasonably warm day to enjoy it.

*Another awesome Christmas surprise ...*The year I turned thirteen, I got a combo Christmas/Birthday gift from my parents. Like any other kid born in December, getting a combo-gift is part of life. It probably dates back to the most important kid born that month; the one born in a manger; the one who became the reason for the season. When you think about it, or when I think about it, baby Jesus was the first to suffer the fate of combo-gift givers. Take the Three Wise Men for instance. They each brought a lovely birthday gift of gold, frankincense and myrrh, but would it have killed them to stop at a little boutique on their way from the mountain, part with a few gold shillings, and pick up a lovely blanket of blue for the Christmas babe asleep on the hay. Or maybe get a little something, something for Mary, like a heating pad for her back and maybe a few OTCs for pain relief? I'm sure she would have appreciated the gesture after the donkey-riding and child-birthing thing. But, alas, the Three Wise Men came without notice and bearing one gift each. I venture to guess if it were Three Wise Women bearing gifts, they would have put the gold, frankincense and myrrh into a gift bag, and made a plan. *"We should call before visiting the manger."*

"And we should bring a Christmas gift. Maybe a basket full of diapers, bibs, and teething rings."

"And we should bring a tree ornament engraved with Jesus' name and birthdate as his birthday gift."

Yeup. Three Wise Women would have figured that if ever there was a kid deserving more than a combo-gift, it was our Lord and Savior. But I digress. I probably also ensured myself a lengthy wait at the

Pearly Gates for that bit of sacrilege, but things just need to be said sometimes. You know?

Anyway, back to the point of this blog … If there really is a point. My birthday being so close to Christmas put me upon the combo-gift-road on more than one occasion. In fact, I began an annual tradition of watching gift-givers arrive to see if their bounty included any boxes wrapped in birthday paper. It was a crapshoot for sure and, on more than one occasion, I felt gypped in the gift receiving department.

I should note, however, that my parents never succumbed to the ease of a singular gift until my 13th birthday. I rolled my eyes and folded my arms when I bounded downstairs Christmas morning and was directed toward my gift, the one wrapped half in Christmas paper and half in birthday paper, leaving no mystery for me to solve on whether it was a twofer gift. All was forgiven when I opened the rather large box and pulled out a suitcase. "Finally, a way of escaping."

"It's not a suitcase, Sheryll Anne. It's a portable record player." The parent-tag-team held the floor and gave an operational lesson.

"You slide this latch and carefully lower the cover which holds the turntable. Make sure you gently snap the cover into the Open position." Snap.

"This arm holds the needle. After you slide the record down this shiny post, you position this lever to the On position, that's when the turntable starts turning. Then you lift the needle-arm and put it onto the 45 or the LP. You have to be really gentle otherwise you'll scratch the record or break the needle."

I listened more intently than I'd ever done before and parroted back an abbreviated version of instructions, "Latch, lower, snap, slide, position, put — do it all gently. Got it." I reached out a trembling hand for the skinny present being offered. I could tell by its size and flatness that it was a 45 record. I tore the twofer paper away with one pull and read the label, "Glen Campbell's, *Wichita Lineman?*" I said my next words in my head. "What the ever-loving fuck!? Who the ever-loving fuck!?" I probably said something way more age-appropriate, but you get the point.

My brother, Donnie, left the room in a fit of laughter, and headed to the serenity of his bedroom. He stopped laughing when I followed him upstairs with my record player in tow, set up shop outside his bedroom door, unlatched the cover, lowered the turntable, and let Glen Campbell have at it. I played that song over and over and over, again. I have absolutely no proof, but I always suspected Donnie broke the needle on my new record player. If he was the saboteur, I wish to God he'd broken the damned 45.

Because I didn't follow the operational suggestion to be 'gentle' and broke the damned needle on the first day, I had to wait a week before I was allowed to walk to Zayres to buy a 10 pack of record player needles. While I was there, I bought my first ever Gary Puckett records. I raced home, locked myself behind closed doors and listened to the leader of the Union Gap sing about a young girl and a woman — one of which I was, and one of which I was becoming. Listening to Mr. Puckett sing about what was waiting on the other side of puberty made me want to become his Woman, Woman.

A bittersweet Christmas ... This year there were no bikes or record players waiting under the Christmas tree. In fact, the thing I wanted most on my last Christmas was the gift of human contact. The embrace of family members, some who would drive a few miles to see me, and others who would travel the Eastern

Seaboard to give and receive a hug. Had I not been diagnosed in November, my brother and sister-in-law would not have driven from Georgia to Massachusetts for Christmas. They always celebrate the holiday down south, choosing to make their annual trek north during summer months so we can all bask in the warmth of family love on the sandy beach in Wells, Maine. This year my 66-year-old brother did the 1,055 mile drive to ensure that I'd get the ultimate combo gift ever! Him.

23. Hardest Birthday Ever ...

For the past year I've been breaking out in tune, singing the first few words of The Beatles song, *When I'm Sixty-Four*. I've driven my family crazy, and have enjoyed every minute of doing so. After receiving **the news**, I became obsessed with having my last Christmas, and my 64th birthday, and another New Year celebration. As I inched closer and closer to the holiday season, I felt more and more sure I'd be getting them. And when I heard that Don and Denise were making the trip north, my anticipation of milestone celebrations turned into sheer excitement at seeing them. I sort of missed the fact that after their visit, they would be leaving and I'd never be seeing them again. That realization inched into my consciousness on Christmas Day, and then banged full-force on the morning of my 64th birthday.

I woke late, barely sipped my morning brew, and sort of settled into a funk. And when deep melancholy tried to take over, I pushed it back so I'd be able to enjoy the gathering set for 2 PM. The expended energy it took to keep from breaking left me fatigued and with a pounding headache. And when I watched my 86-year-old mom slog the walkway all slump-shouldered, and needing help getting into my home by my sister who was lugging presents wrapped in festive birthday paper, it took all I had to keep a stiff upper lip. And when Don and Denise walked through my front door, the one they'd be leaving forever later that day, I discreetly popped the Xanax I desperately needed.

A little background … My mother was an expert knitter in her day. There was never a time when the sound of her metal knitting needles hitting one another wasn't heard upon entering her home. She made hats, scarves, and mittens in a matter of minutes, and pullover and zippered sweaters in a matter of hours. Her trademark creations were her Irish knit, cable-stitch blankets, the ones that took months to make and when finished were works of art. Mom had barely seated herself in my home, when she got up and dragged an oversized bag my way. *"I intended to leave this for you, Sheryll Anne upon my passing, but."* She kissed my head and was helped to her seat by someone. I don't really know because my eyes filled and I willingly jumped into the black hole of nothingness in my head — the place I escape to when things get really hard to handle.

And at that moment, I needed to escape, and since I am not allowed to walk, run, or shuffle away from anything, I sat there with a blank look on my face and leapt into the mental abyss. I heard myself say things like, "Oh, Mom. It's beautiful. Look at the cable-stitch. This is amazing." But on the inside I was hearing the echo of my silent scream, "Oh. My. God. This is the saddest thing. This must be killing my mother." I pushed the tears deep. And when Marjorie gave me a crate full of LPs that had been missing for decades my sadness ebbed a bit until she explained how she spent hours in her spider-filled attic looking for them because she just had a feeling my treasures were there.

Some more background … Marjorie and I shared a room when we were kids. Every night, I'd plop into bed, prop my head on my arm and get ready for the nightly show. Marjorie, my kid sister, the one with golden, wavy hair and sapphire-blue eyes to die for, would enter the room, step to her bed, fold down her quilt, then her blanket, then her sheets and do an inspection for the dreaded spiders she thought might have found their way into her place of slumber. After a good shaking of the linen and an eyeball inspection from corner to corner and top to bottom, she would put the sheet, blanket and quilt back into place and begin the tucking process. Inch by inch she moved down both sides and across the bottom of her twin bed tucking the cloth-wares nice and tight. Then she'd sit her ass on her pillow, put her lower extremities under the top ridge of tucked things and commence the wriggling into her cocoon. As soon as she settled, she'd cross her arms over her chest and breathe a sigh of accomplishment. I particularly enjoyed the evenings when she forgot to turn off the overhead light and had to drag her ass from bed and start the process all over again.

So, the fact that Marjorie spent hours where spiders congregate looking for LPs that I'd long-ago given up hope of ever finding is beyond touching. I pushed the tears deeper. And when my mother and sister made a hasty retreat from my home, supposedly because they didn't want to overstay their welcome, I knew IT was coming. IT began when Denise got up and put on her coat. The room silenced. I stood from my recliner and waited for her goodbye hug. She said her *"I love you,"* and stepped away. We didn't look at one another when we parted. and I tried not to look at Don when he approached, but I couldn't help myself. By the time he reached me his eyes were full of tears.

My brother is a strong man, but he is also a tender-hearted man. There have been occasions when I've seen his tears form, but there have been very few times when I've seen his tears flow. He held them tight when he wrapped me in his arms and whispered how much he loved me. It took a good minute for us to end our embrace. I watched him exit my home and plopped onto my recliner without a single thought I might fracture my ass. Within seconds, he was back inside my house and I was once again in his arms. This time he let his tears fall as he walked away. I insisted Tim help me to the door so I could watch Don and Denise leave. I saw my brother help his sobbing wife into their truck, then lean himself against it before getting in. He pulled the truck forward and parked, flashed his lights to me and I flashed the house lights to him, and then he backed off the driveway and drove away. I didn't bother trying to push back the tears.

I had a horrible headache that night and couldn't settle myself at all. Tim stayed up late with me and tried to distract me from the emotional tsunamis that came and went. And when it seemed as though my sadness was losing its battle to sleepiness, he kissed my head and went to bed. The next morning, he came downstairs and found me typing away. *"What are you doing?"*

"Writing a blog."

He scoffed and asked, *"Oh, God, what did I do wrong now?"*

I cracked up laughing, really laughing, the kind of laugh that has marked our lives together. Our wonderful lives together.

As for Don and Denise, last I heard they were packing their truck with Christmas loot, and two very heavy hearts. I suspect that'll be one miserable trip home.

24. Auld Lang Syne ...

> *I've come to learn that you don't lose friendships, they are simply put on pause.*
>
> *~ Sheryll O'Brien*

Should old acquaintances be forgot? Nope, but one of the sad facts of life is that we meet lots of people along the way, then lose contact with most. Sometimes, we even lose friends, people we really loved hanging with and sharing our deepest, darkest secrets and fears with. I thought I'd lost a few of those tighter-than-tight friends, but I've come to learn that I didn't lose the friendships, they were simply put on pause. For whatever reason, I went one way, and they went another. During our separations, we did some really big things: had kids, raised kids, bought homes, built careers, lost parents, and had grandkids. Mostly, we did a bunch of little things, the day-to-day crap that can be the death knell of friendships — or so it *could* seem.

A little background ... When I emerged from my full-time, stay-at-home, mom-stint, I took a part-time job at the local newspaper in its advertising department. All I had to do during my 15-hour work week was slap on a headset, listen to customers describe what they wanted to part with, type the ad, and be done with it. I quickly discovered I had three learning curves on my new job: 1) push the correct flashing light on the console phone, 2) push the correct button on the computer system to save and not delete the ad I'd just typed, and 3) sort out the rapid fire, Irish-brogue spewing from the worker to my right — the one I asked repeated questions of.

My frequently heard, "What? What? What?" was not a back-to-back-to-back request for clarity about phones and computers, after all I'm not as daft as a mule, but the back-to-back-to-back what questions spewed forth because I couldn't understand her words, the ones delivered on a stream with nary a breath between. I'll admit that on occasion my semi-daftness about phones and computers got her Irish up, causing her to toss her headset upon her desk and come push the damned button on the console or the computer. Whilst she was pushing this and that button, I feared I was pushing hers a time or two too many.

It wasn't long before I deciphered the lilting spew of the Irish One. I really enjoyed her turn of phrase, her sharp wit, and before long I'd found myself a really good friend from across the pond. Jennifer Lane was a bit younger than I and had a way unto herself. She was Irish-pretty, with reddish-brown hair and fair skin, and she wore her clothes really well. I think she was the first person I knew who wore Doc Martens, and she wore the hell out of them. We became thick as thieves in no time at all and spent a few years telling tales of childhood and sharing dreams of adulthood. And then came the pause.

Another background story … When Hannah was in second grade we took her out of Worcester Central Catholic elementary school and put her into a public school in our neighborhood. We thought it best for her to meet the kids who lived nearby and figured the best way to accomplish that was for her to go to the school a few blocks away. I mentioned the change to Joyce McTigue, the wife of Tim's cousin John, who lived across the street from us. She suggested I introduce myself to the Gagnon family who lived further up on Wildwood because their daughter, Amanda, was Hannah's age and they'd probably be in the same class.

I took Joyce's advice and called Debbie Gagnon. I explained the situation and asked if the kids could meet. She invited us to her house and told Hannah to bring a suit for a swim in the pool. The kids got on great and the moms did, too. Amanda and Hannah spent that summer doing things kids do: biking, swimming, and having sleepovers. Debbie and I spent that summer doing the things moms do — shooting the shit. In retrospect, I think I did the majority of the talking. Debbie did a lot of listening and a lot of laughing. She had a great laugh, the kind that caused a few laugh-lines at the corners of her eyes. Those were the only lines on that woman's face. Debbie Gagnon is one of those women, the really pretty kind who needs no makeup and looks dressed up in a pair of chinos and a button-down blouse.

Anyway, we became really good friends and though we lived a stone's throw from one another, we tended to burn the phone lines with marathon gabfests, about this and that, and sometimes about more serious neighborhood goings-on. When Hannah and Amanda headed to different high schools, Debbie and I had plenty of things to share and compare. And when they went off to college, our relationship waned a bit. And then came the pause.

Back to Jennifer ... A few weeks after my blog about my terminal illness hit the internet, I received an email, the subject line read: **It has been at least 25**

years! And just like that, the unpause button was pushed. Jennifer was back in my life and we picked up right where we'd left off — except for the cancer shit, that is. We emailed some and then we talked by phone. It took me a few minutes to sort out the rapid fire, Irish-brogue spewing over the line, but it was positively wonderful hearing her voice. And seeing her face.

A little sidestep here ... One of the things about sitting 24/7 in a chair is that you tend to lose track of which 24/7 day it is, but a day or so before Christmas there came a nighttime knock on my door and there stood Jennifer, half her face covered by a mask, handing off a wrapped gift to Tim. A little more background. On occasion, I'd looked for Jennifer on FB and learned a bit, like she'd gone gray, as I have, and that she'd become an artist, quite the artist. Seriously. Jennifer had beautiful snapshots of her work posted on her FB page. The few messages beneath tipped me off that it was her work. Who knew? Anyway, back to my story. The knock came, she handed a package to Tim, then stood in the doorway while Mr. Wonderful and I pulled back taped paper wrap. To my utter surprise and total delight was the painting I'd made reference to in one of our back and forth emails. I thanked her for her kindness and, as soon as she slipped back into the dark of night, I asked Tim to take my favorite van Gogh (Peach Trees in Blossom) off the wall and hang hers in its place

Back to Debbie ... The day after Christmas there came a knock upon my glass storm door. Standing in the cold was Debbie. She opened the door to the wave of my hand, and just like that, the unpause button was pushed. Debbie was back in my life and we picked up right where we'd left off — except for the cancer shit, that is. *"A banana bread,"* she said as she handed the bag to Jessica who deposited it in the kitchen and headed upstairs. The two of us started rambling. I was saying things like, "Come in. Sit down. It's so good to see you." I think she said something like, *"I was at Amanda's house and she asked if I'd heard anything about Sheryll O'Brien, and then she gave me your blog to read, and I read a sentence, maybe two, then left her house saying I was going to your house and she said I couldn't just drop in without calling, so I took her banana bread, here, I hope that's okay."*

I'm not sure of the order of things, but I think that was the gist of it. She sat in the chair I pointed to and just sort of sank into the cushion, pushed down by the enormity of why we were together again. The pained look on her face made me sink inside, too. When her eyes filled, I pushed my emotions deep and said how happy I was that she stopped in. She said she had to stop, she just couldn't walk past my house to get to hers. Debbie had only read a few lines of my blog, so I filled her in on everything. I could almost see my words layer upon her like bricks.

Before she suffocated from the weight of it all, we swung around to talking about things we talked about before our pause — husbands, kids, and now grandkids. Debbie was one of the few people who used to read my stories before I became serious about writing books. She was thrilled to learn I'd published 23 novels, and positively glowed with happiness because I ended up doing what I always wanted to do. I gave her my last series, the Stony Beach trilogy, and she said she'd read them. I know she will.

I wish more of my friends, the ones who knew about my book publishing and my lifelong dream, had taken time to read my stories or simply given some feedback on this exciting part of my life. A text, a call, an email, or even a thumbs up on social media would have been so appreciated. Writing is such a lonely, isolating process, so hearing from people about the work and getting a 'congrats' on pushing into my dream was wonderful and very needed. And when people who I hadn't heard from in years, like high school classmates of mine, Karen Flynn Larson Gouin, and Sue Leblanc Rohr, reached out with enthusiastic support, it was just so thoughtful. So, to those who brightened my day and life with a painting, a banana bread, or a thumbs up on Facebook, I thank you, and I hope to hear from you in the New Year. Be well, friends. Old and new-again, friends.

An email from Jennifer Lane Courville ...

Your name popped up in my News Feed and brought with it a slew of memories from a long time ago ... If I ever thought when on an occasion you travelled alongside a memory with me that, ah sure, God willing we might bump into each other someday, that assumption was put paid to when I popped on your blog ... and O Fuck!

You might never get this email, you might never read these words, but then again you might. I wanted you to know you added value to my life and I never forgot you. You were brave and beautiful and funny back then .., you are brave and beautiful and funny now. I wish you peace on your journey, and love from an old friend.

25. Some Truth Telling ...

Christmas. ✓ Birthday. ✓ New Year's Eve and Day. ✓ ✓ Now, what? I've been so focused on living long enough to enjoy those lasts that I didn't put any thought into what comes next. That realization hit hard early New Year's Day. "What do I focus on now that the holiday milestones I set have come and gone? Do I choose Valentine's Day in February as my next wanna-see, or stretch beyond that to the first day of spring in March, or should I swing big and go for Opening Day of baseball in April? Or do I just sit back and wait for the telltale signs, the ones that announce my decline and then pick a day or week or month that seems doable — reachable?"

Mr. Wonderful had no response to my question as he headed to the kitchen to plug in the percolator, so the diehard Red Sox fan that I am, sat her ass in the super-de-duper recliner and went it alone on answering that ramble. I chose Opening Day as my new goal. The date I want to reach.

I immediately searched the web to see what date I was aiming for, "March 31st? What the eff? Hey, Tim, I thought MLB Opening Day was always in April. It's March 31st this year." He poked his head into the living room, *"It's only one day earlier."*

"Only one day? Only one day? What if it was the only day you had left?"

Silence. And then a quiet mumble on his way back to the kitchen, *"This might be the only day I have left."*

"I heard that."

Silence. And then my rant. "Is it too much to ask that Opening Day be in April like it's always been? Really, is that too much to ask?" He appeared back in the doorway and moved toward me. I shook my head, "I'm doing math."

He turned and left, *"Oh, Jesus, help me."*

My 'doing math' is never a good idea. Those who know me well know I'm about as good at ciphering numbers as the dimwitted sod Jethro Bodine was on the classic television show Beverly Hillbillies. Still, I needed to know how many days there were between January 1st and March 31st, and the only way to know was to do some goesintas. "Nope. I'll count the days," I mumbled. I searched the table to my left and the one to my right for my phone, but came up empty. Why? That is a very good question. I'm a woman stuck on a recliner in the middle of a living room much like Tom Hanks was stuck on an island in the middle of some body of water. Vastly different people, vastly different circumstances, but like me, Tom couldn't find his cell phone, or maybe he did and he couldn't find his charger, or maybe he had that, but he couldn't find an electrical outlet. I really don't know if he even looked for any of those things, maybe he just looked for the ball, I think he named it Wilson. "Hey, Tim, what did Tom Hanks name his ball in that movie when he's shipwrecked?"

"Cast Away."

"Didn't ask what the movie was called, I asked about the ball. Could you please answer the question I asked?" I hissed.

"Wilson," he groaned.

"Huh, I remembered Tom Hanks was stuck on an island in a movie. Could I remember *Alva*? Nope. See how things work these days? It isn't pretty." Anyway, my phone was MIA and I didn't feel like asking Mr. Wonderful to head a search party, so I did what I could to figure some shit out. By the time I finished the whole, "Thirty days has September, April, June and November, all the rest have thirty-one except February," ditty, I was exhausted and elated that I remembered the entire rhyme. Then I had a little pissy-fit that February only has twenty-eight days and MLB starts in March. "Right out of the gate, I'm screwed out of a few days," I hissed to no one. I pondered my timeframe until Tim brought me my coffee. *"You've been talking to yourself."*

"Uh huh."

"And?"

"I've decided I'm swinging big. I'm going for Opening Day."

"Sounds good," he reached into the pocket of his robe and gave me a surprise baggie of Figgie cookies. *"Happy New Year. I came down around midnight, but you were sleeping."*

"I was Xanaxing."

He laughed. Mr. Wonderful has a great laugh, it's one of the things I love most about him. After a bit of jovialness, we spent a few minutes in silence, then spent a couple searching for my phone that started making some odd, muffled chirping noise. Apparently, I was sitting on the device. How it got between my posterior and the comfy cushion I'd been perched upon for weeks is anyone's guess. Once in my hand, the sucker blew up with text messages surrounded by floating balloons, popping champagne corks, and bursting fireworks — all meant to celebrate my 'success' at living until the New Year. I took pride in the accomplishment though you know and I know the only contribution to the Life and Death game I'm playing is sitting on my ass in the dugout. I appear to be pushing into a baseball analogy or metaphor, so let's see what happens.

Side note and update about my memory issues ... I struggled with writing the book jacket for *Alva*, the last book in my Pulling Threads series. Nancy helped out by sending over a quasi-blurb-book-review that easily could have been used on the back cover, but after reading the synopsis I remembered enough about the story that I decided to use her framework and take a whack at writing the blurb. Every writer has their own voice and I really wanted my voice to finish out the series I'd worked on for years. I felt compelled to try, and I feel tremendous pride having done the work, aided of course by Nancy's prompts.

The reason I mention the memory-slip-and-slide is because I'm mixing up things that I know I know, like the difference between a metaphor and an analogy. For some reason, I'm confusing the two, and I am so tired of checking their definitions that I'm gonna just wing it. So, if you see that I've taken a swing and a miss by using analogy when it should be metaphor, please just tsk, tsk, tsk it away. And when I skip a word or shift a tense in a sentence, please just add them in or switch them up. Guru Jessica has helped with grammatical housekeeping, but when I feel the need to rush a post we concentrate on getting it up, and put striving for an A+ in spelling and punctuation aside. Amazingly, I'm okay with a bit of uncleanliness in my writing which is so not like me. Generally speaking, I am a pain in the ass perfectionist, or I was. Now, I'm not worried about picayune bullshit although I just found 5 misspellings of a main character's name in my *Ashore on Stony Beach* book that caused a slight rise in blood pressure.

Normally, that would have sent me into a bit of a snit because my books are read and reread and reread several times for accuracy during the pre-publication process. Don't know how the snafu happened — don't care, either. Pssssst. I suspect pushing two books through a publication window of two weeks rather than the two months each would normally have been given had something to do with it. I guess I've finally arrived at that place where I don't sweat the small stuff and the Lachlan v Lacklan oversight is so not worrisome now. I kinda like this new phase in life.

Okay, back to the blog ... The month of March has circled through my head on a few occasions. I know in my heart of hearts that I have nothing to do with the date of my death, but I have a lot of time on my hands, and so I fill it in odd ways. Like when I take a bathroom break from my sitting, I do stuff in there I'm not supposed to do, like some light housekeeping and staring out the window at the now bare trees in the backwoods. Please don't fink me out to hospice patrol. Please don't! I don't do much while I'm in there, a little dusting of the linen cabinet, a little straightening of the medicine cabinet, and a little Lysol-wiping of the sink. While I'm upright, I spend some time looking at myself in the mirror. Aside from profound sadness in my eyes (sometimes), nothing has changed. I don't look sick. I know I am dying, but I've been feeling pretty good lately. I've had pain, but I've managed it well with Tramadol. I've had lots of nausea, but I've managed it with Zofran.

I've had increased frequency and severity of headaches and jaw pain, but I've managed them with the combo of Tramadol and Tylenol. Apparently, now that I'm playing in the big leagues, I've become addicted to pain meds and shit. You'd be surprised how easy it is to do. I have a whole new understanding of what it's like to be injured and benched when all you want to do is play the game. I really understand the slippery-slope of pain medication and thank God I do.

I truly believe that barring a curve-ball bone-break, or stroke, or some other catastrophic event, I'll make it to Opening Day. I am always mindful that my cancer is in an advanced stage and is very aggressive, and my game may be called early, but if I'm lucky, I might go into extra innings. I'm gonna be as formidable an opponent in this game of Life and Death as I can be. Now. Having said that, there are some things I need to get off my chest. I have been completely truthful in my writings, but I realize that I haven't been totally forthcoming.

Case in point ... I have heard from so many people that my blogs have become an important part of their lives, especially for friends and family who want to know how I'm feeling but don't want to overwhelm me with calls requiring me to say the same things over and over and over again. I've also heard my blogs have been well received by people I don't know, some who are facing similar health challenges, and may be in the care of hospice.

I admit that I began writing the blog about my journey because I need to write, and I just could not embark on starting a novel when I knew I wouldn't finish it. So while the blog started as a self-serving exercise, it has turned into so much more, and that is so wonderful. The people who have been texting, emailing, and calling with their thoughts on my journey have lifted me on more than one occasion.

The sounds of my cell chirping, dinging, and ringing have put an immediate end to whatever feeling I was working through, or thought I was torturing myself with, or question I was asking that I knew full-well had no answer. With remarkable consistency, the callers have mentioned and marveled at how strong I am. Many have said they'd be rolled in a ball in the corner in a state of hysterics if they'd been handed my set of circumstances. In all honesty, that's where I want to be sometimes, but I know if I allow myself to go there, I won't be able to pull myself up. That's the reason I'm facing the end of my life with as much grit as I can muster.

Truth be told, there's little else I can do. I sure as hell don't want my family and friends to carry the extra burden of a morose or bitchy Sheryll on top of their already heavy load. Believe me when I tell you, there have been times throughout this ordeal when I've been a big old baby. Some in my inner circle might even say I've been a petulant brat. Well, they'd say it to one another — not to me! And they'd be absolutely justified in describing me that way especially when it comes to my aversion to, or more accurately stated, my irrational fear of medical machinery that allows a peek into the human body.

Irrational fear on display: I took the news that I had metastatic breast cancer of the bones way more calmly than when I heard the acronyms MRI, CT and PET scan as part of my diagnostic future. Just typing that sentence has put me into a tailspin, so I'm going to stop this blog, go chit-chat with Tim, and get my accelerated heartbeat under control. And then, I'll illustrate my pissy-ass-pain-in-the-ass-self in my next blog. Don't say I didn't warn you.

26. Medical Machines and Panic Attacks ...

On Monday, October 18th my world began changing. That's the day Dr. Wonderful (no tongue-in-cheek reference because he really is a wonderful physician) told me about the elevated alk phos in my pre-physical labs. By the following Wednesday I learned that the super-de-duper blood work that analyzes alk phos showed the elevation most likely had something to do with my bones. That's when Dr.

Wonderful booked me for a bone scan. I immediately went into a panic, not because the bone scan might show cancer, or because the person conducting the scan would have to inject radioactive materials into my veins, but rather because I'd have to get into some godforsaken machine.

I mentioned in an earlier blog that I avoid medical-research like the plague, but I could not resist the urge to search images of bone scan machinery. There were pages of images, so I narrowed my search to: **bone scan machines used for suspected metastatic breast cancer.** "BINGO." The search narrowed the field to a couple dozen or so contraptions. Looking at each prompted this response, "Shit! Shit! Shit!" That succinct, albeit repetitive, reaction preceded a spike in blood pressure and an abundance of sweat that formed on my brow, upper lip and hands. And when my eyes zoomed to the scanning machine that looked like a big-ass metal box with a tiny circle on the side and nothing else, my response and physical manifestations skyrocketed, "What the fuck, fuck, fuck!?

I stared at that thing for several minutes wondering how the hell the medical torturers got the patient into the little hole. "Must be by gunpoint," I stuttered. Unlike the other machines on the search page, there was no board for the patient to lie upon. "Maybe there's another way in. Nope. Nope. I don't see a way in or out and there aren't any holes punched into the top for air. "What the fuck? Even Donnie and I punched holes into the top of Mason jar lids for the insects we captured. We made sure they had plenty of air to breathe as we starved them to death. Unintentionally, of course." I continued my study of the picture with one eye closed, then with two eyes closed, then with two eyes open, then I enlarged the picture, then hit the 'Go To the Website' option to read some words about the machine. "What the fuck?" I said again. "Nope, nope, hard pass," I choked. Then I pushed myself to think it through, to come up with a reasonable explanation. "Why is that thing completely enclosed? It looks like an effing washing machine." My head and heart automatically went on spin cycle and I almost tossed my cookies — Figgies, of course.

When I settled myself enough, I continued my viewing. I had to, otherwise the frontload machine would be the only image stuck in my head for that night's torture loop. I called Donna, "Okay, what happens if I don't get the scan?"

"You've been looking at nuclear med scanning machines."

"Yes."

"Oh, fuck."

"That's what I said — repeatedly."

She sighed.

"Donna, do you know what kind of machine I'll be forced into?"

She did the whole bullshit thing about it not being her field of medicine, blah, blah, blah. I groaned really loudly and headed toward the metaphorical ledge. She pulled me back a bit. *"Tell me about the other machines you saw."*

"Okay. Right. Other machines. There's one that sort of looks like a big-ass donut with a reasonably-sized circumference for a board to move through."

"Sounds like a CT scan."

"And there were happy, smiling people lying supine ready for their quick trip. I want that one."

"I don't think that's for nuke med, so what else was there?"

"There were a few that fell somewhere between the device I would absolutely stroke-out in, and the donut shop device I could possibly survive in if there was a dozen honey-dipped waiting at the ejection site."

"I'll do some research. You go do something else."

"What?"

"Anything else. Love you."

I pushed away from the computer, left my office and headed downstairs to hang out with my kitchen appliances — friendly machines that held a world of possibilities, none of which included taking me hostage. I pulled my recipe book from the cupboard, and the necessary ingredients to make Joyce McTigue's chicken and broccoli casserole. I think it's her recipe, her name appears at the top of my recipe card, so it must be there for a reason. Right? I don't actually remember her giving me the recipe, although I remember the casserole she delivered to a funeral gathering once and it was delicious enough that I could see myself asking for the recipe. Anyway, while I was stirring the cheese sauce for this 'comfort food' creation, memories from the early 2000s came out of hiding and banged the hell out of my head. I'm going to include a blog I wrote a year ago when life was much simpler and medical crises weren't terminal.

The best gift ever ...

When is tinnitus not just ringing and buzzing in your ears? When the sounds are caused by a big-ass acoustic neuroma, that's when. I'd been experiencing the annoying sounds for several years and complained to my coworkers about them on several occasions. Each of them had to remove their headsets so they could hear my complaints. Ah, the source of the ringing and the buzzing we decided. For them, maybe. For me, the sounds were caused by a tumor that had taken root inside my ear canal. Technically, an acoustic neuroma, also known as a vestibular schwannoma, is a head tumor that begins developing inside the ear. When it grows up, it starts messing with the brain. This type of tumor is slow growing, and stealth as shit. Aside from the tinnitus, I had no other symptoms. No headaches, no dizziness, no facial paralysis or weakness.

Until ... I thought things might be getting serious when cricket chirps and backing-up-truck sounds joined the ringing and the buzzing. In the early weeks of December, some years ago, the cacophony in my head became unbearable. I made a plan to address the situation as soon as the holiday season was over. When I awoke Christmas morning to silence, I truly thought it was a miraculous event — the best gift ever — the plot for a Hallmark movie. Of course, that was before the penny dropped that I was deaf in one ear.

Shortly after the New Year I called for an appointment, "March? You can't fit me in before then? I'm sort of deaf." I could have gone elsewhere as the lovely booking secretary kindly reminded me, but I wanted the best ear, nose, and throat doctor, so I took the March appointment.

As soon as I arrived at the ENT's office, I was taken for a hearing test, which was really a half-hearing-test, all things considered. The results: *"Perfect hearing in one ear, zero hearing in one ear, no mechanical reasons for hearing loss, let's get an MRI to look for a brain tumor."*

"Yeah. Let's."

By the end of that day, I was diagnosed with a big-ass tumor. No hyperbole. Before my husband could say, *"Buckle up,"* and drive us from the parking lot at the MRI facility, I received a call from my ENT suggesting I stop by for a visit ***"On the way home."*** When we arrived, we were greeted by my doctor and a neurosurgeon who already had X-rays of the inside of my head on a lighted board. He didn't need to say a word, or point a finger in a general direction for me to see IT, and I didn't need help reading the expression on the stranger's face to realize that I was in deep shit. *"Your tumor falls into the rare category of acoustic neuromas. As you can see, it is very large and it is compressing the brainstem."*

I needed help with that last part, so he traced the outer edge of the tumor which had nestled itself against the posterior part of the brain responsible for vital life functions like, heartbeat, blood pressure, and breathing. *"This is a life-threatening condition,"* the neurosurgeon said.

Even with only one working ear, I heard those words.

That experience was my first big bump against a life and death situation, it was also my first experience with an MRI machine, the contraption that would have been the torture device selected by Big Brother if I'd been a character in George Orwell's novel, *1984*. Having read the book on more than one occasion, I know for certain I would have ended my days in Room 101, facing my greatest fear of being strapped onto a flat board, my head caged in an iron mask, and moved slowly through a big-ass medical torture device.

I generally subscribe to the notion that knowledge is power; the more you know about something the better, so I decided to learn about the damned bone-scanning machine. I called the nuclear med department at the hospital and asked exactly what kind of device they used. I had the image page open on my computer and when I found the one that looked like the one being described by the very understanding person on the other end of the phone line, I thanked her for her time and disconnected from the call and then I stared at it and bookmarked the page so I could show Tim, and the girls, and myself, over and over and over again.

Comparatively speaking, the machine used by the nuclear med department to determine if someone had bone boo-boos was nothing like the frontload thing or the dreaded MRI machine. Still, it had ready-made features for claustrophobia, so I called Dr. Wonderful's office and took him up on his offer of a little something-something to help me out.

Thankfully, on the day of my test, I was assigned to a very patient nuclear med tech named Maria, who listened to my concerns, gauged my level of anxiety at 10 on the Happy/Sad Face chart, and did everything in her power to help manage my panic so I wouldn't amp up to a Chernobyl-esque meltdown. After her assurances that she'd be with me the whole way, I agreed to the test, so Maria pumped some radioactive agent into my veins, sent me off to wait three hours, and told me to take my Xanax thirty-minutes before my return. Oh, and she reassured me we'd be fine.

"Of course she'll be fine," I hissed at Tim while the plutonium surged throughout my body, "she's not the one getting into the effing machine." Mr. Wonderful squeezed my hand, suggested we spend some time outside then grab something to eat from the hospital cafeteria. I rolled my eyes at the dude, "Is this your idea of a date, cause if it is, it sucks."

"It's not all bad. I'm holding your hand and you're radioactive. That's commitment. And I'll let you get the most expensive thing on the cafeteria menu."

I lived through the scan because of the wonders of Xanax, my first ever experience with my new little friend. Had any of my mental faculties been up and running full-tilt, I might have read 'the clues' Tim said he picked up on when the red light over the scanning-room door went dark signaling the end of the test. Apparently, I missed the stoic expression Maria had when she left the scanning chamber to get a wheelchair, and the absolute insistence that I sit my ass in it until I got into our car, and the tender hand she placed on my shoulder before Tim wheeled me away, and the look he said she gave him, the kind someone might give the owner of a beloved pet right before the shaving of the paw, and the hooking up of the 'nighty-night' IV.

When this nightmare began, I made Tim promise there'd be no secret-keeping, or sugarcoating, or bottling-up of concerns or suppositions. So, after many quiet minutes on I-290 heading west toward our home, he took hold of my hand and said he expected we'd hear bad news.

"How bad?"

"I think you have bone cancer." He gave another squeeze. *"You mentioned Stage 2 the other night, let's hope for that."*

If hopes and buts were candies and nuts, we'd all have a very fine Christmas. Don't know why that little ditty went through my head as we exited the highway at Hope Avenue. But it did.

27. Playing Games Isn't Always Fun ...

Since the diagnosis I've been fixated on having my last Christmas, my 64th birthday, and seeing the beginning of the New Year. As each milestone came and went, I checked them off my list. On New Year's Day, I woke without a plan for the future. I immediately felt myself slipping toward a funk I wasn't going to get to because friends and family blew up my cell phone with Happy New Year messages and congratulatory floating balloons and bursting fireworks and popping champagne corks; all of which were appreciated, and all of which made it virtually impossible to slide headfirst into the 'woe is me' place that beckoned.

The real reason I never made it into the funk I really needed and wanted was because my favorite visitor arrived in her footed pajamas, the ones she'd stuffed into her winter boots for her trek next door. I squealed in excitement at her arrival. "Hadley's here!"

Ever since I told my granddaughter the news, I've been waiting for her to broach the subject with me, and I've been asking Hannah if there have been any discussions at their house about the whole dying thing.

"The night you told her, she slept with me. She cried herself to sleep, woke up a few hours later and did the same thing, woke up a few hours later and said, 'I don't get it Mommy, she doesn't even have white hair yet'. That's it. She hasn't said anything else, but she's been clingy and it takes a long time for her to fall asleep."

I was beginning to worry that the little kid was pushing things too deep, so I asked Hannah if it'd be alright to broach the subject again, if the opportunity presented itself. She thought I should, so on New Year's Day while Hadley was kicking my ass at a game of Snaps, I did some broaching. "Hey Hads."

"Yeah."

"Have you given any thought to what I told you?"

She looked up at me with immediate wet eyes and said, *"That's all I've been thinking about."*

A push of breath left me with my next words, "Oh, honey, are you really thinking about it all the time?"

"Mostly at night. I hear the words you said that night over and over and over again."

Another push of breath and a question caught on a bit of emotion, "That must be upsetting."

She nodded.

"What do you do, you know, to help soothe yourself?"

"Sometimes I call out to Mommy and crawl into her bed, but last night I hugged the monkey you gave me for Christmas, the one that has your voice saying our goodnight prayer. I pushed the button over and over and over again," she said with big, plopping tears escaping from her beautiful blue eyes.

"Did that make you feel better?"

She shrugged a shoulder. *"Can we get back to the game, now?"*

"Absolutely."

"Looks like I'm gonna win again."

"Undoubtedly."

She won three games in a row.

And then this happened … "MammyGrams. Can you tell me about the life cycle?"

"Uh ……. Sure ……. I guess ……. Sure."

A bit of silence. An immediate sweat formed on my brow, and my hands showed a shake so I pushed them under my thighs. "So, you know how in spring trees bud, and flowers bud, and the grass starts to grow?"

"Not Gee's grass," she laughed.

I heard a chuckle from the kitchen where Jessica found herself held captive by 'The Talk' taking place in the living room. I ignored the chuckle and continued on. "Nope, Gee's never been good in the grass-growing department."

"I'll say."

Another chuckle from the kitchen.

"And he sings, all the time," the little one said with the roll of her eyes.

A full-out guffaw came from the kitchen.

I sent a shut-up cough Jessica's way, then pulled the train back onto the tracks before Mr. Wonderful arrived at the station and heard his 'Mini-Mammy' flapping her jaws about his perpetual horticultural failures and songbird tendencies, both of which he swears I purposefully told his grandchild about so she'd occasionally toss insult bombs his way. I have enthusiastically explained to the Paranoid One that the child has ears and eyes, is as sharp as a tack, and needs no help from me on his foibles.

Back to the life cycle ... "The newness of springtime is like the newness of a person's life. Leaves and flowers bud and new baby animals and birds are born, and just like baby humans everything grows big and strong so that they're ready for summer, the really fun season. During this stage of the life cycle, buds turn to big leaves that fill branches, and flowers bloom and spread all along the stone wall."

"And in my fairy garden."

"Yes. You have such a lovely garden with all those new bulbs you and Mommy planted last year."

"The purple Daylilies."

"Mmm, they were so pretty. And they grew nice and tall, like you have from when you were a little girl."

"Like Evie."

"Yes, like Evie."

We were interrupted by a phone call from Hannah suggesting Hadley return home for lunch. The grateful grandmother verbally shuffled her favorite human along.

The obedient child got to the door and said, "I'll be back MammyGrams. Hold your thought."

Jessica came from the kitchen, repeating Hadley's words with a tone of amazement, "Hold your thought? She's something else."

A little background ... Jessica is an ESL teacher currently working with elementary school-age children. I asked her what she thought about the way the conversation was going, so far. *"The seasonal life cycle is working, but when she gets back, don't bring it up again. Let her decide if she wants to move away from the subject."*

"Gotcha."

Hadley came back in a matter of minutes which is surprising because the kid is a very slow eater. She was no sooner in the door when she asked about fall.

Jessica was at the top of the stairs eavesdropping. She decided pretty quick that she was done, and very quietly closed the door leaving me to handle this drama by myself.

I swallowed the lump of anxiety in my throat, then pushed in. "Oh, fall is a really wonderful season and it can be a really long season. I love the fall, it's my most favorite time of year. In New England, it's the most colorful season with big orange pumpkins, and really tall Sunflowers, and trees full of red apples, and the really tall oak, elm, and maple tree branches burst with yellow, orange, and red leaves."

"Is fall a good part of the life cycle for people?"

"Oh, I think so. In people's lives it's when they have everything they want in life."

"Like grandkids?"

"Like grandkids."

There was a bit of silence for which I was very grateful. Then Hadley moved us along. *"Wanna play Buckets, MammyGrams?"*

"Sure."

She quickly divided the snaps into two groups by color, *"I'm red and you're green, okay?"*

It's been that way every time we've played Buckets or any other game. If there's a red thing to move, toss, or flip, it is Hadley's.

"And the youngest goes first, okay?"

I smiled because she always goes first and she always kicks my ass, especially in Buckets. No matter what we are tossing, she always gets the most into the black bucket. This time was no different.

Except, this happened ... From out of the mouths of babes, *"You're near winter. And that's when things die."*

I nodded. She teared and walked toward me. I thought she was going to throw her arms around me as she'd been doing so often lately, but she sat on the floor near my legs and just leaned against them. A minute or so passed before she buried her head onto her knees. I sat near and patted her head while she sobbed. I wanted to go back in time and not broach the subject, or encourage her to play another game of Buckets, but I knew she needed to break a little.

For the past few weeks, at unexpected times, a knock has come on the front door. Before I've had the chance to say come in, my granddaughter is in and has walked the room, wrapped her arms around my neck, and without a word, has given me a hug and gone away. I mentioned it to Hannah, "It's like Hadley is stockpiling hugs." Over Christmas break, she began coming in and extending her hand. The first time she did it I gave it a good old-fashioned handshake."

"Nope. It's a lever, push it down."

I did as I was told.

She did a little twirl of her head and said, *"Jackpot! Pick a number."*

I chose thirty.

She commenced a thirty hug session. If time allows, she comes in and extends her hand, and I choose a number, a really high number because I need to stockpile hugs, too. But back on *that* day, after Hadley's tearful little break, she lifted her head and said, *"I really hate this."*

I nodded, "I really hate this, too." I reached for her hands, and had her come stand near my chair. "There are certain things in life that can't be changed, but there are thousands of things that can be changed."

"Like what?"

"Like today. We're both a little sad right now, but we don't need to stay that way. We can go back to playing games and having fun." She nodded and headed to the front door. "Hey! Where are you going?"

"To get, Spot It! It's a new game I got for Christmas, and I love it! And I'm gonna beat you at it."

"I have no doubt!" Her reply was a delightful giggle. It made me cry a bit. And then she whooped my ass at her new game. We laughed a whole lot.

28. Hospice: What it is. What it isn't ...

Terminal cancer. Those words came out of nowhere. I'd been feeling fine, so it wasn't like I was sitting in a doctor's office because I found a lump, or was unusually fatigued, or had some unexplained bruising, or a prolonged cough. Nope, I was there for my annual physical, the first I'd had in two annuals.

Like many, many people, I didn't go for my routine checkup in 2020. The reason, of course, was Covid. I didn't go on my family's annual vacation to Wells Beach because of Covid. I didn't celebrate birthdays, or Thanksgiving, or Christmas or New Year's with family or friends because of Covid. I didn't do any of the fun stuff or the important stuff because of Covid. Everything I did or didn't do back then was because of that wretched disease because I feared catching it and dying from it. Isn't it ironic? Yeup — a little bit.

I'll never know if my funky alk phos became funky in 2020 or if it would have been found on that year's pre-physical labs or if it would have mattered if it was found. I do know this, by the time Dr. Wonderful learned about the elevation and ordered additional tests and scans, it was already too late for me. There wasn't going to be a treatment plan for me. There was going to be an end of life plan for me. Within a matter of days I went from planning weekly dinner menus for the family to planning a funeral, my funeral. I went from talking about the framework for my next series of books to putting the word 'hospice' into my daily lexicon. As one might expect, I didn't like the sound of the word or the way it made me feel. Just saying hospice out loud caused ripples of fear. It should have, after all, hospice is *that* place. The place where people go to die. Right? Sort of.

This blog isn't intended to inform anyone about hospice. This is simply my feelings about the program based on what I thought before, and what I've heard and experienced, firsthand. I mentioned in an earlier blog that my hospice social worker handed Tim a thick, shiny, pocket folder holding pamphlets and scary-named forms on her way out the door after our first meeting. That was December 10th and I have yet to open the folder. Tim, on the other hand, opened it and read a pamphlet before The Women of Hospice were off the driveway. Within minutes of his speed-reading event, he wanted to explain the stages of death and dying, not because he had some perverse need for a bit of show and tell, but rather because I'd previously posed a casual wonderment if there were hospice stages like there were grief stages. I sort of regretted that curiosity when an uneasiness between husband and wife pushed in and a question started to nudge: should hospice cause marital strife?

"We should discuss the stuff I read," Tim said while waving the pocket folder in my direction.

"I'm good, thanks."

"It might help if you knew about the stages. It really puts things in perspective and—"

I cut him off. "Tim, if I want to know about the stages of death and dying I'll read the damned pamphlet or better yet, I'll experience them firsthand."

Silence. He sat on his mission chair and waited for me to wade into a discussion. We both knew it was going to be a long wait. I don't like being pushed into difficult conversations. Neither of us do, and we both know this about one another. We usually play our 'discussions' like a game of Chess, with each of us making a statement, a brief one, the kind a departing pawn might make as he moves from the front row. Then, after we've made our opening moves, or salient points of discussion, we take time to think or strategize or fume. Tim knows this, but on that day he opened the Chess game with his knight. He moved the horse head piece from the back row, jumped a pawn, slid a space to the left and staked claim. I'm sure there's some Russian name for that opening move, and I respected Tim's bold attempt, but I offered a simple, "Nyet," and went back to the silent treatment. Within seconds, I broke. "Is there a reason why you're pushing into this?"

"The pamphlet really put things in perspective for me." Silence. *"It said you are doing work, the hardest work you'll ever do and you'll be doing it up here,"* he pointed to his head, *"and that you'll be doing it alone."*

"Not so far."

Silence. *"And the pamphlet explained that even if you shared your thoughts, none of us could really understand what you're going through."*

"So the point of this discussion is what exactly?"

He groaned. He continued to push in. *"The pamphlet said the people in your life have to accept that your world has changed and that you're not thinking about the long-term and you may not be interested in the same old, same old, and—"*

I pushed deep the tears I needed to shed, "I'm not interested in this back and forth. Can we be done, now?"

He lowered and shook his head a bit, *"I'm trying to help. The pamphlet said that's my job, to help."*

"Can you please stop helping?"

"Okay, but we'll need to discuss the DNR forms before our next hospice appointment."

"Sounds fun." I watched my poor mate walk away all slump-shouldered. I felt awful. I didn't want to push him away, but I just couldn't have the conversation, or even listen to the things he learned. I knew Mr. Wonderful's need to prepare me was his way of taking care of me, by teaching me. That's what the whole interchange was all about, but I ask you. Can a pamphlet really prepare a person for the process of death? Should a husband have to try?

A shift in dynamics ... Tim and I are partners in every sense of the word. I'm sure people think that I rule the roost and that Tim bends to my will. While it may look like I'm making all of the decisions for our family, the reality is this: Tim and I make all the big decisions behind the scenes, I just move them forward. So, Tim's pushing to have the pamphlet discussion was unusual and uncomfortable and it signaled a shift in our relationship and I wasn't ready for our relationship to change. Tim, on the other hand, wanted me to know he was taking the lead, that he was going to step ahead of me on occasion then wait for me to get back into lockstep with him. We learned pretty quick that I wasn't prepared for his breakaway and didn't like being left behind, especially since this was supposedly **my** journey.

Reactions are complex ... I don't know if the pamphlet lists bitchiness as part of the end-of-life process, but I know it's been part of mine on a few occasions and Tim has borne the brunt of it. It hurts me to the core that we have to have uncomfortable conversations, and that after 35 years of marriage we don't know how to have them. We've had 'what if' discussions in the past, the most significant ones taking place during the days before my brain surgery. We even wrote letters with our wishes about DNR and the removal of life-sustaining machinery.

Understatement here ... It was amateur hour, both in terms of medical and legal knowledge. To help make those long-ago decisions, we tossed a few scenarios out for discussion, each of which had one of us in the hospital with state-of-the-art equipment all around, and brilliant medicine men and women testing, analyzing, and counseling the aware partner about what could or could not be done for the unaware partner. We made our decisions, signed the letters, sealed them in envelopes, and wrote our names and dates across the seal so everyone would know they hadn't been tampered with.

That was a helpful exercise back then, but it has no relevance to what's happening now. It's showtime and emotions are running high, and we haven't had time to practice our routine, and build confidence that either of us knows what we're doing. That's why the seasoned husband and wife team are out of step with one another. We've gotten better over the past few weeks because Tim has adapted to a big change in the way I normally do things. My lifelong philosophy that 'knowledge is power' doesn't hold firm anymore. I want to know stuff, I just don't want to know everything, all at once. And I've adapted to Tim's need to take the lead on a few things and that his push to talk about stuff is really part of his coping mechanism, a really big part.

Joining hospice … I'm not sure if joining is the right word, but it's the one I've chosen. Before a patient can sign-on, hospice has to receive some sort of report from a physician stating he/she has made the clinical determination that their patient is dying. Once hospice receives the information, they make their own determination. Then they make the house call.

During my wait for that call, I imagined the worst. I was sure the meeting would take place behind shrouded windows with me at the pointed-end of a scythe, perhaps a plastic one leaving the real deal for a later visit by the Grim Reaper. I feared I would be forced to cede power and control to strangers who would stand guard until the end. I couldn't have been more wrong. Hospice workers do not want power or control over anyone, certainly not over a person who is in the dying process. Hospice nurses are kind, dedicated souls who are bound by the belief that a patient, a human being, a person who is somebody's everything, should be regarded with dignity, and kept as physically and mentally comfortable as possible during the period leading to, and during their passing.

Comfort is more than pain meds … I'll give an example: dying from bone cancer is painful. I was told by an oncologist that my death would be 'excruciatingly painful'. So right off the top, Dr. Wonderful and Nurse M focused on getting my pain under control and keeping it under control. When 4 doses of Tramadol didn't keep pain from breaking through, they upped the number of doses to 6 per day. And when I complained that I was sleeping way too much during daytime hours, and was unable to clear my head enough to write my blog, I was encouraged to try going without the 1 AM dose. My medical team showed commitment to my physical health, but they also focused on my mental health. They realized the importance of my writing. They knew that my blog is helping me in many ways and that it is a fundamental part of how I will maintain a good quality of life — for as long as I am blessed to have one.

Hospice is a beginning and an ending … Most everyone equates hospice with the ending of a person's life. I have come to learn that hospice is really a beginning — the beginning of a person's final journey. More than that, hospice is the beginning of the most focused care a person will ever receive. Hospice nurses work way outside the 'normal' healthcare box because their work begins at the core of a person, at their soul. These nurses don't try to save their patients. They know they can't. There's no bother with pretense, no reason for hand-wringing, no avoidance of difficult conversations. They come into the relationship knowing that every conversation is going to be difficult.

Setting boundaries … Every question asked by a hospice worker is asked of the patient. So, every bit of focus from Nurse M is on me, on how I'm feeling and whether there is a way to make me feel even better. The concerns and worries of Mr. Wonderful and my daughters are listened to with empathy, and they are answered fully and kindly, but everyone in the room is reminded that I need to lead the discussions and make the decisions — for as long as I am able. That's why my signature was required on the Do Not Resuscitate form, and the Do Not Intubate form, and the Do Not Transport to a Hospital form. It was the hospice social worker who gave the general explanation of what those forms mean during our first meeting, but it has been my hospice nurse who has been in the weeds with me when I have questions about what they 'really' mean. And I've had many questions. "Can I change my mind about the forms?"

"Yes. You are in control of your care."

"And what about Tim or the girls, can they change things if I'm incapacitated?"

"Yes. That's why it's really important that they know your wishes and are prepared to honor them."

"Okay, so let's say I have the dreaded bone break, do we call 9-1-1? Cause you know, it's a broken bone."

"Well, if it's a compound fracture and you're bleeding then you'd call 9-1-1 and then hospice. We would send someone to the hospital and explain to the appropriate people that you are a hospice patient. That's important for the ER staff to know. They will take care of your emergency needs, whatever they may be, get you comfortable, and then they would send you home."

"To die?"

"Given your advanced stage of cancer and overall bone deterioration, most likely yes."

"And if I had a stroke or a heart attack, do we call 9-1-1?"

"No, you call hospice. We'll assess the situation, tell your caregiver what to do, and send someone to your home."

"So basically, if I stroke out or have a heart attack, that's it. There'll be no one coming to render aid, no one coming to try to save me." It wasn't a question, though it felt as though it should have been.

Nurse M leaned toward me. *"That's what the Comfort Kit is for. The morphine would be used to keep you comfortable. Everything about hospice is about the comfort of the patient."*

I wasn't finding the subject matter very comforting and took a not-so-casual look at the clock.

Nurse M caught on pretty quick. *"When was the last time you took Xanax?"*

"Eleven last night."

"You can take one now if you're feeling anxiety."

"Way ahead of you." I had the pill bottle already in my hand.

29. I Am Dying ...

Marjorie, you shouldn't read this one to Mom. You probably shouldn't read it, either. I know I am dying. I've been told that, I've told you that, but the other night, I woke with feelings of anger, and regret, and fear, and loneliness, and profound sadness. Why? Because I realized once again that I am dying. I actually woke in tears and I didn't bother trying to stop them, in fact, I welcomed them, and needed them, and suffered through them. And then I made myself say the words that I'd been holding deep inside. "I DO NOT WANT TO DIE."

When I managed to pull a few steady breaths, I went from being sad to being pissed; really pissed. I wanted to push from my chair and work off some frustration. Instead, I sat my ass in my buff-colored leather prison and let the sadness seep back in. I whispered into the darkness, "I'm dying and there isn't a damn thing I can do about it. I'm dying, and I don't want to be. I'm dying. Dying. What the fuck?" My mind took me to the people I love. I started thinking about how sad they'll be and how much they'll miss me and how different their worlds will be without me. I ached for each and every one of them.

And then this happened … I stopped thinking about them and started thinking about me, about what this means to **me.** In the stillness, I admitted that I haven't been brave enough to go deep into what all of this means beyond the whole physical part of death. I admitted that waiting at the abyss of certain-uncertainty is effing scary and that fear has kept me from going anywhere near the edge for a peek-see into the future, my very limited future.

So like a crazy person, I started angry-talking, raging at the universe. I'm not sure what my first ramble was about, other than to say there was a lot of swearing. When some clarity of thought broke through the outburst, I peeled away the top layers of what I've been avoiding and with the energy of one angry-ass woman, I began excavating and exploring my emotions. My need to do the work was unavoidable. I was on a dig of self-awareness and for the first time during this shit fest I was giving myself permission to be pissed, and profoundly sad, and scared shitless because that's what I've been feeling — sometimes —

all the time — maybe. I pushed in and admitted that I'm pissed that I won't be seeing Wells Beach again, and I'm profoundly sad that I won't write another novel, and I'm scared shitless about what's next and how all of that will play out.

In the light of day… The source of my night-terrors revealed themselves. I'm feeling good right now, but I know that I'll wake up one day and I won't be feeling this way and I know that in due time my twice-a-week visits with Nurse M will become more frequent and it will signal my decline and it will become more difficult for me to get off my recliner for bathroom trips and I'll need more help taking care of myself and my pain will become stronger and less manageable and my nurse will broach the subject and then she'll help get a hospital bed in my living room or arrange care at a facility and I'll begin sleeping more hours each day than I'll be awake and I'll no longer be included in decisions about my life and I will slip away day by day and minute by minute until there are no more minutes, or seconds and it will be the end of my life.

I can barely type through my tears remembering in great detail my need to call out to Tim; to have him come sit with me and how overwhelming the urge was to rage at someone. So I chose God because I knew He was there with me. I've felt Him near me so often lately. Without my reaching out to Him in prayer, I have felt Him near.

In that moment of darkness I was angry at God and I let him have it, not because I blame Him for this, but because there was no one else to be angry with. I know the things happening to me are no one's fault — certainly not His. My faith in Him assured me that He'd take and accept my rage and He'd keep me safe while I faced my truths. That's why I found the strength to call this out in the darkness that allowed such things. "I am angry that I am dying!" And then I said the words that surprised me to my core. "WHY ME?"

Reality sucks … After lots of reflection, I found my way back toward acceptance. My world is different now. I have become a spectator in life. People are coming and going, planning and doing, living and loving. I am waiting to die.

These shit pieces of 'woe is me' makes me almost crush from the weight of guilt and shame. Let's face it, I've been blessed with time to be present in my life, even if it is different, even if I am losing it. I now know guilt is why I didn't allow myself the luxury of a good-old wallow, and fear is what kept me from looking into the abyss. Guilt and fear is why I didn't want to rage at God. I didn't want Him to think I was ungrateful for the time I have because I am so grateful. I am still well enough to forget that I'm sick and dying. I'm well enough to play games with Hadley and to write my blog and to share the grief of a beloved friend who's suffering through the sudden loss of her stepmom and to build friendships with people I am going to have to leave, again. I'm well enough to enjoy a snowy morning, or a star-filled evening and to find joy in the news that babies will be born this summer. But one day, things will begin to change and I won't be well enough to do anything — to remember anything — to feel anything?

My new prayer … "God, I pray that the love of those who will sit with me as I leave this life finds me, and that they feel my love — the only true and valuable thing any of us has to give."

30. Random Acts of Kindness ...

> *Thoughtful expressions are a gift for two,*
> *the recipient and the person who reaches out in kindness.*
>
> *~ Sheryll O'Brien*

I woke this morning a little past four. A soft snow was falling, tiny flakes twirled about, caught occasionally by the light of a near shrouded moon. There was an inch or two of fluff already on the ground and the perfect amount sticking to barren hardwood tree branches and full evergreens. Porch lights in the distance illuminated the scene with the mood of a Thomas Kinkade painting and I was a living, breathing part of the idyllic picture. It was wonderful.

Schools across Worcester County are staying closed because this snowstorm is going to be the first plowable one of the 2021-2022 winter season. It's January, and thus far we've had only two dusting snowfall events, one which fell Christmas Eve. It was perfect, as you can imagine. I think it's safe to say that New Englanders have a love/hate relationship with snow. Deep down, we love it and willingly spend hours watching icy flakes of white flutter past frosted window panes, landing with a hush, and becoming part of a landscape that captures and just won't let go.

Then there's this freakin part ... Snow removal. Ass-high snow drifts are not for the faint of heart. They require strategic planning on how best to handle them. First, there's the bundling up to keep warm and dry in the outdoor elements. A set of long underwear is the best first layer, coupled with at least two pairs of socks, then comes the pants and shirt, and the layering of a sweatshirt, then the scarf, hat, gloves, boots, and coat; preferably a wool or a puffy jacket with thermal lining. As soon as the donning ritual is done, it's time to commence the attack. First off: the shoveling of stairs and sidewalks is a very important part of snow removal. Entrance ways are essential and should be brought to bare-pavement and sanded before you move on to the two or three snow-covered vehicles that have to be cleaned off, heated up and moved, before the backbreaking shoveling or snow-blowing of driveways can begin.

Swearing is now permissible … By the time New Englanders get to their cars, the white wonderfulness of winter has started to wane and the bitching, moaning, and groaning has begun. The shift in attitude doesn't usually take hold until The First Plowable Snowfall arrives. (The initial caps are intentional.) The First Plowable Snowfall is a titled event. As soon as rumors begin about an approaching snowstorm, New Englanders gather around televisions to watch weather forecasts with the same commitment and fervor as when they congregate for a game of their favorite sports teams. Hairy eyeballs and warning grunts hush any who threaten to interrupt the call of projected inches or feet of the 'light and fluffy' or 'wet and packed' winter precip expected along the 495 and Mass Pike corridors. All of the shushing is unnecessary because expected snow amounts are announced ad nauseum and go like this: "Three to five inches on the Cape, six to ten in Central Mass, and over a foot in the Western part of the state." Repeat. Repeat. Repeat. Then. Repeat. Repeat. Repeat. As far as I'm concerned, one announcement should suffice because word of mouth kicks into high gear causing phones to ring and cells to buzz, chirp, or sing text alerts about the incoming assault.

When the first snowflake flits and falls, the real frenzy begins. Reporters from All Points Massachusetts head outside dressed in television station apparel and carrying two things: a microphone and a ruler. Then, for the duration of the storm, the fools freeze their asses off for the sole purpose of sticking a ruler into the snow to prove that there's 4.2" in Chatham, and 6.9" in Worcester, and 11.3" in Chicopee. Back in the day, we'd simply check to see how high up a reporter's leg the snow went. Ankle boot high = 4.2", to the top of a boot = 6.9", anywhere near the knee = knee-high snow. I don't know when or why the 'powers that be' at television stations decided residents of Massachusetts needed precise measurements when all we really need to know are four things: how much snow is expected, when it is going to start, will schools be canceled, and when the storm will end. We don't need or want 'around the clock' television coverage of the snow actually falling and we don't care if Norwood has an inch more than it did two hours ago. We certainly don't want to witness an idiot reporter nearly being hit by a slip-sliding driver whilst said reporter is bent at the waist and measuring snow that's not yet knee-high deep. My personal opinion is this: reporters shouldn't be allowed to measure until a yardstick is required. Watching a 3' long piece of wood being pulled from the sleeve of a snow-covered fool on the eastbound side of the Mass Pike might make for interesting T.V. Just sayin.

That ramble felt good ... Now, a bit of geography. Tim and I live in Worcester at the crest of a hill on Wildwood Avenue, a private street of cozy capes, rambling ranches, and good-sized duplexes. Our place is set way back from the road which means we have a very long driveway. For years, a decade or more really, John McTigue, our across-the-street neighbor and

Tim's cousin, did the snow removal of our driveway, for no reason other than he is a really nice guy who got a snowblower one year and took it upon himself to spend a big-ass amount of time clearing snow from his place and then from our place. Tim offered payment for service whilst on grateful bent knee, but there wasn't ever anything expected from us.

John and Joyce semi-retired to Maine a few years back and took their handy-dandy snowblower with them. I wondered if their move had anything to do with the plowing of 183 though I know their relocation was so they'd be near the ocean at Wells Beach, my favorite place in all the world, though I admit I've been to very few places in all the world. Still, I'm sure I'd feel the way I do about Wells, no matter what. Anyway, as soon as John left, a second snowplow miracle happened. Matt Hanlon, Tim's nephew, moved in next door and started plowing the driveway. For a couple of years, in the dead of night, he'd plow our troubles away. His helpful deed ended when Matt and his wife, Brenna, and son, Shaun, moved to the West Side, the swanky side of Worcester. I don't know if there's an official city ordinance banning parked plow trucks along beautiful tree lined streets in the 01609 zip code, but I think it's very plausible. For whatever reason Matt put his plowing days behind him, and I say good for you, now go out and play in the snow with your son.

As a result of the Hanlon move across town, the O'Briens of Wildwood found themselves with a snow removal dilemma on their hands. The seriousness of which played second fiddle to the whole wife-has-cancer thing. Without mentioning the dilemma to anyone, another winter miracle came via text from Helena and Paul McCarthy, longtime friends of my sister, Marjorie. Helena texted to say Paul would plow our driveway, and no, they didn't want payment they just wanted to do something to help during this difficult time. And when they couldn't come one day, our next door neighbor, Rick Earls, pushed his snowblower up and down our drive because he, too, is a really nice guy who wanted to lighten our load. Tim and I extend our heartfelt thanks to these snow-warriors.

Yummy offerings ... Vegetable soup - Sheila. Tapioca pudding - Annie. Butternut squash soup - Kathy. Warm cookies - Faith. Banana bread - Debbie. Chocolate-covered strawberries - Eileen. Baskets of crackers and candies - Joyce. Caramel apples - Dave. Christmas cookies - Linda. Tins of fudge - Denise. Pizzelle cookies and apple breads - Nicole. Apple pies - Don and Mom. Jams and jellies - Santa? I have no idea who left an array of fruit spreads on the front stoop, but thank you! There may have been others who stopped by with yummy treats, and if I neglected to mention you, I'm very sorry. Every tasty and nutritious tidbit was so appreciated. As I've mentioned, I haven't been in my kitchen to prepare anything since November and on many occasions I've been too nauseated to eat much of anything, so a bit of soup, or bowl of tapioca pudding, or a cookie, or a cracker smeared with jam has been my breakfast, lunch or dinner. And when I've had an appetite, Tim has used gift cards for takeout and for GrubHub delivery thoughtfully sent from his friends at work. Tim and I extend our thanks to these culinary-caregivers.

Beauty, books, and blankets ... I have a gorgeous picture in my living room of a snowy lane leading to a beautiful, wooded area. There's enough light in the painting to suggest a midday stroll is in order, one that might reward the wanderer with a plop or two of snow melt from the burdened trees, or the company of a bunny or lunching deer in the winter wonderland. The painting is sheer perfection and evokes a sense of tranquility. I was given the pleasure of naming the piece, and since the artist is of Irish descent, I've chosen Lána Suaimhneas. I've decided that my last moments on earth will be upon that lane and the final walk of my life will be beautiful and peaceful. ~ Thank you Jennifer Lane Courville.

I received a wonderfully imaginative piece of art and had Tim hang it in my kitchen. Though I am unable to spend time there, I purposefully had it put on a wall I'm able to see whenever I get to move from my chair. The artwork is very unique, and very creative. My understanding is that the artist uses recycled wood that is intricately pieced together to make a 3D image that becomes part of a hand-painted background. I probably botched that description, but I'm giving myself an 'A' for effort. My picture is a vine of beautiful Morning Glory flowers inching their way up a naturally weathered window shutter. The use of the shutter as a base is brilliant, and the blue beauties, a personal favorite of mine, are full of wonderful whimsy. ~ Thank you Phil Gagnon.

I have an adorable stuffed unicorn friend that arrived holding a lovely blue rose and a wonderfully thoughtful card. It came from a woman I've never met, the mother of Guru Jessica. When she learned her daughter was doing the website design for an author, she did what most moms do, she got in on the fun and gave my books a read. Her lovely card offered warm thoughts about my situation, and she made a point to say she enjoyed my books and my blog. What writer doesn't like hearing that? This lovely, kind woman took time to send something for me to hold onto and to bring me comfort. ~ Thank you Linda Charpentier Christina.

I have a beautiful lap throw made by my sister-in-law, the woman who could easily make an entire wedding gown out of a linen napkin, a piece of ribbon, and a spool of thread. This seamstress is like the MacGyver of the sewing world and I'd venture to guess that every member of the O'Brien clan has had her fix a hem, take in or let out a seam, or make something fit better than it did before. As I sit here, alternating between typing and running my hand up and down the soft cloth throw, I smile wide at her talent and appreciate her kindness. ~ Thank you Michele O'Brien.

Things to pass the time … When I tire of writing, I do some reading. I've received books I never would have come upon, but am very happy to have received and read. ~ Thank you, Linda Bushee, Josephine Power, and Suzanne Magaziner.

And let's not forget the many, many, many cards sent by friends, some who I haven't heard from in years, or the good number of pretty paper expressions of thoughtfulness from people I don't know, but who know someone in my family, or have joined a prayer group, which is so lovely. I spend lots of quiet time reading them and basking in the warmth of comfort they bring.

The cards I spend the most time reading are from my editor, The Warden. Each contains a quote from books I've written, so they run the gamut: funny, saucy, emotional, or fraught with tension, and they have wonderful, written thoughts from the woman who knows my work as well as I do. Her little notes are about life, and about our working relationship, and they mean the world to me. ~ Thank you Andria Flores.

I recently became pen pals with my former publisher, a woman who knows a great deal about her author, though I admit I've been at a disadvantage. I knew some stuff about this force of nature, but didn't know the important stuff about The Goddess of the Publishing World. I love that she responded with an immediate, "Yes," when I asked her to tell me tales about her life. ~ Thank you Nancy Pendleton.

New routines … At the end of the tucking-in process at night I ask Tim to give me my stones. One isn't a stone, but it looks like one (I'll explain later). I take the first stone, a palm-sized, naturally smoothed piece that has a cross etched into the center of it, place it on my chest and leave it there. The second 'stone' which is actually a rounded piece of petrified wood that's been buffed and treated with shellac finds its way into my hand. The multi-shaded brown 'stone' is silky smooth and perfect for rubbing my thumb over which is what I do every night while I'm falling asleep. These nightly rituals bring me peace. They help me feel less afraid and I love them. ~ Thank you Father Steuterman and Kevin Mullaney.

Sounds of life and love … Every evening as I fall asleep, I listen to and watch two cell phone videos. The first video is one I made on what will be my last trip to Wells Beach. It lasts a little more than a minute. It was taken at sunrise and at low tide and each time I look at it, I see something new and different. The second video was made at Boynton Beach during a beautiful, sunny day. This ocean recording is much longer and is most often the one that lulls me to sleep. They are just glorious and remind me of how connected I am to the sight and sound and the push and pull of ocean waters. The distant sparkle and white-tipped froth that moves ever closer to the waiting shoreline is something that inspires and fills me, something I long to see again. The gift of the ocean is a most treasured one. ~ Thank you Joyce McTigue.

To the lucky New Englanders who head to warm climates for vacation and a respite from thigh-high snow, if you have my cell number and you happen to be near the ocean please consider sending me a video. It'd be so appreciated. Muah!

Well, this just happened … I was getting ready to send this blog to Guru Jessica when the mailman knocked on the door and handed a box to my Jessica. She opened it for me and handed off a note, which I read and laughed my ass off doing so. Inside the treasure trove were things I've mentioned in my blogs: a box of tea bags, a package of Figgies, and a CD called Pulling Threads with a mystery playlist. Tim slid the CD in our Bose and immediately, *When I'm Sixty-Four* filled the room. I began laughing and ugly crying at the unexpected thrill of someone making me a soundtrack of songs I've mentioned in my blogs and books. We listened to quite a bit then Tim paused it because he needed to do something in the kitchen. I was just about to lose my patience when he returned with two cups of tea and three Figgies for each of us.

"We're doing this — together." He slid the CD in again, and for the next few minutes we laughed and cried as each 'surprise' song began: *When I'm Sixty-Four, Into The Mystic, Wichita Lineman, Woman, Woman, Helpless*. Some of my all time favorites came one after another, and then the surprise of all surprise songs began, a hysterical ditty about 'tea drinking' being sung by a bluegrass singer named Tim O'Brien. The song cracked me up! *My* Tim O'Brien concerned himself for several minutes that his wife was going to die in a fit of laughter at the folly of the evening. In one unexpected moment, Tim and Sheryll were back and we were at a light, fun, happy place, one that had no worries, one that was gifted to us by two wonderful

people. ~ From the bottom of my heart, thank you Phil and Molly McTigue.

A note from Debbie Gagnon …

Lately, I have been reading Sheryll's series of books nonstop. The plot, settings, characters, and dialogue are great. As impressed as I am with her books, her blog is AMAZING!! It is the best rollercoaster ride I've even been on. One minute I'm crying my eyes out and the next I'm laughing my ass off.

Sheryll holds no punches and shows her innermost thoughts, fears, and hopes. It's like she has opened her heart for the whole world to see. Her childhood memories are funny and relatable. When she goes on a rant about something that irritates her, it's hilarious. My favorite is weathermen measuring snowfall amounts with yardsticks. I'll never watch a weather report again without smiling and thinking of Sheryll.

The way that she is handling her terminal illness with strength, courage, and faith is inspirational. To be able to convey in words her heartbreaking and emotional journey shows what a talented writer she is.

Sheryll is a remarkable woman and I am so proud that she is my friend. Her blog has given me an appreciation for things that I sometimes take for granted.

I am beyond thrilled that Sheryll's blog is being made into a book. I truly believe that it will be on the bestseller list.

31. Tim Really Is Mr. Wonderful ...

Meeting the O'Briens. The guy I dated for ten whole months before marrying is a great guy. He was raised in a family of ten kids, born in two groups of five. Tim is the oldest of the second grouping. He has a deep affection for his older siblings, the ones he said were very much like mini-parents; and he really enjoyed being part of the second set of OBs — the ones that ran amuck throughout the neighborhood. I remember being shell-shocked for days after meeting the family for the first time at a weekly Sunday supper of bulkies and deli fixins. Flanked around a huge farmer's table were Nana and Papa (Tim's parents) and their ten children and their spouses and/or boyfriends and girlfriends, and a multitude of grandchildren ranging in age from newborns to early teens. As he did every Sunday, Patrick-Terrence-Francis O'Brien fetched three dozen bulkies from Widoff's bakery on Water Street. I've hyphenated Tim's dad's name because I can never remember which was the real deal. I could easily ask Tim, or look at the online City of Worcester records, or pull the family tree Tim's sister Mary Ellen did, but I sort of think Papa deserves all three names — he was that great of a guy.

Anyway, back to my introductory session ... First impression: it was loud with lots of people asking questions and half-answering them before another round of inquiries were lobbed. Some questions were sent my way, but most others were about seedless v poppy seed bread offerings. In a word, the kitchen was hectic with people passing off bulkies and paper plates like softballs and Frisbees, and little kids elbowing for space at chip bowls. And for the newcomer, it was beyond confusing. "Is that one Annie?"

"Yes."

"And she's married to that one?"

"Tiger."

"Uh huh. And their kids are?"

"Brian, that one, there. And Patrick, that one over there."

"Okay. And that's Noreen?"

"Yes."

"And she's married to that one?"

"Squeaky."

"Uh huh. And their kids are?"

"Kerrianne, she's the baby being held by Kathy."

"And she's married to him?"

"Yes. Tommy Gaffney. You know his older brother Spock."

"Tiger. Squeaky. Spock. Good idea adding some nicknames to this crew of a hundred."

"Tiger's name is Tommy, and Kathy's husband's name is Tommy. Squeaky's name is Brian. And Spock's name is Michael. We already have some of those," Tim explained with nonchalance.

"Right. Duplicates. I imagine that's a forgone conclusion."

Past is prologue … My husband has the patience of a saint. I think it's because he waited in line to use the family bathroom. My husband knows how to communicate with women. I think it's because he has five sisters. My husband comes when he's called. I think it's because no matter whose name Mary O'Brien shouted, all ten of her kids responded. My husband is fine with cereal for supper. I think it's because there was one option for dinner at the O'Brien household — you ate it or you had cereal. My husband is good at keeping secrets. I think it's because he's really bad at remembering who told him what.

Every O'Brien event was huge ... Right off the top, no matter the gathering, the general headcount consisted of 2 parents + 10 adult children + 10 spouses or significant others = 22 grownups; at that time there were approximately ten grandkids and a few on the way. And within stone-throwing distance from the house on Merchant, there were plenty of McTigues, all relatives of Mary O'Brien, many of whom joined in on Sunday supper events. The first few Sunday gatherings caused me a bit of strife. Being one of three children who rarely spoke during family sit downs, I did way more observing than joining in. I'd no sooner mastered Sundays when the 'special event' season came into full swing. Those events put my heart into overdrive and caused a sweat to form here and there and there and there.

Memorial Day — usually held on the land between Tim's parent's home and his sister Mary Ellen's home. Attendees, easily 50.

July 4th — usually held at the same location. Attendees, impossible to tell since it mushroomed with people from all over the Apricot Hill neighborhood.

Thanksgiving night — an open-house tradition that began when Kathy and Tommy built a house behind Nana's and Papa's. Attendees, my guesstimate, easily 50.

Christmas Eve — an open-house tradition that predated me at Annie's and Tiger's house located across the street from Kathy's and Tommy's. Attendees, my guesstimate, easily 60.

It wasn't the number of people that unhinged me, after all, I spent most of my free time as a young adult at elbow-to-elbow concerts. The thing that put me on edge was the need to remember everyone's name and then put it with the correct face. I distinctly remember spending lots of time in Nana's kitchen looking at a cute wall hanging. It had ten different sized walnut shells with happy faces painted on them and a name listed below each. I stared at the 'nut plaque' on numerous occasions and I read the names with my eyes open, then recited the names a few times with my eyes closed. "Franny, Mary Ellen, Eileen, Terrence, Annie, Timmy, Kathy, Joey, Noreen, Jimmy."

For years I wondered who gave that plaque to the family and why the kids were represented by nuts. Over time, I learned the answer to one of those two questions. I'll leave it to everyone to guess which one.

Before leaving the kitchen, I'd stand a bit and wonder why every cabinet and drawer was open. I found it unsettling that everything was left in the 'I'm looking for something' position when there wasn't an O'Brien in sight. I learned over the years that it was really an economical way of doing things. The number of times things were opened and closed in that house could easily have put The O'Briens between the covers of a Guinness Book of World Records. I came to find the Merchant Street habit cute, but I broke Tim of the practice very early in our marriage mostly because I don't arrange stuff in my cabinets, and it's best no one learned that. The cabinet-memory came rushing back to Tim and me one night while watching the movie, *The Sixth Sense*. It was during the scene when the mom leaves the kitchen for a minute and returns to find all of the cabinets and drawers wide open and the kid still sitting at the table eating his cereal. Tim and I cracked up at the scene even though it was scary as shit.

I married into a huge family and watched it grow year after year after year. Bear with me as I try to remember the names of Nana's and Papa's grandchildren: Kevin, Michael, Andrew, Mary Kate, Julie, Jeffrey, Joey, Jill, Terrence, Brian, Patrick, Christine, Hannah, Jessica, Terrence, Patrick, Brendan, Kaleigh, Meghan, Kerrianne, Matthew, Patrick, Shane and Colin (duplicates are correct). And because there just weren't enough kids running around, Franny brought his new son, Mark, into the mix when he married Helen. A most wonderful addition in spouse and child. (I admit I checked with Tim after I typed all of the names because I didn't want to omit anyone).

Thoughtful gestures … Tim is really good at gift giving, but he is off the charts when it comes to thoughtful gestures like this. I wrote Suzanne, during the three-month wait between the diagnosis of my head tumor and surgery. The pressure was on and I needed to do one of the two things I'd always promised myself I'd do: write a book and then maybe see my name on the spine of that book. I pushed myself to get the story written. I needed to prove to myself that I could put a story to paper. When all was said and done, I decided I was a really good storyteller and a really bad writer, technically speaking. Overall, I was very happy that I did the writing part, but I was a bit unhappy that the second part of my dream, the one where my name would be on the spine of a book, would go unrealized.

Or, would it … Nope. I don't think I mentioned this, but Mr. Wonderful has worked in the print industry for decades and he knows who does what in that universe, and who would help him help his wife have her dream. My husband took my unedited, unproofread, sloppy manuscript to a friend who printed 50 copies. Another friend designed the cover with the name *Suzanne* and a 1960s flower-power symbol on a white background. Seeing my words, albeit terribly strung together words, between the covers of a book and my pen name, Anne Hobson, on the spine was beyond thrilling and it proved once again that Tim O'Brien was the best thing that's ever happened to me.

That was then – this is now … The man I married nearly 36 years ago carries the life we led in his heart, and the ups and downs we've had are etched in his face, and the weight of worry he burdens now shows in his slower gait. The sadness he carries every minute of these days have slumped his shoulders, and easily fills his eyes at a tender touch. I feel as badly for Tim as I do for myself. He is losing his wife, his best friend, his comedienne, his pain-in-the-ass nudge, his soft place to land, and the place he goes when he needs some hard truths and perspective. He said recently that he knows he's going to have to work at not withdrawing from life. I suggested he spend our usual morning coffee time with thoughts of us, and then pack them away until the next day. I hope he gives it a shot then I hope he finds new things to do, things he's wanted to do for years and never found the time to get to. "Do you think you might like to take a painting or photography class?"

"I think so."

"I told the girls to make sure you go to Ireland."

"You did?"

"Yeah, so you'd better go. Okay?"

"Okay."

"Do you think you'll ever marry again?"

He answered that question with an F-bomb and a big-ass. *"NO!"*

"Learned your lesson, huh?"

Silence. And then he cracked up laughing. Gotta love him. I do.

I Think I Lost You … So my brother called the other day while I was napping. When I woke, I risked what's left of my life by returning his call while the Patriots were in the process of getting their asses handed to them by the Dolphins. By the way, I hate Florida teams, don't know why, don't care why, I just do! My brother loves his sports; it was always something we shared. Like March Madness, he and I would fill out our brackets and talk for hours about our choices and our wins and losses. Anyone who knows Don Sneade knows not to interrupt him during Saturday college football or on Sundays during NFL season. Given I have a cancer diagnosis, I placed a mid-afternoon Sunday call sure that I faced little to no repercussions. "I was sleeping when you called earlier."

"Yeah. I figured. That's why I left the text about 'Him' and said to call when you could."

I shook my head because I didn't remember getting a text and if I did I didn't know who the hell 'Him' was. I pushed right past that and into a conversation, "I know the Patriots are on and you hate being interrupted, but—"

"Shit. I don't get the Patriots down here," he seethed. *"The fucking NFL doesn't let people outside of viewing areas watch other games. I'm in the Atlanta area so I get Falcons games which is good cause I like them, but just over in Chattanooga, like an hour from here, they get—"*

I zoned out. I zoned in.

"... and so I only record four shows now, NCIS is my favorite. It's in its fourteenth season, and Blacklist, do you know that show?"

I said I did, and I do, but I had a momentary bit of concern that that wasn't the name of the show he said. I zoned out. I zoned in.

"... yeah, so my all-time favorite television show is Magnum, P.I., the original one, but I like the new one cause it's not trying to be the old one, and I fucking love Seinfeld, that's some funny shit. Have you seen The Cigar Store Indian? Funniest damned episode. You should get it online and watch it, and the All In The Family episode when Archie Bunker is locked in the basement and gets shitfaced on booze that's my favorite—"

I zoned out. I zoned in.

"... and Jaws. My all-time favorite move. You know, there are two storylines in that movie, one at sea and one on land. I've watched Jaws maybe a hundred times. I know every damned line. Me and this other guy at work, he's younger and might remember shit better, but I know more shit. Remember at the end of the first movie when Brody and Hooper are kicking back to shore with the barrels?"

"Uh huh."

"I bet you don't know this, 'cause he didn't know this, but there's a scene in Jaws 2, when Brody walks outside and he's on the phone, the planters on the porch are those barrels."

"Didn't know."

"I've been reading your blogs. I cracked up when you said, 'it's wall-to-wall carpeting, so yes it goes from one wall to the other' and when you called Hannah and said, 'get your ass over here, he's asking questions'. I laughed my ass off."

"Good."

"They're hard to read."

"Yeah and to write."

"I bet. You sound tired, but strong. Though I think I lost you before."

"Yeah, I zoned in and out."

"I think about calling you all of the time, but it's too early before I go to work and too late when I get home."

"How about we plan a Sunday call."

"Sounds good. I'll call and if you're napping just call me back."

"Sounds good."

The crack in his voice when he said he loved me was hard to take. A while later, I went on FB and saw a message from Don (not the text that I'd been promised). He said he called, assumed I was asleep, and to return his call whenever. Then he mentioned a blog, the one where I ragged on Tim about wall-to-wall carpet, and that I demanded Hannah come over because her father was asking the hospice nurse questions. **That was some funny shit.** He highlighted the words in his FB post, the one Denise put up for him because when it comes to FB posts, my brother is as dumb as a post. At the end of the message, he said he lost it when he read the birthday blog, the one that mentioned the best Christmas gift this year was Him. I'll admit I lost it when I read his words.

33. Dedicated with Love — Part One ...

I could never express how deeply I love my mother, could any of us, really? I attempted to scratch the surface by dedicating my work to her — all of my works. I wanted my dear mother to see words from me to her when she opened one of my books. On February 1, 2018, I called my mother and read these words. They are from a book I would eventually title, *Bullet Bungalow*.

> **Chapter One**
>
> Kitt Mahoney is doing the two best things in the world — her world anyway. She is watching her daughters enjoy the last rays and days of summer, and she is taking in the sights and sounds of her ocean, the one at Laurel Falls, Massachusetts.

Mom asked what book I was reading and I told her those were the opening lines of a story I would publish one day. She told me to hurry up and write it so she could read it. God bless my mother, she read that manuscript four times before I had the nerve to send it to an editor. As I should have expected, Mom became my most devoted fan — and it wasn't only for my writing.

A little background … After the big-ass acoustic neuroma was removed from my cranium, a couple things happened. I spent a week in intensive care before being sent to a rehab facility where it was expected I'd stay a month or so. I was at the facility for less than twelve hours. Once moved from an ambulance gurney to my hospital bed and settled in, Tim sat near, as he had the entire time I was in ICU. He resumed his ritual of running his hand across my hair and welcoming me back whenever I woke.

And then this happened … The following is how Tim has told the event. When I woke after a catnap, he noticed a faraway look in my eyes, and a slurring of words during our exchange, and then he noticed a wet stain on my pillow, on the side where my skull had been opened and supposedly closed. He rang for a nurse; an aide answered the call. He pointed to the wet pillowcase. He thinks the woman thought he wanted her to give me a fresh case. She moved her hands in my direction, he grabbed her wrist, and demanded she get a medical team in my room STAT. He thinks he actually said that word. The responding medical team knew what Tim already knew — I was leaking brain fluid.

Within seconds an emergency page went out with my room number and countless people descended and began moving this and that, and getting my hospital bed to the corridor where it was met by an arriving ambulance team. I was whisked off to UMass, evaluated in the ER and scheduled for a second opening and closing of my skull. While I was being prepped, the waiting room filled with many of the same people who'd sat with Tim during my first 24-hour surgery. While they paced the halls, I was in some shiny chrome chamber with some big-ass light shining in my eyes and medical people doing this and that, all the while monitoring my level of awareness. During the entire time, I heard myself mumble that I needed to see Ann Leary. Her name went onto a continuous loop. Back then, Ann was an ICU nurse at UMass. She was also a friend of mine, the person who was caring for my ten-year-old daughter, Jessica, who was best friends with Ann's daughter, Megan. I don't know if Ann left her home or her hospital floor in the middle of that night, but she arrived at my bedside just before I was wheeled in for surgery. I remember making her promise that I wouldn't die. She said things I imagine nurses are taught to say, or feel safer saying, things like, *"You're going to be fine, Sheryll. You're in good hands, Sheryll. I'll be waiting for you, Sheryll."*

That wasn't good enough … Even in my weakened state, and from somewhere deep in my messed up, brain-drain head, I knew I needed more. I pressed for more. "I need you to promise me that I will live." Ann Leary, the trained ICU nurse who knew how critical the situation was — Ann Leary, the woman I entrusted my young daughter to while I faced a medical crisis — Ann Leary, the woman I needed most in the world at that moment, gave me the greatest gift. She held my hand as they moved me toward the operating room, and told me over and over that I would survive and that she'd be waiting in recovery for me.

I did. She was.

It took me a very long time (years) to get back to a modified version of who I was before surgery. I had some post-operative things to work through and to compensate for. To look at me, I mostly looked the same, although there was some facial paralysis on my left side and I was deaf in that ear and, since my equilibrium was removed, I had balance issues and lived in a constant state of vertigo. The biggest thing I needed to learn to deal with was some sort of spatial-distance malfunction. I am 5'4" tall, but the folks at rehab determined that when I looked down, the ground measured triple that distance. What that meant was this: when I walk toward a curb or a pothole, I can't tell if it is directly in front of me or 15' away from me. I was told by the lovely whitecoats at rehab that I wasn't allowed to walk anywhere alone. They assured me that once I learned how to traverse a space, I would remember it, sort of like muscle-memory, and I'd be able to move freely in that space. All of that was true, but it left me feeling vulnerable, and it kept me inside my home, the space I learned to traverse.

I had another problem — one I kept secret ... I had this weird belief that I died during surgery and the world around me was my form of Heaven. I wasn't really a part of the whirl and swirl of the day to day, but I was on a continuum with it. I sat long hours perched on a club chair with my feet on an ottoman watching Tim and the girls come and go to work and school. I listened to stories of their days, and smiled when they did, and frowned when they did. There was very little interaction between us because when I tried to connect with them, it felt as though I was looking at the world from inside a fishbowl filled with oil. Nothing seemed clear — nothing felt real — and I had nothing to contribute. Not really.

During daylong periods of silence, when everyone was gone doing their things, I honestly thought I was a spiritual visitor. I mentioned this to the neurosurgeon during a follow-up visit and he kindly reminded me that I underwent a 24-hour surgical procedure on my brain, that I was under anesthesia for that whole time, and I had a second brain surgery a week later. He said it was a miracle that I lived through any of it, let alone all of it. And then he reassured me that I was indeed still alive.

It took many years for my head to catch up with my body. When I was physically better, I started being a wife and mom again. I practiced driving my RAV4 on the side streets in the neighborhood so I could get back to schlepping the girls to their high school. I dipped back into friendships, mostly by phone because I was feeling very insecure and preferred staying inside my house. It was a rarity for me to accept an invitation and an even bigger rarity if I actually ended up going. I'd send Tim and the girls off to Donna's and Clark's for a day of fun, and to the many O'Brien activities and celebrations while I stayed home because I was just too insecure to leave the house. I became reclusive. Everything at that time was a challenge. I remember watching my kids use the toaster, or the microwave, or the blender, and mimicked them. I never discussed any of this with anyone other than Tim because it made me sad, and it felt like an out-of-body experience which is where I wanted to leave it.

Years later ... Jessica gave me her used iPad and taught me how to surf the internet and create documents, and a few other things. I became hooked. The iPad helped me feel connected to the world, and it sort of helped me master technology. (Guru Jessica just spit her coffee across the room because she knows I suck at technology). When I decided to write my first book, I used what I had, and what I had was an iPad. With one finger, I pecked my first and second book — chapter by chapter — in an email — on the iPad. Hannah cautioned me over and over and over that my way of doing things was an accident waiting to happen and she was right. Halfway through my second novella, I lost the damned thing when I was trying to put the chapters onto one email. I don't know how she managed to retrieve my work, but when she did she insisted that I begin teaching myself how to use a computer. That's the year Tim and the girls bought me my HP. Hannah set passwords and IDs, and got *Bullet Bungalow*, and the work I'd done on the second, still unnamed novella, moved from the iPad to the computer.

Then it was my turn. I spent several weeks learning how to create new documents, and do all the layout and margin stuff, and even more weeks trying to understand where to file my documents and how to get them back again. I learned how awesome wireless printers were and I learned I had stories to tell. So, I began telling them — on a computer — like real writers do. And when I finished my second novella, I dedicated it to my mother. I knew then and there that I would dedicate all of my stories to Mom.

Ruth Shirley could barely wait for the second story of what I thought might be a 'trilogy'. When all was said and done, it took 17 books to tell the complete Pulling Threads saga. As soon as I started pulling Mahoney, Maxwell, Watts, and Serpico threads, I realized my characters had rich backstories that pushed the series forward, and forward, and forward. As I suspected she would, Mom fell in love with Fred Serpico in *Bullet Bungalow* and her affection for him never waned, but she always had a soft-spot for John Maxwell, so I made him the central character in *Netti Barn*.

Mom fell more deeply in love with John Maxwell during this story and, no matter what I did to that character or what I had him do to others, she always jumped to his defense. As a writer, I took great pleasure from that. For those of you currently reading the Pulling Threads series, I won't ruin your fun with anymore teasers. I will, however, tell you the first three stories of PT are set in the fictional seaside towns of Mayflower and Laurel Falls, along the North Shore of Massachusetts. After the happenings in *Cutters Cove*, the third novella, I took my characters on the ride of their lives. Truth be told, Fred, Kitt, John, Joy, Mike, and Annie decided where their lives were headed — I just went along for the ride. And what a ride it was!

A note from Ruth Shirley Bodreau, my mother ...

How does a mother look forward to the next blog coming out knowing the writings chronicle her daughter's last days?

Sheryll's enormous talent still shows in her writing as she conveys her thoughts and feelings about each day. Some of the blogs are extremely difficult to read and some of them tickle my fancy as she describes joyful times from her school days, and with her loving family and friends, and about her faith in God.

Marjorie reads the blogs to me and at times we are either laughing or crying together. Don and Denise share the blogs in much the same manner. It has become a family thing, our family's thing.

Although Sheryll's blogs cover her daily struggles and how she is dealing with her days ahead, she is also blessed with many days of joy spent with her devoted family. She thinks ahead to certain happenings and uses them as goals such as: Red Sox Opening Day, birthdays, Easter and Mother's Day.

She treasures the simple joys of looking out the window at a beautiful sunny day, or a bird perched on a branch of her Rose of Sharon bush, or her granddaughter skipping home from a day at school.

Sheryll lives each day to the fullest! She hears that she is reaching and comforting people she has never met and the outpouring from the public continues full scale.

Sheryll's heart is breaking along with ours and we pray she will be safe in the arms of Jesus. I wish her blogs could go on forever as our love for each other will!

Love, Mom

34. Dedicated with Love — Part Two ...

When I began publishing the last three novellas in the PT series, the dedications to my mother became a bit reflective. I knew the end of the story was in sight. I always intended on finishing the Pulling Threads novella series with a big-ass blockbuster book. I had the entire framework for *Alva* written in my head, but when the time came, I just could not put it to paper. The central story, the thread that ran through every PT book — the mystery of who The Body was and what his plan was had to be told. But I just couldn't do it. Why? Because I knew some of what I had in store for my characters, and I just couldn't bear saying goodbye to my friends.

Over the course of three years, I cried and laughed with my men and women. I helped carry the burden of their suffering and became giddy during joyful times. I loved each and every one of them — even those I detested. As my unproductive time dragged on, I questioned if it was normal that a writer just couldn't finish a story or a series? I silently wondered if I was experiencing some sort of traumatic writer's block? I had no idea what was going on, but I sure as hell was suffering from something. I slapped a band-aid on the festering emotional wound by writing the dedication for *Rebound*, the last novella of the series, the one that set the stage for the big-ass finale. The dedication was ambiguous, to say the least. It gave me an out, should I never be able to write *Alva*.

My mother knew I was struggling because I complained ad nauseum. She offered words of encouragement, and tried to help me figure out what the issue was. She'd been party to some hand-wringing over storyline difficulties in the past, but I'd always pushed through, so this total block and whining crap was a whole new experience for Mom. One day, I was yakking away about the shame of it all. "I have some really good shit to write, some really big stuff happens, but it's all stuck in my head, in one jumbled mess, and I can't find the thread to pull to get off and running."

The little old lady who wouldn't drop an F-bomb if her life depended on it got all up in my face. *"Okay, that's it. Write it or don't write it, but I'm telling you right now, Sheryll Anne, you'd better effing tell me what happens. You better tell me what the hell The Body's plan is, and who pays the ultimate price. I've read these damned books a hundred times each, so you'd better tell ME!"*

My mother, and Donna, and Marjorie, and Helena, pressured me over the years for hints about what was around the corner, and I never cracked. But on that day, the one when my Mommy yelled at me, I cracked and told her in minute detail what was going to happen and I even told her the big-ass ending. She said four words and hung up on me.

"Write that fucking book!"

While all of the *Alva* back-and-forth was going on, I'd started a new series because, why not? By the end of summer 2021, I'd written *Ashore on Stony Beach* and *Adrift on Stony Beach* and had begun writing *Awake on Stony Beach*. On several occasions, I lamented to Andria and Nancy that I still couldn't get focused on *Alva*, and so I decided to push into *Awake* and then try to circle back. I was two-thirds of the way through the final Stony Beach story when I got an urgent sense — a really deep dread that if I didn't write *Alva*, right then, it would never get written. I put *Awake* aside and reread large sections of the last three Pulling Threads books. I needed to get back into the heads of my characters and reconnect with the storylines and the pacing of that series.

I pulled a thread and decided how the final book would begin — with one of my central characters alone in a room. I got in there with her, crawled inside her head and focused on everything she saw, every move she made, every longing she had. Without question, the opening chapter of *Alva* is the best work I ever did. For the next month or so, I pushed *Alva* along and simultaneously worked on *Awake*. I would get up at 3 AM and work 15 hours straight. I was a mad woman on a mission — finishing two totally different stories from two totally different series. There wasn't a day during that time when Tim came down for coffee and found me anything other than a hysterical mess. And then one day I was all smiles. "I finished!" I proclaimed.

"Which one?"

"Both!"

"Are you shittin' me?"

"Nope. They're done." I broke with the emotion of it all, pushed back in my recliner, missed our morning coffee, took a power nap, woke refreshed and began the work of 'first edit' on my manuscripts.

And then the shit hit the fan … I was given a death sentence. I told the wonderful women I work with about my diagnosis before I told family members outside 183. All three of them broke emotionally for me and then put my work front and center. They did the lion's share of first, second and third edits, all of the proofreading sessions, and worked together to set a publication plan. Guru Jessica worked around the clock with social media postings for my books and handling the announcements about my illness, all while she was redesigning her own business and preparing for a major launch. This young professional is beyond talented and full of grit and stamina and she loves me, which is just delightful.

Andria. Nancy. Jessica. The Warden. The Goddess. The Guru. Their teamwork definitely made my dream work. In two months' time, those three women got three Sheryll O'Brien books edited, published, and promoted and because they did, I had the privilege to write this *Alva* dedication.

Mom,
All good things come to an end.
What will never end is my love for you.
Sheryll

That's the last Pulling Threads dedication, a heartfelt shoutout to my mother. The woman who traveled every road with me on my journey as a storyteller. Now, a little about the Twisted Threads series. Ruth Shirley loves reading books with lots and lots and lots of pages. She was practically giddy when she received the most recent *Outlander* and learned it has over 900 of them. My novellas run 200-250 pages. They are part of a series, but each is written with a specific story within the overall story, so each could be read as a standalone novel. The only complaint Mom ever had about my books was that they weren't long enough. I shook things up when I wrote the Twisted Threads series — I went long and I went **dark**. An ad I placed in an online magazine for *Her Scream* and *Stay Safe* has this warning: *Read At Your Own Risk*. One relative said she read each book in one sitting because she was too afraid to leave her locked bedroom to go pee. And as for my mother, suddenly, my books were too long and too tense.

"I had to take the damned book to the bathroom," she nearly hissed.

"Because you were scared?"

"Yes, but also because I had to pee and I couldn't put it down."

Hand to God this happened — and since I might be meeting Him soon and am very reluctant to bullshit about Him, you can take this as fact. Donna said the same thing as Mom when I called her. "What are you doing?"

"Taking a pee and reading Her Scream."

"Thanks for sharing."

"Your fault. I can't put the thing down. I'll call you when I'm done."

"Peeing or reading?"

"Reading."

I dialed back on the nail-biting-tension in my next series. The Stony Beach books have lots of threads to pull and are jam-packed with suspense and intrigue, and they have lots of love, lies, and lust — my trademark in storytelling — and it's got a Scotsman to die for. Why? Because my mom has a thing for the Scots. Anyway, the last three dedications for those books were done after my diagnosis. There was so much to say, but I just couldn't put into words how I was feeling, or any comforting words that would soothe my mother's very hurt heart. But I tried. The final written words to Mom were in *Awake on Stony Beach*. They are the most significant words I ever wrote.

Mom,
Be faithful,
Sheryll

And then this happened ... The retired storyteller penned one more book, *Be*, and a final dedication.

My Dearest Hadley,

Between the covers of this book you will find loving advice from MammyGrams. I hope my words help you grow to Be whomever you are meant to Be. Take the book on your journey through life. When times get tough, as they surely will, your Be book might help remind you that people are good by nature, that there is joy right around the corner, and that every moment is worth living, sharing, and cherishing.

So, to my wonderful, spirited, intelligent, sweet girl; embrace all of the special things that make you who you are. Then ... Be anything, Be everything, and most of all, Be happy.

I love you, Hadley, now and always,

MammyGrams.

So, there you have it, the end of my book writing days. I started living my dream late in life and it is ending way too soon for my liking, but when I first set out on my writing journey my goal was to write a book. I wrote 23. I wanted to see my name on the spine of a book, and I did.

Along the way ... I learned a valuable lesson or two. When I reached far beyond what I knew I could do, I learned I was destined to do a whole lot more. And I discovered that being successful is a personal thing — it's something you get to define and claim for yourself. At age 61, I put my fears aside and did what I wanted and needed to do — *for me*. I became part of the periphery of my 'normal' life and lived the life of a writer, waking before the sun so I'd get a few quiet hours in before Mr. Wonderful came for coffee, and I set goals that seemed unattainable. I never concerned myself with making money, I only hoped that people would read my stories and find enjoyment.

And now … I am writing the most personal and important thing I will ever write. Preparing for the loss of my life is really painful, and it is scary, and it is lonely. But through this blog, I have found strength and support from people I know and people I will never meet. I have learned that I want and need to live every minute of every day. Being lashed to my recliner 24/7 since December 1st would be miserable if not for the many people who have reached out in support and offered encouragement.

It seems fitting that I dedicate this work … Beyond saying thank you to friends, old and new alike, I'd like to dedicate this blog to all who are reading along. You are helping me carry my load.

And to you, Mom, I give you all of my love.

35. Donna. Sort Of …

My bestie, Donna Eaton, is many things. Truth be told, every one of us is a mix of a whole bunch of things, but people tend to grab onto something that becomes the first thing used to describe the multi-faceted human beings we are. I suspect the word that comes to mind by most everyone describing Donna is: strong. My friend has weathered far too many storms in her life and has shouldered many for her family and friends of which the woman has many. When we met, we hit the ground running with our friendship, and apparently we ran forward. I have known Donna for 30 years. I cannot tell you where in Worcester she grew up other than to say she was raised in a house.

A little background … Worcester is known as the City of Seven Hills. I'm going for broke here and am going to try to name all 7 without help. When my mind was working at the top of its game, (before the whole Swiss cheese of cancer), I relied on a well-honed organizational thought process when trying to figure out mundane things such as this. I put A before B before C, and eventually arrived where I wanted to be. I'm going to try that here by alphabetizing the hills, writing them down, and seeing where we land: "Airport Hill, Bancroft Hill, Belmont Hill, Burncoat Hill, College Hill, Deadhorse Hill, Green Hill, and Vernon Hill. Phew! That felt great, I named the 7 hills of Worcester." Then I counted. "Right off the bat I'm wrong. I named 8 hills." I counted again because I suck at math and math starts with counting. "Eight." I thought for a minute, the kind of thinking I would have done back in the day when Trivial Pursuit was all the rage. I would have realized I was close to the correct answer, so I would have pushed in and reasoned it out.

A total digression here … The person who I *never* wanted to compete against in Trivial Pursuit, the person I would always beg to be on my team was Donna Rosetti. She and I went to the same high school, though she was a year behind me. Apparently, *that* was the year everything was taught to the students at South High. Donna R. passed away a handful of years ago. I think of her most every day because it was she who introduced me to some of my favorite music — Jackson Browne and Fleetwood Mac are most definitely at the top of the list. I listen to music all of the time, ergo I think of Donna R. all of the time. I hope to hell we bump into one another in Heaven. I suspect she'll be in one of the rec rooms whooping some scholar's ass at the pie game while spinning Jackson's *Late for the Sky* album.

One more digression … I doubt it, but whatever. I played a very rewarding game of pie one time. I was on fire and was successfully pulling useless tidbits of random shit from wherever they reside and making it to the center circle in record time. I was going to win a game! I could feel it! I could taste victory!

And then this happened … Question: *"What was John F. Kennedy's biggest mistake while in office as President of the United States?"*

"Going to Texas," I boldly said.

"Nope, the Bay of Pigs."

I knew that was the answer, but all things considered, I strongly believed going to Texas was his biggest mistake. I argued the point, suggested we contact the makers of the game for a judgment call, all to no avail. I lost the game, but I still say I was right.

Back to my 7 hills riff… I tried talking through the list of 8, pretending this was for a piece of Trivial Pursuit pie. A sweat formed along my brow and upper lip. "Okay. The naming of the hills must date back a long ass time — definitely before there were airports, so I must be wrong about Airport Hill. But I live on that hill." Before I finished that thought I remembered Indian Hill and added it to the list, "Great, now I have 9." I called out to Tim who was boiling water for his nightly Lipton, "What are the 7 hills of Worcester?"

"Airport, College, Bancroft, Grafton."

"That's it?"

"That's all I can think of, but Pakachoag Hill might be one, but I think that's called College Hill."

"When I named them, I came up with 9."

"Can I borrow two?" he asked.

"That'll still leave you short by 1."

"So what'd you come up with?" he asked while passing three Figgies my way.

"I named mine alphabetically."

"Naturally."

"Airport was first, but I've already decided the hills were probably named before there were airplanes and airports, and since Worcester has a rich Native American history, the hills were probably named Nipmuck or Tatnuck."

"Or Pakachoag?"

"Yeah." I looked at my list again and tried to use a more historical filter. "Indian Hill — it's a bit politically incorrect in today's world, but it might have been the White Man's way of paying tribute to Native Americans who lived in Worcester and were 'asked' to vacate their property."

"Are we about to do a research project on Native Americans?"

"Not yet, but soon. I want to talk about Deadhorse Hill, first."

"What about it?"

"When I was a kid, someone told me it was called that because horses would die trying to get to the top of the hill."

"Oh, God."

"First question. How many horses do you think needed to perish before a hill was named in honor of the deceased beasts?"

"Could have been just one horse."

"No way! It had to be lots of horses. If it was only one, the hill would be named after that horse, like Trigger Hill, or maybe after the equine's breed, like

Appaloosa Hill or Palomino Hill. Nope not palomino. I don't think that's a breed, I think it's a color and the breed might be the American Paint, so the hill would have been American Paint Hill. Kinda a mouthful, though."

Mr. Wonderful sipped his tea and offered a shake of his head, *"When was the last time you took your pills?"*

"When you were napping. Hope you enjoyed the four hour snooze fest."

"Yeah. I must have needed it. Did you sleep?"

"Yeup. I woke up ten minutes before you, that's when I took my pills."

He laughed and headed to the kitchen, *"Want anything?"*

"Yeah, I want to whittle my 9 hills down to 7 and I want them to be the correct 7."

"Tell me what you came up with?"

"Airport, Bancroft, Belmont, Burncoat, College, Deadhorse, Green, Vernon, and Indian. That was a last-minute add on."

"Wow, you did good."

"Well. I did well. Thirty-five years, Tim. Adjectives. Adverbs."

"Shut up."

"I have cancer."

"I heard." We laughed. I took a minute to ponder the 'did well — did good' debate that was suddenly raging in my head, and how we got here — not the cancer 'here' but the conversation 'here'. Tim checked the clock. *"You wanted to watch a movie at eight, so you'd better figure this shit out."*

I moaned loudly. "I really *need* to figure this out. It's good for me to push in when I forget things."

"Then go for it. You're probably close. Push in to the contemporary names 'cause you and I aren't gonna know the Indian names for the hills."

"Native American names."

"Shut. Up."

I laughed my response, "So let's whittle down my list. I read it again. "Airport, Bancroft, Belmont, Burncoat, College, Deadhorse, Green, Vernon, and Indian."

Tim started whittling. *"We live on Airport Hill so let's keep that one. And Bancroft Hill and Belmont Hill sound right, but I don't think Burncoat is a hill."*

I don't know why, but I suddenly began mimicking that British game show host, "Burncoat Hill — you are the weakest link, Goodbye."

Tim groaned.

I laughed and started on the list, again. "Okay, so we're keeping Airport, Bancroft, and Belmont, and we should keep College cause it's a big-ass hill, and Vernon cause it's another big-ass hill. That brings us to 5."

"So what's left?"

"Deadhorse, Green, and Indian."

"Indian Hill is a lake. Take that one off."

"Should we flip a coin on the last two?"

"Deadhorse or Green? Let's go with Green. So what's our list?"

"Airport, Bancroft, Belmont, College, Green, Vernon."

"That's only 6."

"You suck."

"Put Deadhorse back on the list and look this shit up on the internet."

"That's cheating."

"Who cares? The movie starts in five minutes."

I reluctantly searched the web and read the **real** list. "1) Pakachoag Hill is where the largest number of Nipmuck Indians lived. Good for you Tim, you got one. 2) Sagatabscot Hill aka Union Hill. Ooo, we forgot about that effing hill. I think that's where Jackie McTigue works."

"I thought she worked at City View."

"And that school's on a hill, I wonder which one."

"Just continue reading the list — please!"

"Okay, 3) Hancock Hill was once owned by John Hancock. Ooo that reminds me, did you pay our life insurance bill cause you know, you'll be needing the money."

"All set. You've got two minutes."

"Before I die?"

He laughed. *"Maybe. You've got two minutes before the movie."*

"Oh, okay. 4) Chandler Hill aka Belmosy Hill near East Park. So that must be Belmont Hill. 5) Green Hill named after the Green Family. I wonder if Helena is a relative?"

"One minute, let's go."

"6) Bancroft Hill named after the well-known historian, George Bancroft. I'm thinking old George should have written this shit in a history book, then maybe we'd know it."

Tim turned on the television.

"Okay. Okay. 7) Newton Hill. It says it used to be farmland and is now a public park. I wonder which one?" The movie music started, so I put my computer aside and tuned in with the hubby.

An hour later he asked the question. *"Why were you interested in the 7 hills?"*

"I'm writing a blog about Donna and I don't know where she grew up, and I sort of went down a rabbit hole."

"And dragged my ass down with you. And by the way, Donna grew up on College Hill."

"Why didn't you say so?"

"Why didn't you ask me?"

"Shhhhh, the movie's back on." We watched the movie, mostly in silence, although I got onto a tangent when the main characters began talking about ice wine. "Ooo, I researched ice wine when I was writing *Her Scream*. I bet this movie is set in Upstate New York." I gloated when we learned it was. At 10 PM Tim tucked me in. At 4 AM I opened my eyes and this Word doc and got back to the blog about my bestie.

Donna is a very strong woman. She's gone through things that would bring most people to their knees, and keep them there. She has an enormous capacity for love, and a very strong moral compass. She's a straight-shooter, and rarely misses her mark. And as soon as she's fired off her round of reality, drawn blood, and holstered her six-shooter, she's all open-arms waiting to shoulder your pain. I can count on one hand the number of times I saw my bestie cry. I've seen her eyes well on countless occasions, but she always manages to push her tears back and swallow them hard. So, when I answered the phone a few days ago and heard her sputtering words between anguished sobs, I quickly read caller ID to make sure it was Donna, then I immediately thought the worst, "Oh My God, what happened?"

"You're dying. And I read your blog. And I'm gonna miss you. And you're so brave. And I don't know how you're doing this. And what will I do when you're

gone. And how are you feeling? And you can call me in the night if you're sad."

She took a long racking breath and I pushed in. "Looks like I chose the right person to deliver my eulogy."

We both cracked up before she started in again. *"And I'm fucking pissed!"*

"About the eulogy crack?"

"No. I'm pissed that you're dying! I mean seriously, what the fuck!"

"Ah. Finally, something I can work with. A pissed off Donna."

When my bestie is faced with the option of crying or bitching, she always heads toward the B word — or more likely the F word. Her proclivity for the F-bomb is one of the reasons we're such good friends. Unlike me, though, when some tragedy befalls an individual or thousands of individuals, Donna immediately dives headfirst into the deep end of the angry pool while I head to the stairs at the shallow end, shake a bit with fear and anguish before dipping my toes into the water.

Examples ... "Princess Diana is dead," I said through racking sobs. *"Fuckin' drunk driver,"* she snapped. "The World Trade Centers are collapsing," I said from the corner of my living room where I'd curled myself into the fetal position. *"Fuckin' terrorists," she growled.* "Betty White died," I said the other day. *"Two weeks before her 100th birthday — what the fuck is that about?"* she rightly lamented.

Diversion ... When I heard the news about Betty White, I called upstairs to Jessica to tell her. I am a huge Golden Girls fan, so my daughters grew up with the show on the television nearly around the clock. They know everything about the characters and about the actresses who played them. I heard about Betty's passing from Hannah, who called in tears to tell me. It's difficult to bring my older daughter to tears, although she's become a bit of a weeper since hearing my news and was emoting freely at the death of Betty. Anyway, "Hey, Jessica," I hollered from my perch. She came halfway down the stairs and poked her head over the banister.

"What?"

"Betty White died"

"Oh, no! How old was she?"

"Ninety-nine."

"How'd she die?"

"Skydiving accident."

"Really?"

Silence. Lots and lots of silence ... The penny dropped. We cracked up laughing and in walked Hannah. *"What's so funny?"*

"Betty White died," Jessica answered.

Hannah turned and left with a few choice words on her tongue.

Anyway, back to Donna and that phone call. I listened to my bestie's anguish and it broke my heart. And then it dawned on her that I am the one who's dying. *"I'm sorry,"* she moaned.

"Yeah, me too."

"I can do your eulogy."

"I know." The reason I know Donna will do a really good job delivering my eulogy is because my bestie is strong. And she's so much more than that.

36. Life's Little Surprises ...

Mr. Power - I would like to mention and thank my junior year, high school teacher, Mr. Andy Power. I think it is fair to say Mr. Power expected much from his students. I know he gave much in return. I'm sure there are lots of students who have a Mr. Power story, or two. Since this is my book, I'm going to share my favorite story.

Swamp Monsters ...

I showed up for class, having forgotten a writing assignment at home. When Mr. Power finished walking the classroom collecting the students' work, he singled me out, *"Miss Sneade, you didn't hand in your paper."*

"No, I didn't, but there's a really good reason."

"I doubt it, but please stand and tell the class the reason."

"I was reading my paper on the way to school, and when I got to Beaver Brook, this enormous, foul-smelling, swamp monster jumped into my path, drooled and spit, then grabbed my paper and sank back into the murky water."

"Well, that is a really good reason. Rewrite the paper and submit it tomorrow. The highest grade you can receive will be a B."

On the day Mr. Power handed back our papers, he neglected to give me mine. My hand shot up, "Excuse me Mr. Power, you didn't hand me my paper."

"No, I didn't, but there's a really good reason. I was reading your paper on the way to school, and when I got to Beaver Brook, this enormous, foul-smelling, swamp monster jumped into my path, drooled and spit, then grabbed your paper and sank back into the murky water."

The class erupted in laughter. Mr. Power gave me my paper the next day. I received an A. Thank you Mr. Power for all that you brought to your classroom.

You demanded respect. You easily earned it.

I recently received a call from Joyce McTigue saying she read my *Ashore* book and she raved about it. That's not relevant to this blog, but it sure the hell is relevant to this author. Anyway, Joyce mentioned the acknowledgement in that book. She asked if I knew that Phil McTigue was very good friends with one of the Power kids and wondered if it would be alright if Phil shared the acknowledgement with his friend. "Share away," is what I think I said. I've since heard that Mr. Power's children were pleased and touched to know that one of his former students thought highly enough of their father to include him in the front matter of a novel.

There was a beautiful obituary written by two of his daughters, and referenced on FB by a classmate of mine, the former Karen Flynn. I immediately found and read the loving words. The things I didn't know about Mr. Power could fill several blogs. What I knew, in a very personal way, was that Mr. Power was the best teacher I had in high school. He didn't just stand in front of the room and lecture, he moved about. I think it was his way of getting and keeping his students' attention. He could have stood as still as a statue and kept my attention, not because he was lecturing, but rather because he was teaching. Not only about the topic at hand, but also about life. He always found a way to connect the past to the present — the prologue to the epilogue.

I carried many lessons from my junior year English class. Words Mr. Power spoke that year have come around and around during my attempt at writing books. The words that are coming around now, as I push hard at writing this blog about cancer and dying are these. *"The written word is only part of a writer's story. The most important part is what moved someone to write it in the first place."* Surprise #1: isn't really a surprise at all. Mr. Power is still teaching me.

> *A note from Josephine Power ...*
>
> Love the new blog!! It is really wonderful. My family loved the Acknowledgement because it captured our dad so perfectly; we could totally see him as you described what happened. Your blog spoke to me on so many levels...enjoying every bit of life each day and each minute. Your writing style is brilliant--your humor is the exact humor that I love that I inherited from my father (as did my four siblings); you make the daily events that happen in your life so worth reading about...
>
> I wish I'd gotten to know you sooner, but we are friends right now. Be in touch later today. Fondly and (gentle) hugs.

Marjorie - My sister walks through life in service of others. She spent many years as an elementary school teacher putting in long hours doing the ABCs of learning. She was a familiar face outside the classroom, spending oodles of time cheering-on students or pitching-in at after school functions because she wanted her students to know she cared about all parts of their lives. Most generously, she spent money she didn't always have on kids' school supplies, and Christmas coat drives, and giving trees, and, and, and.

As a kid, whenever anyone asked Marjorie what she wanted to be when she grew up, she'd say, *"A mommy."* That was the constant in her life. It was her dream and her passion. And when life didn't just hand her the opportunity for motherhood, she became a certified foster parent. And when a little girl named Nicole was placed in Marjorie's home and heart, my sister became the adopted mommy of the little girl who needed her — the little girl of Marjorie's long-held dream.

After the passing of our stepfather, Roland Bodreau, a truly wonderful man who left this world without warning and way too soon, Marjorie expanded her home by adding an apartment for our mother. I'm not sure how many years Marjorie and Shirl have cohabitated, but I'd venture to guess it's been at least fifteen years. And when Shirl slowed down a bit and stuck closer to home, Marjorie became whatever Mom needed or wanted her to be. And when Covid hit the elderly with a vengeance and Marjorie was still working outside the home, she set a decontamination center in the mudroom where she stripped to her skivvies upon entrance and disinfected herself before moving further into the inner sanctum.

Marjorie has always done for others. She would most assuredly be in servitude to me 24/7 if she could be. But there's really nothing she or anyone can do by way of fixing things. So, my kid sister tends to my mother's broken heart, as she does her own, and then she finds ways to lift my spirits and remind me that I am way more than a hospice patient. With increasing regularity my sister texts photographs from when we were kids, dating back to the time when we played together and looked out for one another, and from the time when she took care of her baby dolls and idolized her older sister. Surprise #2: isn't really a surprise at all. My kid sister is caring for me through little acts of kindness.

Hadley - Saturday morning brought with it a knock on the door. It came from the light of my life. *"I'm here,"* she shouted from outside.

"Thanks for the warning," I shouted from inside, as I have most every time she's announced herself.

The seven-year-old ushered in a blast of frigid air, kicked off her boots and headed toward my chair, *"Can I sit on your lap and cuddle under the blankets?"*

I shook my head, "No, I'm sorry we can't, but let's do this." I called out to Tim, "Can you bring Hadley's bench in."

"Sure. Where do you want it?"

"Put it there for a minute, then move this end table away from my chair .... okay, move the bench next to me .... okay, Hadley, hop onto the bench." She got onto her knees, leaned over the arm of my recliner, and hugged me tight. Tim covered us with a big blanket. "There, now we can cuddle under the blanket."

She kissed my cheek and tried to hide her wet eyes.

"You okay, kiddo?"

"Yeah."

"So what's on the agenda, today?"

"I'm going to Daddy's for an overnight."

"I bet you'll have fun."

"Yeah. I'm bringing my Barbies. Do you think I can take the monkey game I gave you for Christmas?"

Yes, folks, my granddaughter gave me a monkey game for Christmas. Monkeys are our thing. Upon either of us uttering the word or hearing the word in passing, we both scream 'monkey'. It's something we started doing years ago and neither of us plans on stopping anytime soon. Anyway, I answered her previous question, "Of course you can take the game."

"Daddy will love it." Hadley went to the kitchen table when she learned her Silly Saturday breakfast was ready. When she was finished, she and I played several games of Snaps and Buckets. She whooped my ass and had way too much fun doing so. When it was time for her to leave, she extended her hand, I pushed the lever, and she commenced on giving me thirty hugs. I gave her a kiss for each one. As soon as the door closed behind her, I took the recording device I'd turned on at the knock on the door, pressed rewind, and relived my morning with Hadley. I plan on leaving the recordings for her, so she can have me near — sort of. Surprise #3: isn't really a surprise at all. Hadley is the greatest gift of my life.

Dr. Wonderful - I got a text from my doctor on a Saturday afternoon saying he was just checking in on me because we hadn't spoken in a couple of weeks. The text included the reminder that I could contact him if I needed anything. Surprise #4: isn't really a surprise at all. My doctor is what all healthcare providers should aspire to be — caring people.

Donnie - I got my Sunday afternoon phone call from the Dude in Dixie. We took a verbal stroll down memory lane, one that had twists and turns and a few surprises here and there. We shared stories we'd never told one another. My favorite of his was a tale about an act of kindness he did for a family member who was battling addiction — his favorite of mine was a tale about an act of kindness I did for a complete stranger who was battling addiction. Neither of us set out to discuss those stories, but we ended up at that place and I'm so very glad we did. When we ended our call, I spent some time reflecting on who Donnie, Sheryll, and Marjorie grew up to be — three very caring individuals who find ways to help others without seeking praise, or even thanks. Why? Because they were raised by a woman they call, “Mom.” Surprise #5: isn’t really a surprise at all.

37. Who Has the Time ...

Okay, so you’re given a death sentence and you’re given time, so what do you do with it? My suggestion is you get down to business. If you have a will, review it. Maybe give your lawyer a call to make sure everything is still current. Tim and I signed our most recent will in 2016. We called our attorney, explained the situation. He did a review of things and asked Tim to stop in and resign a bunch of stuff. We weren’t changing anything significant, but it was suggested that a sit down between Tim and Attorney Wonderful (yeup, he’s wonderful) was a good idea. If you don’t have a will, my suggestion is you get down to business. I am not an attorney although I pretend to be one when I bestow that profession on one of my characters. Still, I think it’s sage advice to put your things in order.

With or without a will, it’s a good idea to discuss your intentions with your children, and maybe give each one a little something, something while you are still here, a piece of jewelry, or some little thing your child or grandchild or friend thought was special. Sharing your bounty is a sure-fire way that they’ll remember you. Just kidding! It’s a sure-fire way to make a wonderful last and lasting connection. Each of us spends a lifetime gathering belongings, things that tell the story of who we are, where we’ve been, and what matters to us, so go ahead and share them, watch for yourself the pleasure gifting things brings to the people you love. I did this during the Christmas holiday.

A little background ... Tim and I live in a duplex; we on one side, and Hannah and Hadley on the other. It is the absolute perfect living arrangement. The proximity means that my best little person in the whole world opens her front door, skips a few steps my way, opens my front door, and lands in my arms. Oh, what joy it brings to my heart when I hear that Hadley is on her way. The side-by-side homes were perfect for this past Christmas. Hannah hosted her first Christmas brunch — the one I hosted for the past 35 years. Tim's sister Annie has a huge Christmas Eve bash for the O'Brien clan and most of Worcester County — which is pretty much the O'Brien clan — and then Tim and I have my family, all 10 of them, to our home Christmas morning. With Covid rampant, once again, we needed to make a plan — a safe plan — for my family to spend this last holiday with me.

The plan ... Everyone visiting 183 took a sacred oath to do a rapid Covid test Christmas morning, don two masks each, use hand sanitizer on the way in and on the way out of cars and homes, congregate en masse at Hannah's side, eat drink and be merry there, then come visit me — two by two. During the inner sanctum visits with Yours Truly, the Sneades, the Bucks, the McCarthys and Mother Bodreau kissed the ring of the Godmother much like the Tattaglias, the Barzinis, the Cuneos, and the Straccis kissed the ring the Godfather. My 'family' exchanged happy hellos before anguished goodbyes. In between the giggles and tears, I 'bequeathed' my jewels.

What that really means is this ... I handed each of the women in my life a small black velvet bag that had a little something, something inside. Whatever trinket was gifted to me over the years was now being gifted away. One of my most favorite 'bequeathings' was to my sister-in-law, Denise.

First a little background … from a blog I wrote a couple years back.

The engagement …

April is a wonderful month, once you get past the tomfoolery of its first day, or in my case, the 'timfoolery' of its first day. Mr. Wonderful popped the question on April Fool's Day. I think.

Tim and I attended the same high school, though we didn't hang out together. I knew who he was, everyone knew who he was. Tim O was the all-around, go-to guy at South High. The classmate who interfaced easily with teachers and students, the one who did things off-campus at the behest of administrators, the president of the inter-high student council, the young adult who roamed halls freely whilst the rest of the 'kids' remained shackled to desk chairs. I, on the other hand, wasn't really part of my school's social scene because I spent most of my time with my boyfriend — a really gooood-looking jock from a school across town. (The extra oooo-s in gooood just sort of wrote themselves, so I'm leaving them).

Anyway, after high school, Tim started college, had to leave to have major back surgery, suffered through a lengthy recuperation, went to art school, then moved to The Woodlands, a sort of suburb of Houston. While he was doing all of that, I was climbing the stepstool of success, earning some cash, buying concert tickets (you name them, I saw them), and tooling around in my midnight-blue Datsun 280Z 5-speed. I was living moment to moment, and enjoying every damned one of them.

For ten years, neither of us had a single thought about the other of us. That tidbit didn't matter a lick because when the man recently back from the Lone Star

State, and the woman wearing a dress that screamed, "Welcome back to the Bay State!" found themselves in the same reunion hall, it was a damned yeehaw moment. On the umpteenth time our eyes locked from across the room, Tim raised his beer bottle in a sort of salute, pulled a long sip, and nodded his head in what I assumed was some sort of Texan mating ritual. I was lassoed. I leaned close and whisper-drooled to a classmate who knew Tim really well, "Barbie, that's the man I'm going to marry."

She nudged me nearly off my 4" stilettos, and laughed, *"Doubt it."*

On April Fool's Day, Tim O'Brien asked Sheryll Sneade to marry him while at Dino's, a wonderful Italian eatery with red and white checked tablecloths, Chianti bottle centerpieces, each with a melted to the nub taper, and a roasted pepper pizza to die for. At a booth for two in a quiet nook off the main-seating area, Mr. Wonderful pushed his meal aside and said, *"I've been thinking a lot, but I haven't really planned anything yet, you know with rings and things, but I think we should get married."*

After a minute or two of silence I asked, "Are we engaged?"

After a minute or two of silence he asked, *"Did you say, yes?"*

After a minute or two of silence I asked, "Did you propose?"

He reached across the table, took hold of my hand. He asked. I said, yes.

Okay, back to the Christmas story … Tim never did 'the rings and things' proposal because I suggested we use my mother's wedding set. She 'bequeathed' it to me upon my parents' divorce — there was a hiss involved but, still, the event was charming — not really. The set was really beautiful. The bands were primarily yellow gold, but the engagement ring held a half-carat round diamond set in platinum, and the very thin wedding band had a row of itty-bitty round diamonds, also set in platinum. I don't really like wearing rings, so I never planned to wear both pieces. Tim and I took the wedding band to the jewelers, purchased two thin gold bands and had the three pieces made into one wide band. Into the drawer went my mother's engagement ring.

And then this happened … Don was getting engaged to Denise. I offered him Mom's engagement ring. It pleased my mother that two of her children happily used her rings. It pleased me that my new sister-in-law loved the ring and the sentiment. This Christmas morning, thirty years or so later, I handed Denise a black velvet bag that held my wedding band, "I think it's time we put the set back together." Mom, Marjorie, and Denise shed tears during the sentimental moment, Don and I pushed ours back and swallowed them hard.

This 'bequeathing' story is my long-winded way of suggesting that those with limited time in their lives, bits of time on their hands, and trinkets in their drawers might want to give them to loved ones. The sheer joy on the recipients' faces is priceless — even if your jewels are not.

Planning your funeral … I'd made the decision years ago that I would be cremated. My somewhat rational decision was born from my irrational fear of confined spaces — like coffins. Even though I'd be dead, the thought of being in an enclosed box gave me the panics. I partly blame Mary Higgins Clark for my over-the-top fear of coffins. I believe it was she who wrote a book where the female darling was kidnapped and buried alive in a century-old cemetery plot. Fortunately for the young woman, the grave just happened to have an old-fashioned above-ground bell attached to a string that hung down into the grave. The author explained things this way: it was common practice that the 'bell-ringing emergency system' would be used by a prematurely dirt-packed, still alive soul. He or she would find the string and ring the bell, altering whoever was roaming the graveyard that a mistake had been made.

Ingenious, but fuck that shit. Coffins. Graves. Claustrophobia! Nope. Nope. Hard pass. That was it for me and cemetery plots. Just sayin! Anyway, cremation is my preferred way to go, and there were other things that I wanted done my way — I don't want a wake, and I don't want a church funeral, but I do want an open-house type gathering where family and friends can just hang out and shoot the shit.

I can have what I want — sort of … Since Covid is still an effing curse on those living and those who won't be for long, like Yours Truly, things can be planned with a funeral home, but they may not be realized. In other words, it'll be a crapshoot if I get what I want, but this is what I want. I've decided to have an open-house gathering, a 'stop by' anytime between 11 and 1 or 2 and 5, and be lulled by the sounds of the Atlantic Ocean piped in courtesy of surround-sound, and watch a little slide show of random thoughts by Yours Truly, and listen to Father Dude plead my case to the Big Guy, and to my brother say nice things about me on behalf of my family, and to my bestie tell the truth about me.

Planning the best party you won't attend … You might as well plan your party, your last hurrah, your final send off. After the open-house gathering, there will be a quick drive past my childhood home, a stone's throw from the Knights of Columbus where family and friends will gather, and my favorite tunes will be played, courtesy of Hannah who has put together a playlist, and where lots of laughs will be had, most likely at my expense, but I'll be dead, so whatever.

A trip to Breens … My sister-in-law, Noreen Hanlon, is the Sam Malone of Cambridge Street. She owns a bar/café called Breens. Many members of the Hanlon family have been part-owners of the joint for decades — that's the length of time I've said these words. "I have never stepped inside Breens. When I was young, I was a Blarney Stone girl, when Tim and I were dating we were more inclined to share our drinks at home before hitting the sheets, then I had kids, then I became a recluse.

So, this is the plan … When I die, I want my urn to be taken to Breens for a private, family-only toast or two." So there you have it. I was given time to plan things. And so I have!

38. All About Tim …

The year was 1957, the month was February. Mary O'Brien, moter of 5 delivered her 6th child. A boy named Timothy James. The first set of OBs: Francis, Mary Ellen, Eileen, Terrence, and Ann Marie, ranged in age from 13 to 4. Tim became the oldest of the next grouping of OBs: Tim, Kathy, Joey, Noreen, and Jimmy.

Time warp … I surprised Tim with a 50th birthday party at one of his favorite eateries, Chuck's Steakhouse. It was an open house, drop-in-when-you-can buffet event held on a platformed section of the massive bar — the focal point of the restaurant. While the business-as-usual patrons were enjoying pints of beer, games of pool and watching strategically placed televisions broadcasting the Patriots game, Tim's family and friends were celebrating his birthday.

The bash was an Irish-themed shindig with men in black top hats and women in glittery gold ones. There were strands of green Mardi Gras beads strung here and there, and End of the Rainbow gold pots that served as whimsical centerpieces, filled to the brim with gold-wrapped chocolate coins for Good Luck. And the surprise of all surprises was a very surprised birthday boy, surrounded by widely smiling family and friends because we got him good. My gift to Tim was a hardcover, coffee-table book, *What a Year It Was! 1957*. The nostalgic book covered world news, human interest, sports, fashion, entertainment, science, medicine, and enough tongue-in-cheek stuff to keep you interested for hours; it also served as a journal for guests to write a little something in remembrance of the day — more on that later.

So, here we go, back to 1957 ... Drive-in theaters were all the rage with more than 4,000 of them nationwide. Men and women interested in risqué, black-stocking and black jacket flicks, but who didn't necessarily want the public to know about their darker proclivities, appreciated the anonymity of watching racy movies whilst slumped in car seats rather than theater seats. Drive-in owners quickly seized on the mass appeal and went a bit more 'mainstream' with their movie showings. Theater audiences headed to the drive-in in droves (couldn't resist the pun), and Saturday night dates behind fogged windshields became 'the thing' to do.

An Affair to Remember was the #1 drive-in movie in 1957. Rock Hudson was the top male star, Sophia

Loren was the top female star and, *Around The World in 80 Days* won the Best Picture Academy Award. Hollywood lost actor Humphrey Bogart, and comedian Oliver Hardy, as well as co-founder of MGM, Louis B. Mayer. Future Hollywood film stars: Geena Davis, Melanie Griffith, Daniel-Day Lewis, Michelle Pfeiffer, and Rachel Ward were all born in the wonderful year of 1957.

In the world of television … 'Living Color' sets hit the market, making black and white ones obsolete in a matter of a few years. Families sat around their sets for the debut of Kermit the Frog on the Tonight Show, the premiere of Leave it to Beaver, and the rise of Dick Clark's American Bandstand from its rank as a regional hit to a nationally televised sensation. Future television stars born that year were: Katie Couric, Fran Drescher, Paul Reiser, Ray Romano, Katey Sagal, and Vanna White.

A digression … When Tim's sister Ann Marie White was expecting her third child, her two young sons wanted to name their sister, Snow or Vanna. Annie and Tiger chose the lovely name of Christine for their beautiful baby girl. I smile whenever I remember the boys' disappointment that parents got to make such monumental decisions without their consultation. I always wanted to write a book called, *How Parents Chose Their Kid's Names*. Everyone has a story to tell about the Baby Name Game. I already shared how Tim and I named our kids and I've heard countless stories over the years, some fun and some frustrating, about friends' ordeals in the baby naming process. Given I ended up with three nephews on Tim's side named Patrick, an author might find the stories repetitive, but still interesting. So, for the person out there who might want to dig deep on a fun project, go for it!

Okay, back to 1957 ... Elvis Presley topped the charts in music — no surprise there, Pat Boone and Fats Domino each had three #1 hits, and the Everly Brothers released *Wake Up Little Susie* and *Bye Bye Love*. John Lennon and Paul McCartney met for the first time at a church garden party, and Berry Gordy, Jr. started Motown Records. Future recording artists born in 1957: Gloria Estefan, Vince Gill, Lyle Lovett, George Strait, Donny Osmond, and Eddie Van Halen.

Over in the world of books ... Dr. Seuss got a publishing deal after receiving countless rejections for *The Cat In The Hat* and *How The Grinch Stole Christmas*. Within days of the books' releases, they became a hit with adults and children alike. And miles away from the rhyming sensations of tall cats and green outcasts, Jack Kerouac's 'stream of consciousness' novel, *On The Road*, became *the* book about the Beat Generation, and Allen Ginsberg's poem, *Howl*, was seized by U.S. customs officials on grounds of obscenity.

In other news ... Dwight David Eisenhower was president, Teamster official Jimmy Hoffa was arrested on bribery charges, the 'Little Rock Nine' enrolled in Central High School in Little Rock, Arkansas, Cuban rebel leader, Fidel Castro was interviewed on a CBS documentary, Princess Caroline of Monaco and Caroline Kennedy were born, Elvis joined the Army, and Martin and Lewis broke up their comedy team.

During the festivities, Hannah and Jessica roasted their dad with a witty repartee of his parenting-style. Their speech was a ramble of life's situations and the readymade clichés their father dispensed as wisdom. Just about every platitude known to man made it into their schtick.

Papa's Platitudes …

Every cloud has a silver lining … Tomorrow's another day … There's no use crying over spilled milk … If at first you don't succeed, try, try, again … The bigger they are, the harder they fall … Don't put all your eggs into one basket … Take the high road, there's a lot less traffic on it … Seems you're caught between a rock and a hard place … Looks like you bit off more than you could chew … If it ain't broke, don't fix it … Don't bite the hand that feeds you … Don't look a gift horse in the mouth … Don't put the cart before the horse … That's as useless as tits on a bull.

The girls' favorites.

You can't unscramble an egg … You can't unring a bell.
You'll only ever have one father …
You'll be sorry when I'm gone.

He didn't have to tell them that.
They knew it deep in their hearts.

The girls' performance brought laughter to the room, and there were times I thought Tim would need to be resuscitated from his complete enjoyment of their schtick. Oh, and more than a few bar patrons left the Patriots game and joined in on the fun — always a good thing!

The next blog will shock the hell out of you. Don't say I didn't warn you.

38. All About Tim — Part Two ...

Nine years after I had my brain surgery, this happened. It was a Sunday afternoon, Tim went to buy a new pair of work shoes at the Greendale Mall, and on the way home Mr. Wonderful was in a fender-bender on Park Avenue. Not to worry, his awesome shoes were bubble-wrapped, tucked inside a cardboard box and resting comfortably on the floor in the back whilst his body was taking the full impact of the hit.

A young girl operating a vehicle whilst texting a message didn't realize my beloved had stopped for a red light. The attempted murderer did enough damage to the back end of our car that a police officer suggested Tim go to the E.R. by ambulance. The dude I'm married to (the one I think I'll describe as the dumbass I'm married to for this story) came home instead and within a few hours he could barely move his head from side to side, so off we went to get him checked out at the aforementioned E.R.

Some background info ... Tim had major back surgery when he was 18 and has two Harrington Rods that run the length of his spinal cord. To those of you who've wondered if the 'really nice' guy goes toe to toe with his strong-willed wife, he does, and he's quite successful since his spine is shored up with two steel rods. Just sayin.

Back to the story ... Even though he was only complaining of neck pain, Tim was sent for a CT scan because the medical team wanted to check his steel rods and spine. Everything seemed fine and he was sent on his merry way. A week later he received a registered letter (on a weekend) from the Radiology department at the hospital saying Tim needed to get in touch with Dr. Wonderful, as soon as possible. On

Monday, the physician who's been at the center of a lot of O'Brien shit over the past 15+ years told Tim to come into the office for a discussion. In case you are unaware, when a physician suggests you have a face-to-face discussion it is never a good thing and you should prepare yourself accordingly.

As it turned out, Tim O'Brien had a brain tumor. Bet a few of you just said, WTF! Cause we did! A pituitary adenoma showed up on Mr. Wonderful's CT scan. Thankfully, the typical X-ray prescribed for most whiplash-likely patients was upped to a CT scan for Tim. Otherwise the brain tumor would have gone unnoticed.

So here we go again … Nine years to the same month, with the same neurosurgical team, Mr. Wonderful underwent surgery to remove a pituitary adenoma. There wasn't going to be an opening and closing of his cranium to get the grape-sized tumor out and since I'm still skeeved about the surgical procedure he had, I'm gonna let you search the internet to read about it for yourselves. I'm going to jump to the fun part, the one immediately following his two-hour surgery.

Tim's procedure was delayed seven hours because the surgical team was called in for an emergency situation. And since we'd already been separated, and he'd been prepped for surgery, Tim was alone in the pre-surgical area that entire time. While the patient waited impatiently, he was getting concerned that his 'team' might be too tired when they finally got to him. Then he remembered the chief neurosurgeon worked on me for 24 hours straight, so my mate relaxed a bit.

I, on the other hand, spent those hours in a waiting room reading decades-old People Magazines, some with celeb wedding photos, and others announcing the couple's divorce proceedings were already underway. Worst of all, I was forced by my girls to help with a 1,000 piece jigsaw puzzle they grabbed from a shelf of puzzles I hoped, I prayed, they wouldn't see. They saw. They conspired. They tortured me.

For the record, I hate jigsaw puzzles. The only puzzles I find any enjoyment in doing are the kind two year old kids do, the ones with the knob on top of thick cardboard pieces. You put the five pieces into the perfectly odd-shaped cutouts, clap happily with the smiling tot and be done with it. The takeaway from this ramble is that Mama wasn't happy with the seven hour wait or with her husband's children.

As soon as Tim was taken to recovery, I was tracked down by the two neurosurgeons, Dr. Miracle who painstakingly removed my big-ass tumor and Tim's little-ass tumor, and the less miraculous doctor who neglected to adequately close my cranium. I guess I'm still a bit bitter about the whole drip, drip, drip of brain fluid, oh well. Anyway, before the men in surgical garb had a chance to say bye bye to me, Dr. Miracle got paged to Tim's bedside, apparently the surgical patient who was medicated heavily so he wouldn't move his head was sitting upright, vomiting his guts out because he was having an allergic reaction to morphine. By the way, sitting upright and retching was absolutely not part of the post-op plan.

Concerned about a brain fluid drip or some other complication, Tim was whisked off to the ICU. He was stabilized incrementally as the effects of the morphine lessened, and when I was finally allowed to see him, it was after 3 AM. His surgery had been scheduled for 9 AM, so the girls and I had been at the hospital a long-ass time. I'd kept his family apprised about the delay, but by early evening the shit hit the fan and so the news hit the airwaves. One awesome thing about the OBs, because there are so many of them, there's a family call tree, so all I had to do was call Person A who called Person B who called Person C. Within a matter of hours, all 973 of them were caught up to speed. And because Tim has two sisters who are nurses, all I had to do was say a few medical terms I heard from Tim's doctor, and they took it from there. They gave me a thumbnail of the situation, maybe suggested a few questions for me to ask, then made their plans to get their asses to the ICU to find out for themselves what was going on. What was happening at that point in time ended up being a blip on the medical screen when the real shit hit the fan.

A couple days after that incident … A stabilized Tim was sent home. Within two days, things went from moderately okay to, *"You should bring him to my office."* Dr. Miracle took one look and sent Tim by ambulance back to the ICU where he spent six days, and then another handful of days on the 'regular' hospital floor. Tim developed something called diabetes insipidus, an uncommon disorder, not related to type 1 or 2 diabetes. Diabetes insipidus causes an imbalance of bodily fluids which demands a high volume of fluids going in and coming out. Almost drop by drop the in-fluids and the out-fluids were measured and analyzed because Tim was really sick. There is no cure for diabetes insipidus, but focused treatment can help get fluids back in line. My understanding is a healthy adult outputs 1 to 2 quarts of urine per day. Tim was outputting 20 quarts per day and that significant increase causes an imbalance in the blood: important things like sodium and potassium get all out of whack which can lead to weakness, imbalance, and confusion. Tim had them all, in a very big way.

All in all … Mr. Wonderful spent two weeks in the hospital for what should have been a one night, post-op observational stay. When my 6'2" man finally returned home to stay put, he was as weak as a lamb, and acted as though he had a few bats in his belfry. He'd leave bed for a quick bathroom trip and I'd find him many minutes later sitting outside on a chair, under a tree, on his barren lawn, wearing only his pajama bottoms. I'd grab my cane for balance and do the vertigo-wobble to him. And there we'd be, outside, before dawn, Mr. and Mrs. Wonderfully Looney, he in his bottoms and me in my nightgown asking, "What'cha doin?" He'd stay silent for many minutes then shrug a shoulder. He did enough of these wacky trips that the first question people asked when they checked in on Tim was, *"Where'd you find him this morning?"*

I suspect if I hadn't already been given an expiration date for this whole cancer crap, Tim might consider offing me for this blog, but I figure his brush with a critical health issue and the fact that both parents of our girls had head tumors, it was worth the risk mentioning it.

It took a few weeks for Tim to get back on sure footing, and to keep his ass inside the house until he was fully dressed. The experience pushed me into Mama Bear mode. I found ways to cope with things on my own, and to put on a brave face out in the world, particularly at hospitals when I really felt like withdrawing. And I spent time taking care of the guy who'd done so much for me over the years. We spent the next three years living a normal and uneventful life and then the shit hit the fan. I had breast cancer, and it became the beginning of the end.

40. Turn Turn Turn — Part One ...

> *To everything there is a season, a purpose, especially when the season is living.*
>
> ~ Sheryll

Writing a blog ... I started writing one because I just can't live the remainder of my life without writing something, and since I'm not able to lay out a bunch of threads for characters to pull and solve some mystery, I'm keeping things short and telling my story. Surprise of all surprises, I'm still writing mysteries because I never really know where my blogs will take me. What I do know is this: my writing was supposed to give me a creative outlet, a way to help assemble information that was coming fast and furiously and to provide a dumping ground for overwhelming emotions. My blog was supposed to help **me**. It has become so much more.

The writings about my final journey are touching people in a variety of ways. People I know, and people I've never met and will never meet have been reaching out, mostly through email. They are sharing stories about themselves, or about a loved one who went through hospice, or about someone who passed suddenly leaving important messages of love unsaid. Mostly, the people who reach out want to offer support, to me, a complete stranger. The support has come in a variety of ways: the mention of a book someone found helpful, or the link to a music video of a song I mentioned in a blog or one they thought I might like to hear, or a heartfelt expression of thanks for an acknowledgement I wrote in one of my novels. Universally, those I know and those I do not know have all mentioned or marveled at how strong I am and how my acceptance has made them think about how they would handle such news or if they could handle such news. So, the purpose of this particular blog is to push into a question I asked myself this morning. Am I in a state of acceptance or denial?

During the days and weeks between funky blood tests and body scan readings, I told Tim and the girls that if things were really bad I wasn't going to fight a fight I couldn't win. I was going to accept the diagnosis and live the life I had left and be grateful for every second of it. Of course, those words were said when I lived in 'The Land of Ignorance'. A lovely corner of the universe where the words, *"You have bone cancer from your skull to your knees. You are terminal,"* hadn't yet been spoken. So while I really had no idea what I'd do when someone lobbed those words my way, it turns out, I did exactly what I said I'd do. I accepted my reality.

I am going to die … My acceptance of that fact was not without misery. I hurt so badly and wept so powerfully that I could hardly pull air sometimes. I remember the wrap of Tim's arms and the burying of my head into his chest. I can still feel his tears drip onto the back of my neck as they slipped silently down his cheeks, and his repetitive, *"I'm so sorry."* I remember pushing away from his hold and rambling a list of things I'd be missing out on, and how sorry I was for my family and friends, and how pissed I was that my writing was coming to an abrupt end, and that I'd never see if my books caught on. I remember almost collapsing with worry about my eighty-six-year old mother suffering a profound loss near the end of her life, and about my seven-year-old granddaughter carrying a profound loss for the rest of her life.

And still, I accepted my circumstances … I think part of my accepting the word 'terminal' has to do with what I'd been through all those years ago. The head surgery was big and it definitely felt like a bump against death. The breast cancer crap felt more like a bump in the road in comparison, but it felt serious nonetheless. And though both experiences could have ended very badly, I sort of knew, from somewhere deep, that I wasn't going to die from them. This go around I never had any sense of ease, still I knew from the outset that I'd be blessed. Reading some of the stories people have shared, has left me with this realization: even though I know how aggressive my cancer is, and how advanced it is, and how brittle my bones are — I am blessed. And even though I know the cancer is spreading to areas where I've never felt pain before — I am blessed. Why?

Look at my blessings through this filter … I've learned new things about myself, and about those who are reaching out, and about those who are not. During this time of reflection I've come to believe, really believe that I am a very strong woman. I can take a punch, shake it off, and take another. I've learned that I can help carry the load for people I love even if that means I carry my pain in silence, and even if that means my mother, sister and I hide our true emotions behind happy, chirpy, singsong, "Hellos," because it's just too exhausting to do anything else. At some point, we entered into an informal pact where we protect one another from our heartbreaking feelings as often as we can. What else can we do? I don't want the time we're sharing to be all about grief. There'll be time for that when I'm gone, so we chirp our way through talk about the weather and little nonsensical things then we say,

"I love you," a handful of times before our voices crack and the phones go silent.

I've come to learn things about others, too. About people who have the capacity to look beyond themselves and send emails of reintroduction and encouragement, or knock on doors and ask what they can do to help. Many old and new friends have shown genuine expressions of sadness. They have reluctantly accepted my predicament, have expressed anger that my new little life as an author is being cut short, and have extended promises that my girls will always have a place to go for comfort or guidance. In other words they've turned thoughts of love and promises of service toward someone they are about to lose.

In the dark of night ... I remind myself that my time is measured, that I should make every minute count, that I shouldn't leave this world with unfinished business. I accept that I am going to leave behind things that should be dealt with. I think we all will leave a bit of untidiness. There are some difficult conversations that should take place, but I am not pressing into them. Not at this stage of my life. Not when there are new areas of pain popping up here and there. Not when reality hangs overhead. There are things I am not going to get into as my life is hitting the shits.

And this just happened ... I wanted to put something about regrets, and I wanted to quote a singer and an iconic song as a lead in. I couldn't find either in my head so I yelled up to Mr. Wonderful. "Hey, Tim!"

He came to the top of the stairs. *"Yeah?"*

"Who's that singer? The big one who isn't Bing Crosby."

"Perry Como?"

Growl. "No! Someone good. And big. And really popular."

"Como was good."

"No he wasn't. The big guy. Not Tony Bennett." Tim is downstairs now because I'm getting a little pissed.

"Big? Can you give me something else to work with?"

Pause. Pause. Pause. "His daughter wore boots."

Pause. *"Nancy Sinatra?"* Tim questioned incredulously.

"YES! Frank Sinatra. Thanks." I immediately went to the internet to find the song he sings about regrets. BTW, the song is, *My Way*, but you probably already knew that.

The lines I wanted to use are these ...

My Way ...

Regrets, I've had a few,
but then again, too few to mention.
I did what I had to do and saw it through
without exemption.
I planned each charted course,
each careful step along the byway.
And more, much more than this, I did it my way.

(Written by: Paul Anka)

I guess my bottom line is this: I regret that there are conversations that won't take place, but I'll leave it to others to sort that shit out for themselves.

I'm happy with where I am ... I've done many things during my 64 years. I've made commitments, set goals, faced challenges, looked beyond myself, and helped others through small acts of kindness and charitable contributions. I've held jobs that served disenfranchised populations and those in need, and trained as a volunteer counselor for assault victims. I pushed through grief and helped others shoulder the pain of loss, and am now appreciating those who are doing that with me. Most importantly, I am happy with the life I shared with Tim and our daughters.

Another little story … Thirty years ago, we purchased our 'starter home'. We are still living there. The primary reason we never moved was education, ours and the girls. Tim always regretted not getting a postgraduate degree, and I always regretted not getting an undergraduate degree. We agreed very early on that helping our girls get a quality education from preschool through college was our top priority. We were all-in in the pursuit of higher education for our girls.

That wasn't the case for me. Right out of high school, I took a couple courses at a community college because the school was located directly across the street from a bank where I'd landed a part-time job in the afternoons/early evenings. In order to afford my dream school, UMass-Amherst, I needed to bank some bucks. In the meantime, I killed a few morning hours taking whatever class was available to non-matriculated students, then I played a little pool in the college cafeteria, then I took my life into my hands as I bolted across West Boylston Street to the bank's processing center where, for the next six hours, I canceled checks by typing in account numbers and check amounts in batches of thousands. It was blindingly monotonous work, but I did it because it was part of the master plan.

Things became different after my parents' divorce and I needed to get a full-time job. I landed a really good one as executive assistant to two V.P.s at Hanover Insurance. I had stellar secretarial skills and carried myself with confidence, and I was very well read, knowing just enough to carry on conversations with individuals on the upper-floors of life, though I admit I didn't know enough about anything to whoop Donna Rosetti's ass in the pie game. An obvious sore spot. As soon as I began pulling in some good money, my priorities changed. I ignored the call of higher education and honed in on how the business world functioned and how I could use that knowledge to get a little further up the stepladder of success.

Back in the day … In certain industries, experience combined with a go-get-em attitude was as valuable as a college degree. So, my new plan was to play up the skills I had, learn what skills I needed to have, and figure out a way to get them. I worked for a few years for the insurance V.P.s, going from a green-behind-the-ears support staffer playing dress up and mimicking seasoned professionals, to a bona fide executive assistant who ran the professional lives for the V.P. of Personal Lines and V.P. of Commercial Lines at a major insurance carrier. During my leisure time, I wrote greeting cards for two very different companies; Blue Mountain Arts, a lovey-dovey company all about the pastels of life, and for a company that catered to the more vulgar side of life. These two creative outlets were the perfect combo for Yours Truly — sweet and smut, a natural fit, thank you very much.

I left Hanover to work for an insurance agency that specialized in malpractice insurance, learned everything there was to learn, then applied for a job in the risk management department at UMass hospital, a job that required a bachelor's degree and was a stretch for me to land on a good day. I talked up my experience and convinced the human resources rep into submitting my resume. I received a call from the director of the department, went for an interview and landed the job. My puzzle-piece on-the-job experience + teach yourself what you need to know attitude paid off rather well. While I was doing all that, I volunteered at city and state democratic campaign offices because I was a budding political junkie back then. I'm a full-fledged one now.

And while I did all of that, I did this ... I spent nearly all of my free time attending concerts. You name them, I've seen them, although the ones that got away were Queen, Bowie, and The Rolling Stones. That's pretty much it. I saw all the biggies and those hoping to become biggies. In the 70s and 80s I would take an occasional day off from work so I could sit on the damned phone hoping my call would be answered by some ticket-mastering agent before the much sought-after seats were sold. I always purchased 2 tickets because someone in my circle of friends would be down for whatever concert was being held from Maine to Pennsylvania and any state between. My friends and I considered ourselves 'roadies' because we'd drive anywhere for a good show. On many occasions, I bought someone else's 2nd ticket and was introduced to soon-to-be superstars like Bonnie Raitt, and the multi-talented Charlie Sexton who went on to open for David Bowie's Glass Spider Tour, to which I was unable to get tickets. Sore spot.

Okay, back to the point of this blog — if there is one ... It's amazing how my mind is working, or not working, depending on your perspective. In the middle of a thought, I'll find myself at 'Who the eff knows where'. I'm pretty good at staying focused during conversations, so long as no one interrupts my sentence. (Hellooooo Tim! Please read this and stop interrupting. Thank you, kindly). And texting is fine because of the short nature of things. I even managed quite well when I got dragged into a game of 'I Spy' with Joyce McTigue the other day. That was absolutely the best time. She took a wide-angle shot of her living room and typed a brief description of something on display. Then I had to find the object. It was a hoot of a time. I'm down for a game with anyone. I've got lots of time on my hands! Anyway, I just scrolled to the top to find out what this blog is about and found that it is about finding purpose and counting blessings.

That's so nice ... I'm going to spend a few minutes pulling a thread on the blessings of our girls, the ones who began draining our financial coffers in junior high and continued through their college years. We made sure they carried part of the financial load of their higher education by taking federal loans, and they needed to apply for scholarships, and earn money for books and supplies, but Tim and I did the heavy financial lifting. The girls are both very happy in their chosen professions, and are drawing strength from friends and coworkers, and from one another during this shit fest of a time. They are with me often, and come running when I need something or am having a tough go of it. What more could a mother ask for? Nothing.

Overall, the life of Mr. and Mrs. Wonderful consisted of a series of lean years where we robbed Peter to pay Paul, and less than lean years when we lived it up with an extra vacation in Wells. Tim and I ultimately did what we set out to do, we lived in a home that we were proud of and comfortable in, and we put our money where our mouths were as far as education was concerned. We explained the value of higher education to our girls when they were young, told them our regrets at cutting our education short, and then helped pay for theirs when they took our advice to go places and learn things. And even though there were lean years, we always managed to dig our toes into the sand once a year at Wells — our nonnegotiable. We might not have stayed an entire week, but we always got there.

A little diversion … I suck at math. Mr. Wonderful knew that from the get-go, but for whatever reason, we put me in charge of household finances. Tim was working very long hours supporting a family of four, so he threw caution to the wind and let the female version of Jethro Bodine have at it. As long as bills were paid on time and checks didn't bounce I would remain in the role of debit and credit mistress of the family. I kept that job because I had a system!

My system … Write a check for $15.45, subtract $20.00 from the register. Write a check for $70.01, subtract $80.00 from the register. Back in the day, everything was done by checks, so there was a lot of extra money going into our bank account. Now, let's look at why I did this.

Reason #1: Sheryll Bodine.

Reason #2: I'd never bounce a check because the account always had extra funds in it.

Reason #3: I'd have spending money saved for our trip to Wells.

Two weeks before we packed the RAV to head All Points Maine, I'd close out the bank account flush with Bodine funds and open a new one for the following year. Say what you will about my effed up math program, and I'll counter with this: I never bounced a check and our pockets were lined with vacation money. And furthermore, you shouldn't judge the sick one. Just sayin.

Life was good back then. Life is good now, too. I'm counting my riches in very different ways because they are showing themselves in very different ways. As I said at the beginning of this blog, there is a purpose to every season. Writing this blog is definitely part of my purpose, although there are so many other purposeful things. You'll see.

41. Turn Turn Turn — Part Two ...

> *To everything there is a season, a purpose, especially when the season is living.*
>
> *~ Sheryll*

Reconnecting with friends ... You know I've reconnected with Debbie and Jennifer, and I mentioned that Debbie heard about me from her daughter Amanda, who was besties with my daughter Hannah all through grade school. Amanda has become a texting pal recently, and I appreciate getting her texts, her little 'Amanda' personality popping through each one. Anyway, proximity played a major role in Debbie's stopping by the day she learned about my situation. This reconnection required a BBBDK strategy: **B**log, **B**anana **B**read, **D**etermination, **K**nock on the front door. Easy-peasy. She said she mulled whether she should just do it, or make a call first, or think about this or that first. Bottom line for her was that she'd have to pass my home to get to hers to do the calling or the thinking.

Ultimately, Debbie did what felt right and she stopped and knocked. And it was so right for me. I needed to see her face even if it'd only be for that one visit. She's been back a couple of times, once with a carrot cake in tow. Amazing! It has been like old times. Shooting the shit with someone who knows tons about me let us slip right back into the familiar give-and-take of comfortable conversations. Given the circumstances, we have shared a few moments of choked-back tears, but mostly it's been a ton of laughs.

See, I'm still living … Jennifer used a computer to reconnect. I recently asked her for specifics on the where and the why for. Two caveats before I begin: the Irish One does a rapid-fire, brogue-speak-thing that requires some rapt attention and quick deciphering on my part. On a good day, it's a challenge, and now, well I'm quite sure I'm only getting a smattering of 'facts' from she who spews. Assembling and keeping 'facts' straight from anyone is not currently my strong suit. I'm gonna give it a whack though, and she can correct me if need be.

Jennifer said that over the years she'd looked for me on FB with no success. I had a page under the name Anne Hobson which wouldn't have meant a hill of beans to her or anyone else, really. Anne is my middle name and Hobson Avenue was the street I grew up on. I used the name/street formula of choosing a fictitious name because of Whoopie Goldberg. The comedienne was asked once how she got her name. She said it was common practice for strippers and other performers to use their middle name and their childhood street as their 'stage' name, so Whoopie gave it a go. She said the process failed her because her stage name would have ended up being Elaine Martin Luther King Boulevard. Obviously a schtick, but I gave the process a whirl for my pen name and ended up with Anne Hobson. Kinda nice.

When it came time to publish, it dawned on me that I wanted to see my name, Sheryll O'Brien, on the spine of a book, so I kicked Anne to the Hobson Avenue curb. I didn't really care about amassing friends when I had Anne Hobson's FB, I only ever used it to occasionally snoop on my daughters' lives, (Hi, Hannah. Hi, Jessica. Tsk, tsk, tsk.) and to learn a bit about social media for a book I was dabbling at years ago.

Anyway, back to Jennifer's dogged pursuit ... She is FB friends with someone from the Columbus Park neighborhood where I grew up. I'll call him Mike because I haven't seen this guy in forty years, and he may not want to be dragged into this saga. Anyway, Mike became FB friends with Jennifer, and he was also FB friends with Tim's best friend, Kevin Mullaney, who now resides in New Mexico. Jennifer and Kevin don't know one another from a hole in the wall, but Kevin put up a FB post about me and Mike saw it and shared it. Jennifer finally hit paydirt when she saw the unusual spelling of my name magically appear on her feed. She pulled the thread which brought her to my website where she learned about my illness. Within the beat of a saddened heart, she took to email and gave each of us the gift of reconnection.

The Irish One has been back to visit a couple of times, and it has been just what I needed. We slipped right back into the familiar give-and-take, and shared some tears of sorrow and side-splitting fits of laughter. The other day, was the be all and end all of enjoyment. I've found that my circumstances have let me push a few envelopes.

Like this ... I handed a child's book to Jennifer and asked her to read it to me. For those of you who are unfamiliar with the book, *The Wonky Donkey,* I'd like you to take a minute (4:17), go to a search engine and type in: "Scottish woman reading Wonky Donkey YouTube." Watch the video and meet me back here.

Four minutes seventeen seconds later … That's what it was like when Jennifer consented to my request to read me a little something on her most recent visit.

Making deeper friendships … Joyce McTigue lived across the street from me for thirty years. We've chit-chatted about grade school happenings, and laughed at our kids' Halloween costumes, and commiserated when our kids got sick, or in her case when Michael got poison something or other one summer, and when he broke his collarbone sledding, and cut his foot skating, and God only knows what else. The poor kid had a run of really bad luck and his mom suffered along with him. I don't have a clue why I remember that stuff and for the record, there's a very good chance none of that happened.

Things are getting weird in my head. I'm forgetting a lot of things, and I'm struggling with finding words while I'm speaking and writing, and my penmanship sucks now. There's been a recent addition of new catch-all phrases in the household because I just can't find the right word. The other morning when I wanted a piece of toast I said, "Jess, can you get me a whosy-whatsy, you know the … the … the bread thingamabob." Don't know why I'm channeling Ariel, or how Jessica manages to get whatever it is I'm wanting, but she does. And I have a story about a unicorn that I'll save for another blog that will illustrate a new weirdness in the noggin. Not to worry, I've written a note to remind myself to write about the unicorn. I have a stack of notes about blogs I want to write, but the actual writing of them is taking more and more time to do, so don't hold your breath.

Back to the problem ... I'll be saying the words in my head, the ones I intend to write. I've come to learn that it means very little. After each paragraph I go back and read the text. Honestly, the stuff on the screen is gibberish sometimes. I'm going to do a blog and leave a paragraph or two the way they come out, so you can see that the old brain is on a slippery slope. It pains me when I see bits of myself chipping away, especially my ability to write intelligibly, but I'm doing what I can, cleaning it up as best I can, and finding occasional humor where I can. I should probably have Nurse M read this, you know, in case I forget to tell her.

Anyway, I totally digress ... I scrolled up a bit to get my bearings and apparently I was writing about making deeper friendships, so back at it. Joyce was dealt one emotional blow after another in a very short span of time a few years back. Mr. Wonderful and I often remarked about her strength, and wondered how she put one foot in front of the other, day after day, without complaint and still offering a neighborly smile and wave. We knew damned well her journey was difficult, for her, and for those who leaned heavily against her for the support they needed. And yet she rose to the challenge of dealing with loved ones lost and the grief left in their place.

Now that I'm terminal, this woman is offering herself in so many kind ways, knowing full-well that she'll be losing me, too. She's pushing in when she very well could be running away. She sends pics and videos of beaches, and from celebrations we both attended over the years, and she's called often to give me a safe outlet for something I might want to say. Best part, Joyce shocked me to my skivvies when she said this, *"I'm fucking sick and tired of death and dying."* That was the first time I ever heard this lovely woman swear. It was a profound experience for me. I could feel those words deep to my core. They were alive with raw honesty. Painfully alive.

See, I'm still living … There are other women with whom I am building deeper relationships at this late stage in the game and I am so grateful. These women are courageously navigating unsure footing after having life-altering surgeries, cancer diagnoses, and strokes. I've been surprised to learn how much they have endured. Sadly, I'm not surprised to learn they kept things bottled up, their fears and insecurities, about who they are, and about the deep sense of loss over who they were. I remember those things post-head surgery, especially the feeling of loss over who I used to be.

<u>The fun mommy</u>. The one who had neighborhood kids in her house and yard all the time, the one who hosted themed sleepovers on the living room floor or in pop-up tents on the deck, so the kids could use the slider when they'd had enough of outdoor noises and wanted the familiarity of the living room floor. <u>The home goddess</u>. The one who kept a reasonably clean and orderly home, the one who worked hard in 'her' garden, the one who crocheted and did needlepoint long into the night. <u>The hopeful writer.</u> The one who typed words into a clunky, old, desktop word processor then printed pages of crap so family and friends could read them. God love them.

A diversion … I am a storyteller. I can take a reader from here to there and hold their interest, but that does not mean I am a writer by any stretch of the imagination. Way back when, I knew nothing about the fundamentals of writing: first person, third person, past or present tense, or point of view and, with a loaded pistol to my head, I wouldn't have been able to identify an omniscient narrator in a lineup of subjective and objective narrators. Huh, I wonder if that's real stuff I'm spewing? I'm not going to stop to look it up because then I'll be forgetting and scrolling up to find out what this ramble is about. So let's just keep pushing in. I bought a few *Creative Writing for Dummies* books (not kidding) and got to reading. The books are stored somewhere in my basement. They're most likely next to a handful of manuscripts I wrote, very bad manuscripts (technically speaking) but very good stories. I'm going to try and name them: *Suzanne. The Caller. The Gutter. The _____. Dancing with Deception. Dancing with _____. Dancing with _____.* Well, that was a bust. I had a momentary thought about rewriting the manuscripts before I started writing the blog, but there was no way I would have had the concentration to go page by page, chapter by chapter, but Nancy, if you're up to the challenge!

Back to the conquering women ... They have battled and have won the game of Life, though it is very different from the life they were living before they got the news, whatever the news was. Every person going into surgery, or for treatments, or who survives a catastrophic event knows they will be different, but what that truly means, what it looks like and feels like, lives somewhere in the abstract, in the place of unknowns, the place where there is hope just beyond fear. And when you become one of the lucky ones, the ones who make it through, the ones who beat all of the odds, it's hard to utter any words that may be interpreted as being ungrateful. So, you suffer the insecurities in silence, and you mourn who you used to be in silence, and then you offer to the universe gratitude that you're still alive because, after all, you get to carve out a new place for yourself.

I mentioned to one of the remarkable women who is pushing through and moving on in spite of her heavy load, and uncertain road that, "It's tough to keep a tough woman down." Her reply was succinct and spot-on, *"We've always known that, haven't we?"* Indeed! Her remark speaks to the indomitable spirit of women.

Another digression is needed … The other night I watched a Hallmark movie. This time I actually watched it. I'm not sure of the title, but the female lead was an overly organized, tightly-wound woman who'd just turned thirty. One of her gifts was a time capsule her mother put together before her death and buried in a flower garden in the backyard. The gift wasn't to be opened until the daughter's big 3-0. In typical Hallmark fashion the young woman opened the gift while bathed in bright sunshine, with singing birds doing a beautiful job on harmony, and her loving father sitting nearby solemnly paying witness to the moment. Inside the unearthed shiny, chrome cylinder were several items from the woman's childhood, and a stack of ribbon-tied envelopes that held six challenges.

An observation and suggestion … Hallmark needs to do some work on authenticity. If I ever wrote a scene where a woman dug through a garden and pulled a long-ago buried time capsule from a bed of soil, and it was in pristine, spit-shiny condition, my editor, The Warden, would have sweetly suggested I dirty the thing up. And you can bet your ass I would have.

Anyway, back to the story … Not the original one, the side story, or maybe the second side story. Who knows at this point? So, anyway one of the challenges for this thirty-year-old woman was to find something she was afraid of doing, and do it. In other words the mom wanted her daughter to face her fears. With the encouragement of a guy she **just** met, they drove to some big-ass remote mountain where there was a long-ass suspension bridge over rocky terrain and a rushing river hundreds of feet below. For reference, the bridge looked like MacGyver constructed it out of popsicle sticks and gimp. Anyway, the dude started walking across the bridge, leaving the terrified woman to inch after him in tortoise-like pursuit. While she was edging along, death-gripping the sides, she was singing, *London Bridge is Falling Down.* I looked at Mr. Wonderful with one hairy eyebrow raised, tilted my head leftward and sneered. He instantly knew I was readying for a tangent and I'd be dragging his unwilling ass along with me.

"Okay," I began. "Who the eff would sing that song? She's terrified about walking the bridge, so she chooses a song about a bridge falling down. That crap would have brought a pant and a glisten to The Warden. And furthermore, there's absolutely NO woman who's terrified of bridges who would have gotten onto **that** bridge unless there was a loaded gun pointed in her direction. And furthermore, going off with some random dude to God-only-knows-where should satisfy the challenge of doing something you're afraid of doing and something that's recklessly stupid, just in case that's one of the unopened envelope challenges." He laughed. He waited for more. "And for fuck's sake, just once I'd like Hallmark to shake things up and have the woman say, 'Are you fucking kidding me right now? I'm not walking across that damned MacGyver bridge for anyone, including my dead mother.'"

And for the record ... Hannah and Jessica, I won't be leaving you any challenges, you'll have enough. And please keep your asses off of suspension bridges, and I've already warned you against going anywhere with strange dudes, but I suppose it wouldn't hurt to say it again. Don't go anywhere with strange dudes!

Family friendships …

Kathy Gaffney - is easily an enviable woman. She's the female half of a gorgeous couple. She's tall, thin, fashionably cutting edge, has a recognizable and readily used laugh, and she owns the room when she enters it. Kathy worked for many years as an E.R. nurse and is enjoying her retirement going wherever she and her husband, Tommy, feel like going which is usually far, far away from the pack of 973 OBs. Coincidence/Plan? You decide.

Anyway, the early-retiree can effortlessly flip a switch from, *"I purchased this bottle of wine in Italy,"* to *"Hold my glass,"* at the sound of anyone in distress. None of the normal people will have heard anything to raise concern, but the well-honed 9-1-1 receptors of Nurse Kathy sensed danger, pushed her to her feet, and got her to the kid with a sliver in a finger, or someone in real medical distress. While 972 OBs passed the salad tongs, Nurse Kathy had triaged the patient, stripped off the fashionable scarf she bought on the streets of Milan, and used it as a tourniquet. Kathy has received more than her fair share of calls from worried siblings and siblings-in-law about every medical situation known to man, woman, and child. And when Tim and I were unsure of something medical, we'd unison, "Let's ask Kathy." That's what I did when I suspected I was in medical trouble.

From my very first call about the funky alk phos, Kathy and I became close. I think we both knew there wasn't going to be a ton of time, so we'd better get on with it. From Day One, she was on her medical game, asking just the right questions, and explaining things in a way I could understand even when the information was scary and overwhelming and let's face it, all of the information was scary and overwhelming. And when the daily barrage of incoming slowed a bit, she gave me a little space. Keep in mind, this shit fest started on October 18th and by early November I went from delightful ignorance to, "Oh, my God. I'm dying."

Kathy called me every one of those anxious-filled days, helping me inch my way toward the place where I could handle the news that was surely coming. And when the diagnosis came, she listened to my fears and anger, and encouraged me to let my feelings out. Not an easy thing for me to do. We talk every week now, and if something more urgent is happening she calls every day. She does all of that because of who she is by nature and nurture, but she also does that because she cares deeply for me, Sheryll the person who just happens to be her sister-in-law. There have been countless times when her words of sorrow are lost in her emotion, and her pride at how I'm handling this is almost motherly. There is sincere joy at hearing me say, "I'm having a really good day," and an exhale of relief or maybe gratitude that her prayers are still being answered.

Kathy Gaffney is all-in with me. I need and want her to be, but it's hard for me knowing the toll it's taking and will take on her. She's come to know me, really know me, without the pretense of superficial relationships. I no longer need to be anything more than what I am at this very minute. Today is all that matters because it's all I'm certain of.

When Kathy visited before leaving for her three month vacation to Florida, we hugged and said the 'L' word. It's the first time we've said that face-to-face. I truly believe neither of us said it that day because that visit might be our last time together. We said it because we feel it. Kathy called yesterday. She and Tommy were driving to Florida and were somewhere beyond Virginia. I asked how her hip was handling the long ride, and she asked how I'm feeling and listened to a long story about my very bad weekend (I'll explain it in an upcoming blog). When we ended our call, I told her that I plan on being here when she gets back from vacation. She agreed wholeheartedly that I will be. So, that's that.

A little sidestep … I knew all of my sisters-in-law on Tim's side as well as I possibly could, having lived a secretive-semi-agoraphobic life for the past couple decades. ***** I can't tell you how freeing it is for me that people can understand now that I wasn't intentionally being antisocial, I just couldn't bring myself to socialize face-to-face, not without a lot of mental prepping and heart palpitations. Hand me a phone and I'll talk myself hoarse, but up close and personal was up close and uncomfortable.

Denise Sneade - is the wife of my redneck brother. Don met the tall, brunette, mini-hurricane of a woman when he lived in the western part of Massachusetts. In my mind things went like this: they met, they whisked off to live in Rome, Georgia, they staked their claim, built their dream home, cultivated acres of land, and turned into the Clampetts minus the oil strike.

Within minutes of arriving in the Peach State, Denise had a southern accent. Amazingly, it didn't feel fake, like that time when Madonna slapped on a British accent after living in London for a hot minute. The southern drawl of Mrs. Sneade is as natural as if she'd been born in Georgia. I figure it's because she was meant to live there, in that Godforsaken, sweatbox, land of chiggers. Oops, did I type that part out loud? Yeup and I'm leaving it.

Everything about Denise is circular. She moves about in a circular motion. She's there, then she's over there, then she's hovering God knows where and all of the movements are done in a silent Tasmanian Devil-esque twirl and swirl. The wife of my brother is rail-thin, but she's sexy in a sporty sort of way. I don't think an ounce of fat has found her bones, ever. I think it's because she doesn't sit her ass down long enough for anything to find her, let alone stick to her. She is one of those delightfully unaffected women. She is who she is, wears what she likes, doesn't bother with fitting in, so she just does. Denise is a damned hard worker, and an all around good egg. If her boss asked her to stay an extra hour, no problem. And when her boss said he moved the company an hour and a half away from Rome, no problem. Denise is quick to decide if things fit in her life, and if they do, then there's no problem. There's no bellyaching, and not a whole lot of cussing. At least I never heard it, but I admit we hadn't been closey-close all these years.

Sheryll O'Brien and Denise Sneade were leading very different lives for the last three decades. I was living in Massachusetts where we tend not to enunciate the letter 'R,' and she was living in Georgia where they tend to turn a monosyllabic word into a forty-second song. Case in point, *"Dooooooooooooooooooooon's sittin by the fiiiiiiiiiiiiiiiire."* In the early days of their relocation I was paying by-the-minute for long distance calls, so I wasn't making many of themmmmmmmmm.

Mrs. Sneade can do lots of things, but what she can really do is cook. When she says she's making the redneck dude a filet mignon, or baby-back ribs, or prime rib, I believe her. She was absolutely genetically gifted in the culinary area of the DNA strand associated with cooking utensils and appliances. Having said that, she could very well pass squirrel or possum off as finer cuisine. I kinda like thinking she may have done just that on an occasion or two.

In any event, no matter what Don feels like eating, Denise will cook it, and it will be beyond edible. For those edging toward the fallacy that if you can read a recipe and set temps on an oven, you can be a culinary whiz, don't bother going there. I can read and set temps but I can't cook like Denise Sneade.

Now for the other circle of Denise. When you get on the phone with her, it's like hopping blind-ass drunk onto a merry-go-round, and tossing your drunk ass onto a semi-affixed horse that's rising and falling out of sync with the other equines. Denise will start a convo, stick with it for a handful of seconds, take a sharp right onto a semi-related subject, then a hard left onto some other tract, then take a final right and left that brings you back full circle. That's the go-round part of the merryfull conversational style of Mrs. Sneade. The other part is the never-ending word creations she does. Denise makes up words as she goes along, and you just have to figure out the correct ones. It's a challenge, what with the whole southern drawl and all. Denise's communication style is simply endearing.

New friendships ...

Josephine Power - the daughter of Mr. Power (my high school teacher), emailed me to express how happy she and her siblings were to learn about the acknowledgement I wrote about her dad.

She pushed in on how she could absolutely see him doing and saying the things I wrote. She mentioned her long-standing relationship with Phil McTigue, and mentioned a dear friend who recently went through brain surgery and was readying for a series of treatments. And just like that, we were off and running. In a rapid series of emails, we learned and shared more about ourselves than I know about lots of people I supposedly 'know'. Aside from learning about a really interesting person, there were lessons for me. I learned that all it takes for two people to get to know one another is a willingness to open up. Not incrementally, not guardedly, just freely. I guess I no longer need to care what people think of me, I only need to be my authentic self. At this moment in time, that happens to be a person who's dying. I figure I owe it to myself and to all of you to just put myself out there. You might as well know who the hell I am.

I think she's a perfect example of someone who lives her life the way she wants. She threw herself out there, to a total stranger, with an easy attitude of, this is me, wanna play? I've decided she's a genuine individual, one who knows who she is right down to her core. There is absolutely no pretense with her, no hedging when she wants to know something about me or my illness. No matter what she asks, it feels like it comes from a place of genuine curiosity, and a desire to learn in case she can help in some way. And she has, in very ordinary, and extraordinary ways.

The topic of her dad's obituary came up in an email because I used parts in a recent blog. I told her I was working with my family on writing my obituary, that Tim, Hannah and Jessica, Mom, and Donnie and Marjorie all wrote something. Then I told her I wanted to have the last thing written about me — to be written by me. Weird, I know, but whatever. Anyway, Jo said she and her sister worked on their dad's obit and that she/they would be happy to proof and/or edit mine.

Nancy and Andria read the piece for accuracy and mechanics, but both admitted they didn't 'know' anything about where I live and how things of this nature are presented in Massachusetts. I considered asking someone close to me to review it, but that felt really weird and unnecessarily painful. So, I went all-in, with a complete stranger, and sent her my obit. She made assurances that she'd share it with no one and I believe her. I call that 'freedom' and it feels wonderful.

Freedom's just another word for
nothing left to lose.

42. Mr. and Mrs. Not-So-Wonderful ...

Tim and I ran into a rough patch recently. It followed a really bad weekend I had. Saturday started early (before 4 AM) when I was woken by nausea. I popped a pill, munched a few square salt crackers, put on the Hallmark channel for a distraction, and hoped I'd fall back to sleep. I put an abrupt end to that unsuccessful attempt at 5 AM, took my handful of morning pills, one of which was a Tramadol, and got on with things. I pulled my laptop onto my laptop and tried to blog something. Tim got up late because .... I can't remember, but we got to coffee late, maybe 6:30. By then, the nausea pill had kicked in just enough for me to enjoy my time with Mr. Chase, Mr. Sanborn, and Mr. Wonderful. When I lifted my big-ass mug I noticed some pain in my shoulder area. "Hmm, that's new."

"What?"

"Pain in my shoulder." I moved the other one, "Hmm, pain in that one, too. That's concerning."

"Because the Tramadol isn't working?" He posed a reasonable question.

"No. Well, yes. But it's concerning because I have pain in places that've been pain free. My arms and fingers were the only bones from my skull to my knees that were cancer free. Shit. I want to keep writing and I won't be able to if—"

"Let's not get ahead of ourselves."

"Right, and since I've had really good luck lately, there's probably nothing to worry about," I growled and it was only 6:30 AM." Four hours later, I popped another Tramadol because I was having breakthrough pain here and there and there, too. "Hmm, I'm having pain in my right outer shin area. I've never had pain there before."

"And still in your shoulders?"

"Yeah, and in my left foot near the toes, I think."

"I don't like that you're having breakthrough pain."

"I wonder how long I've been in pain in those areas and how much degeneration is going on? Hmm, I never thought about this before."

"What?"

"I've been happily thinking Tramadol was masking the crap that I knew about, you know, the cancer in my femurs and spine and ribs and shit, but the Tramadol is probably masking pain in new areas that are now being eaten away by that effing cancer mouse. I'm probably decaying all over the place, like my arms and fingers." I started to cry.

Throughout the afternoon Tim hovered, and asked, *"Do you want anything? Can I get you anything? You haven't eaten all day. How about some toast and—"* He held back the T word, smart man.

By late afternoon I was growling, "No thanks, I'm good," to all of his offers. Inside my head I was screaming, "I want you to go away. Can you get the eff away?" His need to care and comfort was interfering with my need to worry and weep. My nausea hadn't let up all day, so by suppertime I hadn't eaten anything. And my pain hadn't let up, which meant that Tim hovered and asked his questions a hundred times.

And then this happened ... He suggested we call hospice.

I said. "Nope. Not yet." Inside I was thinking, "Not if I were dying." Yeah, yeah, I know I'm dying. And yeah, yeah, I know morphine can help with pain. But I also know morphine is a gateway drug and the gateway I'm preparing for is Saint Pete's (hopefully) and I'm not ready, yet. So, at the risk of arriving at Tom Petty's gates of hell, I stood my ground and I didn't back down.

"But you haven't eaten and you're in pain."

"I'm aware."

"I should call hospice."

"I don't want you to, and you'd better not call behind my back."

"Why don't you just take a little morphine?"

"I'm not ready to go there."

"But—"

"I want to take a nap."

He put my phone on silent, shut the front door (which is our signal to the world-at-large that I'm resting), and he went upstairs. I knew I wasn't going to be able to sleep, I just wanted him to go away. He came down around 7 PM. He could tell instantly that I hadn't slept and that I was in a lot of pain — everywhere.

"Okay. We need to call hospice. You need *some morphine."*

I knew he was right, but in my head, taking morphine was the signal that I was turning that corner. To me it meant that I was giving up and giving in. That the first bitter taste of that medicine meant I was ready to climb upon my deathbed and morphine myself away. So I adamantly refused to let him call. Two things worked in my favor: 1) I can hold my own in a toe-to-toe with most people, and 2) Tim knows that hospice patients need to keep control until the time comes when they are no longer able to make decisions. He knew I was making the wrong decision and I knew I was making the wrong decision. But it was my decision to make.

By 9 PM something weirdly awful happened. I'd been having occasional headaches for weeks. Not the pound-pound-pound kind of headaches, more like a pressure kind of headache, mostly situated on the left front skull area, the place that has cancer in it. And on occasion I've been having lower jaw pain on the opposite side of my head. On this night, I realized I had a skull.

Let me explain what I mean ... We all have elbows, but unless you smack your funny bone and feel the tingle, you don't go around all day saying, "I have an elbow and it has a funny bone." And we all have a heart, but unless it's beating rapidly, or oddly, we don't really think about our heart. It does what it's supposed to do and we let it. On that night I knew I had a skull and it felt like it was a helmet, one that was way too tight. And when I touched my face, particularly the bones under my eyes, it felt like the slightest pressure would break them as easily as if they were pretzels. I kept my mouth shut, made my nighty-night trip to the bathroom, my walker taking a bit of punishment along the way. I looked out the window at a very dark yard for a few minutes, then returned to my fabulous leather prison, took my nighttime Tramadol and Xanax, grabbed hold of my comfort stones and sent Tim away.

I was pissed and I was scared shitless, but I just couldn't take the morphine. I just couldn't. I wasn't being stubborn, I just couldn't go there. While I waited for sleep that didn't come, I wondered how affected my skull was and how much cancer had found its way to my brain. At 1 AM I took another Tramadol and was rescued by sleep — or I passed out. Potato – Po-tah-to.

Tim woke me around nine Sunday morning to get ready for our conference call with a representative from O'Connor Brothers Funeral Home. Yipeeeeee! We both put on pleasant voices and I explained what type of services I want, what type of casket I want so my Mommy can spend a few minutes with her girl, and what urn I'd like to spend my days in until someone scatters me at sea — or until I end up in the vacuum because Butterfingers Tim drops my urn and I'm scattered across the carpet — the wall-to-wall carpet that goes from one wall to the other in our living room.

When the $9,500 restful slumber conversation was over, I texted back and forth with Kathy about Harry Connick, Jr. and, after many minutes, I texted that I finally remembered his wife's name is Jill Goodacre. A personal triumph! I shut off my phone and dozed here and there until early evening. When I turned it back on, a call came in and I found myself on the conversational merry-go-round with Denise, then finished my night with a short chit-chat with Dooooooooooooooooooon.

As for Mr. and Mrs. Wonderful, we shared very few words that day, and those we did share were on the snippy side of things. I've mentioned I've been forgetting things, big things: like my final book, *Alva*, and little things: like I'm wearing my glasses and bitching about the fact that I can't find them. "Where are my damned glasses?" I'll call out.

Tim comes running from upstairs to help in the search, and points to my face. *"They're right there."*

I touch the tortoiseshell frames and roll my eyes, "Good to know. Now maybe you should go look for Carmen Sandiego, I think he/she (?) is still missing." That exchange was said in jest, back when we were still on the same page and the page had quotation marks on it because we were still speaking to one another.

A sidestep here … To illustrate how 'off' I am in the noggin sometimes. I called next door and this is what transpired. "Hannah, why does Hadley think unicorns are mystical?"

"Because they are."

"What are you talking about?"

*"What are **YOU** talking about?"*

"Unicorns were real once."

Hannah laughed, *"When were they real?"*

"I don't know, but Hadley showed me a video this morning and it said unicorns used to live in Argentina. Ask her."

Hannah called Hadley to the phone, *"Hadley, are unicorns real?"*

Hadley laughed, *"No, they're mystical."*

"MammyGrams said you showed her a video and it said unicorns once lived in Argentina."

Hadley laughed her ass off, *"Wooly rhinos once lived in Mongolia."*

See, noggin problems … Long story short — too late! Sunday, we were living in the land of Husband Hibernates Upstairs — Wife Wallows Downstairs. I feel the need to offer a defense because Tim is usually the one that garners empathy during any raised voice altercations between Mr. Wonderful and that woman he married. I tried to explain to Tim why I was reticent about calling hospice. "I need two things to keep me sane and relatively happy while I await the arrival of the Grim Reaper. I need my arms and fingers so I can type, and I need my brain so I can think about something to type. My brain is already messed up. I'm quite sure morphine will make things worse. It'll help the pain, but it will make me stupider, or more stupid, or whatever. I've accepted that I have to sit my ass on a recliner 24/7. I've accepted that every time I get up to pee I fear I'll hear the snap of a bone. I've accepted that I'm going to die soon. I've done some really hard work and gone to some really dark and lonely places thinking about leaving my loved ones, so is it too much to ask that I not have to take morphine yet?"

He went back into hibernation … Things were really tense all-day Sunday and early Monday morning. Nurse M was coming so I asked Tim to get me my purple V-neck tee shirt. He brought me my purple turtleneck. I growled. I wanted to smack him.

At the snap of a decision he made, he dragged my ass into a metaphorical game of chess. He quickly jumped my pawn and moved a space to the left, *"It's really cold. You should wear the turtleneck."*

I metaphorically tipped the board, "I'm sweating my ass off from the cancer pill I'm taking. I want my tee shirt. Jesus, Tim, could you please just bring me what I ask for and, by the way, stop finishing my sentences. If I'm struggling to find a word, let me find it, and when I tell you I don't want something, can that be it? Or do I have to say it 2, 3, 4, 5 times. Pick a number, so I know what the damned rules are."

"For fuck's sake, I'm trying to help."

"Don't!"

Jessica appeared at the bottom of the stairs wearing a concerned look and whatever the hell she sleeps in, *"What's going on?"*

"She doesn't want to wear the turtleneck," he snapped and stormed upstairs.

Jessie went to get me the purple tee shirt I wanted, waited for me to dress, then sat across from me as I railed against everything, ending with the thing that was bothering me most. "Just because I'm different, and losing words, and getting close to the place where I won't be able to make decisions, I'm not 'there' yet and I want people, I want him, to stop making me feel —"

Nurse M knocked on the door and walked in. She found us in tears. *"So, how are things going?"* she said with a tone that I read as though she knew the shit fest had hit the fan.

I jumped right in, "Tim is hovering, he's pissing me off, and he might need your nursing services if he doesn't leave me alone."

"Okaaaaay. Tell me what's going on."

"I had a bad day on Saturday and Tim wanted to call hospice and morphine my ass up, and this morning I asked for .... for .... something and he brought me something else. I can't remember what it was I asked for, but he's doing shit like this all the time. Like if I ask him to put my pen on the end table, he puts it in the drawer, and I repeat that I want it on the end table, and he says it might fall off during the night so it's better in the drawer, and I say it might be better in the drawer, but I want the fucking pen on the end table. I don't know why it matters to him where I put my pen, so long as I don't impale him with it, and shouldn't my word be the last word?"

She nodded and said, *"Yes."*

I smugly sneered at Jessica. My smugness ended pretty quick.

"Tim was right about calling hospice," Nurse M said.

"I know and I knew it then." I told Nurse M all the stuff about turning corners and giving up and giving in, and not wanting to be so drugged up I missed the rest of my life, and I ended with, "And I know Tim is hovering and trying to do things because he's trying to fix something he can't fix. He feels helpless and he's trying to offer comfort in the ways he can and he doesn't want to see me in pain and he needs to take care of me. I know all that, but he's already taking care of me, for Christ's sake, I'm not even allowed to walk to the bathroom unescorted. I've had just about all I can take with people doing and suggesting. I know I'm losing it in my head, but I'm still here."

"Yes. And you need to help us keep you here."

When a hospice nurse lectures you, you listen … In a very nice way, Nurse M reminded me that I have already lost my battle with cancer — that I am going to die from the disease — that it just hasn't happened, yet. She explained that my body is fighting a losing battle, but it is still fighting. And so far I am doing really well. But when my body tells me what it needs, I need to listen. When I'm tired I need to sleep. When I'm nauseous I need to take the meds and try to eat something. When I'm in pain I need to take all of the normal meds. And when nothing is working I need to call hospice. *"Sheryll, we want you to keep eating and we want you to have peaceful sleep and we don't want you in pain. So if you need morphine to get you over a bad spell, you need to call hospice and take the morphine."*

"But taking it feels like I'm waving the final white flag, the one the Grim Reaper is waiting to see."

She assured me that it is a very common thing for patients to balk at the first dose of morphine, for the same reasons I was giving. And then we entered into an agreement: I wouldn't suffer with nausea or pain for more than a half-day. That if my regimen isn't working I need to make the call. And then she hit the clarifying nail on the coffin. *"Because you dug in and didn't take the morphine, you suffered all day Saturday and slept most of Sunday. There are a finite numbe*r of them left, and you need to do everything you can to enjoy them."

My bad — but him, too ... Tim always makes an appearance at my nurse visits. There was an audible sigh of relief from Nurse M when he came downstairs. Jessica read the nurse's thoughts and cracked up, *"See, he's still alive."*

Nurse M cracked up, *"I was wondering."*

Tim cracked up, *"I've been the topic of conversation I see."*

"Yes!" I pushed in, "and you need to stop trying to fix me, and stop interrupting my sentences, and stop telling me to do things your way, and stop hovering — oh, and I should have let you call hospice."

"I know," the Smug One smugged.

So I learned my lesson and Tim learned some of his ... He's still bugging the crap out of me, occasionally. But things are what they are. Neither of us asked for this huge helping of crap, and neither of us should be expected to handle it well all of the time. At the crux of it all, there is a husband and a wife who struggle with the dynamics of this shit fest and even on the best days, and admittedly our recent days haven't been good, let alone best, we're sharing them as best we can.

And one last thing about hospice ... I pray none of you are ever told that you are terminal and there isn't any hope from a medical standpoint. But if that happens, I'd like you to know this: There is always hope in hospice. The hope is that you live a pain-free day. What more could you ask for? Nothing, really. And I want you to know there's hope that Tim will survive MY terminal illness. See — Hope Floats.

43. Dream a Little Dream of Me ...

I'd venture a guess that most people think of The Mamas & The Papas when they hear this title. And I suspect many of you have taken a second to sing the opening lines, *'Stars shining bright above you, night breezes seem to whisper, I love you.' Or* you went directly to the chorus, *'But in your dreams whatever they be, dream a little dream of me.'* This song became Cass Elliot's 'signature' song, but years before her cover made Casey Kasem's American Top 40, it was released by many recording artists. There are two worth mentioning, in my opinion: Doris Day and Dean Martin.

Side step #1 ... I love Doris Day. I love everything about her. She starred opposite Rock Hudson in *Pillow Talk* (my favorite), *Lover Come Back*, and *Send Me No Flowers*, and the two movies she made with James Garner, *Move Over Darling*, and *The Thrill of it All*, are some of the best romantic comedies ever made. Ms. Day starred in many other works with all of the greats from back in the day, like Clark Gable, Jimmy Stewart, and Cary Grant to name a few. I just swooned a bit at Cary and my heart did a little rat-a-tat-tat. Nice to know it still skips a beat for a dude and not only because of the plethora of drugs circulating through my system.

Anyway, the song Doris Day is most identified with is *Que Sera, Sera* (whatever will be, will be). The tune flutters through my brain a lot, mostly at night if I wake and have trouble getting back to sleep. Sometimes the 'whatever will be, will be' is about my future, given that it is surely limited, but so often my wondering is about Tim, and the girls, and Hadley. It's the wondering about my girl and how she will manage all of this that's heart-wrenching and unrelenting. My sweet little girl is losing her MammyGrams, the woman with whom she's lived from the minute she returned home from the hospital at birth until she and her mother moved next door when Hadley was 6 years and 46 days old, but who's counting.

I remember … nights when Hadley was an infant and I would push back in my recliner and she would sleep on my chest because Hannah was beyond exhausted.

I remember … smiling brightly at all of her firsts, and knew from three months old that she'd be a lefty, always reaching up from her Boppy pillow, or her play mat with that hand outstretched and grabbing at the air or some hanging toy.

I remember … singing the classic nursery rhymes, and putting a few Sheryll O'Brien spins on them when I was tired, or just being silly.

"You are my sunshine, my only sunshine, but
even sunshine goes to sleep.
You'll never know dear,
how much I need you
to sleep and sleep and sleep."

And when she was old enough and began her trek downstairs each morning, she'd call out, *"I'm coming down, MammyGrams,"* and I'd answer, "Thanks for the warning!" And whenever she wanted a cheesy egg, I'd drag a chair to the counter, let her choose which egg to crack, let her put a pat of butter into the pan, let her tear a piece of American cheese to little bits, and then start singing a little ditty while she scrambled the egg in her favorite mug.

> "You've got to toss it and slop and stir it up, and twirl it all around in the cup, and when you're done scrambling, you're gonna have a great egg."

Fridays are cheesy egg day and we're still singing the song. The only difference now is that she and Gee (Tim's granddad name) do the egg selection and cracking, then she comes into the living room with mug in hand and fork in mug and we sing our little ditty while she scrambles away.

We have a truly wonderful, and remarkable grandmother/granddaughter thing, but there is no question that Hannah and Hadley have the best little relationship as mom and daughter. There is sheer joy and squeals of delight when they reunite, and they share the most relaxed form of sharing space and communicating, and they've developed a keen interest in and shared preference of music. Hannah has an antique record player and has amassed an extensive collection of LPs. She/They listen to music all of the time, as I once did with my girls. Hadley knows the classics and can identify Grateful Dead, Marshall Tucker, Queen, CCR, Fleetwood Mac, Stones, or Dean Martin tunes with ease. The other day she came into my house singing *Ophelia*, by the Lumineers. And one day her Auntie J was spewing about something or other and Hadley entered the room and did a Taylor Swift on her, *"Who hurt you?"*

Last summer, I listened to Maya Angelou's poem *Phenomenal Woman* on loop. Someone got the thing trending on Twitter and I could not resist listening to her fabulous voice, her throaty, luscious voice. So whenever the Tweet with her poem came up, I pressed play and it played no matter the activity in my home. As children often do in the summer, they run in to grab a jump rope, then sprint back out, then run in for some water, then back out, then in for God knows what, then back out. Hadley did the in and out enough so that when she was coloring at the kitchen table one day and I was cooking something or whatever, I heard her say: *"Pretty women secret lies. I'm not cute or built to size. It's my arms, my hips, and lips. I'm a woman. Phenomenally."*

Okay, first, the child has some sort of ability to remember every word of every cartoon she watches or conversation she hears and, while her recitation of Ms. Angelou's poem was choppy, she had the gist of the initial lines. On some level I should have figured she'd remember this and that if she heard it often enough and she'd repeat it, but seriously, she was in and out. It's not like I sat her down and did the Maya Angelou hour starting with that particular poem. BTW, that was my defense when I told Hannah this story.

Hannah is a very devoted mom who has already influenced Hadley in the importance of education, and finding out about and respecting the world and the people who share it, near and far. If Hadley is on the internet, you can bet her mom is close by and Hadley is listening to some cartoon character explaining pointillism and that Seurat developed the painting technique, or hearing about the mummification process which she explained in minute detail and I casually considered until she got to the organ removal part.

The little girl with waist-length blonde hair and big blue eyes that are always behind colorful rimmed glass frames, the girl who's turned her arm into a lever to determine how many hugs she'll get on any given day, the little girl who sits on a bench next to my chair instead of on my lap while we alternate reading from a Nancy Drew, Clue Crew book, is going to take my death hard. There is no question that I am Hadley's touchstone. She trusts and believes everything I say, right down there in the deepest places in her heart and soul. She knows I have never and will never lie to her.

My seven-year-old granddaughter knows I am dying, and yet she has put that knowledge away someplace, and finds ways to enjoy each day with MammyGrams. She comes over every morning for breakfast, and when she's finished, she goes on a hunt for something I've asked Tim to hide for her. Many days, she's in search of a Beanie Baby that once belonged to her mommy or her auntie. Or she's looking for a keychain that I buy in bulk because she loves the damned things. I recently had to get carabiners for her to slide the silly shaped things onto and lock them down just so she can carry them about.

Make no mistake, though, when she's visiting it's not all fun and games for the child. She takes my illness seriously, and gets involved by offering 'Hadley' ways of helping. When I need to use the bathroom, she takes my blanket off my legs, uses the remote control for the recliner, moves my walker into place, puts her little hand onto one of the handles and moves slowly with me. When I go behind closed doors, she turns the walker so I can step right into it then calls out, *"Let me know when you're ready to come back!"* She runs off to the living room, balls my poofy blanket into a soft landing place, climbs onto the upraised recliner and goes for a little slide off of it over and over and over until I call that I'm ready for my escort back to my perch.

She knows I've been recording some of our conversations and the other day she came in and said, *"You might want to record this."* As soon as the red light went on, Hadley went on a tangent about a girl at school who, *"Annoys me all the time, MammyGrams. You have no idea how much she hangs on me, hugs me, and follows me."*

"Have you told her it bothers you?"

"Every day. I say _______, please stay this far away. And I put my arms like this. And I say, do you see the masks we're wearing, it's because of Covid, and we shouldn't be getting close. But does she listen? Nope. She just barrels in, grabs hold of me, and if my hands are free I cover my face, but if my arms are locked I have to wait until she's done squeezing me to death."

"Do you think you need to talk to a teacher about it?"

"I have. They tell us to work it out for ourselves. That's not gonna happen."

"So, what's the plan?"

"I'm gonna continue hiding at recess."

"Could work."

"I don't know, she's pretty good at finding me. When we get outdoor recess again, I'm hiding behind a snowbank."

The other day Hadley came in and told me a few things she wants to have on the recorder, *"MammyGrams, I'm gonna go to the top of the stairs, make sure you tape this."* I knew what was in store.

When she was at the top, she started our schtick, *"Hey MammyGrams, I'm coming down."* To which I replied, "Thanks for the warning."

Side step #2 … I love Dean Martin. I love everything about him. The years he played straight man to Jerry Lewis. The years he played opposite starlets who craved his attention. The years he did his variety show pissed as a fart. And especially the years he roasted the asses of the brightest stars in Hollywood. Most of all, I fell in love with the crooner and played his CDs often enough that my girls knew all of the words to all of his songs when they were in grade school. It took me many years to settle on a favorite Dean Martin tune, but I did.

Innamorata …

If our lips should meet Innamorata.
Kiss me, kiss me sweet Innamorata.
Hold me close and say you're mine.
With a love that's warm as wine.
I'm at Heaven's door Innamorata.
Want you more and more Innamorata.
You're a symphony, the very beautiful sonata
my Innamorata.
Say that you're my sweetheart,
my one and only sweetheart.
Say that you're my sweetheart, my love.

(Written by: Harry Warren and Jack Brooks)

Back to the point of this blog … Since December 1st, I haven't had a single dream (I had a snippet once, maybe). I became aware of my dreamlessness one night when I woke because I was in pain. I searched my mind to see if there was something there, some little fragment from a dream that disappeared right before I opened my eyes. There was nothing. Since then, I've tried to push into that space when I first wake to see if maybe there's something. Consistently, there's nothing about dreaming.

I had a facepalm moment though ... I've had a question on my mind since the oncologist said, *"You have terminal bone cancer. There is nothing that can be done. You will die an excruciatingly painful death."* None of those words were particularly enjoyable to hear, but the last ones have been the ones that have caused bone crushing fear, no pun intended — okay, a little pun intended.

Question ... Why is bone cancer so bad? ***Facepalm answer ...*** Because there are bones from the top of the skull to the tips of the toes. Think skeleton. Apparently when someone dies from cancer of the liver, the pain will be concentrated in that area, and death by lung cancer will be painful in and around the rib cage, but Yours Truly won the jackpot! I have full body bone cancer, ergo it's gonna hurt like hell everywhere. I am in no way comparing or minimizing the pain associated with death and dying from any type of cancer, it is all intense and horrible and tragic, I'm simply trying to pull the thread on why my pain will be excruciating. Okay, that's done.

Back to dreaming ... Living without them is a nightmare. Or it was. I had a dream the other night. The most wonderful dream. Tim and I were dancing along the sand at the shoreline at Wells Beach. I know we were there because that is our place, and I think I recognized every grain of sand. When I say we were dancing, we weren't Fox Trotting, or even Waltzing, we were just wrapped in one another's arms, swaying to and fro to the sound of Dean singing my song. Tim and I were holding hands and they were sort of tucked between us chest high, the others were wrapped around our backs. I had my eyes closed most of the time, but when we turned, I knew I'd be facing the ocean. I opened my eyes and followed the moonlight trail across the inky black water. When the song ended, he and I walked hand in hand toward the far jetty. When I arrived back to where we started our dance, I was alone, in fact the beach was empty except for Hadley who was flitting in circles with her arms wide open. When she saw my approach she ran toward me, her arms flailing with joy. She threw herself into my outstretched arms. We twirled and twirled on the now sunny beach. When her little feet landed on the sand again, she said, *"That was so much fun, MammyGrams.* I agreed, and suggested we do it again, someday.

Dream a little dream of me.

A conversation with Hadley O'Brien …

"Hey, Hadley, what do you like about MammyGrams?"

"You're funny, and cuddly, and caring. You're good at making Jello, and you're good at sharing, and you are very smart."

"What do you like to do with MammyGrams?"

"Have sleepovers and make crafts, like toilet paper tube bird feeders. Oh, that reminds me, MammyGrams, you're clever. And I like when you watch me do yoga, and when we watch Barbie movies, and Big City Greens, and when you play restaurant with me."

"Is there anything you miss doing with MammyGrams?"

"Having you do my hair every day. Silence. And hopping onto your lap for a cuddle."
~ My granddaughter.

44. Andria, or ~ A, As I Came to Know Her ...

Heaven,
where everybody knows your name.

~ Sheryll O'Brien

For those of you who are reading my blog, but have not read other parts of my website, I'd like to make something abundantly clear, I consider myself a storyteller. I know enough about the English language to get by, but my strength is the story, in the crafting of it, and the telling of it. I wrote three stories, *Bullet Bungalow, Netti Barn*, and *Cutters Cove*, and was ready to do the hard work with an editor, so I found one, unfortunately, he was the wrong one. He wanted me to change most everything about my books. Some suggestions made sense and I was willing to change things up, but there was a bottom-line for me and it was the word 'boobs'. Mr. Editor thought the word was crass and suggested I not use it. My response was beyond crass — no surprise there. Still, my desire to present my stories in the best light, coupled with a huge dose of inexperience, nudged me toward making decisions that ultimately turned my dream of writing and publishing into a nightmare. In the process of trying to make things better, I made them worse.

Boobs aside, I took his advice and hacked away parts of each of the three stories I'd written, and combined them into a single book, a 350 page book. It wasn't long before Mr. Editor and I mutually parted ways and I went in search of the right editor. I paged through options on Thumbtack and saw this introduction.

> As a freelance writer and editor, I am committed to communicating every message accurately. My strength is preserving the author's voice without sacrificing excellence in language. I am prompt, professional, and friendly — and I love collaboration!
>
> ~ *Andria Flores*

The words: **My strength is preserving the author's voice without sacrificing excellence in language,** was all I needed to see — ***this*** editor will let me say boobs! ***This*** editor is the one I want! I wrote an introductory email, she wrote back, we exchanged a few more emails, and she suggested we talk by phone. When I answered the call a few days later, my heart was racing and my hands were sweating. And when I heard the soft, sweet, almost songlike Texan drawl on the other end, I immediately wondered if 'boobs' were indeed in my future. Andria sounded so 'Cinderella'. I envisioned her standing at a window with a blue ribbon in her hair and a bluebird upon her finger enjoying a lovely moment before her feathered friend lifted the corner of a page in the book Cinderella was editing. I briefly explained I was writing stories and an editor read one and portions of another and objected to the use of the word 'boobs'. The woman with the 'soft, sweet,

Texan drawl' said, *"The editor must have been a man.* I laughed. She continued, "C*an you imagine Samantha on Sex and the City saying breasts?"* the Texan asked through a breathy giggle.

That was it – I'd found my editor … But I wanted her to read a few pages first. She agreed, so I sent off the prologue and a few pages of Chapter 1. To my complete delight, Andria agreed to edit my book and several days later, she wrote these words in an email:

> Hello Sheryll...just a quick note to say I love your story! Not only are you a wonderful storyteller, but a fabulous writer. There are many clever things you do with words that are funny, brilliant, or playful. I am having the best time working on your book. (I just finished reading about the faux, faux date! ;)
>
> ~ A

As time went on, Andria learned I do clever things with words that aren't always funny — to her, anyway. Like when I just make them up, or turn perfectly good nouns into verbs. As soon as I received her edited work on *Bullet Bungalow* and saw the comments suggesting we might want to stick to the English language, I gave her the playful name of, The Warden, and accepted her advice here and there. She eased in when she really objected, but she lived by her words to 'preserve the author's voice without sacrificing excellence in language' and she was savvy enough to know that I didn't want to be micromanaged. Trust me, I wasn't always the easiest author to throw-in with.

As soon as I went all-in with the Mahoney-Maxwell-Watts-Serpico group in my Pulling Threads stories, I knew the first three novellas had legs, so I dragged Andria along on what would become a 17 book series. She dragged Nancy Pendleton into the shit fest when she agreed to get back into the publishing game with us. That's when the three of us traveled the world together without ever leaving our office chairs. We left the North Shore of Massachusetts and went to France, and Italy, and London, and Canada, and South America, and Australia, and Spain, and cities and towns all across America.

We worked hard. We had a blast. We became friends.

And then this happened … The final book of the series, *Alva*, was written, but not yet edited, or proofread, or formatted, or uploaded, or promoted, or, or, or. I'd happily moved on because my job on the writing team was to write. I was several chapters into writing a new book, *Treble Clef,* and the publishing team members were all doing their thing. A publication schedule for the final book of the Stony Beach series and the Pulling Threads series were agreed upon and Guru Jessica was creating covers and ads and social media announcements. Life was looking good.

I learned my future was looking bleak … I told Andria Flores, Nancy Pendleton, and Jessica Champion, their writer, their friend, that I wouldn't be doing what I loved anymore, and they wouldn't be coming along on any more fictional trips across the world because I was terminal. What do you do when your writer emails you out of the blue and says she's dying? If you're Andria Flores you rearrange your editing schedule with other clients, and push all-in on editing Sheryll O'Brien's final books.

Then you do this … On what has seemed like a daily basis, I have received brown Kraft paper envelopes with a return address in Texas. Inside the pretty-scripted envelopes there have been handwritten cards from my friend, Andria. On the front of each card is a quote from one of my books, on the inside are her thoughts about the quotes, or about us. I am going to share some with you.

Words in books. Words from the heart.

"Boobs" — she said, "boobs" ... *And that was how 'it all began'. Boobs. You told me on our first phone call in your northern accent that your previous editor told you not to say boobs. Ha! Didn't take me long to learn not to tell Sheryll O'Brien to refrain from saying anything she damn well pleases. Muah! ~ A*

"**After the law enforcer leaves to do law enforcing things."** *Yep! You said that. In print. And for the record, I let it be! I love your Sheryll-isms. I love you! ~ A*

"He is wearing an anxious expression on his face and a hole through the carpet." *Yes, you are a storyteller. There's no question about that. But with lines like these, you are an exceptional writer – my personal fave! Muah! ~A*

"You have lighted my darkest days and have shown me how to move through rough waters." *Such a beautiful line. Love, ~ A*

"Holy the fuck, what?" *I love how you even crack yourself up with the shit that comes out of your mouth! You, my friend, are a real piece of work. ~A*

"For weeks, those words have looped incessantly, frayed her nerves, and shredded what remains of her heart." *Hmmm ... isn't that the truth? Even in fiction, you have the gift of capturing what's real. The next line reads,* **"She forbids this**

new set of tears from falling." *I don't do it every day, but today I'm forbidding mine. Love you big! ~ A*

"He bangs through life with wrecking ball precision." *Gosh, I love this line – and a million others just like 'em! You are one of a kind, that's for sure! ~ A*

"The words came from behind Rocco and Joy, who were mid-ting of a champagne flute toast." *I love all of your words! I especially love your perfectly imperfect made-up words. Don't tell The Warden. ~ A*

"Their hands find their homes." *I love the way you write subliminal, seemingly automatic gestures with such meaning. ~ A*

"The man loved me to distraction." *I have always loved this line. It is very steamy, and reckless, and solid as a rock. ~ A*

"I'm happy, Kittridge." — "Me too, Fred." *I love it every time they make this little exchange. It says so much. Kitt and Fred and three small words with the weight of a thousand. I love you, ~ A*

"...Callie sings from the kitchen in tune with 'Hey Jude' — the soundtrack of my life." *What's currently playing on the soundtrack of your life? I'm sure some of your soundtrack is loud and noisy, but I hope most moments are filled with love, with gratitude, and with peace. ~ A*

"...Sage headed to the terrace for an afternoon with her precious array of floral friends. She'd taken to calling each by name and telling stories, much like she did with her Momma before things got bad." *This scene and so many others, are imprinted in my memory as if I'd actually seen it with my own eyes. What a gift. ~ A*

“Big tears begin wetting her lashes as they take to their journey. One by one they slide across and down her cheeks, some pooling in her ears, others finding her pillow.” *You have a way with details. You seamlessly describe common experiences to readers in a way they haven’t even realized for themselves until they read your words on the page. Impressed. ~ A*

“What. A. Fucking. Heirhead!” *I’m probably breaking a dozen social and grammatical rules by writing the F-bomb on the front of a greeting card. But my favorite author breaks the rules of writing — All. The. Fucking. Time. — And it serves her well. Muah! ~ The Warden*

“By the end of that year, Curtis had moved on from Bertha.” *Even your backstories make me swoon. I always loved Mama Girl and her story. ~ A*

There were many other brown envelopes … I can’t include some cards because they give away a little too much storyline, others because they are more personal in nature, but you get the gist of things. My editor is a very busy editor with many important clients, yet she carved out time from her days to handwrite cards to me, to remind me of the stories I wrote and the characters to whom I gave life and words. She kept them alive for me and kept our relationship vital and new.

And then this happened … Yesterday afternoon I asked my daughter, Jessica, to organize all of the little brown Kraft paper cards I’d received from Andria in chronological order. This morning I opened a word doc and began writing this blog. Twenty or so minutes in, I received a text.

Andria: I ’m reading your blog, the end of Turn. Turn. Turn.
Me: I’m writing your blog. It’ll be 44. You know how I love my double numbers.
Andria: Hahaha! Yes ma’am. I’m reading #42. I’m at the part where the hospice nurse enters mid-shit fest.

Andria then shared a personal text about the passing of her mother. We’ve shared many conversations over the years about the deep love the women shared, and the difficult path Andria has walked since her mom’s passing. In the past few months, my dear friend has expressed concern for Hannah and Jessica as they prepare for what lies ahead. Always the thoughtful, sweet woman from Texas — caring about those whom I love.

Her text went on to champion my right to call the shots while I can and warmly reminded me that Tim has a right to want to help me because ‘he loves you so’. She loves me, too. I feel it every day and it is on full display in the many cards she’s written. And on a day like today, when she’s reading a blog of mine while I’m simultaneously writing one about her, I know there is a little heavenly intervention at play.

In one of my books, I think it’s *Rescues*, I have my detectives head to San Antonio. While there, the men meet a bar-owning-broad, a character loosely based on Andria’s mother. I think she owned her own bar, or ran one as though it was her own, way down there in the Lone Star State. Anyway, real-life mother, Paula, loved the show Cheers, so I gave my character Sam Malone’s last name and thus a character was born — Paula Malone. I honored my friend and the woman she misses every day in the only way I could. Andria and I have discussed a possible meeting between me and Paula. I hope when we do meet we'll pull up a couple stools and tell stories of Our Girl. Today's events make me think Paula might be on my welcoming committee. Heaven — where everybody knows your name.

A note from Andria Flores …

Sheryll O'Brien and I connected on the internet. If it would have been on a dating app, her profile might read: 'Discontent story-teller longs to divorce current editor and connect with one who really gets me. Loves long walks on the beach, making up my own words, and calling people names.' After a few years, I learned her name for me was The Warden. As an editor (who still allows her to 'verb' a noun), I take it as a compliment that I've been able to keep some grammatical boundaries intact, even if they feel like prison bars to her.

On our very first 'check each other out' phone call, I immediately loved her Northern accent, and I think she may have been charmed by my Southern. What sealed the deal for me was hearing her describe a scene in which some female characters are sharing glasses of wine and chatting when one of them comments on the other's boobs. Sheryll said, "My former editor won't let me use the word boobs. He wants me to say 'breasts' instead." We both laughed. Hard. "Women don't talk to each other like that," I snorted, "You have to say boobs!" We've said boobs a lot since then.

I had no idea the gift God presented to me that day. But I fell in love with Sheryll's writing. She is my favorite author, not just my favorite client—I mean, the best author I have ever read. Her stories are complex and smart and playful. Her character development is flawless. I know her characters so well that I think of them long after the edits are over. They become old friends who I want to text just to see how they are doing. Sheryll raises the bar exceedingly high with her dialog. There's no need for 'he said' and 'she replied' because you know the characters so well, it's as if you are in the same room with them. You recognize their voices. And don't get me started on her sex scenes! Yes, there are boobs—and all the things. But it's not the trashy smut of grocery store romance novels. She writes sultry, pins-and-needles exchanges that well… leave you needing a minute.

From our very first phone call, we were a great fit as an author and editor. But then something sweet happened. Something personal. One day I told her by phone that my mom would have loved her books. It led to this whole conversation about how my mom had recently passed, about how she always had a book or a People magazine in her purse or on the dashboard of her pickup truck, about who she was and why I loved her. And somehow a connection formed that grows to this day. Sheryll is not old enough to be my mother, and I don't think of her as a mother-figure. She is my friend. At the same time, she is one hand holding mine and another holding my mother's. I am absolutely certain that once Sheryll finds Mom in Heaven they will compare notes on me, and I will have gained another guardian angel, one who calls me Babycakes.

Sheryll has written my mom into her books, my husband, even me. Just like everyone else she knows, there are snippets here and doppelgangers there of family, friends, and celebrities in every story Sheryll tells. Sheryll and I have actually never met in person, nor by Zoom, nor have I even seen a photo of her except from her honeymoon with Tim. Rather, Sheryll and I have developed a life-changing friendship in the margins of her manuscripts as I comment this and she rebuts that. We've exchanged countless emails, some texts, a handful of phone calls, and in recent months notecards by mail. I love Sheryll. She has impacted my life forever.

45. Roid Writing — Part One ...

It's 3 AM on Saturday and we're going for a ride, metaphorically speaking, of course. I'll be sitting my ass in my warm recliner and, if you join me, you'll be banging around inside my head, which is full of untethered stuff that's tumbling about at high speed — think clothes dryer gone amuck. First, let me set the scene. It's dark outside. Crystalized tree branches from a daylong frozen rain storm are being brought to sparkling life by the soft glow from a light outside my front door. The gentle tap of sleet hitting the bay windowpane is a clear reminder that no one should go anywhere on a night such as this. I haven't a choice, but you still have time to reconsider joining me on our little mental jaunt. Fair warning: I've had very little sleep over the past few days and I'm putting no thought into what this blog will be when it grows up. I'm going to do a brain dump and see what tumbles free. I make no promises about this writing exercise except this, given my current state of hyped-exhaustion I suspect Blog 45 will be a hot mess. If you still want to come along, buckle up!

As many of you know, I've been having a lot of trouble with headaches and memory loss recently. One recent Saturday things got particularly bad, and I should have let Tim call hospice to help with some skull crushing pain I was having, but I didn't. And yes, I've learned my lesson, it was a hard lesson, one that cut deep to the bone, which is where all of my problems begin and end. I've accepted (reluctantly) that as things progress with this whole dying thing, I am going to have to relent one day and let someone make life and death decisions on my behalf. Take a minute and think about what that means, for me, and what that means for you should you find yourself in my shoes. I suspect you might balk at saying these words, "Sure, honey, you decide."

Keep in mind, the 'honey' in this case has never, not once in 35 years of marriage, gone to his car to leave for work, or the market, or wherever, and remembered to take his wallet, or car keys, or cell phone. But when the time comes, I'll be putting my life into his hands. God knows they won't be holding his wallet, or car keys, or cell phone because they'll be holding my hands. I take pure comfort in that, I really do. I tease a lot about Tim, but there's never been anyone who's loved me more deeply than he, or from a place of more rock-solid certainty. How fortunate am I?

Back to the question I posed a minute ago, or many minutes ago, they sure do tick by slowly in the middle of the night. Should you find yourself in my uncomfortable shoes, would you have concerns about giving up control of your life? And, should you happen to be a control freak like I am in certain areas, in all areas, then I double-dare you to try these words on for size. "Sure, honey, you decide if it's time." It's not easy. None of this is easy, but it is tolerable.

When I told Nurse M about the events of that weekend and the pressure and pain in my skull, she again suggested we add a steroid to my lengthy list of medications. She'd explained a few days earlier that taking a low dose steroid could help with the noggin fluid, which could help with the headaches, which could help with the memory loss, but it could also have some side effects. I'm on a lot of medications. All of them help with some cancer related conditions, and help control my blood pressure, and deal with diabetes issues. All of them can cause some other condition, so all of them need to play nice together, that way the medications don't aid and abet the slow murderer named Cancer. Therefore, before there's a pharmaceutical addition or subtraction, there's always a discussion about what can and should be done, and when it can and should be done.

Whenever I mention a symptom, Nurse M does a nod of understanding. She is, after all, a professional hospice nurse and I am a patient who is traveling a well-worn path, though she never makes me feel that way. I always feel as though I am her only patient and most certainly the only person in the room that matters. Nurse M is smooth. She knows where I'm fitting in in relation to the stages of dying, but she keeps the death march of Sheryll O'Brien strictly to herself. She knows what I can and can't handle and what will keep me up at night, irrespective of the 'Roid Runner' in my head. Beep-beep!

On my first meeting with hospice, I jumped from, "Hello, please have a seat," to "when will I be climbing onto my deathbed and when will you pump me full of morphine and who's going to take care of my needs, you know my personal care?" I'm very sure I shivered and teared at the words. Nurse M homed in and realized my fear about dying was second to the ordeal of having loved ones or strangers having to do the personal care. Odd perhaps, but this is my death story and those were/are my concerns. And, Hello! It's called personal care because it's supposed to be personal. She reigned me in and kept me focused on things that needed to be done in the immediate and said we'd discuss the other things when the time came. Okay, but all that other stuff is still on the horizon and, in the dark of night when I'm not sleeping, I'm thinking about a whole lot of uncomfortable and sad things, and personal care is among them. Just sayin.

When I mention a new or persistent physical thing: a new pain or ache, a new eye and lip twitch, or new area of swelling, she scrolls through my chart reading this and that, and when she stops her search, I assume it's at my lengthy list of medications which I'm pretty sure she knows by heart. There's usually a bit of scrolling up and down and I can almost see the wheels turning in her head, good thing because I can't read her face as it is always behind a mask. Hmm. I've never seen her face. Probably some plot by the Grim Reaper.

Anyway, after the events of that weekend ... Nurse M informed Dr. Wonderful who prescribed Dexamethasone. The day I took the first pill I developed cold-like symptoms. My nose opened like a faucet, my throat became scratchy and sore, my right ear started to hurt a bit, and I felt like crap — the good kind of crap — not the kind of crap I've been feeling because of the cancer shit fest. By late afternoon, I'd used half a box of tissues. I asked Tim to take my temp a handful of times, which registered nothing more than a low-grade fever. That was enough for him to start doing the whole, *"We should call hospice,"* song and dance.

I said, "Okay." See, I learned my lesson.

By early evening the after-hours call to hospice was made, Tim gave the skivvy about my faucet-face, got the medical-scoop from another lovely nurse (must be a prerequisite for the job), and handed me a fuzzy-tipped-stick that I stuck up and swirled around the insides of both nostrils. I handed it to Jessica, who'd arrived at the scene of spontaneous parental bickering when Tim dropped something from the test kit and I groaned and rolled my eyes in a way that suggested he'd dropped a newborn on its head. She patted his hand, *"Don't worry,"* gathered the pieces, walked away from the two of us, stood at the counter silently opening foil packs and plastic test tubes, calmly stuck the snotty test strip into a fluid-filled holder, set the timer and pronounced, *"Ten minutes."* Her father and mother stared at her. *"Still gonna take ten minutes."*

Jessica is carrying a great deal of anxiety over this situation, though she is no longer asking questions about when, probably because she sits in on all of my hospice checkups and when the pronouncement from Nurse M comes that I am stable, my beautiful girl smiles wide, bids farewell to my nurse, then touches my hand as she heads upstairs to do yoga or lose herself in a book. Her new ways of destressing. Sure wish she was reading one of my books, but they cut too close to her bones now, too.

Anyway, back to the story … Within ten minutes we knew I didn't have Covid (big-ass sigh of relief), but we still concerned ourselves that I might have gotten a head cold. Let's face it, at this stage of the game of Life, I don't want to get anything! Tim offered me something to eat, and though I was hungry, I couldn't really eat anything because my throat really hurt — "DRATZ!"

We're going on a sidestep … When I was diagnosed, and my world was upturned, the standard rules and regulations of Dr. Wonderful changed, or eased a bit. At least they did on my end. For a couple of years I'd been monitoring my blood sugar and had changed my diet because I caught diabetes. I didn't catch diabetes, I lived a lifestyle that primed me for the disease. In any event, I became a statistic and I began, in earnest, watching what I ate and did the whole finger-testing twice a day. I typed the foods I consumed into some online app-thingy (see Guru, I can talk the talk) that calculated where I was on fats, carbs, good and bad, and proteins. Overall, I did really well and didn't really find the 'diet' restrictive, except for my having to cut way back on my favorite food – lasagna.

Another side step … Throughout the Pulling Threads series, several characters serve lasagna, or order lasagna, or brag about their culinary skills in making lasagna. They do that because I MAKE THE BEST LASAGNA IN THE WORLD. I shit you not! My personal schtick is this: "People who don't like me invite me to events if I promise to bring my lasagna." One of my characters, Shelby Webber, uses that line in one of my books. Couldn't even begin to tell you which book, but it's in the Pulling Threads series. As for my lasagna. There are two secret ingredients. And I'm not telling! Although I did tell Denise Sneade and she never asks me for cooking advice!

Anyway, back to the blog … Scrolling up. Okay, I'm back. Steroids. We were talking about my newest little friend, the one I think might have opened the faucet in my head and let my brain drain out my nose — gross, sorry. Basically, I was feeling like I had a head cold, and I was feeling way less fluid pressure in my head, AND I was clearer in my thoughts. But, I was hyped as hell. A warned-about little side effect. Tim offered me a cup of tea. Wait for it. Wait for it. I accepted! He tucked me in with a kiss to the top of my head and placed his left hand onto my cheek, our new goodnight ritual, then went upstairs to sleep. I stayed on my heated leather recliner and went to Bug-Eyed-Insomnia-Ville — a lonely little place where sleep evades, and feet start pumping air at rapid rates, and fingers start tapping chair arms at even more rapid rates, and the change of minutes on cable boxes slows way down.

That first night, I was awake until 2 AM. I grabbed hold of my next scheduled Tramadol, swallowed the thing without water, and started a chant, "Come on. Come on. Come on. Do your thing. Okay, I know you're for pain, but right now I'm feeling the pain of being awake and when I'm awake, I'm thinking and believe you me that is fucking painful! Come on. Come on. Come on." I fell asleep. Tim woke me when Hadley arrived for breakfast, a non-negotiable four-and-a-half hours of sleep later.

That was then, we're back to now … I'm reclining. You're tumbling in my messed-up head. Tiny ice pellets are gently tapping at the windowpane, and I honestly don't know what I'm writing about. Scroll to the top. Are you effing kidding me right now? I'm still writing about steroids? Okay. New Plan. This entry just became Part One. I'm going to try to close my eyes for a few, or maybe try to get lost in a Reba rerun on Hallmark; either way, I'll meet you back here after I spend some time with Mr. Chase, Mr. Sanborn, and Mr. Wonderful — whenever the hell the latter of the three drags his ass from bed and brings me coffee. I know I shouldn't drink it, but you can bet your ass I will drink it. Peace out.

46. Roid Writing — Part Two …

It's still Saturday. I've had my coffee, I'm still on my recliner and those of you who made the reckless decision to tag along are tumbling about my roid-filled-head. I suspect you've taken a liking to my rambles and, therefore, went all-in on this twisted trip. Therefore, I'm assuming you've read the blog where I said lovely things about my sister-in-law, Kathy, the scarf-twisting, blood-stopping, world-traveling, superhero nurse. The one who is now at the top of my shit list.

She Devil … I got a text message a few days/weeks ago — I haven't any idea because I'm riding a roid-wave and have lost track of time. Anyway, the text was from Kathy and it contained rows of yellow, green, and gray squares. *Hmm*, I thought. Is that the Irish flag? I could have sent a text to the Irish One to ask, but that could have ended badly, so I asked my sister-in-law, the she devil, who sent the odd text, what it was.

Me: "What is this?" I asked upon receiving the first text.
Kathy: "It's a game called Wordle. There's a new word every day and it only has five letters. Started in the UK. Go online, check it out, and let me know what you think. I have Adrienne and Arianna hooked on it. My brother Joey does it with me daily. It's good because it's only once a day. You only have six tries to solve it."
Me: "Perfect. Just as my brain is turning to mush. It sounds like fun."

What I really wanted to say was,
"Are you out of your effing head?"

Over the course of the next few days a few more yellow, green and gray texts came, like *really* early in the morning. "Huh. She probably does them while she's having her morning coffee. She's in Florida, though. I'd be looking at the ocean, but whatever," I mumbled, which is becoming a whole new thing with me. Anyway, I sent a smiley emoji, then went back to the things I'm currently working on, like my blogs and my death march. I successfully ignored the pull of Wordle.

And then this happened … I sent a text of my own.

Me: I sort of hate you for dragging my demented brain into this torture game. Just wait until the next blog.

Well we're here! At the next blog. Hellooooo Kathy ...

I went online and found Wordle The Archive Edition. It has about a trillion puzzles to lure you, torture you, and when you're ready to cry UNCLE, you're already a bloody, battered heap of emptiness in a corner somewhere, singing the alphabet with certain letters missing. That was me after playing the effing game for six hours straight and losing 30 'games'. Consider this, Wordle is a word game. I'm a damned wordsmith. I earn my livelihood by draining Tim's bank account because I sure as hell don't make money stringing words into sentences, into paragraphs, into pages, into chapters, and into books. But still, that's how I earn a few bucks here and there, so given that I spend my days and nights with words, one would think I ought to be able to Wordle with the best of them. Right? One would be wrong.

My dedication to writing notwithstanding, I have had a love affair with words for more than five decades. For fun, I used to take a dictionary to bed, open it, point to a word, read the definition and when I found a word I didn't recognize in the definition, I'd look for it in the dictionary, read the definition and continue playing my game until Marjorie came into the room and did the whole bed-untucking, sheet-shaking, spider-scouting, linen-tucking, ass-scooching routine. Apparently my devotion to words helped me not one bit with Wordle. I called my sister-in-law in a huff, spewed about the damned game, and laughingly teased that I'd get her good. I meant it. Here's your Wordle of the Day, Kathy.

B __ T __ H

Could be BATCH. Could be BOTCH. Could be BUTCH. Have fun playing! Love you!

Mr. Thoughtful ... As many of you know, Kevin Mullaney, bestie of my Mr. Wonderful, did the most thoughtful thing for me and nearly stole my husband's moniker. But since Tim really is Mr. Wonderful in so many ways, I've given Kevin his very own nickname. Mr. Thoughtful. It may not be original, but it is spot-on.

For those who don't know, I am a diehard Red Sox fan. I have been a fan forever. As a kid, I used to sit outside on the stoop while my grandmother, Meme, sat in a lawn chair beneath the shade of a gigantic limb that hung over a fence separating our yard from our neighbor's yard. Whilst Meme listened to the game being called on a transistor radio, she'd have her house dress pulled to her knees and her feet resting in a basin of cold water. On occasion she'd ask that I add some water from the hose. I would, then I'd sit my ass back down and listen to the game.

Years back, my mother gave Tim and me a really cool antique-looking, table-top radio. At first glance you'd think it came out of the 60s with its pull up antenna in the back, big round dial on the front, and metal-casing like the ones from days gone by. This radio, however, is state-of-the-art and could probably tune into China's airwaves. On many days, Tim and I would turn off the television and tune the game in so we could listen to the announcers call the plays just like I did with Meme.

I think it's important to note that I was such a fan that I didn't date anyone (for very long) who wasn't all-in on the Red Sox, and when I had children, I took my fandom seriously and raised my girls to love them. I scored a run with Hannah and struck out with Jessica.

A side step ... Debbie, you'll remember this story. Jessica O'Brien was signed up by her parents to play T-ball at the local field. We'd signed Hannah up a couple of years before and she loved the game, so we just assumed Jessica would follow suit. To put it mildly, we assumed wrong or wrongly. I don't know and I don't care.

Anyway, the rule in the OB house was if you joined in, you stayed in until the end. The reality in the OB house became this: getting Jessica to the field for practice was a skirmish, getting Jessica ready for game day was an all-out battle. But God love her, every Sunday she'd put on her green jersey, matching ballcap, and sneakers and go to Ty Cobb Little League field to strike out, and fall down, and run the wrong way around the bases, and throw dagger eyes, or wet eyes my way as she was having 'fun' on the field.

Debbie and I would cheer her on from the bleachers, then sit back and watch her strike out at T-ball. Hello, the ball is on a stationary stand. You swing, you hit. That was not Jessica's experience, ever. At the end of every game, Debbie and I would get what we knew we'd get — five-year-old Jessica stomping to the stands, her glove landing wherever and her ensuing spew readying on her lips, *"I hate this game."* Off would come her green hat. *"How many more games are there?"* Off would come her green team jersey. *"Can I go to the shack for a freeze pop?"* Off she'd go.

On the last day of the season, Jessica took to the field when she was told to, stood at the T when she was told to, and sat on the bench whenever she was allowed to. And when the final play of the final game of the season was called, she pulled open the gate, raced to the bleachers, tore off her green stuff and proclaimed, *"I can't wait to play next year!"*

"What?" Debbie and I simultaneously choked the word.

"But I only want to play if I can be on the red team. It's my favorite color."

I'm going to follow my current brain dump… I guess we're all-in for another Jessica story, or two. These are my favorite stories because they showed me from a very early age that Jessica would make things interesting.

It's the summer of 1992. Tim and I moved our family into our 'starter' home — I absolutely love saying that because we've never left our 'starter' home. Anyway, Jessica was outside with her sister and their cousins, Kerrianne, Matt, and Pat, playing in the front yard. I'd been on the front steps watching, but I needed to shut off the timer on the stove, so I headed inside. Within a minute's time, Jessica was crying and moving quickly into the house.

"What happened?"

"I hurt my toe!"

Up onto the counter she went, her boo-booed foot headed my way for an inspection. "You hurt this foot?"

"Yesssss. My toe. My toe." Tears.

Off came the sneaker. Off came the sock. Mom went in search of the boo-boo. Mom sees nothing.

"My toe. My toe." Tears.

"Honey, I don't see anything. Which toe did you hurt?"

"The one that ate roast beeeeef."

Like an ass, I stood there and sang the damn song until I found the toe that ate roast beef. I kissed the boo-boo I didn't see, asked if she was better, put her sock and sneaker back on, handed her a freeze pop and sent her on her way, marveling at her clever communication style.

Last Jessica story, for this blog. "Jessica, stop jumping on the bed," I called up the stairs.

"Okay, Momma."

"Jessica Kathleen, stop jumping on the bed!"

"Okay, Momma."

"Jessica Kathleen O'Brien, stop jumping on the bed," I said as I climbed the stairs. When I arrived in her room, she was mid-flight. "Jessica! Stop jumping on the bed!"

"I'm not jumping, Momma — I'm landing." Gotta love her. I do.

Back to Mr. Thoughtful for a bit... The dude knows how to impress a girl — this girl, anyway. All it took for him to make me fall in love was for me to see my name on a big-ass green sign at Fenway Park. I still can't believe he found a way to do it, that he took the time to do it, and that I lived to see it. Yes, I know my name was up there because I have cancer. Yes, I know I didn't do anything to warrant the attention lavished on me, but I *am* dying of the wretched disease the Red Sox Foundation has been trying to end through their decades-long fundraising initiatives for The Jimmy Fund. My Team has gone to bat year after year in support of those stricken ill with cancer. I am one of those who had her name on The Sign and it moved me beyond words. Someone thought exclusively about me, took the time to help me **Feel The Love** through a wonderfully grand gesture.

A few blogs back, I mentioned that living through my first goal of Christmas, my birthday, and the New Year left me with an overwhelming need to choose a new goal, a new date to try to reach in this battle I'm losing. I chose Opening Day of the Red Sox season as my new target date. You can bet your ass, I am energized to meet that goal. I am going to muster all I have to make sure I see my Team take to the field — and if I am unsuccessful, I hope you will all remember to **Feel The Love** on that day and every day. Gotta love, Mr. Thoughtful. I do.

Another side step … I've often said that when you have more than one child, you become more than one parent. The way in which I parented Hannah wouldn't have worked on Jessica because they are two very different individuals. Certainly, the parenting basics remained the same, but the finessing, the subtle manipulation, was completely unique.

Hannah, from birth, was a low-key kid. Put her in a swing or a crib and she'd entertain herself with fingers and toes for hours. Put her outside to play and she'd run the yard, skip, hop, jump, or whatever, and she'd do it without any need for anyone to join in. She was Hannah, just Hannah. She was easy. She was the reason Tim and I got tricked into having Jessica, the kid who never shut her mouth, the one who needed and wanted a playmate every second of every day. The one who fascinated me then and continues to fascinate me, today.

My very different daughters. Jessica likes attention. Hannah does not. So at the risk of cutting my life shorter than expected I'm telling you a Hannah story.

Hannah's favorite animal is the sloth. She loves their whole vibe and if she were part of the Animal

Kingdom, a sloth she'd be. Real-life Hannah has some sloth like, slow-moving, mellow tendencies, but she's not the least bit lazy, In fact she is a really hard worker at her place of employment, at her new home, and in her role of mother. But, dare I say, you'd never find a more laid back, relaxed, uncomplicated, cool chick than Hannah O'Brien. I know the word 'chick' is dated, and maybe not even appropriate anymore, but that's how I see her. She's just a cool chick. Except for when it comes to my blogging about her, so I'm going to make this brief.

Hannah had an awesome teacher in third grade. Mrs. Brigham taught all subjects, but based on the papers Hannah brought home, I venture to guess Mrs. Brigham's favorite subject to teach was language. She had a Literary Center the kids earned points to go to. Whenever Hannah brought home a borrowed book from the Literary Center she treated it with the utmost respect. Most often she chose stories about famous women in history, although her favorite story was about Elijah McCoy, an inventor who designed an oil lubricating system for locomotive trains. Don't ask how I remembered that.

Anyway, Mrs. Brigham's students were deep in the learning block of writing structure — beginning, middle, end. They had done several practice sheets in school where they organized sentences into paragraphs and then into short stories. You get the idea. Hannah's papers showed a clear understanding of the order of things, so imagine my surprise when I was asked to come to school for a meeting with Mrs. Brigham. I went into Ludlow after the morning bell, as I'd been instructed. Waved to Mrs. Brigham from the hall, as I'd been instructed. Then waited while she busied her students with *busy* work.

When she opened the door, she had a stern expression upon her face. I'd never seen it before and it unnerved me. Then she said, *"Are you aware of the final writing assignment?"*

"Yes."

"The students had to write a short story, concentrating on organization and punctuation."

"Uh, huh."

"Did Hannah tell you what the students were instructed to write about?"

"No." *Oh, shit,* I thought.

"They were asked to write about the thing that they would most hate to be in the whole wide world."

Oh, shit, I thought again for good measure.
Mrs. Brigham handed me Hannah's paper. I read the title: **Toilet Paper - The thing I'd hate to be.** I read the paper. I got a really good laugh because my daughter presented a very good case. Gotta love her. I do.

My favorite side step ... Hadley was over for breakfast this morning, it's still Saturday, by the way. Tim set her at the kitchen table and she and I talked from one room to the other. At one point I asked her to come to the living room. She skipped in. "Hadley. Can you put the fan on, just on low." I waved my hand in front of my face because I was having a major hot flash from the cancer pill. She turned on the fan, positioned it so the air was blowing toward my face, then asked me why I was sweating so badly. "It's a side effect of a medicine I'm taking."

"Is it the same medicine that's making you stay awake?"

"How'd you know about that?"

"I heard Mommy ask if you got any sleep last night and you said no."

"I should have said not much. I did get a few hours."

"But you can't sleep because of the pill?"

"Yes."

"Can you stop taking the pills so you won't sweat and you can sleep?"

"No, I can't."

"Why not?"

"Well, the pills are helping me stay alive."

Pause. *"Then you'd better keep taking them."*

Off she went to finish her breakfast. When it was time for her to leave, she did the whole lever thing. I gave her a lower number of hugs (7) because she and her mom had plans to leave. The door slammed behind her and I watched her round the corner for home, then I saw her come back around, climb the stairs, and open the front door. "Did you forget something?"

"Nope. Just wanted to remind you to take your lunchtime pills." Gotta love her. I do.

Looks like this blog is going to Part Three.

47. Roid Writing — Part Three ...

It's still Saturday. In a recent blog I mentioned Auntie Fifi, a woman who finagled her own chair in Mary O'Brien's kitchen. The events surrounding that accomplishment predated me, so I can't help with the specifics, but it is noteworthy to me that she had her own seat at the table, so I am noting it.

Why is a chair a big deal? Two parents plus ten kids three meals a day. Right there, there's a whole lot of people sitting around a sizable Farmer's table day and night. But Mary O'Brien's kitchen wasn't only a place for meals, it was *The Place for Everything* — chit-chatting about nothing serious or delving deep into weighty discussions. It was where cups of tea or coffee and a slice of Irish bread or Coffee Cake were always at the ready, and an empty pair of hands were always being offered for a fussing baby. It was the heartbeat of the home because a mother of ten made it that way. Patrick-Terrence-Francis O'Brien was head of that household. But, Mary McTigue O'Brien was head of Her Kitchen.

By the time I entered the picture, six OB kids had taken spouses and the remaining four were about to. Math recap: Two parents plus ten kids plus ten significant others plus a healthy smattering of *OBs: The Next Generation* either parked their asses or darted about the first floor at rapid speed. This made for a very busy room. I married into this big Irish family and learned firsthand that none of them think anything about the size and scope of their daily life.

For me, however, it was a big deal. I'm the middle kid of three, my family fit around an ordinary-sized table, we didn't need to fell a mighty Sequoia to build a place to set our nightly dinner plates. Nor did we need to turn conversations into a contact sport. The dinner table experience at my childhood home was about eating food and partaking in small-talk. When it was your turn to open your flap, you opened your flap. The OBs conversational style was more akin to chatter one might hear while traversing Grand Central Station; noise coming from all sides of the room like blasts of water coming from a super-soaker spray gun. Everyone got wet. Some were listening well enough to know why they were drenched. It was years before I knew why I always felt soggy upon leaving 15 Merchant.

A little geography lesson before we get back to whatever this blog is about. Not to worry, I'm better at geography than I am at math. Tim and I live in 01603. That of course is a zip code, but it is so much more. It's an area in the south part of Worcester with distinct neighborhoods tucked up and around the three main-drags, Main Street, Park Avenue and Stafford Street. If you were from 01603 you grew up in segmented neighborhoods known as Columbus Park, Downing Street, Crystal Park, Bennett Field, Hadwen Park, Deadhorse Hill, Heard Street, or Apricot Hill near The Rez. When you hit puberty, it didn't matter what neighborhood you were from, everyone knew about The Rez, a small, wooded area that's perfect for a stroll through the thicket along a babbling stream or for underage bending of elbow shenanigans that took place after nightfall.

There were large families in all of the 01603 neighborhoods, but the families associated with Our Lady of the Angel's parish had more than their fair share of 6+ kid families. (Disclaimer: I might be off on the number of kids). The O'Briens: 10. The Dowds: 10. The Gaffneys: 10. The other Gaffneys: 7. The Pettys: 6. The McTigues: 6. The Vales: 11. The Pratts: 13. The Gibbons: 7. The McCarthys: 6. I know I've missed a few of the gargantuan OLA families. I extend my apologies. Anyway, I came from Columbus Park. We had a couple families with 6+ kids, but the average family could be counted on one hand. So, for me, walking into Mary O'Brien's kitchen really was like walking into Grand Central Station. It was loud, active, and fun, and it was a never-ending game of musical-chairs unless you were Auntie Fifi. Seats were a commodity. So having one designated to you was a big deal. At least in my mind it was.

Alfreda McTigue stood out amongst the O'Brien clan, all of whom were fair of skin and thin of frame. Fifi was of Polish descent, hailed from Buffalo where winters are brutal and family roots settle deep so one doesn't wither on a vine in the Upstate tundra. Fifi was formidable in frame, had a full, expressive face, and poofy hair the color of a Twinkie. I know I'm wrong about the color, but that is what popped into my head, so I'm leaving it, absolutely NO offense intended.

From the moment my ass was moved out of Fifi's chair, she moved into my heart. She took an interest in me, she wanted to know where I came from, where my ancestors came from, how I met Tim, and wanted an immediate answer as to whether we'd 'stick' as a couple. Tim and I were twenty-eight when we first started dating, and right out of the gate we knew we were a good fit, so I told her I thought we would. On several occasions, Fifi invited Tim and me to her home which was a stone's throw from the OB house. Sometimes it was the three of us who hung out, and other times one of her children was in town for a visit and we'd be invited up. She told me often that I was good for Tim because she could tell he enjoyed my company, *"An important thing for the long haul,"* she said.

Things happened quickly for us as a couple. Dating led to a quick engagement and to a quick wedding and to a fun-filled honeymoon year. Shortly after our first anniversary, I learned I was pregnant. Tim and I thought I'd have the baby, put her in daycare and head back to my office located across the street from the Old North Church in Boston where it is said that Paul Revere spoke his famous words, *"One if by land, two if by sea,"* the signal that preceded the Battles of Lexington and Concord during the American Revolution. It would have taken that type of battle to get me to leave Hannah. I never returned to that job. I became a stay-at-home mom to the utter delight of Auntie Fifi. *"She won't know if you live in an apartment or a house, but she'll know you're there to kiss her boo-boo."*

I sold my Datsun 280Z to Kevin Mullaney, ditched my business suits for mom jeans, and when I had the energy, I loved every minute of my new life. When Hannah turned one, our little family moved to June Street and lived in the 01602 part of Worcester. We were a one-car family and so my relationship with Fifi continued mostly by phone. We chatted about all sorts of things, but we shared a love of crafting and that became our thing.

I'm getting to the point of this blog ... In the summer of 1990, I bought a stamp-patterned, cross-stitch, red tablecloth that I planned on giving to my mother for Christmas. The tablecloth was really big. In the center there was a Currier and Ives village scene with a steepled church, barren hardwood and evergreen trees, and stars and snowflakes everywhere. Along the bottom of the piece were Christmas trees, probably two dozen trees of varying sizes. I remember opening the package, seeing the amount of work, calling Fifi and lamenting that I'd never finish the tablecloth for that Christmas or probably any other Christmas in my lifetime.

"Put the time into it. Eventually you'll finish."

I put the time in and got physically ill sometimes with the repetitive cross-stitch. Oh, did I mention that every stitch was in white. EVERY STITCH WAS IN WHITE. Two years later and a few weeks before Christmas, I was finishing up the border work and the end was in sight. I maybe had a half-dozen trees to go before I finished. *And then this happened …*

The Tablecloth from Hell ...

Scene: I was sitting on a beautiful recliner in my quiet den of a second-floor walk-up. A lighted Christmas tree was set in a corner near a beautiful pair of pocket doors. On my lap was a draped tablecloth, the part I was stitching was pulled taut in a cross-stitch frame. A gentle snow was falling outside, and my little ones were tucked in and fast asleep. Life was grand.

A second later, a cry was heard from one of my children's rooms. I stuck the needle into the cloth, gathered the long material and placed it onto the floor. I lowered the legs of my seat and in the process of getting up I somehow knocked a drinking glass off a side table, the contents of which spilled all over the tablecloth from Hell. I grabbed the material, gave it a few shakes to get the brown soda off, threw it onto the chair, went to my daughter's room and joined my child in a good cry.

The next day I called Fifi before it was socially appropriate to do so. I was still in tears when I explained what happened.

"Bring it to me."

"It's ruined."

"Bring it to me."

"Fifi, the tablecloth is red, the stitching is white, there's nothing that can be done. It's ruined."

"Have Tim bring it to me on his way to work."

Several days later, a knock came upon my front door. There stood Alfreda McTigue, sturdy of frame and standing straight-spined with an obvious sense of accomplishment. She handed off a plastic bag, the kind that zips across the top, *"It's all set. You'll have to finish the final trees, but it's cleaned, and pressed, and you should be able to give it to your mother for Christmas."*

"But. How?" I stammered, "how did you get the soda off the white stitches without having the red dye run all over the place?"

"It did run in a couple places, but I cut those stitches out. You'll need to do that area over."

I opened the bag, took out the table cloth, laid it across my table and inspected it. Actually, I gawked at it because it was beautiful and it had been lovingly saved by Fifi, the woman who never considered any obstacle too great to overcome, the woman who never gave up.

When I gave my mother the tablecloth for Christmas, I told her I never wanted to see the thing for as long as I lived. Then I told her about the two-year journey of my work and the almost tragic ending to her gift. My mother never used the tablecloth at mealtime, she would place the cloth somewhere on display and every year we'd reminisce about its creation and salvation.

My elderly mother gave me the tablecloth for Christmas this year. It came tucked inside the zipped plastic bag Alfreda McTigue handed me thirty years ago. As members of my family came into my home, two by two, to spend time with me, the story of Fifi saving the tablecloth was told over and over. Sitting in the corner of my living room is a chair. I pointed to it and said, "That's Fifi's chair. She died on my birthday, you know." My mother knew and smiled a smile that said she was so happy I'd had a Fifi in my life. Gotta love them both. I do.

I stopped writing for a few minutes. I was a bit overcome with emotion, but I'm back and I'm determined to finish this blog. Many people credit Mark Twain with the quotation, *"The only two certainties in life are death and taxes."* The saying actually originated in a 1789 letter from Benjamin Franklin to Jean-Baptiste Leroy, a prominent French scientist. I mention this because it's still Saturday and Tim and I are doing the prep work for our taxes which will be taken to our tax preparer tomorrow morning, Super Bowl Sunday. We have had our taxes done on that day every year of our marriage. We do not like things hanging over our heads, so we don't let them. As soon as we collect our tax crap, we confirm our appointment, get them done, and put the grueling experience behind us. Then we celebrate our version of 'Souper Bowl' with crocks of French Onion soup and Tim's souper-de-duper stuffed mushrooms. Trust me, they're the best, ever!

Tim and Sheryll O'Brien are creatures of habit, it'll be these little things that will be hard on Mr. Wonderful when I'm gone: our mornings with Mr. Chase and Mr. Sanborn; our nibbling Figgies before bedtime; our tradition of putting up the Christmas tree the day after Thanksgiving and taking it down on New Year's Day; our Souper Bowl Sundays; our annual 'Staycation' at home during our anniversary week in June; our annual vacation in Wells in July; and all of the other little things we did that made us who we are as a couple. They are going to clang my loss over and over.

I've made Tim promise me that he will go places and do things when I'm gone. I really hope he makes a trip to Ireland. It's really the only place he's ever wanted to visit, to **see**. Tim was an art major in college and he's always wanted to see the greens of Ireland — supposedly there are countless shades of the color. I *want* him to see them. And I want him to visit relatives throughout America. And I want him to visit Kevin in Albuquerque. And I want him to visit the Lone Star State and meet Mr. and Mrs. Pendleton, and Mr. and Mrs.

Flores. So that is my clarion call to those who know and love me. Encourage Mr. Wonderful to travel.

From my publisher's husband – J.E. Pendleton ...

How is it that an old Fort Worth man spends a portion of each day thinking about a New England woman he's never met?

I'm the Fort Worth guy and I asked myself that very question. I guess it started over twenty years ago when I had one of my hair-brained ideas. That idea was to write a book. Sounds simple and it was; at least getting it into rough draft form. I had eight hundred handwritten pages, and no idea what to do with them. Into a drawer they went, and there they sat for years.

When my wife and I retired within a month of each other we suddenly had time to focus on what we wanted. One day she asked me what I was going to do with the book. I shrugged. She gave me 'her look' and said "That's not good enough."

Long story short, she took my scribbles and typed the manuscript, then spent days upon days researching just how to self-publish. My wife, Nancy, never gives up, and she finally figured out how to go from four spiral notebooks to a paperback and ebook, and suddenly I was a published author.

An editor we met along our publishing road and became friends with, started including my wife in some of her projects. Nancy, by working with Andria, helped several writers get their books before the public. A couple of years ago Andria asked Nancy if she was interested in working with a new writer, she jumped on it, and Sheryll O'Brien entered our world.

As we sat in our study together, me surfing the web, Nancy working on books, I'd hear about the books, I'd hear about emails between the two, we would laugh at the witty comments, or the snappy come-backs. As I heard more and more, I was witness to the forming of a bond between these two women.

As the months rolled by, so did the books from Sheryll. I had never seen anything like it. No sooner would Nancy complete the publishing of one book, when a new one would arrive. At times it was a book a month! These women were churning them out like crazy. Twenty-four books published in under twenty-four months! As a writer I was astounded.

I listened; I'd hear Nancy cuss at the computer, I'd hear her rant about issues, I'd hear her laugh at something Sheryll had sent her, and laugh just as hard at something she sent Sheryll. I sat and listened as Nancy read me snippets of books, or emails, and I was impressed with Sheryll's talent. But what really grabbed me was that I realized these women were alike, there are so many similarities. I was witness to a true bond, a treasured friendship developing between these two.

So Sheryll, we've never talked, never traded emails, or text messages, but I feel I know you. You are a part of my life. You live in my mind and heart, just as you live in Nancy's. And it all started because of a simple idea we shared – I think I'll write a book.

Fondly, Jim

Delightful Surprises … When Debbie traipsed back into my life, her daughter skipped back in, too. Amanda was Hannah's bestie all through grade school. An adorable, always smiling kid, with long, very curly brown hair and big brown eyes. She was a great kid to have around the house and she was around the house all of the time. The girls were close until they went off to different colleges, and different life experiences, and are now back living in their childhood neighborhood raising their own children.

A few weeks back, I got this text from Amanda.

Amanda: Good morning Sheryll, this is Amanda. I just wanted you to know I'm thinking about you all the time and reading all your blogs, they are so beautiful and wonderfully written. I'm so happy you were able to enjoy the holidays and your birthday with your family, and I'll be praying for you for Opening Day.

Happy emojis went back and forth. Then a few days later.

Amanda: I wanted to mention you used to make a dish for Hannah and me when we were younger and I THINK you used to call it hamburger mush, just letting you know it's one of Elliot's favorites and I always think of you when I make it.

Happy emojis went back and forth. Then a few days later.

Amanda: Hi, I just wanted to check in and let you know I'm thinking of you.

I'd just finished a visit with my hospice nurse when that text came in. I texted Amanda back saying the nurse just left and declared me "stable" and I decided on the spot that I loved the word. Rather regularly now, Amanda checks in, always hoping I'm still stable, and when she hears I am, she sends me happy texts. A week or so ago I received this text.

Amanda: Thank you so much for the copy of *Be* for Elliot. I'm going to start reading it to him tonight. Hadley is a very lucky little girl to have you as her MammyGrams.

And then came the announcement on Facebook. Amanda is expecting her second child. I'd been let in on the secret before the announcement, so when it came, I texted a congratulations and asked if I could mention the happy news in my blog. She enthusiastically consented. I wondered if the baby might make an appearance on Amanda's August birthday and I said I had a feeling about the baby's gender. She texted back immediately wanting to know my thoughts. I told her she'd have to read the following week's blog to find out.

So, here you go, Sweet Amanda. I think you'll be having a girl. Just putting it out there. No matter the gender, I know the baby will be very loved and very lucky to call Amanda, "Mommy."

It's still Saturday. Tim tucked me in an hour ago. He kissed the top of my head and put his hand onto my left cheek. *"Do you think you'll be able to sleep?"*

"I'm tired, so I hope so."

"Do you want me to sit with you so you're not alone?"

"No thanks."

He gave me another kiss and touch and went upstairs. I sat in the dark and heard him open the door at the top of the stairs a couple of times. He was checking to see if I was still awake and whether I'd put the television on for company.

I was awake and softly crying. When I'm alone in the dark now, I'm not afraid. I used to be afraid of what I was leaving and losing. The tears I shed now are about what I've had and what I have. This exercise in Roid Writing was a wonderful reminder of my blessings. It was a thoughtful nudge to Feel and Share the Love. It was an acknowledgment that the people in my life will continue to live wonderful lives and bring new ones into this world.

Feel The Love … It's all around you. And for the record, this blog is a very good representation of the hyped-up state of things in my head. We covered:

Steroids. Wordle. The She Devil. Mr. Thoughtful. Boo-booed toes. The Green Team. Bed Jumping. Sloths. Toilet paper. Medicine reminders. Alfreda McTigue. Tablecloths from Hell. Death and taxes. Clarion calls. And delightful surprises. Welcome to my world, friends. My wonderful, wonderful world of steroids.

A note from Linda McTigue Bushee ...

No one wants to talk about dying.

Tim called early last icy cold November 12 to share, through tears, the news that Sheryll had terminal bone metastases. He shared the link to her blog, said I may want to take a look at it. I have been riveted to it ever since.

To call this a blog is an understatement.

Sheryll has given us an intimate portrayal of what it's like to receive a terminal diagnosis. It's also a story about beginning to live life to the fullest before your life ends.

She says all of the things that no one wants to say or hear about dying, and she shares the road she's traveled-her fear, her pain, her anger, her incredible love for her family, and her happiness for accomplishing a life long goal.

I have laughed, cried, remembered happy stories, and felt painful memories. I've wanted to be back in Worcester. But most of all I have felt honored that Sheryll has taken us on this journey. She has invited us into her home and her heart and has shared with us all of her emotions. She has made it known, with many twists and turns along the way, that death is a part of living, and that you can accomplish unbelievably wonderful things when your time is limited.

I do not want her blog to end, as I do not want her life to end. I have learned and felt so much. But because of her artistry, her family and friends will forever have a treasure to read again and again.

Thank you Sheryll. Thank you for your honesty, your bluntness, your bravery, your anger, for sharing your pain, and your love. And most importantly, thank you for your incredible gift. It will never be forgotten. You are loved.

~ daughter of Alfreda 'Fifi' McTigue

48. Opinions. Facts. Reality ...

Decisions.
Some you can live with, others not so much.

~ Sheryll O'Brien

Someone recently asked me how my cancer got so far along without anyone noticing. At the risk of opening a can of Covid worms, I'll answer the question truthfully.

A little lesson on my cancer history: I was diagnosed with breast cancer in 2012. I did the surgery, radiation, and drug therapy for five years. I had a super-de-duper genetic test done on my tumor and was told I had a 14% chance the cancer would return in that breast, a low probability and very good information to know. From 2012-2017, I went for diagnostic mammograms twice a year. This type of screening is more sophisticated than a typical one, they take a lot longer, there's a whole lot of squishing with images taken from many angles. Every time I had one — EVERY TIME I HAD ONE — I wondered if the squishing could push some errant cancer cell out of my breast and into my body. I'm not kidding. I mentioned it on many occasions to Tim. Then we laughed at the absurdity.

In October 2017, I was five years out and elated when I walked the oncologist's hallway and heard the ring of a bell letting me and anyone in earshot know that **I was in remission**. What a great word, what a great feeling — what a triumph. I beat breast cancer. So there! I continued going for my breast screenings and annual physicals until 2020. Like millions of people, I feared getting Covid, so I hunkered down in my home, wore masks when family members came home from their brief, but necessary trips out, declined visits from friends, sprayed agents on anything that moved, donned plastic gloves and doused food deliveries with disinfectant, and while I did all that, I waited impatiently for a vaccine to be approved. Because I fell into a high-risk category, I rolled up my sleeve as soon as I could and took a single-dose J&J Covid vaccine. Then I went home, hunkered down, wore masks, and sprayed everything because I was still fearful. I was a cancer survivor and I met four out of five high-risk categories. I had every right to be fearful and to stay out of circulation and far, far away from medical facilities where Covid patients filled waiting rooms, ERs, and intensive care units. And doctors' offices, well they were the frontline in the battle against Covid. I stayed as far from the frontline as humanly possible.

During that year, I stopped seeing my eighty-six-year old mother and sister who live five miles away, and when Hannah and Hadley made an infrequent trip off of Wildwood Avenue, I would double up on masks and count the days until we knew they hadn't been 'exposed' to Covid. When enough time had passed and it was safe to play together again, I'd open my arms and Hadley would race into them for the hug we craved. I wasn't seeing people — **by choice** — because of fear, real fear. I was filling most of my days and nights writing, and some time reading the local newspaper online. Soon, I began seeing names and faces of people I knew, or sort of knew, listed on the obituary page. I began reading the 'Covid Obits' and thought the families were brave, and determined, or pissed off just enough to let readers know their loved one died of Covid.

Without exception, I'd spend a few minutes after that sad experience opening the CDC website to get the statistics, then watched news reports to get an idea about how people were processing the events, and I'd finish each day watching Governor Charlie Baker's press conference, and the daily White House briefings, and, and, and. Through it all, I kept a keen eye on what was happening in Worcester County. Overall, it seemed as though things were working until such time as hospitals started filling to capacity, and family members were no longer allowed to stay with their loved ones, and elective surgeries, and some not-so-elective treatments were postponed or canceled altogether. And then, the DCU center — the place to go in Worcester if you want to be entertained or enthralled by a performer or an awesome sports team was turned into a makeshift hospital for the overflow of Worcester County patients — Covid patients.

To date, 913,000 Americans have died from Covid. I suck at math, but even Sheryll Bodine knows that is a lot of dead people. I could itemize the number of those who died before there was a vaccine, and the number since the rollout, and the percentage of those who died without having been vaccinated, but that isn't what this blog is about. Those numbers, those facts can be found elsewhere. At the beginning of this blog, I said I was opening a can of Covid worms. I should say, emphatically, that I am not interested in anyone's opinion on this subject. I'm not even interested in my own opinion, anymore. I educated myself on Covid, I did everything I could to protect myself and my loved ones. I tried to persuade people to dig deep into research and make decisions based on facts and science. I am still very passionate about this shit fest because it remains a danger for all of you. But, I am more interested in what Covid has cost me, and continues to cost me, and what it will cost my loved ones.

In 2019, I had a normal alk phos; normal is 20-140. I don't know what my alk phos was in 2020 because I didn't have pre-physical blood work. No need for blood work unless you intend on following it up with a physical examination. For already stated reasons, I planned on sitting my ass in my hermetically-sealed home instead of venturing out into Covid-World. I made that choice. So, if you want to blame me for where I am. Go ahead. But before you close the blog, at least grant me the opportunity to say my piece. I think I've earned it.

By the time I had blood work done, it was October 2021: on the 14th the result was 618 and on the 18th it was 645. NOT. GOOD. We all know what the elevated level meant for me. Before I even knew I was sick, I had already lost my battle with metastatic breast cancer of the bones. **I had already lost my battle.** To cancer and to Covid.

I was right to fear Covid then, and now. There were so many things to fear about this disease, the one that quickly became political, the one that caused families to break apart, the one that caused bloodshed over mask wearing, the one that brought our country to its knees, the one that ripped our healthcare system to shreds, the one that's left our children to suffer the loss of parents and grandparents and siblings and teachers and friends, the one that has stripped away their chance at a normal childhood.

I've no doubt that this generation of children will be called The Covid Kids, or Generation 19, or some stupid shit. It doesn't matter what they are called, what matters is that they aren't being allowed to be children. The youth of today have become casualties of Covid 19. They have become casualties of the choices we make. It doesn't matter how well-intentioned we think our choices are; our children are the ones who are suffering.

A sidestep … A year or so ago, Tim took Hadley to the drive-through at McDonalds at Tatnuck Square. They donned masks and went off for a little time together. He went up over Airport Hill, grabbed her Happy Meal, then headed home via Mill Street. He'd barely stopped his car on our driveway when Hadley bolted through my front door.

"MammyGrams! MammyGrams! Guess what I just saw!"

"What?"

"Two kids were playing outside on their front lawn! They were playing catch. With a ball!!"

How fucking sad. How fucking pathetic. My granddaughter reacted as though she'd seen a unicorn, not a couple of kids doing what they ought to be doing, what every kid ought to be doing: on ballfields, and playgrounds, and front yards, and everywhere else in America — being children. I suspect people reading this are thinking I'm going to get onto a high horse for this side or that side. I'm not getting onto anything. I can't.

Remember, I'm dying of cancer — bone cancer. I'm not allowed to get up and walk to my kitchen for fear that one of my bones will break and that will be the end of Sheryll O'Brien.

My Reality ... The other day, I gathered the courage to look at the images from my nuclear medicine bone scan. I mentioned, in a previous blog, that I don't do online medical research. It freaks me out, and besides, I don't understand half of what I read. I knew I had access to my bone scan and other test results, but I'd resisted the urge to take a peek. For some unknown reason, I threw caution to the wind and accessed my medical tests and scans. Heads Up: the My Chart online medical record at UMass Hospital is a portal to Hell. I opened my chart and went to the titled section: Nuclear Medicine Bone Scan. I clicked my mouse on the pretty blue arrow. I wish I hadn't looked. I wish I could get the images out of my head. I cannot. With complete honesty, and without hyperbole, **I am filled with cancer from my skull to my knees**. The devastation of what this disease has done to me is indicated by black marks and swaths across my skeleton. My skeleton should be white. My skeleton is not.

I have two black sections on my skull. My entire spinal column, from the base of my head to where my back meets my butt is black. My rib cage has black markings reminiscent of those on a tiger's back. My pelvis and hips are black front and back. My femurs have black sections here and there and holes that run from the front through to the back. My knees look like two huge black marbles. One physician told me it would be impossible not to lose sleep after looking at my scan.

One physician told me I might survive six months if it was just the cancer, but a fracture was my most imminent concern. One physician mentioned something called a spinal collapse.

The other day, I told Nurse M I looked at my bone scan. She stopped emptying her backpack of the tools of her trade and stared at my face. The air was sucked from the room. And time stood still. My eyes filled with tears. "How on God's green earth am I still alive? How did I not know I was sick? How am I still alive?"

She gave her head a tiny shake, leaned her elbows on her thighs and moved into my space, even though we were a few feet apart. Her body language sent the signal that she was all-in with me — on the conversation we were about to have — and the pain I was experiencing. She gave her hands a tiny clap, *"Honestly, Sheryll, it's because you are who you are. You're a fighter. You've decided you are going to do whatever it takes to live the remainder of your life, your way, and for as long as you can."*

I nodded, had a moment's cry, shook it off, and readied myself for the battle I won't win — the battle I've already lost — the battle I'm still going to fight.

When the nights are long and lonely, I sit and wonder how I will die. I used to fear climbing onto my death bed, but given the option of a slow decline on morphine or a sudden fracture or spine collapse, I'd like the decline, please. Truth be told, there are other things I would like. Correction, there are other things I need and I may not get to have because of the wretched curse of Covid. My preference, and goddammit, I should have my preference, is to pass away at a hospice facility. I'd like to stay in my home until such time as I need around the clock care. I don't want my husband or my daughters doing anything for me other than holding my hands and telling me they love me. But because of the rise of Covid again, I may find myself without a hospice bed and if I am lucky to find a bed, Covid restrictions may make it so that Tim, and Hannah, and Jessica, and my eighty-six-year old mother, and Marjorie, and Don, and Donna, and Kathy, and Eileen, and my religious guide, and my, and my, and my won't be able to visit let alone be with me when I die. And when I do die, I may need to wait a week or more for cremation availability. I know I will be dead, but I will be alone for a week or more, and my family will have to wait to say goodbye, and I may not find the peace I seek, the peace I am entitled to.

So again, I don't give a damn about anyone's opinion about the can of worms I've opened. I do care that I am **absolutely** a casualty of Covid and the politics and passion that has run amuck. I do care that I, and millions of others just like me, won't be counted as victims of Covid even though we most certainly are. So, at the end of the day. If you've had a shot or if you have not; if you wear a mask or if you do not; if you object to my writing this blog or you do not; none of it matters to me, anymore. I am going to be dead soon. Maybe I would have had a chance to beat cancer if I learned about it in 2020, none of us will ever know the answer to that. I guess I'll leave that for all of you to bicker about when I'm gone.

49. Minesweeper ...

I used to love playing this computer game. For those who don't know what it is, and for those who might have forgotten, the objective of Minesweeper is to make it through a grid of gray squares without being blown up by hidden bombs, 10 to be exact, although the higher levels have 40 and 100 bombs. HA!

So, how do you traverse the board without stumbling upon a landmine? You don't, not for a long while if your name is Sheryll O'Brien.

The opening move on Minesweeper is a crapshoot, you'll either hit a bomb or you won't. If you don't, you will be given hints as to what your next move should or should not be. A series of numbers will appear on the board around the move you just made. The numbers range from 1 to 5 and they let you know how many landmines are touching the square you just cleared. For example, if you click on a square and you reveal the number 3, that lets you know there are three landmines touching your square. When you think you know where a bomb is located, you put a flag onto the space as a reminder not to click on it, then you continue playing the game.

Minesweeper is challenging, for me anyway. If you'd asked me a couple of weeks ago before the whole Wordle dustup, I would have suggested I suck at Minesweeper because it involves numbers. But, thanks to a certain sister-in-law, who will remain nameless in this blog (Kathy Gaffney, the She Devil), I no longer have the luxury of thinking numbers are my only shortfall. Empirical evidence is now overwhelming, I suck at computerized games with numbers and games with words. Give me a deck of cards and I'll beat-your-ass at Pitch or Poker or Gin Rummy, or, or, or, but don't bother me with computerized games, please, I'm dying. That ought to be enough punishment.

I taught Hadley how to play Minesweeper a few years ago. I use the term 'taught' very loosely. I explained the rules, then went about getting my ass blown to smithereens, over and over and over as I tried to show her how to play the game. My seven-year-old granddaughter caught onto Minesweeper pretty quickly and moved the field with confidence, counting out spaces, throwing up flags, and getting nearly to the end of each game before she found herself blown to bits. At the end of the day, even she found the last sequences difficult. So there.

My girl used to sit on my lap when we played, and while we played we chit-chatted about whatever little thing that popped into her little head; a trip to the playground or an episode of PJ Masks, it didn't matter what we chatted about, it mattered that it was MammyGrams and Hadley time. The other day, she hopped onto her bench that is permanently set beside my chair now and asked if we could play Minesweeper. She really wasn't interested in playing, she just wanted to hang out, or perhaps she wanted to reminisce through action. Before long, we were chatting about her day at school and about an award she received.

"Mommy said the Kindness Award is the nicest one of all to get."

"I agree and, knowing you the way I do, it was the perfect award for you to receive. I couldn't be prouder of you, Hadley." Silence. "What do *you* think about the award? Was it a good one for you to get?"

"Absolutely!" Pause. *"It isn't easy being kind to _______."* Hadley shrugged her shoulder, *"She's always hanging on me."* Another shoulder shrug, *"I guess she just can't help herself."*

My girl played a few more grids, then moved on to more sophisticated, solitary computer games while I mentally traversed my very own real-life game of Minesweeper.

February to June … Consider the months laid out like a Minesweeper grid. <u>February 26th: Tim's birthday.</u>

My beloved turns sixty-five this year. We began dating the year we both turned twenty-eight, so for the past thirty-seven years Tim and I have shared every life experience, stored every memory we made, and whispered every hope for our future. The years between high school and our tenth-year reunion were ours to live and we lived them. We answered to no one, went where we wanted to go, did what we wanted to do, and sowed our share of wild oats. So, when we finally met up again, we were ready to settle into a serious relationship.

Almost ten months to the date of our reunion, we married. I was a confident June bride — Tim was a nervous groom. His vows went something like this.

Greendale People's Church …

"Timothy, do you take Sheryll to be your wedded wife—"
"I do."
"to live together in marriage?"
"I do."
"do you promise to love her—"
"I do."
"comfort her—"
"I do."
"honor and keep her for better or worse—"
"I do."
The minister put a hand onto my groom's arm, *"I'm going to finish the vows. I'll nod to you when I'm finished, then you can say, 'I do'. The groom nodded. The minister continued, "—in sickness and health, and forsaking all others, be faithful only to her, for as long as you both shall live?"*
The minister nodded.
The groom said, *"I do."*

The congregation laughed at the sweet moment.

Tim took his vows seriously. It might be because he said them over and over and over at our wedding altar. Nope, he took them seriously because that's the kind of man he is. He was raised by very decent people, parents who put their family first, weathered their storms together, and made commitments through word and deed then lived up to them, thereby setting an example for their children.

Playing the field... My time on my own let me know what I wanted for my future, more importantly, it let me know what I needed from my man. When Tim came along, I knew, deep in the places where insecurities can root and grow, that I wanted a man who had lived a little, one who'd been out on his own and responsible for taking care of himself, one who'd be all-in on any vows we might take. Most importantly,I wanted someone with whom I could laugh my way through life. I learned Tim was *that* guy at my mother's retirement party in 1985 (she was a young retiree).

A sidestep first... My parents divorced when I was in my early twenties. At that time, Mom, Marjorie and I were living with Meme, and for the foreseeable future things were going to remain status quo. And then came a chance meeting between my mother and Roland Bodreau, a man my parents knew through the Elks Club, but with whom they never socialized. Roland had been a widower for a few years. When he heard about my parents' divorce, he let Mom know of his interest in her. They had a secret thing for a few months (so cool) and when my mother told Meme, Marjorie and me about her steady beau named Bodreau, I think she feared pushback, or whatever. She got none. My mother deserved to be with a man like Roland Bodreau — a salt of the earth kind of man. The kind of man I wanted for myself, one day.

Anyway, back to Mom's retirement party. It was at a place in Auburn called Periwinkles. I'd arranged the thing, invited family, a few of Mom's friends, and several of her coworkers. Dinner was supposed to be served at 5:30. By 6:45 the owner made an appearance to offer apologies, a free round of drinks, and promises that food would appear on the table by 7:00 at the latest. Tim and I snuck outside for a butt and some fresh air; oxymoronic statement, I know. I lamented to the starving dude about the poor service and bitched and moaned about my own state of hunger. Tim nodded and pulled a drag of his Marlboro. I pulled a drag of my Newport menthol and groaned through an exhale of smoke, "I'm so hungry, I could eat a horse."

Without missing a beat, Tim stomped his foot as though it was a hoof, bent at the waist, whinnied, neighed, and snorted, and banged his head against my shoulder. Then he stood upright, smiled a big-ass smile that went from ear to ear.

I laughed my ass off and surrendered
a piece of my heart.

It was more than his sense of humor that took me head over heels. There is absolutely nothing about Timothy James O'Brien that is flashy — nothing fake. He is cut from a clean cloth and along a straight seam which I found sexy as hell. When Tim put his hand to the small of my back, I'd get tingles of excitement. When he held my hand — he always held my hand — it made my heart skip a beat. I loved him then. I adore him now. I don't want to die on his birthday.

March 5: Jessica's birthday. My second-born daughter was supposed to be born on March 21st, my grandmother, Meme's birthday, but I developed a serious condition when I was six months pregnant and needed to have my gallbladder removed. I was not a candidate for laparoscopic surgery because of the pregnancy, and I couldn't delay surgery until I gave birth because the fear was that a gallstone could get dislodged and block something or other and that would threaten my unborn child, so I had the big-ass type of gallbladder surgery during my second-trimester. That doesn't even come close to being the big thing that happened during my Jessica pregnancy.

In January 1990, two months before Jessie was due, Hannah and I were taking a noontime nap in our second-floor walkup. There came a knock upon the back door which I ignored. Several minutes later, I heard a loud bang coming from the first floor. Several minutes later, I heard another knock on the back door. Concerned that our elderly first-floor neighbor needed me, I left Hannah on the couch and waddled to the kitchen, arriving just in time for the back door to be kicked open by a home invader who moved aggressively into the room. Hannah had made it to my side, had wrapped her little arms around my legs and buried her face into my thighs as he moved closer.

I don't know why the robber turned and left, but he did. I scooped up my toddler, grabbed the cordless phone from the wall, and went to the enclosed front porch and locked it behind us. I stood with my girl in my arms and watched the bastard make his way down June Street toward Newton Square. I don't remember much about the actual phone call I made to 9-1-1 other than I repeatedly said my brother-in-law was Tommy Gaffney, a WPD officer.

A necessary side step … Does anyone other than me find it extraordinary when you hear a tape recording of someone who's called 9-1-1 because they've severed an arm, or have tripped over a loved one who's been bludgeoned to death, or some other horrific criminal event has taken place, and the caller is like, *"Hi, this is so and so, and I live on Windsor Lane, you know, the pretty cul-de-sac off of Parker Lane, well anyway, there's a dead body in my living room. I hope you can send someone over. Okay, thanks."*

What the hell is that? I'm sure it's helpful to the 9-1-1 dispatcher to receive a calm, cool, and collected emergency call, but HELLO PEOPLE, the dispatcher is the one trained to be calm, cool, and collected. You don't need to be calm if someone is bleeding out on your Persian rug. Just sayin. As for my call to 9-1-1 — it was an emergency situation, so I emergencied myself all over the place. There was a whole lot of spewing going on, and there was zero pleasant chit-chat — I assure you.

Anyway, the police and EMTs arrived within minutes. I was examined from the perspective of being a pregnant woman, and also because I'd recently had major abdominal surgery. I had a smattering of contractions, I think I was given a shot of some sort, and was eventually sent home to bed which was located behind locked doors — newly installed, steel constructed, deadbolt locked doors. That is where I stayed until the decision was made to deliver Jessica three weeks early, on March 5th. I did what was best for her then. I want to do what's best for her now. I don't want to die on her birthday.

<u>April 4: Hannah's birthday.</u> There were no dramas during my pregnancy with Hannah; that in a nutshell is why I think she is nearly unflappable. I am in no way

implying there hasn't been cause for her to flap on occasion, there certainly has been, but she takes things in stride. Remember, she's the cool chick. Aside from having two surgeries of her own before she turned thirteen, and weathering the many health issues I've had, and being the older sister of jabbering Jessie, and the daughter of Yours Truly, Hannah could rightfully claim a bit of wackiness.

After the break-in, Hannah said no words other than, *"Bad man, bad man,"* for approximately two weeks. She was twenty-one months old at the time and was looking forward to being a big sister. We'd moved her from the crib and into a big-girl bed with ease right after Christmas, then moved her back into the crib when we woke one morning and found her bed empty. The poor little kid had gone into the nursery, crawled under the crib, and spent the night surrounded by dozens of stuffed animals. Our toddler needed to take a step back, so we let her. We tucked her into the crib that night, the place she'd comfortably slept for nearly two years. We let her stay there until she was ready to move out. It took about four months, and it coincided with Jessica's move from her bassinet to the crib.

That's pretty much how Hannah's life has always been. She's set her own pace, gone about her business, did what needed to be done, and in the course of things, she paved the way for her kid sister, and made things very easy on her parents. As her Momma Bear, I kept a close eye on her, and put my heart and soul into helping her feel safe in this world. I responded to her needs as best I could then. I want to preempt her needs now. I don't want to die on her birthday.

May 1st: Marjorie's birthday. My kid sister is a May Day baby. May Day is celebrated around the world either on May 1st or the first Monday of May. The earliest celebrations date back to the Roman Republic with the festival of Flora. American May Day festivities date back to 1627 at the Merrymount Plantation on Massachusetts Bay. It was there that the first Maypole Revels took place.

A sidestep history lesson ... Maypole decorating has roots in ancient Pagan festivals celebrating the beginning of the pastoral summer season. The pole is made from a young tree that's been stripped of its branches and secured in the upright position. The pole takes on the masculine role of the dance. Maidens would weave through and around one another while wrapping the Maypole in ribbon and foliage. The springtime tradition was a hopeful celebration for livestock fertility, plentiful land bounties, and health and happiness for the people living off both.

I don't remember a twirling ribbon or crepe paper celebration around a maypole for Marjorie, but there most certainly should have been. There's something very colorful about Marchrie (my nickname for her). When she was a kid, she had sunshine yellow hair and gorgeous sapphire-blue eyes. When she was old enough to choose her wardrobe, she most often chose citrusy colors; the kind that look great on a select group of people; the kind that always makes my mouth water and sends me straight to Friendly's for a cone with orange sherbet scooped high. I can easily imagine Marjorie barefoot, in a flowy, cotton ankle dress, with a flower wreath atop her long, lioness tresses, leading the systematic draping of a maypole. Ahhhhh, a perfect image. I wanted happy celebrations for her then. I want beautifully decorated maypoles for her now. I don't want to die on her birthday.

The other night, I told Tim I was moving my death-date goal post. I know that I still have more than a month before I will reach MLB Opening Day, and that in and of itself is an ambitious goal, to be sure, but, I feel; I believe; I desire; I hope; that I might make it June though it is a bit problematic in the Minesweeper Game of Life and Death. Kathy's birthday is June 6th. My thirty-sixth wedding anniversary is June 20th. Hadley's eighth birthday is June 28th. Yeup, June comes with a few landmines. I suggest we cross that grid when we get to it.

A side step … I mentioned in a previous blog that Hannah was born on her great-grandmother's birthday. Interestingly, at least I think it's interesting, Hadley was born on her great-grandmother's birthday. Sort of cool. There's that word again in relation to Hannah. Yeup, like I said, she's a cool chick.

Back to my personal game of Minesweeper. For the next five months, there are many days on which I do not want to die. You know I am so not a numbers person, but I suspect the odds are kinda high that I will manage to avoid those days. I sure hope so. I already know that no matter when I die it will be a really bad day for them — all of them.

50. Misfires. Music. Memories …

It's long past midnight. Tim tucked me in with a kiss and a touch and went upstairs a couple of hours ago even though he wanted to stay near and hover a bit longer. The reason for his attention: I had some lumbar pain around suppertime. It came during that not-so-sweet-spot when I'm nearing the end of efficacy on one dose of Tramadol, and readying myself for the next.

The discomfort I get during those times is called breakthrough pain. I've come to realize the intensity of pain depends on where the breakthrough is on my body. Intense pain is usually felt in my thigh area, particularly the right thigh, and the pain can also get pretty bad along the upper part of my back, on both sides of the spine, several inches below my shoulder blades. Pushes of sharp pain definitely cause a cessation of whatever limited movement I can do in a chair, and always emits an audible moan. I know everything about this body of mine now and can usually tell how long the painful session will be, and I usually tough it out without much fanfare.

I have other bouts of pain, mostly manageable pain that pokes through here and there. It took a few times of breakthrough pain in new areas before the penny dropped. Tramadol is a strong pain medication. It is keeping me from feeling pain in areas where I know the cancer rodent has already done deadly damage. Ah, the Catch-22: Tramadol is keeping me from knowing about new feasting areas, about new areas of deterioration.

And then there was today's pain. A totally new species. The pain I experienced today wasn't breakthrough pain; it was more akin to the pain I would suspect someone feels when they break their back — their lower back. It felt as though I'd been kicked by some brute in a steel toed boot. SMACK. Then, almost as soon as it came, it left, though it left a lasting impression. It scared the ever-loving crap out of me. Tim, too.

You all know my spine is a cancer zone, from top to bottom. The wretched disease is everywhere, but my L1 is of particular concern and has been from the very beginning. During the months before I knew anything was wrong, I had a lot of lumbar pain. I'd nestle against a heating pad, toss a few OTCs into my mouth before bed, and assume an ache here and there was part and parcel of being in my early sixties. When I had the bone scan, and a set of reclining X-rays, I had to stretch out on a hard surface. The experience was excruciatingly painful. Seriously, just lying on a table caused silent tears to flow. My lumbar area felt as though it was cement and it was resting upon an equally unforgiving surface.

I remember putting my nightgown on when I got home from the scan. I ran my hand across my lower back. It was a surreal experience. My skin and the soft, poofy area that should have been just beneath the skin's surface felt like concrete. An unusual sensation to be sure, and an experience I've shied away from repeating. That isn't like me. I tend to check things over and over. If I have a bruise, I'm one of those people who touches it to see if it still hurts. It always does, probably because I keep touching it. I'm not sure what that says about me, but I'll toss this out there, as soon as I felt my concrete lumbar region, I've had no desire to touch it — I'm not sure I ever will.

Getting back to the story ... I'd just taken a Tramadol and was minding my own business when it felt as though someone took a sledgehammer to my lumbar region, just one quick smack to the right side. Pain pushed hard, took my breath away, and left in its place an aftershock of physical reactions. They UNSETTLED the hell out of me. It felt as though my internal electrical system was having a malfunction. My heart did some sort of rat-a-tat, thumpity-thump, twirl thing. Pins and needles shot down my arms and legs, did a turnaround at the tip of each finger and toe and headed back up at lightning speed. I began to sweat profusely from everywhere, and when I called out to Tim I didn't recognize my own voice.

He was at my side within seconds and the look on his face mirrored the internal shit storm inside me. *"What happened?"*

"Pain. Back. Bad."

"You have no color, and you're sweating, and you're shaking. And—"

Before he finished whatever it was he'd planned to say next, everything corrected itself. It was as though someone plugged me back in and rebooted the electrical system. I cooled down, and settled down, and marveled that there was only the tiniest twinge of back pain.

Again, Tim asked what happened.

"I don't know, really. I'd just taken my suppertime pills, was watching a show and all of a sudden, I had this smack of pain in my back and everything inside seemed to go haywire. I'm fine now." I extended my hand to prove that I wasn't shaking anymore, and he said my color was back. We discussed calling hospice then we wondered what they could possibly do about something that was already done and over with. And then we had a conversation, a sort of a whispered one for fear our words would find space in the universe. We tend to shy away from letting the Grim Reaper know some shit is hitting the fan at the OB homestead.

"It's just a matter of time before something like that happens and it doesn't correct itself," I said through tears.

He nodded through misty eyes.

"You're the one who's gonna have to call hospice — like by yourself."

He nodded, again.

"Something like that could be the end, you know, it could be that sudden."

Silence. "I really don't want it to be that sudden. I'm not prepared to die that way. How *do* I — *can* I prepare myself to die that suddenly?"

He kissed the top of my head and went to the kitchen. He returned with an apricot danish which you should note I have become addicted to in recent weeks. As soon as my appetite came back, it came back with a vengeance for apricot danish. There's a place in Worcester called Culpeppers Café and Bakery on Southbridge Street. They make the best danish of any flavor anywhere and the apricot is a huge seller, so Tim has taken to buying a dozen at a time and tucking some into baggies for the freezer so we have some on hand.

I accepted the tasty treat with a smile, leaving the 'what if' fears and anxieties about sudden death scenes for another time. I spent the remainder of the evening pretending to watch a show on Hallmark. Tim spent the time with his eyes glued to me and when he knew I'd had enough scrutiny and was about to snap, he went upstairs. I heard him walking the floors late into the night. I couldn't sleep either, but since I am lashed to the leather, I grabbed a piece of paper, and jotted a few notes about things I wanted to cover in upcoming blogs. I make these lists often, but the stuff rarely gets into one of my writings.

For the most part, I don't outline or even think things through before I start typing. It was the same way with my books. I'd start with a blank page, put a sentence or two down, and let my characters take me on a ride. The story essentially wrote itself, and then on the first rewrite, I'd go back and put in the color, the setting, the description of the characters, all the oomph-stuff that makes readers fall in love — or not.

I fell in love with my characters — my men. I miss the ease of Fred Serpico, the guy who makes you think you've known him your whole life even though you're still shaking hands of introduction; the guy who's comfortable in his own skin and wears the hell out of it. I miss the intensity of John Maxwell, the guy no one really knows; the guy who catches the eye of every woman, lusts after a few, but loves only one. I miss the sophistication of Rocco Fiancetti, and the mischievous sex appeal of Manuel Xavier, and the prowess of the legendary Malcolm Price, and the wackiness of Randall Parker, and the boldness of Mathis Reynolds.

I'm not sure why I took you on a little walk down memory lane with my guys. Maybe it was to introduce you to the 'people' I've spent the past three years with. The ones to whom I gave life. The ones who gave it right back to me. And now that you know who I've been hanging with, it's time to get back to business.

All things considered ... I am doing really well. Sometimes I forget that I'm sick. Correction: sometimes I forget that I am dying. Like this past Saturday, I had Mom and Marjorie over for a mid-day dinner of chicken pot pie and whipped potatoes. No big deal. A very big deal.

Two lovely young women with whom Jessica works, Molly and Haley, sent a chicken pot pie to our home; an unexpected treat, for sure. Tim put it in the oven, and we had dinner guests. Everyone grabbed a seat in the living room, put their plates onto laps, and mouthfuls of yumminess into their no longer flapping traps. When chit-chat began again, there was no talk of cancer, or hospice, or funeral preparations. We talked about the beautiful, unseasonably warm day, and the many wonderful people who have done considerably kind things for a woman they know, or one they think about because they have a friend who is hurting and they want to show her they care.

Guess who made a reappearance later that afternoon. Hint: He came in a package and was delivered by our postman, Jose. Yeup, it was Philip McTigue. He's been reading my blog and taking time out of his busy life to create a musical treasure trove of CDs for me. Tucked inside the package was a lovely note and two more musical trips down memory lane. Tim went to put the CDs into our system.

"No, don't!" I shouted.

"Don't what?"

"Play them."

He shot a look that said, *"What the eff is she up to now?"*

"Don't play them. Not now." My mind was twirling and swirling. A wonderful idea was taking shape in my head, but sadly I wouldn't be able to pull it off without help. I probably would have enlisted the aid of Hannah and Jessica, but Mr. Wonderful was there, impatiently waiting for me to say something. "Don't play them. I want to save them."

"For what?"

"I want to have a date night with you."

He lowered his head and looked at the floor. When he looked my way again, he had a smile, the one that spreads wide and causes line-dimples to run his face. His eyes lit with excitement. I melted. I don't know if I ever told you, but Tim has really pretty blue eyes. The thing that makes them unique is a circle of yellow around the pupil. They are like starburst eyes. I've seen them flash with excitement hundreds of times before, but then again, never like this.

"When. When's our date?"

"Next Saturday. It's your birthday." So, here's the skivvy. No one is invited to Tim's 65th birthday. February 26, 2022. Do not call. Do not come. It is a party for two.

Whenever Tim and I had date nights at home, we'd have shrimp cocktail, green grapes, sharp cheese, pepperoni, a variety of crackers and a bottle of sparkling cider. So that, my friends, is what we'll be eating. As for what we'll be doing. In my mind's eye, I'll be dancing with my man. to the tunes of Mr. Philip McTigue. Music has always been my connection to the good and not so good parts of my life. I'm not unique in that, but I'm one of those people who can, or could, name the singer/group who recorded the song, whether it was an original or a cover recording, the year the song came out, the album it was on, or the flip side of the 45, and most often who wrote the music and lyrics. I suck at math, but I was the bomb at music.

My very first 'concert' was with my mom at Fitton Field at Holy Cross stadium when I was ten, or so. I saw Bobby Vinton. I knew his songs because my mom and Meme listened to W.O.R.C. the music station in Worcester. Morning, noon, and night the station played Vinton's tunes leading up to his visit to Wormtown, an affectionate nickname of my hometown. Here's a link to an article if you want to know about Worcester.

http://www.golocalworcester.com/lifestyle/inside-guide/

Since I'd never been to a concert before that day, I had no way of knowing if I'd enjoy it or not, but it was wonderful being on an outing with my mother, just the two of us, a rarity, for sure. Anyway, when Mr. Vinton sang *Blue Velvet*, I knew then and there that my ass would be sitting in concert halls and nightclubs and tiny venues for the rest of my days. I became addicted to live music. My first 'real chosen concert' and I say that with some tongue-in-cheek, was a Bobby Sherman show, somewhere in Worcester. I was probably twelve or thirteen and I remember seeing several faces from my neighborhood at the show. I think I remember seeing Terry Canavan, Linda Fitch, and Susan LeBlanc in attendance. I'm probably wrong, but in my mind's eye, they were there.

Those kids had long ago gone from my mind and had stayed away for decades until very recently when I received an email through my Pulling Threads website. It was from a girl with whom I went to grade school. Let me tell you what I think I remember about her. Susan LeBlanc, she doesn't go by Susan anymore and she changed her last name when she married, so technically, the girl I knew as Susan LeBlanc is Sue Rohr, now. Her name may have changed, but the person I remember is still there.

I didn't pal around with Susan outside of school, she lived in Columbus Park, but she lived down from the rotary at Lovell Street and I lived up from it. We could have made the trek, it wasn't all that far, but there were plenty of kids on either side of the rotary, so we often spent our time in our own little neighborhood corners. That didn't keep me from 'knowing' or at least forming an opinion of Susan, the kid with the goofy smile (we all had one), the kid that fit in with everyone (we all tried to), the kid who didn't make waves, the kid who probably didn't even choose sides. Susan was just there, always there at the ready when someone was cast away or edged out. She was part of the safety zone in the playground.

From what I recall, she was really smart, too and never one to cause a raised eyebrow from a teacher. We all have kids like Susan LeBlanc in our grade schools. They're the ones who are happy to sit next to you in class pictures or on an infrequent bus trip on a school outing. To some extent, we are all those kinds of kids, or we should be. Truth is some kids shine more brightly at that age while others are comfortable being who they are. Susan LeBlanc was comfortable being who she was. How lucky for her.

During the formative years you get to know who's who in the way you get to know pieces on a checkerboard. The pieces in your life are here and then they are there and then they are gone from the game board called 'grade school'. They move on and arrange a whole new checkerboard in high school. They become adept at moving diagonally across black and red squares, forming new friendships, the real kind, the ones with a certain amount of depth and substance. They take the time to lean into those relationships before jumping onto life's big checkerboard, the one that takes longer to play and requires strategy and effort. That checkerboard is for keeps. It's where people build new lives with husbands and children. And where they lose loved ones before they've fully realized how much they need them. It's where they tend to their daily lives never expecting an opportunity to take a trip back in time.

It is the fortunate few who see a chance for reconnection with someone from their past and grab hold of it without expectation without reservation. Sue is that person. She reached out to someone she knew once upon a time, someone who wrote a book. She wanted to help celebrate the accomplishment and she did and it made me very happy to hear from her. And then no sooner had we become email buddies, she learned that our time was going to be cut short that I was going to be ending my game of checkers. She held nothing back, not her anger, nor her sadness.

The person who reached out to celebrate with me a few months ago may go by the name Sue Rohr now, but the person who sends a weekly email full of comforting words is Susan LeBlanc, a girl I knew way back when. And no sooner had I heard from Susan, I heard from Karen Flynn Larson Gouin.

I met Karen Flynn in high school, a time when you sit near or across from kids you never knew before. My memories of Karen seem to involve times that took place outside of classrooms. Maybe gym class — God I hated the uniforms we had to wear. And I swear every damned fire drill that took place at South High school took place during my gym class. The bell would ring and the whole lot of us had to vacate the building and stand in an alleyway with the whole student body staring and laughing.

I can't say for certain if Karen was in the alleyway being snickered at or not, but I think she was and I also think she was a classmate of mine in Mr. Power's class. I'm sure she'll let me know if any of my memories are real in a future email, the ones that have turned the corner from fun chit-chat to the telling of meaningful life experiences.

Karen first reached out when she received a copy of my first book, *Bullet Bungalow*, as a birthday present. She expressed very kind words and has kept me in the loop as she moves through Pulling Threads and we move through an email friendship. One I would have enjoyed continuing.

Tonight I had a really scary episode … It reminded me that I am a terminally ill woman and that I am going to die sooner rather than later. The experience kept me awake longer than usual and set me on a path of remembering who I was and what I was doing before my world was turned upside down and all of the important parts of who I am were dumped by the wayside.

Tonight I gathered the pieces of my life, took a quick peek at what they meant to me and what they mean to me, still. From misfires, music, and memories came an opportunity for me to be me. It allowed me to hang with my mother at a concert way back when, and with characters who I've come to know and love, and with people who came into my life, not once, but twice. It's true that the memories were fleeting, finding me in the still of the night, but I'll take it.

51. Unleashing Memories — For Others …

I have said it more than once, my end of life 'flash of memories' are more akin to a slow motion slideshow. Images appear then click away, followed in time by another image. There has been no urgency, no rapid-fire succession of snapshots, no movie reel on fast forward. For now, it appears I'm on a slow-motion-move toward death. Fingers crossed!

So far, I'd say I've had a really great end-of-life experience. Let's face it, my body is a mess, my skeleton is a mess, my internal organs are another story. As of November, my body scan showed no cancer involvement in my heart, lungs, liver, zero, zip, zilch; in my intestines, kidneys, bladder, no, nope, nada. The projected life expectancy of Sheryll O'Brien back then was six months, provided I didn't break anything. So far, so good.

For those of you who have been following along since the beginning, you'll remember my prayerful mantra since Day One was to be given no more than I could handle. Without question, there's been lots to handle, and lots to learn. First lesson: dying is difficult work. Second lesson: living while you are in the process of dying is difficult work. But, if you're a writer with hours and hours to kill, and you have to kill it while sitting on your ass, and you have a laptop computer, and a few of your faculties are still intact, then I ask you this very important question. Could my non-walk toward death be any more perfect? No, it could not be.

At the risk of sounding greedy, I'm going to throw this out there — no matter the pain, physical and emotional — no matter the lashing to the leather, day and night — no matter the inability to grab a glass of water or a solitary trip to pee — I want my six months. I want every single day, hour, and minute of the optimistic life expectancy I got a few months ago.

I find it funny that my death sentence of six months feels optimistic now. Back when I first heard those words, optimism wasn't part of my thinking. Perspective makes all the difference! To that end, I'm doing the two things that will keep me alive for as many of those days, hours, and minutes as possible, 1) I'm taking handfuls of pills around the clock to manage my pain and fluid on the brain, and 2) I'm sitting my ass in a chair 24/7. Since last fall, I've been on my ass: morning, noon, and night. If it sounds daunting, it is.

Here's a challenge. Sit down and plan on sitting there for one day. Now, don't move. If the doorbell rings, ignore it. If you want a snack, wait until someone you live with walks through the room and ask for one. If you want to breathe in some fresh air, wait until someone you live with opens a window for you. And how about that blanket across the room that you'd really like because you're cold from air pushing through the window that's still cracked a bit. Should you wake your slumbering housemates, or can you wait until you need to pee and kill two birds with one stone? And when you need to pee, don't forget to call someone to escort you — even if it's 2 AM. And before you get tucked back onto your seat make sure your groggy-eyed assistant gets the remote or mouse you dropped hours ago so that when you can't fall asleep you can watch television or play a computer game.

No Kathy, not Wordle or Nerdle. A game. You know, something FUN.

Breaking News: CIA to use Wordle and Nerdle instead of waterboarding as a new interrogation technique. Just sayin.

Okay, I'm back to the point of this ramble, and apparently we're talking about going pee. How delightful! Anyway, it's the middle of the night and you don't need to pee, so you don't disturb your loved ones for the window and the blanket, ergo, you don't get the remote or the mouse either, ergo, you'll have no choice but to sit and think. And think. And think. That's when most of my memories come. That's really what the 'flashing of my life' is — it's my memories being released. For me, they are ones I didn't even realize had made the grade of becoming a memory. Weddings, the arrival of a baby, the loss of a loved one, those are easy memories for us to find. These end of life memories are way more esoteric and *way* better.

To date, my memories are of good times and nice conversations. A recent memory was of my father-in-law, Patrick-Terrence-Francis O'Brien and me sitting in a small den off Mary O'Brien's kitchen. Grand Central Station, a mere ten feet away, was in full swing that fall afternoon. The den, on the other hand, was full of hopeful tension. Papa and I were watching a Red Sox game — a 1986 World Series playoff game. The patriarch of the OB clan was a Red Sox enthusiast, but he was also a realist, one who cautioned his new daughter-in-law not to get her hopes up. Sage advice coming from the man who waited year after year after year for the team to break the curse and win a damned series.

I, on the other hand, am a Red Sox romantic, a girl who loses the ability to reason the minute her boys of summer take their places in the infield or outfield, on the mound or behind the plate. I believe wholeheartedly, every year, that this is going to be our year. Worse than that, I am one of those who thinks she somehow dictates what happens during the game. If my team is winning, I do not move from my seat for fear I'll shift momentum. So, on that afternoon in 1986, one of us was sitting back and enjoying the game; one of us was leaning forward, legs in motion, hands sweating, and heart palpitating because she needed to pee and refused to go.

In 1986, the Sox came *thisclose* to winning it all. *Thisclose* means squat in the game of life and baseball. The team, my team, lost to the Mets in the seventh game. I took the loss hard, Papa took it in stride. I pushed from my seat in a huff, "Bunch of heartbreaking bums," I might have said.

To which he definitely replied, *"You're a corker, Mrs. O'Brien."*

I'll never forget the words because it was the first time I'd been referred to as a corker, and it was the first time Patrick-Terrence-Francis O'Brien called me Mrs. O'Brien. That recent memory brought a smile to my face and filled me with comfort. Isn't that just wonderful!

Before adding the steroid to my pharmaceutical intake, the slideshow in my head was all over the place and my blog writing reflected that. I sort of remember doing quite a bit of rambling and scrolling up and down to find out what I was rambling about. I don't read my blogs once they are posted, so I'm doing this bit of memory recall from a time when I had no memory recall to speak of. My writing is sort of a brain dump experience, now. I'm okay with that.

My 'life passing snippets' come from wherever they've been stored all these years, released by a song, or a conversation with my brother, or photographs from my childhood that Mom and Marjorie have been spending hours going through. Their scavenger hunt in the basement and attic unearthed a treasure trove of things that date back to when my mother was a little girl living in Shelburne County, Nova Scotia. I'm going to tell you a bit about my mother, and I'm not going to ask her for any help. I may miss the mark on accuracy, but her story will be here.

Ruth Shirley Thomas

The blonde, blue-eyed girl of four or five held onto her older brother's hand at the graveside of their father, Clark Robin Thomas. With them was their mother, Ruth Hannah Lyle Thomas, a woman in her mid-twenties, a widow in her mid-twenties.

The young family of four lived along the shore of the Bay of Fundy, a body of water between the mainland of Canada and the peninsula of Nova Scotia. The family was young and beginning to settle in for the long-haul, and then their lives were changed, forever. Clark Robin Thomas, a tall, strapping, red haired, bearded fisherman died hundreds of miles away from the waters surrounding his homestead.

A good provider for his lot, Clark fished the coast of Canada three seasons of the year, then headed to Massachusetts during the coldest and most brutal months to work as a ship hand for a wealthy Worcester industrialist. I'm not sure how the connection between the two men came about, but each year Clark Thomas would leave his family behind and head to the States for a few months — it was in Worcester that he became ill with pneumonia and died.

It is said his widow, my grandmother, Meme, went temporarily blind from the shock of the news. Within a matter of weeks, the body of Clark Robin Thomas was escorted back to Nova Scotia by an employee of the Worcester industrialist. A handful of years later, the employee, Tom Duquette, married the young Canadian widow and moved her and her two children to the States, to live in the home that would one day become my childhood home.

On her first day of school, Shirley Thomas met a girl named Margaret McKim, and the two embarked upon a lifelong friendship. Peggy passed away a handful of years ago, but she is thought of everyday by her forever friend.

A quick sidestep ... One Sunday night, Donnie and I were talking about my plans for my funeral, that's not really a funeral, but more like an open-house gathering. "I'm keeping things simple," I said. "There will be a milling about at the funeral home where people can take a look at some pictures and some of the things I've mentioned in my blogs, the Irish cable-stitch blanket Mom made me and the tablecloth from Hell I made her, and after a few words from Father Dude, and a eulogy by you and Donna, there will be a quick procession up and around the Lovell Street rotary, a quick pass by our childhood home and a quarter of a mile later, people can storm the Knights of Columbus hall for a party."

"Sounds perfect," he said with a catch in his voice.

"The girl from 01603 is leaving her earthly home via that zip code."

My brother thought it was great that we'd be passing the handyman's special we grew up in. After a few minutes of my waxing poetic about the barn red house with white trim and pretty rose bushes outside the kitchen window, he said, *"I don't know who the hell built that house, but there wasn't a damned 90 degree angle in that place. There wasn't a wall that was straight, or a single corner that met. It was like someone threw a pile of lumber in the backyard and a gust of wind whipped the wood into a house."*

"And insulated it with newspaper," I scoffed. "What the eff was that about? Behind the walls there was newspaper, nothing else. What. The. Eff?"

"Damned miracle the tinderbox didn't burst into flames."

"I used to pull newspapers out from behind a baseboard and read them."

"Jesus."

We have arrived at the point of this blog ... I received a text a few weeks ago from my niece, Kerrianne Barreto, née Hanlon. The young mother of three and busy nurse wanted to know if we could FaceTime. She heard her brother, Matt and his son, Shaun, spent time with me via that technology, and she wanted in. We scheduled our chit-chat for a Wednesday morning after her older two children were dropped off at preschool, and during a time she felt her youngest boy, Charlie, might nap or quietly play with his toes, or whatever.

I was beyond thrilled when I saw the pretty, vivacious blonde on my cell phone. The thing about Kerrianne is this, she lights up the space she fills. She's bright — like a little glare of sunshine when she enters an area. As such, you respond the way you would on a nice sunny day — you smile. Kerrianne started right in by saying she got the biggest kick out of the blog about Mary O'Brien's kitchen and the wall hanging with the walnut shells with each OB kid's name on it. She said she hadn't thought about that in years.

I told her that her dad used to do the New York Times crossword puzzle in pen every Sunday, which amazed me then, and amazed her now. And we talked about Covid, and what being a nurse during these sad times means to her. And then the conversation turned to me, she wanted the latest skivvy on my hospice visit and vitals and whether I was still Stable Mabel. She smiled that Kerrianne smile when I exclaimed that I was. Then she marveled, lamented is probably a better word, at the whole stealthiness of metastatic breast cancer.

After that go around, we got down to serious business — my blog. She's been reading, and she's been enjoying it, but she took exception with my proclamation that I make the best lasagna. She didn't belabor the point, probably because I'm on a time limit and shit, but she pressed in a bit about her hubby's lasagna.

And then this happened … A car pulled onto the driveway Super Bowl Sunday, I leaned forward to look out my picture window and sure enough the busy mother of three, ray of sunshine niece of mine was exiting her car with a tinfoil covered pan in her hands, a rectangular pan, the perfect shaped pan to hold a lasagna. She put it onto the front stoop, *"I know you're having French Onion soup for the game. Marcio made this and said it could wait until tomorrow night."* Mrs. Baretto waved and said, *"Marcio's parents are from Italy, you know.* ***This*** *is the best lasagna."* And just like that, we were in a smackdown.

And this is what happened next ... Tim put the Barreto lasagna into the oven Monday afternoon. A wonderful aroma filled the air and by the time the food cooked and cooled enough to cut and plate, my mouth was salivating. And when Tim handed me my dinner, I knew I was in for a treat. Most importantly, I knew from the get-go my lasagna and Mr. Barreto's lasagna were going to be worlds apart, at least continents apart.

I ate. I moaned and there wasn't a breakthrough pain being felt. I fired off a text.

Me: Okay. So apparently, I don't make lasagna. I sure the eff don't make THAT yumminess. My lasagna has marinara sauce — you know like the lasagna in AMERICAN restaurants. THAT pan of loveliness is like some gourmet treasure. So, here's the thing. I make the best FAKE lasagna in the world and Mr. Barreto makes the best REAL stuff. Thank you.
Kerrianne: I read Marcio your message and he was grinning ear to ear. He loves to make people food that they love to eat. I'm glad you enjoyed it.
Me: Bravo to Marcio. A job very well done. Muah!

Another food delivery came on Super Bowl Sunday. I slept through the event. Christine McTigue Mullaney, must have peeked in my front door and saw me conked out on my chair and went next door to Hannah's and handed off an Irish bread and a lovely plant. When I woke, Hannah delivered the two and the note left by Christine. She said I could share her story.

Christine McTigue Mullaney letter to Sheryll ...

Sheryll,

I wanted to thank you for sharing your blog. I don't know how you have the energy but your honesty and humor are a gift. I have remembered things that I haven't thought of in years when I read the blog. It puts a smile on my face, and at times a tear, but I expect that proves what a wonderful writer you are.

When I read the section about Auntie Fifi it brought me back to my kitchen at 176 Wildwood. Every holiday I would wait in anticipation for Aunt Fifi to stop by with her famous loaf. I loved her Irish Bread.

My mother once told her how fond I was of her bread, but how I wished she used more raisins. I couldn't believe that my mom told her that, but sure enough the next loaf was tweaked. Auntie Fifi told me she had adjusted her recipe to make me a special loaf. Then she gave me the recipe card. Wow!! I felt so special. I try and I try, but never does my loaf compare to hers. Maybe you and Tim can enjoy this with a cup of tea!

Love, Christine

When Tim realized there was an Irish bread in our home and it was a creation from Auntie Fifi's recipe, there was an audible moan. The reason? When I was diagnosed, Mr. Wonderful decided on the spot that he needed to get healthy because he needed to be here for our daughters for the long-haul. His solution? Become a vegan. With the snap of a finger, Tim did away with everything he's eaten for sixty-five years and began consuming sawdust and nuts. Hannah has lived the vegan lifestyle for quite some time, so she took him under her wing and fed him things of the vegan world.

The thing about Mr. Wonderful is this: his strength is all about making decisions and commitments, and never shall either be broken. Unless there's an Irish bread thrown into the mix. Mr. Wonderful eyeballed the Irish Bread, went online, saw eggs and buttermilk as ingredients and pushed another moan, then offered a shrug of his shoulder, *"Oh, well. Looks like I'm cheating tonight."*

Mr. and Mrs. O'Brien had tea and bread for supper. Christine, it was every bit as good as Fifi's. A job well done, indeed! Even the Irish One raved about your loaf when she visited the next day.

Now, back to my mother's trip down memory lane. It has been a bittersweet experience for Mom to look at photos from my youth, and from the big days of celebration: my graduation from high school, my wedding day, and the trips home from the hospital with my new babes in arm. The deeper she went in the boxes, the more she unearthed from her life, the one that preceded me.

On a recent visit, she handed me an envelope. It was weathered by time, had a postmark dated January 31, 1946 from Nova Scotia, and was addressed to: Allan & Shirley Thomas, #10 Hobson Avenue, Worcester, Mass, U.S.A. It contained three letters, one dated November and another dated January, both written by my mother's grandfather, and one note without a date written by my mother's grandmother. I'm sharing the letter from November.

Hello Tiddlywinks,

How are you getting along, by this time suppose you are big as ever and go to school every day. I bet none of the kids can beat you in school unless you are different from what you was when you was in Barrington. We got a rainstorm today and I am just keeping a fire going and doing nothing but eat and I guess I went to sleep in the chair once or twice. Mickey is stretched out good. I guess he has been eating something outdoors. He catches a rabbit sometimes. If he can find one. Asleep now. Grammy has gone on Cape Island for a few days. Wish you could see the big boy up to Donald fat as butter and come good. Always laughing. Hardly ever cries only when something hurts him. He is cutting teeth now and they are coming hard. Suppose you are giving music lessons now quite a piano player. So I hear. I went hunting one day with a couple men. We got a nice deer and saw several moose. Well guess must stop. Love to all, Grampy

The art of letter writing … It's changed over the years. In fact, our generation doesn't do it often enough. When people take the time, we find the central elements of the practice haven't changed one bit. My mother's grandfather pulled his memories together and shared them with his granddaughter. Christine McTigue Mullaney pulled her memories together and shared them with me. She very easily could have dropped off the tasty treat she took time to bake without mentioning her trip down memory lane, but she didn't. She shared her fondness of a woman who meant the world to her and to me. I guess that's the legacy of a life well lived. Someone you care about might pull a recipe from a cupboard one day and spend time with you by kneading some dough. Someone might dig through a memento box and find letters from their long lost grandfather, a man who called her, Tiddlywinks.

Imagine my delight knowing that I played a very small part in Christine's memories of Auntie Fifi. Imagine my pleasure in reading words from a man who died more than a half-century ago, words he wrote to his granddaughter, the child who would one day become my mother. One day, my granddaughter, Hadley, will read my blog and she will learn about me and about the wonderful people who pressed into my life when I was losing it. When I needed their company the most and when I needed the reminder that memories matter, my dear Hadley will know who helped me on this journey. At the end of the day, at the end of our lives, memories are all we really have. So go make a few. I still am.

52. 1-800-Call-A-Priest and Prepare for Hallucinations ...

Donna came to visit! The reason you haven't heard much about my bestie lately is because I haven't seen her since early December. Think back. Remember now? The last time I mentioned Donna Eaton visiting me was when she dragged a priest to Wildwood for a little tête-à-tête. The guy who hung out with us that day wore a clerical collar, but that did nothing to cloak Father Dude's relaxed vibe, conspicuously on display with a pair of jeans and a sweatshirt. I can't say for certain, but in my mind's eye, that's what he was wearing.

As you may recall, I decided on the spot that 'he's the one that I want, ooo, ooo, ooo, honey, the one that I want' to pave my way toward the Pearly Gates. BTW, that little ditty flew through my head courtesy of Miss Olivia Newton John. Thank you very much and now I'd appreciate her jumping off the loop inside my head. Thank you very much. And, hello Phil McTigue. Please feel free to exclude that song from any future CDs. Seriously. I don't need the Grease tune. I'm suffering enough, don't ya think?

It's kinda early in the blog for a sidestep ... Before we get to the point of this ramble, and to be perfectly honest I don't know what the point is yet, so it's a fine time for us to take a little detour. When this blog grows up and is ready for Guru's posting, I will title it. At the moment, it is numbered 52, but before long it will have some weird title — ooo, the suspense is killing me. Given it's a little after 3 AM, and I'm having enough breakthrough pain in my right thigh and shin to keep me from sleeping, we're going places in my head, undetermined places, isn't that just wonderful?

I had a hospice visit earlier today, technically it was yesterday given the hour and all. I pronounced myself Stable Mabel while my nurse did her decontamination process by wiping everything within arm's reach with an array of antibacterial, antifungal, anticootie cloths. In this day and age of the Greek alphabet of Covid, I am thrilled with her dousing techniques although I'd appreciate the cessation of an aerosol blast of Lysol my way. Just sayin.

Anyway, my vitals were awesome. My heart did the appropriate number of rat-a-tat-tats, and my lungs expanded on inhale and deflated on exhale, and sounded great. And while my legs are freakishly swollen, think tree trunk in appearance from my thighs to my ankles, there was only moderate pain when Nurse M did her touching and poking here and there thing, each touch usually accompanied by a preemptive apology.

During the question and answer round of our time together, my answer was, “No,” to any breakthrough pain since her previous visit. And, “No,” to any current pain. I threw in a joke that I’m feeling so good I’ve begun wondering if I even have cancer. Then raised the possibility that I’m part of some wacky experiment.

“Hey, let’s get some 64-year-old dumbass, tell her she’s terminal, scare the crap out of her so she doesn’t move a damned muscle, lash her to a leather chair, and see what happens.”

If not for the pain I’m currently in I could believe that scenario. And I wouldn’t be the slightest bit pissed. Just sayin.

Back to the sidestep ... I really don’t plan what I’m going to write about. I make lists from time to time that contain things of note: like the envelope my mom gave me, the one that had letters from her grampy. I knew at some point I’d make reference to it, but the when and why was a surprise to me. It’s very lovely how things find their way into one of my blogs. Having said that, there is a blog that’s been banging in my head for months. It is not going to be a nice blog. It is going to have a whole lot of anger associated with it.

I’ll give you a hint. When an oncologist walks into a room, introduces herself to a woman who’s sitting on an exam table wearing nothing but a hospital johnny, and tells the nervous woman she has terminal cancer and there is nothing that can be done to stop or reverse course, the conversation, in my humble opinion, should turn to an expression of sympathy and the assurance that pain management has jumped to the forefront of medical care being considered. Again, in my humble opinion, there shouldn’t be a full-frontal, scare tactic assault and emotional shakedown of the nearly naked woman. That is what I believe happened to me.

My shakedown started with the next words spoken that day, *"And you are going to die an **excruciatingly painful death**."* Those words paved the way for me to make decisions, unmake decisions, and regret the eff out of the ultimate decisions I made. That blog isn't this blog. But, it is sooooo coming! And be forewarned. I am carrying a lot of emotional baggage about what happened back in November and December. I will be writing about it. I have to write about it. I'm just not there yet.

So, getting back to this blog, the one that isn't pissing me off. One of the things I recently noted during a dark winter night are the differences in what people bring or send or create for the hospice patient. There have been many deliveries: breads, soups, puddings and lasagnas. They were delivered by hand, then gobbled up around bouts of nausea. And there were deliveries that hang on my walls now. They bring me lots of enjoyment. And there were deliveries of music. some of which I'll be listening to on date night.

You've heard about those wonderful arrivals, but there were two others of note that I have been remiss in mentioning. They've made the lists, but I never read my lists. Tonight, I remembered them on my own.
During the holiday season, I received two lovely and tasty Edible Arrangements from Eileen McTigue McDonald — yeup there's another McTigue! The gift-boxed arrangements had an assortment of goodies, but the hand dipped strawberries most definitely deserve a shoutout. The exquisitely shaped and ripened to perfection strawberries were the size of a small child's hand and beyond delicious.

The second lovely and tasty treat was a beautiful assortment of candied and carameled apple sections from one of Tim's coworkers. (The Warden probably did a facepalm because carameled is not a word. It is now! Teehee). Anyway, the apple slices were dipped in yumminess and had lots of crunchies and munchies sprinkled across the top. And they were to die for — appropriate, all things considering.

When it comes to deliveries, however, my bestie doesn't fool around. She doesn't deliver food, she delivers human beings, and the one she brought me was of the ordained variety. I choose besties rather well, don't ya think?

Now, getting back to the reason Donna hasn't visited since the Presenting of the Priest, she had extensive surgery done on her foot or her heel or her tendon or her ankle. I don't know exactly what part of her pod was worked on because I can't stand hearing about injuries and surgeries which is absurd on the face of things because I'm telling all of you about my medical crap.

You should note … If I was reading this blog, I'd skip the medical stuff and I would skip the stuff about tomb-like scanning devices and stick to the stuff that doesn't skeeve me out. In any event, the surgery Donna had on her foot rendered her immobile for weeks. So, while I've been lashed to the leather in Worcester, Donna has been sitting her ass on a sofa or in a wheelchair in Oxford waiting for her heel to heal. Between you, me and the lamppost, I've done a lot less bellyaching about the 24/7 sitting thing than Donna has done, but, whatevs.

Three weeks ago, her cast came off and a big-ass boot contraption went on. After a week or so of time-measured-ambulating, five minutes here, five minutes there, Donna got the go-ahead for some upright, weight-bearing roaming privileges. She roamed to 183 Wildwood Avenue.

The former medical professional came prepared for a visit with the hospice patient. She was double-masked, offered proof of a negative rapid Covid test, and I think she held her breath as she hobbled across the room and plunked onto my sofa. We stared at one another for many seconds, then said the same thing at the same time. "You look really good. I'm feeling really good. Good. That's good."

Once that banal crap was over, we were off and running. Blogs. Priests. Eulogies. Kids. Grandkids. Husbands. Weather. Pain killers. Old Orchard. Hospice. **My mother.** Donna always asks about my mother, then says something sympathetic through a trail of caught emotion. When we were nearing the end of our time together, I brought up the Priestly One. "I need to call him."

Silence. "I should sort of tell him what kind of thing I'm having and find out if he still wants to advocate my getting into Heaven." Silence. "I'm guessing he's gonna want to say something at the gathering, you know, to sort of commiserate with my peeps about my departure and prepare the Big Guy for my arrival."

She laughed. *"Give him a call. He'll come by."*

"I called once and planned a get together, but I needed to cancel. Can't remember why, snow maybe." I shrugged then said what was really on my mind. "I'm sort of trying to stay on the downlow. You know, out of sight, out of mind. Kinda hard hiding out from God if I invite a holy dude into my home. I imagine the Big Guy has some sort of **GPS**: **G**od**P**riest**S**atellite capability, so I intend on staying off radar. Actually, I think the prolonged sitting is working. There's no attention being drawn by Sheryll O'Brien, and as long as Mr. Wonderful dusts me once a week, it's all good."

"If you don't want a visit, just give Father Dude a call."

"Huh. 1-800-Call-A-Priest. Never thought of that."

That's why God gave us best friends. When one is daft from skull cancer, the other has her finger to the pulse of the problem. I'm going to place the call soon. I need to discuss a fear that's digging deep in my bones during the long, lonely nights, huh, digging deep in my bones, might be the source of the breakthrough pain in my legs. Psychosomatic? Nope, the pain is from the cancer-eating-rodent.

Anyway, I've been brought to the brink of discussing my fears on three different occasions, with three different people. I'm not going to name them because each person shared a personal end-of-life story about a loved one that included bits and pieces about hallucinations. Full disclosure. Having hallucinations is the part of the death experience that has rendered me scared shitless. I haven't had the guts to spell it out, but the people with whom I've skirted the issue were astute enough to pick up on my fears. The heebie-jeebie shivers and upper lip sweat probably tipped them off well enough. So, here it is folks, the point of this blog. **I am terrified about what's next.** I can put those words in a blog. But, I haven't had the guts to say them out loud. **I am terrified about what's next.**

I recently wrote a book for the hospice patient and their loved ones. *Be, still* is similarly fashioned to *Be* the book I wrote for Hadley. The headings are identical, the content is very different. I wrote *Be, still* because I've learned an awful lot about myself while in the care of hospice and I learned a whole lot about hospice itself. And though I know what this experience is to me, I haven't a clue what it is for anyone else.

When I was told my life expectancy, on the long end, was probably six months, I pulled the immediate threads and found there were things I needed and wanted to do right then, that day. Prepare my family members, get my things in order, keep myself from going insane. ✓. ✓. Eh. The other threads that needed pulling were personal to me. Keep my creative juices flowing. Write a blog. Write a book for Hadley. Write another book? Yeup. The last one just sort of found its way to me a couple of weekends ago. *Be, still* was a labor of love for me. It's only been through my end-of-life experience when I've put myself first. I am still a wife to Tim, and a mother to Hannah and Jessica, and a MammyGrams to Hadley, and a daughter to Shirley, and a sister to Don and Marjorie, and a friend to many, but the role I have for those people changed the second I learned my fate.

I no longer have the luxury of a bunch of tomorrows. I won't be able to help my girls through their grief. I won't be planning anymore annual vacations in Wells, hell, I won't even be going on this year's trip. The focus of this time has become a bit myopic. I think about today and this minute because it's just too fucking hard to think about all of the other days, the ones I am not going to have. And when I started feeling guilty about not joining in on conversations, and plans, and hopes, and dreams that everyone else gets to continue having, I had to find my way to a place of acceptance. I had to find me. The person who is going it alone and when I found her, I needed to give her permission to support and comfort herself. During my hospice process, I realized I needed to Be kind to myself, and I needed to Be thoughtful of others, and I needed to Be strong for everyone.

I know I am strong… I am handling this shit fest remarkably well if I do say so myself. Fortunately for me, countless people have said I'm showing remarkable strength. People whose opinions I value, like my sister-in-law, Kathy, who often remarks about my strength. Just hearing her say so helps keep me strong. Truth be told, though, I'm scared. I fear what will come with morphine. Hallucinations, I fear.

I'm going to include two sections of *Be, still* in this blog. They are ones that I will be referring to time and time again.

Be Strong

You've learned you are terminal — perhaps you've battled valiantly against cancer — the surgeries, the radiation, the chemo — or perhaps you've struggled for years with breathing issues and now find drawing a simple breath is anything but simple. No matter what illness brought you to death's door and brought you to the decision to enter hospice, you are here now. You may be weary and think you are without any reserve of strength. Dig deep. You might be surprised at how much strength you have left.

When you can … Be strong enough to make the decision to enter hospice. And then … Be strong enough to allow strangers into your home — and strong enough to be honest with them about everything. Be strong enough to tell family members what you want by way of Do Not Resuscitate, or Do Not Intubate, or Do Not Transport to a Hospital. Be strong enough to feel the pain that will become your constant companion. Be strong enough to ask for help when the pain becomes unbearable, even if it means moving to the next level, morphine. Be strong enough to face the long, lonely hours that come night after night. There is so much to learn when the world is still. You'll have times of fear, but there will be times of comfort. You may want avoidance, but if you lean in, you may find acceptance. It is in the stillness when you will learn that grace helps shoulder all burdens.

And then ... Be strong enough to ask for help, or a hug. No one should go through death alone, so when life really challenges you, and it will, reach out to the people who will comfort you, then lean in.

Please Be strong.

Be Fearless — Not Reckless

There are going to be times when you don't want to turn the corner and follow a well-worn path toward death. That corner usually involves the decision to take morphine, even just a little, just enough to take the edge off of pain that just isn't being handled through the normal course of things. That is a very difficult corner to turn, but staying where you are will cause you and your loved ones emotional pain. They do not want to see you suffer. It's really that simple for them, but taking that first dose of morphine is anything but simple for you.

And know ... You may want to tough it out but there is a cost to digging in and tolerating too much pain. You may fear what is next if you take that first dose. The reality is this, you are dying. It is a painful process. Admitting you need a little something stronger is not a sign of weakness, it is a sign of acceptance.

Please Be Fearless — Not Reckless.

I hope that when the time comes for me to act upon the hardest of all these words I have the courage to do so. And I'm just going to throw this out there, in case He is still listening to my prayers. Please don't give me more than I can handle. Amen.

A dedication to the hospice patient and the people who love them …

This book is written with the hope that it will bring comfort, through understanding, about what a final journey can be. When I entered hospice, I thought I'd be putting all of my hopes and dreams aside, that I'd be giving up control, that I'd crawl onto a bed and wither away. I was wrong. I gave up nothing and I learned that this has been the most rewarding time of my life.

The time you spend under the care of hospice can be whatever you are able to make it. Some days will be challenging, pain may be your only companion and fears may keep you awake, other days may bring a flood of memories of dreams fulfilled while others may awaken a desire to write your first poem, or read your first sonnet.

There is no escaping the emotional and physical pain of your final journey, just as there has been no way to avoid them during your life's journey. My hope is that the passages in this book offer gentle reminders to you and your loved ones that while your days are few, there is still a lot of living and loving to do.

Please spend a few moments together, choose a page, read it, share your thoughts with one another, reminisce, laugh, and cry together. You may find that this time is the most important time of your life, so live it, and then —

Be, still …

Fondly,
Sheryll O'Brien

53. Hadley Day and Night …

It is 4 AM Saturday morning. It's Tim's birthday and 183 Wildwood is on lockdown from the outside world beginning mid-afternoon. Hadley will be heading off for an overnight at her dad's house around 1 PM, and the general plan is this: whatever needs to be done in the OB household needs to be completed before Tim and I do the most important thing on this day, take a nap.

That is a very big part of our plan and it is scheduled to begin at three and end at five. Since we're planning on staying up past bedtime, correction: since I'm planning on staying up past bedtime which technically is whenever one of the pesky Tramadol pills conks me out, I'm going to need to do some preemptive resting of the bones.

As for Tim, he usually tucks me in at night, heads upstairs, and hits the hay whenever he can turn his mind off. Today's afternoon nap is part of my birthday present to my old man — the man who loves taking an afternoon nap. The man who rarely gets to take one. So, when Hannah leaves with Hadley, Mr. and Mrs. Wonderful will shut the front door, silence our phones, and close our eyes.

I'm doing a little more blogging before that bliss. I think it is very evident that I adore Hadley. I eagerly await her daily breakfast time, and her return home from school. I love hearing about her adventures in the great world beyond Wildwood Avenue. This past week, there wasn't much by way of traveling near or far from home. Hadley was on February school vacation. That means I've had plenty of time with my favorite human in the whole universe. It has been wonderful. It has been exhausting. It is paving the way for one hell of a nap.

Before my mid-day slumber can commence, there's the pesky business of Tim's birthday. The family festivities are set for this morning because Tim and I are having our date night, tonight! So, in order to fit everything in, Hannah and Hadley will be having breakfast at their place while Tim and I kick back with Mr. Chase and Mr. Sanborn. Then, while he's getting ready for the day, Hadley will sneak in for 'Operation Celebration' and Hannah will hang back at her place until she hears Hadley's knock on the wall between our two homes. Let me tell you how 'Operation Celebration' came to be. After much discussion with Hadley yesterday about what I could and could not do by way of executing a birthday soiree, Hadley decided she was ready to go it alone.

"Don't worry, MammyGrams, I'm seven. I can handle this. First, I need to make Gee a card." So off she went.

A little sidestep … My office is upstairs. It's set in Jessica's childhood bedroom and, when I was finished arranging and decorating it, it was everything I'd envisioned for my writing room. The walls are dove gray, the area rug is a patterned Berber in chocolate brown, a bit darker than the scallop-edged swag burlap curtains on the window. The furniture: desk, end table, and glass-enclosed bookcase are black and Colonial in design, and for a subtle pop of color I added a console table in distressed navy and a big-ass recliner in denim. My favorite piece in the room is a small, electric black iron fireplace.

I used to spend hours in my writing room either sitting at my desk, or kicked back on my laptop editing my work or researching. I'm not sure I ever mentioned this, but researching was one of my most favorite parts of the writing process. Over the course of 17 books, I took my Pulling Threads characters across the globe — a most perfect way to travel for someone who didn't like going across the street. But, that's a story for another time and I think I already covered it in a blog so let's get back to the sidestep in the blog I'm writing.

On one wall of my office, I have black frames with my book covers proudly displayed. For artwork, I have a canvas print of my favorite painting, Monet's *Impression Sunrise*. It hangs over the console table and is softly lighted from below by a beautiful antique brass lamp. Across the room, I have a canvas print of *Café Terrace at Night*, by van Gogh. This is a bold, colorful painting — not my usual taste, at all. When it comes to Vincent's work, I am drawn to his softer pieces, particularly his *Pink Peach Tree*, a canvas I had hanging in my living room until that knock came upon the door before Christmas, and the Irish One was offering me a painting I casually mentioned liking. That wall space is now occupied by *Lána Suaimhneas*, the painting done by Jennifer and named by Yours Truly.

At the moment, I'm not sure where Vinny's piece is. I should track it down and find a place for it just on the odd chance I run into the artist during my stint in the afterlife. I would rather be able to say it's hanging on a wall somewhere in my house, than having to admit it's tucked behind a piece of furniture or worse yet, hanging in my upstairs bathroom. It could be for all I know. The horrors. I need to ask Tim about this potential pitfall.

As for *Café Terrace at Night*, the picture is exactly as I'd described a place in Nice, France, in *They Run*. I was shocked when I saw Vinny's painting. It was as if he'd read my scene and painted it for me.

Anyway, back to my sidestep .... I spent a lot of time choosing pieces for my very first home office. When Hannah and Hadley moved into their own place, Tim and I claimed our home — every square inch of it, for us, for the first time ever. He'd already set office space for himself when the pandemic hit and he started working from home, so establishing personalized space for me was about me, what I wanted, redecorating the upstairs was about us.

Tim painted the hallway walls dove gray to match my office walls, then painted the bathroom walls a medium-dark blue. The color is Distance, SW 6243, in the Sherwin-Williams line, if you're interested. The fixtures in both rooms are antique bronze, and the swag window curtain and shower curtain, as well as the throw rugs and decorative towels are linen, in color and fabric. The bathroom has a very spa-like vibe and I love it. I loved it. I haven't seen my office or any part of my upstairs since December 1st. Several pieces of my furniture are now in my living room because that is my new office space. I am so incredibly fortunate that I can still do what I love to do, and surround myself with my things, but I miss hanging out upstairs.

There is another space upstairs that had a makeover, way back when, and it is all about Hadley. The closet in my office was the perfect size for a small office for a kid, so we took the door off and made it a dedicated office space for our girl. We put a white rattan desk and matching chair in, put a hanging shoe organizer on one wall, filled it with tools of trade for an elementary school aged student: pencils, erasers, post-it notes, crayons, stapler, tape, and, and, and, then finished it all off with twinkling lights wrapped around and around the crossbar normally used for hanging clothes. We finished it off with a big-ass red *Hadley* sticker on one of the walls. While MammyGrams wrote her stories in her office, Hadley did her remote learning for nearly a year in her very own office. It was a perfect setup for both of us, another way for us to be together. MammyGrams and Hadley. Mr. Wonderful says we're a pair that could beat a flush. I agree, completely.

The writing of this blog is a little different from all others. I knew what I was going to write about going in — Hadley's February vacation and what we did together. She and I planned some things ahead of time and other things just sort of happened along the way. First off, each morning after breakfast she needed to do 15 minutes of online math and language work assigned by her teacher. Then, it was no-holds-barred.

For years, even the years when Hannah and Hadley lived in my home, Hadley would spend every other Saturday having a sleepover with MammyGrams. Think about the logistics of having a sleepover with her grandmother, the woman with whom she lived. Come sleepover time, she'd grab a pillow and a blanket and a hundred or so stuffed animals from her upstairs bedroom and relocate them to the living room. She did the schlepping with the excitement of a kid heading off for a bona fide sleepover with friends. Bless her little heart. The every-other-week events meant I'd be camping out on a recliner in my living room and my overnight guest would mull her options a bit then pull up space on the floor, or ask for her cot to be set up, or simply flop on the sofa.

Ever since the Hannah and Hadley homesteading took place next door, sleepovers involved a little more effort. Hadley needed to walk all the way from her house to my house. The schlepping took several trips for the armfuls of stuffies and blankets and pillows and whatever toys and games we were going to play. With each opening and closing of the front door, the excitement built and built. For her, and for me. I loved every minute of our special time.

I am a creative thinker, so every sleepover had a special theme, some were low-key, i.e., everything needed to be brown: burgers and chocolate milk for dinner and brownies for dessert; others were done up big. If it was a safari adventure sleepover, she'd spend some time looking for hidden Beanie Babies native to the Serengeti: lion, elephant, giraffe, zebra, and then nestle in for a dozen or so episodes of Wild Kratts.

If it was a scavenger hunt sleepover, I'd give it a theme: fairy tale princesses, witches and wizards, or pirates and treasure chests. I'd write all of the clues specific to the theme in rhyme, print them and scroll them, then Tim would hide them throughout the yard. The only rule was this: if she happened to see a scroll but it wasn't the one she was seeking, she had to leave it be. Without question, the scavenger hunts were Hadley's favorite.

She also enjoyed her Barbie sleepovers. She'd arrive in a pair of themed pajamas, pull her hair high, run a little eyeshadow over her lids (and mine), and a little blush across her cheeks (and mine), and a swipe of Bonne Bell Lip Smacker onto her smackers (and mine), then nestle in for a Star Light adventure, or Princess adventure, or one of the gazillion Dreamhouse

Adventures. My personal favorite is the one where Barbie, Skipper, Chelsea, and Stacie stay at their grandmother's house and each sister adopts a puppy: Honey, Rookie, DJ, and Taffy. OH. MY. GOD. Moving on now and yes, I'm a little embarrassed.

Since my diagnosis, Hadley and I have been having half-sleepovers. They usually begin around 3 PM and they end at 9 PM, or earlier, if need be. The theme for the half-sleepover heading into vaca week was Campout. She came schlepping her sleeping bag (purple with bright pink splashes here and there), a purple thermos, and a pink plastic lantern. She and I played a few hands of Go Fish and sang a few campfire songs. Then she headed to the kitchen to toast marshmallows and shake the hell out of a Jiffy Pop — raise the top — popcorn fun fest with Gee. The sound of her laughter filled me with joy.

During the rest of the week, we spent time reading passages from *Be* and a Nancy Drew: Clue Crew book. She worked on her first ever paint-by-number set, and played a math game with two enormous sponge dice. Hadley loves to set rules for everything, the dice game was no different.

"I'll toss a die and you'll toss the other one. We'll guess a number and whoever comes closest will decide if I do addition, subtraction, or multiplication with the numbers."

As soon as the numbers settled Hadley went about her math business and Sheryll Bodine checked her math business. I handled the equations with ease. Seems I'm fine with adding, subtracting and multiplying digits 1 through 6. Thank you very much. And if you are judging me, you really shouldn't judge the infirmed. Thank you very much.

We played countless computer games, even a battle or two of Minesweeper, and we did lots and lots of chit-chatting, all of which I got on tape. I know the intent of the tapes is for Hadley, but I've taken to listening to them at night. They make me laugh. They make me cry. I suspect they will have the same effect on my girl.

Now, back to Hadley's plan for Tim's birthday … She spent time in her upstairs office making his card, a beautiful creation, by the way. When she got to the top of the stairs to come down she hollered.

"I'm coming down, MammyGrams."

To which I replied, "Thanks for the warning."

She laughed that wonderful laugh of hers. When she got to my recliner, she showed me three things she took from her office.

"MammyGrams, I'm going to put these into the Memory Box you gave me for Christmas because when I look at them I think of you." She held out a Happy Face mouse I got for her first day of remote learning. Then she held out a picture she drew of herself on her last day of remote learning. *"I was happy about going to school."*

I took hold of the picture, "You sure were. Look at that big smile on your face."

"I was a little scared, you know."

"I know."

Silence. *"I'm a little scared about you."*

"I know."

"But mom said I can Be strong."

I turned tear-filling eyes away before she showed me the last thing she wanted to put into her Memory Box. It was a pocket calendar I gave her a couple years ago. She flipped through the pages and showed me little pictures she'd drawn and words she'd written, all misspelled and with some alphabet letters written backwards. It was all so wonderful.

"Do you think I could have another one of these?"

"On it." I grabbed my laptop, opened Amazon, and scrolled through the pages of calendars until she chose what she wanted.

She waved the one in her hand in my direction, *"I'm putting this one in the Memory Box."*

"Good idea." I suspect Hadley will make a notation in her new calendar commemorating Tim's birthday celebration. And for the record, Hadley was absolutely correct when she said she could handle the festivities. She even handled the birthday cake.

As soon as she burst through the front door this morning, she went to the kitchen. I heard the opening of the pantry, then the freezer, then the silverware drawer, then the cupboard where we keep the paper plates. A minute later, she rolled her little table into the living room, put it in front of Gee's chair, then made a few trips back and forth to the kitchen.

"I'm making Gee a pancake birthday cake."

I turned on my cell phone and taped the kid as she made a 7-layer frozen pancake and strawberry frosted creation. After spreading each layer with bubblegum pink frosting and stacking them high, she did a full go-around of frosting, then added green, yellow and blue sugar crystals on top. She finished it off with a 6 and 5 candle that I ordered from Amazon weeks ago.

She quickly cleaned up her work area, ran to the staircase, banged hard on the wall, the signal for her mom to come over, continued upstairs to wake Auntie J, told Tim to stay put until she called him down, then raced back downstairs, arriving at the same time as her mother. She grabbed hold of Hannah's hand and dragged her to the kitchen. *"Wait until you see the cake I made Gee."*

"You made him a cake? Did Auntie J help?"

"Nope. I did it all by myself."

"Where is it?"

"Hiding in the microwave."

I heard the micro door snap open and a bawdy laugh came from Hannah. *"You made that? What is that?"*

"A pancake birthday cake."

"Oh. My. God." Hannah peeked into the living room. *"Did she think to do that?"*

"Yeup."

"Oh. My. God."

The birthday boy was called down by Hadley. She presented him with the plate and he blew out the candles. Then Hannah took the pancake birthday cake to the kitchen and laughed her ass off as she tried to cut it.

"Hey, Hadley."

"Yeah."

"Did you microwave the pancakes before you frosted them?"

"Nope. The frosting would have melted."

Hannah laughed again and continued sawing through the 7-layer, frozen pancake birthday cake.

I'm no longer able to plan and execute a party. Apparently, I no longer need to because Hadley has it covered. Sort of bittersweet.

54. Date Night — Part One ...

Mr. Not-so-Wonderful almost ruined Date Night before it even began. For the past 35 years, whenever Tim and I planned a Date Night it included three things: 1) an outdoor playday for the girls, 2) an early bedtime for the girls, 3) some dinner, a movie, a little dancing, and an early bedtime for the adults. In order to make numbers 1 and 2 happen — so number 3 could happen — Tim would take Hannah and Jessica to Rocketland, a playground in Auburn. That's where he ran them ragged.

The rocket playground was themed in honor of Robert Hutchings Goddard, the American engineer, professor, and physicist, who is credited with inventing and building the world's first liquid-fueled rocket. Goddard was born and raised in Worcester, but the maiden rocket launch took place from a parcel of land that currently sits between the Auburn Town Library and fire station located at Drury Square. The town got bragging rights for the first ever 10-9-8-7-6-5-4-3-2-1 'liftoff' and used those bragging rights wisely when they named the children's park.

Anyway, back to the ramble … Tim would take the girls to Rocketland and let them ride bikes around the quarter mile track, or climb up, around, and through, an awesome wood structure with moving walkways, chain and rubber ladders, twisty tunnels that eventually deposited them at a gravel playground with bucket and tire swings, a climbing apparatus worthy of Cirque du Soleil trainees, and plenty of vertigo-inducing spring mechanism animal seats that move back and forth, and left and right, simultaneously. I'm not sure which inventor came up with those dizzying-doozies, but just watching my kids move in all directions caused my innards some distress.

While Tim was doing a preemptive tuckering out of our tots, I was home preparing our soiree. Our menu was set way back when on our first at-home Date Night and never varied. For 35 years we had: Shrimp Cocktail, the easy-peasy, delightfully delicious must-have of our nibble fest. I have some skills in the applianced room of my home, but I am not a culinary queen by any stretch of the imagination. If a recipe calls for a honey-mustard dipping sauce, I'll grab honey from my cupboard, mustard from my fridge (upping my game by grabbing the Grey Poupon), mix the two together and call it a voilà day.

Not only am I not one to mix a sauce from scratch if I don't have to, I am not one to skin or devein any land or sea creature I am readying to eat. So, my shrimp preparation boils down to this: I open a plastic bag and remove from it 32-36 pieces of big-ass jumbo shrimp, drop them into a kettle of cold water, bring said kettle to a boil for the appropriate number of minutes, drain and rinse the pretty pinkish prawn under cold water for 2-3 minutes, then pop them into the fridge for several hours. We always make extra so there are some to nibble during Date Night afterglow. Bow, chica, bow, bow!

Another sidestep ... Way back when, when the rugrats returned from the park, all rosy-cheeked, and too pooped to pop, they'd walk into the house and unison, *"What stinks?"*

To which their mother would reply, "Your dinner if you don't get upstairs and into the tub right now."

Their little feet would take to the treads before I finished my sentence. Tim would follow them up with a 'well done' nod, prepare a bubble bath for two, dump in a ton of bath toys, and depending on their age, would either park his ass on the closed hopper to supervise, or mill about the upstairs while bubbly bath water bubbled the day's dirt and sweat off of our cherubs. Upon their return downstairs, they'd both unison their delight at their dinner offering: spiral or elbow or Spongebob mac and cheese.

"Yes!"

I would send a smile Tim's way and we'd do a little checklist rundown. "Sufficiently tuckered?"

"Check."

"Bathed and ready for bed."

"Check."

"Full bellies for a full night's sleep."

"Check."

"Early bedtime."

"Yes, please."

"I meant for the kids."

"Uh huh."

That conversation happened every Date Night — Mr. and Mrs. Wonderful are nothing if not predictable. Or are they? This past Saturday, Tim was responsible for the shrimp prep, so into the pot went 12 pieces of shrimp. Why so few in number you might ask? Was Sheryll experiencing nausea and the thought of munching on cooked-to-perfection crustaceans generously dipped in cocktail sauce too much to bear? NO. It was because my husband decided to go vegan on me and no longer had a Brad for shrimp.

Having a Brad ... Another sidestep. Decades ago, Tim used to work with a guy named Brad Hankin. Also, decades ago, whenever Tim wanted something out of the ordinary to eat he'd say something like, *"I have a hankering for Chinese food."* One night, he had a slip of the tongue and said, *"I have a hankin for Chinese food."* We laughed at his slip, then the two of us skipped happily toward OB lunacy. Before the conversation was over, we'd turned the silly slipup into lasting lingo. Ever since then, whenever we have a hankering for something out of the ordinary, we say we have a Brad. We've been doing it for so long now, and have said it in front of enough people, and in the presence of our kids often enough that, "Having a Brad," is understood in our tiny universe. It's also a nice way to remember a guy Tim enjoyed working with all those years ago. So while I was having a Brad for shrimp — Tim was having a Brad for something else. When to tell the wife became Tim's dilemma.

Another quick sidestep ... When we were young and divvying up duties, of which I did the lion's share because I was a stay-at-home mom and Tim spent long hours at work, he latched onto grocery shopping as his primary divvy-duty. He enjoyed doing it, God only knows why, and weekends afforded him a good chunk of time for traipsing aisles.

I was fine with his schlepping and shopping for the family for three reasons: 1) I never liked grocery shopping. I found it boring, probably because I didn't visit the culinary aisles where the cool people shopped for things they use in homemade sauces and stuff; 2) I no longer needed to plan out menus for the week, Tim would do that as he shopped. If he had a Brad for stew and lemon meringue pie, I'd find that out when I put the groceries away; 3) on my last big shopping trip to Shaws, when Hannah was about four or so and sitting in the cart handing items to me for placement on the conveyor pad, I heard her begin the opening lines from, Ding Dong the Witch is Dead, you know, from the Wizard of Oz movie.

I smiled at my daughter then dropped the smile when I followed her stare and her pointed finger toward the woman standing in line behind us, the woman who looked exactly like Margaret Hamilton aka Almira Gulch aka the Wicked Witch of the West. **Ding. Dong. Dead Ringer!**

I have absolutely no recollection as to what happened next, there may have been apologetic words from me or not, there may have been a few more choruses from my child or not, there may have been a ball of fire tossed my way or the releasing of a horde of pissed-off flying primates or not, and it matters not because that was the last time I did the grocery shopping, thank you very much.

I have absolutely no idea how we got to this particular place in the blog and I'm not sure what the exact purpose of this blog is, so I'll scroll to the top for a little light reading and be right back. Okay. Got it. Back to Tim's appetite abandonment of his wife, the woman standing, the woman sitting at death's door. The woman who had the brilliant idea of having a last Date Night with her husband. The woman whose excitement was ebbing a bit. "You're effing kidding me, right? You're not having shrimp?"

"I don't eat seafood anymore."

I pushed in, "And you don't eat sharp cheese and crackers anymore, either. Right?" I said the words in a tone much more appropriate for a wife learning about an act of infidelity, not dietary changes.

"Cheese no. Crackers if they're vegan."

"So, our Date Night dinner of shrimp cocktail, sharp cheese and crackers, and green grapes has been reduced to green grapes."

"And sparkling apple cider."

"Well, this Date Night sucks, already."

"I have a plan."

"Does it involve you eating shrimp?"

"No."

"Better be a good plan, dude. You do know this is our last Date Night, and so far it kinda sucks."

"You already said that."

"Deserves repeating."

"I know. I'm sorry.

"Me, too," I said through a spring of tears. Some of those tears belonged to Date Night disappointment, most of them were because I'd been experiencing breakthrough pain for days and was exhausted by the ordeal. More on that in a future blog.

"I have a plan," he said while taking a seat across from me.

"Okay."

"I thought I'd prepare everything for you, and then Hannah and I could have vegan Chinese food from Nancy Chang's, and Jessie wants a gluten-free pizza, so I'll just grab all of that and as soon as dinner is done, the girls will head to Hannah's."

"Tim, at the risk of sounding bitchy—"

"Too late."

"—and condescending."

"Oh, God."

"I managed to get our toddlers, tweens, or teens out of our hair for Date Night countless times over the years. The one time I let you take the reins, dinner for two is now dinner for four, and I'm eating oxymoronic jumbo shrimp by myself."

He laughed. *"George Carlin was a riot."*

"Don't George me when I'm pissed."

"Okay, so dinner isn't perfect, but by seven they'll be gone and we'll be back on track." He headed to the kitchen to open and close a few doors and drawers, *"So, how's 12 shrimp sound?"*

"Perfect. Some for tonight, and some for lunch tomorrow."

A few minutes later.

"Okay, the shrimp's on the stove. I put it into a big pot so it won't boil over and I set the timer for ten minutes. That's how long it should take for the water to reach a boil. Call Jessie down when the timer goes off and tell her to let it boil for a couple minutes. I have an errand to run."

"Cocktail sauce?"

Silence. "Forgot the cocktail sauce, did ya?"

"I'll be back."

"Yipeeeeee."

"Love you, too."

Before the timer rang, the pot boiled over. I grabbed my phone. "Hey, Jess, the pot on the stove is boiling over."

"On my way."

The door opened at the top of the stairs and I heard an exaggerated gag because Jessica hates shrimp, hates **everything** about shrimp, she certainly hates the smell of shrimpy water boiling onto a back burner. She banged down the stairs. *"It smells like low tide down here. Jesus, Mom, this is awful."*

"Shut off the unit. Drain the shrimp. Rinse it under cold water. And go away."

"As soon as humanly possible."

"My thoughts, exactly." She did the straining and draining without further commentary, then skimmed her hand along my arm as she passed by. It's become her non-verbal expression of love.

"Love you, too." I squeezed her fingertips before she moved beyond my touch.

As soon as Tim opened the front door he grunted, *"What happened?"*

"Shrimp boiled over."

"How?"

"I don't know for sure, but I think it had something to do with water being brought to a boil."

"I didn't put that much water into the pot."

"Uh huh. And heads up, Jessie's upstairs gagging."

He laughed. *"She hates the smell of shrimp."*

"She said it smells like low tide in here."

He laughed, really laughed, *"She's not wrong."*

The Bickersons were laughing. A glimmer of hope was on the horizon that Date Night might be saved.

Rules and Regulations ... Tim and the interlopers were having dinner at the kitchen table while I was perched upon my leather prison with a beautifully laid out tray of Date Night nibbles. In between bites, I called out to the Traitorous One, "As soon as Hannah and Jessica leave, the cell phones get turned off. Deal?"

"Deal."

"There's no calling, texting, or emailing by phone. Deal?"

"Deal."

"So, if there's anything you need to do for work, you should do it now."

"I'm good. Oh, by the way, you got a letter from Guru Jessica."

He handed it to me. I opened it. I read it. I knew instantly that I was going to break the 'no phones' rule, as soon as humanly possible. Before I did, I hopped onto YouTube and found a song Guru recommended on the handwritten, multi-page, front and back letter. I pressed play on a song called, Oceans (Where My Feet May Fail) by Hillsong United.

In recent weeks, I learned The Guru is quite an accomplished singer and, according to her letter, she tends to belt out this particular song. I put it on and within seconds the chit-chat in the other room ceased, and their flapping traps were used exclusively for the food they were consuming. Like me, they turned their attention to the music and lyrics of Oceans.

The version I chose on YouTube is a live, outdoor performance from the Sea of Galilee in Israel. Taya Smith is lead singer, and upon first look she reminded me of Sinéad O'Connor, à la shaved head, a killer set of pipes, and passions that run deep and display easily on a beautiful, expressive face. The energies of the two singers, however, are vastly different.

Okay! What the eff is the point of all of this? Oh, right, Guru sent a letter, the contents of which made me need to fire off a text, just a quick one because she took the time to write a playlist for me. We'd discussed sharing our lists during a recent text chain, and she laughed her ass off when she learned I intended to type my list instead of jumping onto any millennial-developed device to create a playlist and whoosh it to her via text or email. She, of course, planned a guru-esque delivery system.

As soon as the front door shut behind Hannah and Jessica, I sent Mr. Wonderful to the basement on a bogus errand, grabbed my phone, powered it up, and fired off a text, telling her to expect an email. I grabbed my laptop and banged out an email.

Subject: Date Night Interruptus.

I love you. I love the song. Oceans are my thing. Oceans is now going on both of my funeral playlists. I hope you enjoy them. Gotta get back to my date. I sent him on a bogus errand in the cellar.

To the email, I attached two Spotify playlists Hannah made me. One will be used at my funeral home gathering and one is for the party afterwards. Bottom-lining this. The computer-savvy-tech-genius sent me a paper and pen playlist because I'm a dolt at computers. I one upped her by sending an email link to the soundtrack of my life courtesy of my computer-savvy-tech-able daughter. BTW, as soon as the 'no phones' rule expired, I began getting texts with Guru's commentary on how many songs are on both of our playlists, and though she is thirty years my junior, there are many, many duplicates.

Okay, back to the blog ... Tim arrived upstairs from the bogus errand sans the book I asked him to find.

"I think we donated that book to the library."

"I think you're right. Oh, well."

On his way into the living room, he locked the front door, then headed to the Bose system to put on one of two Phil McTigue CDs. As you know, Mr. McTigue has been reading my blogs, and maybe a Pulling Threads book or two because the first CD he made me had songs from both of those writings. Anyway, since receiving his first CD, I've mentioned several other songs in my blogs. I'm doing this from memory so there'll be omissions, but I made reference to *Dream a Little Dream of Me, Blue Velvet, Que Será, Será,* and my favorite Dean Martin song, *Innamorata*. I was sort of primed for one of them to be the opening song of my newest gift from Phil McTigue, who I now refer to as Wile E. Coyote. I haven't a clue why, but whenever I think of Phil McTigue, up pops Wile E. Coyote. So. There. — Beep! Beep!

As it turned out, none of the aforementioned songs started our evening. This did! A recording of a 7th inning stretch stadium singing of *Take Me Out to the Ballgame.* **That** is what came blaring through my

Bose speaker system! It brought Mr. and Mrs. Wonderful to a fit of laughter. And kept us laughing through the whole damned song. What Fun!!!!!

Tim and I spent nearly an hour chit-chatting with 'McTigue's Musical Madness' in the background. And then we got down to business. Serious business!!!!! You'll read all about it in Date Night — Part Two.

A note from Jessica Champion ...

The working relationship I shared with Sheryll quickly grew into more of a friendship. Sheryll never fit the typical client mold. Did she fit the typical anything mold? We had a very unique "flow" to our work exchanges — Sheryll would make a request and I would make it happen. Interpreting Sheryll-isms and learning her language, letting her push past the formalities and procedures expected of "normal" clients, and later, becoming the conduit for her very personal blog, afforded me a transformation that I couldn't feel taking place but, looking back, I can see how huge it was.

At the time of deconstructing the original blog to replace it with the memoir-esque body of work that it has become today, Sheryll and I had already been in each other's inboxes almost every day for about two years. You develop an affinity for someone, a fond familiarity, working with them on such a regular and personal basis. Translating others's art has always been my work, but my relationship with Sheryll rapidly became a "first" in my field and an extremely personal experience.

Upon learning Sheryll's tragic news, I felt a renewed surge of dedication to her work. Upon witnessing her grace, strength, optimism, openness, and powerful love for her family and world around her, my mission became more important than ever: give life to her words and honors her voice, her story, her urgency, and her potent ability to draw people in as though she were another beloved character in her own books.

It isn't for the faint of heart. It's intimate. It's confronting. It can be scary. And yet, I marvel at her bravery. Her willingness to share what's going on in her heart and in her mind while we all read about what's happening to her body. Just as I'm wiping away a tear, I'll burst into laughter because that's the way Sheryll writes — and dare I say her gift has only intensified in this late stage. It's truly amazing to be a part of. It's like I'm really in it with her. In her head, in her thought process. It gives me such comfort and joy to hold this space with and for Sheryll.

55. Date Night — Part Two ...

Dear Tim,

Our night got off to a rocky start, but Date Night was everything it was destined to be, time spent in our hallmark way, laughing. Sure, there were moments of sorrow and a few shed tears, but the laughter from that night and from our life together fills the corners of my mind and lifts my heart when I need it most.

As for your ability to remember the details about our special night — don't worry — I've got you covered. I recorded the evening so you can listen and laugh whenever you'd like.

Happy Birthday.
I love you, Sheryll

When I planned Date Night, I did so whilst lashed to my leather prison, so, straight off, I knew the dancing part of our evening wouldn't take place. That was disappointing because dancing, a little swirl here, a little twirl there, was a regular in our household mostly because we always had music on at 183 Wildwood. If by chance I wasn't with Seger on Main Street, or having a one-night stand in Shaky Town with Jackson, or swooning to the crooning of Martin, or tripping down Penny Lane with The Beatles, or getting all redneck with Lynyrd or Marshall, or, or, or, then my songbird, Mr. Wonderful, was filling the air with a musical ditty from his vast array of tunes.

Tim is one of those people who can hear a song a single time and know all the words. Not me. I've screwed up lyrics for years, decades, even. A prelude to making up words when I write, I guess. Anyway, for the past 35 years, Tim has been singing, morning, noon and night. He used to go all The Band/Van Morrison and sing me to sleep with *Tura Lura Lural* when we were first married. A very sweet memory. You should note that Mr. Wonderful has a very nice singing voice and recently said he might join a choir, imagine that. It brings a smile to my face when I imagine that.

The point of this background ramble is to establish that music was the backdrop to our lives and as such, I'd often find myself in Tim's arms taking a little dance across the floor. When we were young, our spontaneous dances were fun and flirty, always ending with a smooch or two and a wink or two of what our nights would hold. As the years went on and the 'Dizzy-Dame' as he started calling me post head surgery couldn't really swirl and twirl anymore, our dances were about holding one another as we swayed to whatever song filled the air. Our date nights, however, *always* ended with a dance to whatever song happened to be playing on the soundtrack of our lives at that particular moment. But, on June 20th, every year, bar none, for the past 35 years, we've held one another and danced to our wedding song.

Let It Be Me …

I bless the day I found you, I want to stay around you.
And so I beg you, let it be me.
Don't take this heaven from one,
if you must cling to someone.
Now and forever, let it be me.
Each time we meet love, I find complete love –
without your sweet love, what would life be?
So never leave me lonely, tell me you'll love me only –
and that you'll always, let it be me.

(English version written by: Manny Curtis)

No matter the number of times I've heard it, or have sung it in my head, those words filled me with the surety that Tim and I were meant to be with one another. I feel every one of those words, I believe every one of those words, as though they were written and sung for us — only us. I knew going into our most recent special night that there wouldn't be dancing. Truth be told, I considered risking it. I thought I might be able to get upright and into his arms for a little sway or two. I had conversations with myself, "You get up a few times a day to pee. And you do the whole sponge bath routine, and wash your hair in the kitchen sink a couple times a week, so would it really hurt to have a little dance?" And then I'd imagine the worst. My spine collapsing and my body ending in a heap at Tim's feet as Don and Phil Everly serenade us. After my last debate, I shrugged a very sore shoulder. I'm quite sure the cancer nibbling rodent is doing a fair amount of damage there, now. Then I made my decision. You could do it. You should not do it. It could be the Dance of Death. So, I conceded our final date night would be without dancing, but we could still do dinner and a movie, right? Wrong.

If you read my previous blog, you know I learned rather late in the game that my date and I would be dining on different foods, in different rooms, with uninvited guests, the daughters to whom I gave life, the ones I hoped would live that life elsewhere for the next few hours. Anyway, not having 'our' cuisine pissed me off, and my frustration was expressed in typical Sheryll O'Brien fashion with a few well-placed, "What the effs?" In my defense, though I don't think I need one, dinner, dancing, a movie, and whispered 'sweet nothings' was our version of a perfect evening together. Perfect was no longer in the lexicon for Date Night. And the realization was bittersweet.

Before the evening began, I knew we wouldn't be dancing, or smooching, or winking and wooing, and as for watching a movie, I've banned everything except the Hallmark channel on my living room television and, therefore, have watched said channel 24/7 since December 1st which means I've seen every Hallmark movie 24 x 7 already. So, I put the kibosh on watching a movie. Now, what's a girl to do? Think. Think. Think. You may be surprised to know that I have lots of time to think, think, think, whilst lashed to the leather, and believe you me, my mind tends to go wherever the eff it wants to go. So, as soon as I received my newest McTigue CDs in the mail and I stopped Tim from playing them until Date Night, I knew I needed to come up with something new. Something fun. And I did.

"We're going to play the Newlywed Game," I mumbled to myself, pleased with my ingenuity. For those who might not know, or remember, the Newlywed Game was a wildly popular television show that ran from the mid-1960s to the mid-1970s. It was hosted by the handsome, and always smiling, Bob Eubanks. Each week, four newlywed couples would show the world how much, or how little, they knew about one another. The rules of the game were very simple: husbands and wives would take turns answering questions while their spouses were backstage. When one half of the couple had answered four questions, the other half of the couple returned, answered the same questions, and hoped for a match. Each correct answer garnered a point. The vying couples hoped beyond hope that they'd get the most points, that week's bragging rights, and a bottle of dish detergent or whatever that week's prize was.

I thought it might be fun to play the Newlywed Game with the old dodger, the man I've been married to forever, and who I hoped might get an answer or two correct. I went to Amazon, had the same old debate with myself about how I shouldn't be a slave to Jeff Bezos and fuel his narcissistic need for dominance in worldwide purchase and delivery systems, then did a bit of rationalization: I am the perfect consumer for his business model — order it and you can have it in twelve seconds because let's face it, I'm on a time limit and every second counts. I scrolled the pages of Amazon, learned I could purchase an 'original version' of the boxed game for $99.00, or a video version for some lesser amount, but since I didn't want to play a video game and I didn't want to indulge Mr. Bezos on that scale of finance, I decided I should drag my ass to the 21st century and find something new, and fresh, and fun to play. And I did. I bought a boxed card game called a couple of hearts that promised we could ask a few questions, get a few answers, and have lots of laughs. “This could work,” I mumbled to myself. I’m always mumbling to myself these days. C’est la vie! Remember my letter to Tim, the one at the beginning of this blog? Well, the tape I made him will ensure that every question asked during the playing of this game and every answer given is the real deal. Hello, Tim! Every question asked, every answer given, is on tape. Not sure if that’s making you smile or sweat! A bit of both, I suppose.

You should note: I shuffled the cards sufficiently before we began playing and we pulled them in the order in which they settled. It was astounding to both of us, and remarked upon by both of us, that the cosmos had a hand in who got what question to answer. You’ll see.

Time to play A Couple of Hearts ... The boxed set of questions is divided into two sections: sexy and romantic questions; all other types of questions. I figured there was no need to torture ourselves, so I grabbed a handful of cards from the boring pile, put the rest away, then waited for the Unsuspecting One to park his ass on his recliner. After singing and laughing our way through *Take Me Out To the Ballgame*, we did a bit of chit-chatting during a few more songs.

“Do you think you’ll do some traveling?”

“I’d like to.”

“I hope you go to Ireland.”

“I think I will. Someday.”

“Thinking won’t make it happen, Tim.”

“You really want me to go.”

“I really do.” Pause .... “Are you going to retire?”

"Nope. I want to keep busy."

"Don't work until the bitter end. Okay?

"Okay."

Pause ……. a good, long pause. "Sixty-five, can you believe it?"

"Nope."

"Time goes by so damned fast. Especially the middle years." Pause ……. "Even now, I still think of myself as being in my forties."

"The only time I think about my age is when I look in the mirror." He ran his hand through his white, cropped beard.

"My Gorton's fisherman." I sang the tune.

We shared some laughs. Seriously, before I got sick, I had to push in and think about retirement, that we're at the age of retirement because in my head I wasn't there yet. And with my writing, I could have done that for years, so—"

"— so retirement always felt way off in the future."

A pause to listen to another song. "After this song, I want you to stop the Bose because we're going to play a game."

"Okay ……." The word was said with a bit of concern. *"What game?"* The words were said with a note of trepidation.

I laughed. Sometimes I cackle when I laugh. I cackled. "I think I'll shuffle these cards and let you wonder a bit more."

He laughed. Sometimes he moans when he laughs. He moaned.

"What a beautiful day it was." He tried to take the edge off his concern about the game by filling the time with idle chit-chat.

"Cold, though." I played along.

"Yeah. It's always nice after a snowstorm, clean and crisp. Couldn't have been a nicer day."

I shuffled the cards, over and over, drawing his attention to me.

"So what's the game?"

"I wanted to get the Newlywed Game, do you remember that?"

"Yeah. Questions like, what's your favorite color?"

We laughed. "Well, it was a bit more sophisticated than that."

"Not much."

I laughed. "But the game on Amazon was a video version and I didn't want that and I didn't want to spend a hundred bucks on a boxed anniversary edition of the board game, so I got this. It's a box of questions, called A Couple of Hearts. We'll each take turns pulling a card and asking the question. So when I ask you a question, do me a favor, just answer it, don't go all Tim O on me and dissect the question.

Groan.

"Do you want to go first? It's your birthday so you should go first."

"Okay."

"Okay, here's your question: What surprising thing did you find out about me during our relationship?"

Pause ...... a really long pause ......*"During our relationship? Because I knew you in high school, so does that count? Or is it just when we started dating?"*

"Oh God."

He laughed.

I did not.

"This is what you meant about me asking a bunch of questions."

"Uh huh."

"But it isn't clear."

"Pretty clear. Let me read it to you again: What surprising thing did you find out about me **during** our relationship? Good god, almighty."

"Okay. Got it.

"Doubt it."

Pause .... Pause .... Pause .... "Oh good god. You know I'm dying, right? And I'm sort of on a time limit, right?

"You had to know I'd ask questions."

"Yes, but this is a game, not a test. There aren't any right or wrong answers."

"Bullshit. There are wrong answers. Tons of wrong answers."

We laughed — a lot. "Fair enough. Just answer the question, would ya?"

"How strong you are. That's what I learned. How strong you are."

"Jeez, and I thought you were gonna say, patient?"

He laughed then pulled a card. *"What fictional character do I remind you of?* He started laughing and shaking his head.

"Why are you laughing?

"Just going over the list of things you call me."

"Like what?"

"Mr. Magoo."

We laughed. "I'll try to stay away from cartoon characters, okay, Goofy."

He laughed. I laughed. "Ooo. Ooo. I know, Forrest Gump."

"Should have seen that coming."

"And, yet."

We laughed. I absolutely love Tim's laugh. I enjoyed it a little bit, then read the next card. "Nope. Nope. I'm putting that card back."

"What do you mean? You can't put it back."

"It's too easy."

"What's the question?"

"Who is the strongest person you know and why?"

"Well you, of course."

"See. Wait, go ahead and answer, but you can't say me."

"Okay. Is the person living or dead?"

"Oh good god! It doesn't matter."

"But I have to know them, right?"

"Perhaps I should read the question again. Mr. Gump, who is the strongest person you **know** and why?"

"Me. I'm the strongest person I know, and you can figure out why."

"Already have." I said laughing hard. "Go ahead and read the next card."

"Complete this sentence: When I look into your eyes, I feel."

"Protected, safe, loved."

A bit of silence. A long bit of silence and a few tears from me. I pulled it together and asked the next question. "What is your favorite photo of me?"

"The one from our honeymoon. That one." He pointed a finger toward a framed picture that'd been on his bureau for decades and is now on our fireplace. *"I'm taking it to the funeral home."*

Some more silence. A long bit of silence and a few held tears from him. I brought him back around. "Read the next question."

"What makes us special as a couple?"

"That all of the big things, all of the big decisions in life, we were in perfect sync on. All of the plans we had for us as a couple, and for our kids, they were agreed upon, almost immediately. And it didn't matter how simple our life was. We had everything we wanted, a family."

"I agree."

"I know."

We sighed the kind of sigh that said, "A Job Well Done!" I pulled a card. "What's one thing you would never do for me?"

"Never do for you?"

"Never do for me."

"There's nothing I wouldn't do for you."

"Would you lie for me? Like if I committed a crime. Would you tell a lie for me?"

"Yeah, sure."

"Really? So how far would you go?"

"Pretty far."

"Ooo, okay. So, I committed a crime. I didn't mean to, but no one is going to believe me, and I already started covering things up so it makes me look guilty. Do you lie to the cops for me?"

"Yeah. If they asked if you were home with me, I'd say, yes."

"Well, if the crime took place tonight, you wouldn't be lying because I can't leave the house."

"Well, technically, you could leave the house."

"Ooo. You dastardly devil."

"Actually, tonight would be the perfect night for you to commit a crime."

"Ooo. Mr. Wonderful has a dark side."

"Better be careful answering your questions, Mrs. Wonderful."

We spent some time laughing — really laughing. "I'm writing a blog on this, you know. Wait until Kathy tells her detective husband that you'd lie for me."

"Maybe you should leave this question and answer out of the blog."

"Fat chance."

"You probably won't remember this part, anyway."

"The memory-bank is working pretty good now that I'm on steroids, so I'll remember this conversation. And for the record, I won't be lying for you."

"Shit."

Both of us laughed like idiots. "So, let's recap. Detective Gaffney knocks on the door and says your wife was seen on Main Street at the scene of a murder? It was a DWR."

"DWR?"

"Driving while reclining." He shook his head and mumbled something. I continued. "So, I'm involved in a DWR, you say what when the detective asks you about it?"

"I'd point to your recliner and say, I don't think so, Tom."

"Wow, you really would lie for me."

"Yeah."

"There has to be something you wouldn't do for me?"

"Nope."

"So, I'm on my deathbed and I ask for an extra dose of morphine, you're gonna give it to me?"

"Maybe I'll give you a little extra, but I'm not gonna do anything blatant, like pump you up or cover your face with a pillow."

"Good to know."

We started laughing our asses off. *"God. I hope you're not taping this."*

"Yeah. It'd be kinda tough explaining this to Detective Gaffney."

Tim could barely *breathe,* he was laughing so hard. And when he finally stopped, he turned serious. *"I couldn't ever hurt you. And if I could take all the pain you've been feeling, I would, in a heartbeat."*

I started crying. When Tim listens to this tape, I'm sure this part of our evening will resonate with him. He pulled a card. *"If you could go back in time, what moment in our relationship would you like to relive?"*

"The last five minutes." Laughing .... for a long time. "That's an easy question. And you'd probably want to relive it, too."

We answered in unison — Institute Park.

"That's the night I fell in love with you."

"That's the night I fell in love with you."

"I wish we could go sit on that bench and talk for hours like we did that night."

I pulled a sigh and shed a few tears. See, our final Date Night was bittersweet. I pulled a card. "What was the best advice I ever gave you?"

"To take the job at Donnelley."

"Yeup. I agree."

He pulled a card. *"What was the craziest thing I've ever done for you?"*

"The craziest thing? That's hard. You don't do crazy. Although the whole lying for me would certainly count as crazy." His facial expression suggested he thought he'd done crazy. I was having a hard time remembering crazy from Tim. "Have you done crazy things for me?" He smiled. I love his smile.

"I'm thinking of a few and they all have crazy elements."

"Get out! A few? Crazy things? What are you thinking of?" He mentioned a few things — they **will not** be part of this blog. Thank you very much. He ended up tossing out a blog-worthy crazy thing.

"Throwing you a fiftieth birthday party after you threatened bodily injury if I did it."

"Yeah. That was pretty crazy and risky."

"And it could have ended really badly."

"It was wonderful and thoughtful." I sat with the memories for a few minutes then pulled a card. "What's your funniest memory of me?"

"Oh, God, there've been so many."

"Yeah, I've been like Lucy, so this could be a long list, Mr. Ricardo."

"Yeah, you're always doing crap."

"You love it."

"I do." He pulled a card. *"When was I there for you when you needed me?"*

"So, this is the card that's equivalent to my asking you when I'm funny because you're always there for me. But, let's see. When were you really there for me? Got it! When I was having an MRI for my head tumor, and I was in that godforsaken, effing machine and you talked to me and touched my hand and gave me that tactile connection. I would not have been able to stay in that machine without you. Pause .... You've been there for me with all the medical crap I've been through."

"Like staying with you 24/7 at rehab."

"Yeah. Rehab. Remember the day you were in the shower and my physical therapist came to take me for my session and I yelled out to you, 'I'm going to the gym.'"

My husband started laughing and nearly passed out from the experience, then and now.

I repeated it for fun. "Five words you never thought you'd hear me say, 'I'm going to the gym.'" I enjoyed watching his fit of laughter. Tears were streaming down his face, and he was incapable of talking. I piled on. "And then that whole bullshit about me having to go down to the kitchen and cook an egg before they'd let me leave rehab. Meanwhile Marjorie's coming and going from the place as she sees fit, and she didn't know how to boil effing water let alone cook an egg."

And you rat-finked her to the occupational therapist."

"Damn straight. Lot of good it did. The whitecoats did nothing. They just let her come and go while the woman who'd had a lobotomy had to cook an egg and make a bed before I could leave. What the eff?" Laugh. Pause. Laugh. Pause. "Who the hell's turn is it?" Laugh. Pause. "Whose turn is it? Stop laughing."

"It's my turn." He continues laughing. *"Ask a question."*

"What talent do I have that still impresses you?"

"Your writing. That was easy." He pulled a card. *"Are you happy and content right now?"*

Well, yes. Right now. But an hour ago, I wanted to smack you." Pause. "You know, this whole vegan crap would be a problem for us, long term."

"I wouldn't be vegan if you had long term. Pick a card."

"We're stranded on an island. What five items would you like to have with us?"

"Your recliner."

"Are you serious right now? We're on an island, you know, with sand, and surf, and sun, and you've decided I may as well be dying there, too? Before you answer, these are the ground rules. I'm healthy and I do not need a recliner."

"Okay. So five items. We should be practical. We'll need food and water."

"We have food and water on the island."

"Oh, we do?"

"Sure, it's an island. There's probably a coconut or two and maybe a bird we can kill and we can fish. Oops, I forgot you're a vegan." I growled. "Okay, we're on the island that Harrison Ford and Anne Heche were on in—"

"Six Days, Seven Nights."

"Yeah, so we're on that island and we have food and water, so what 5 items do you want us to have?"

"We'll need a fire."

"We have matches. So what 5 items?"

Pause .... Pause .... Pause .... *"I'd probably look for a way to get off the island."*

"What? Why? Why do we want to get off the island?"

"I didn't say we. I said I'd look for a way off the island."

Laughter. "Okay. Let's try this. We're on the island and we're staying there."

"Okay, so we don't need clothes."

I started laughing.

"And we don't need sunscreen."

My laughter increased.

"But we'll need towels."

My laughter turned to tears and there was a whole lot of ugly laughing and crying going on because he's now the last person on earth I want to be stuck with. "Dude. How about a record player so we can have music. Or how about books so we can read."

"Let's go back to the record player. The island we're stuck on has electricity?"

No, we have a battery pack."

His laughter started. *"You know, the normal 'getting stuck on an island answer' would be food, water, fire."*

"And a bottle of gin. We should have a bottle of gin on the island."

"You don't even drink."

"I'll start."

"So the island is a Sandals resort. Nice."

"Forget it. I'm leaving the island."

"Good, you're off the island."

"How long have you been waiting to say that?"

The game stops for fits of laughter. "Whose turn is it?

"Yours." He pulls a card. *"You're writing a book about me. What would the title be?*

"An interesting question, don't ya think?"

"I'll say."

"So, I'm writing a book about you and I get to title it." Pause ……. "Poor Tim."

Lots of laughter. I pulled a card. "What is the first movie quote you can think of?"

"Tomorrow's another day."

"Okay, Scarlett."

He laughs. *"Complete this sentence: I feel _______ because of you."*

"All of the things I said about your eyes."

"You said something about my eyes?"

"Active listening wasn't on the schedule tonight, I see." Laughter. "I said I felt safe and protected and something else when I looked into your eyes, but whatevs. So let's see ……. I feel blessed because of you. At the end of the day, I'm blessed."

"Snap out of it."

Laughter from him. Tears from me. *"Are you okay?"*

Sniffles. "I'm fine." Pause ……. Pause……. I pulled a card. "What five words would you use to describe our marriage?"

"Comfortable. I don't need five words."

"What about fun?"

"Okay, comfortable and fun."

"And simple. Our marriage has been really simple. There haven't been big dramas, there haven't been any dramas at all. Not personal dramas between us. The only dramas we ever had were medical ones. You're right, we don't need five words."

"Comfortable."

A heavy silence filled the space. I pulled a card. "Oh my god."

"Is this another 5 things question?"

"No but this is so ironic. Ready?"

"I doubt it."

"If I lost my memory, what would you do to make me remember our love?"

"Take you to the beach."

"Ohhhhh ...." a few tears — and then .... "I need some clarification, are you taking me to a beach beach, or to the island we got stuck on, you know, the one you want to get off of?"

"We're going to Wells, always Wells." He smiled wide, his long dimples running the length of his face and his eyes twinkling. He threw in a wink for good measure then pulled a card. *"What do you remember about our first kiss?"*

"I don't remember for sure where our first kiss was, but I think it was after the movie, *Jagged Edge*, when you walked me to the third floor of Houghton Street. You leaned me against the door and kissed me. Not sure if it was our first kiss, but it's the one I remember."

"Pretty sure that's where it was."

"And I remembered that I wanted you to do it again. So, there you have it."

Tim got up, walked a few steps, and leaned his hands onto the arms of my recliner. Then he kissed me. He went back to his seat and just stared at me. There were several minutes of silence. And when I couldn't stand it anymore, I pulled a card. "Which three words do you think describe you best?"

"Neat. Flexible. Relaxed."

"I'd say you nailed that question." I pulled another card. "What's been your happiest moment so far and why?"

"Everything happy came from us getting married." He realized I pulled two cards in a row. *"You need to answer that question. What was your happiest moment?"*

"Having kids and marrying you are the expected answers, but I'm going to try to think of something different." Pause ……. "Something happy for me. Oh, the day you brought me home after spending time in rehab. I remember coming here, and the girls were away at the Cape with Mom and Marjorie, and Donnie and Denise, and the two of us walked into the house hand in hand. That made me happy. It was quiet, and I was home."

"And you felt safe."

"I did."

"It was so nice to be home after being gone for five weeks." There was a lot of silence. I'm not sure what Tim was thinking about, but I was thinking about him being alone, here. Soon. I pulled myself together. "What was the worst date we've ever had?" I cracked up and preempted him with an answer. "The one we're living right now."

He cracked up. *"Our worst date? I don't know."*

"Ooo. Ooo. I know what our worst date was."

"What?"

"Jefferson Starship at the DCU when the dude puked all over you."

Growl. *"That was awful."*

"Your car smelled awful."

"For months." He waved the last card. It was for me. *"What was the best present I've ever given you?"*

"My diamond heart pendant was the best gift you ever gave me, but the nicest present we gave each other was buying our first Christmas tree and decorating it in lights and tiny red velvet bows."

"That's all we could afford, back then. That was nice."

"Or the nicest present could have been when you did the bedroom over while I was on a business trip."

"Yeah."

"Or when you had *Suzanne* published so I could see my name on the spine of a book."

"That's what I was thinking of."

"You did tons of nice things for me." Pause. "Did I ever do anything nice for you?"

"You gave me our last Date Night."

We sat quietly for a few minutes, just sort of got lost to our own thoughts. He kissed my head on the way to the kitchen, and when he was finished tidying, I was already nodding off. He escorted me to the bathroom and when I came out he was leaning against a wall, his stance very reminiscent of the way he was standing when I saw him at our 10th year class reunion.

I laughed — then I cried.

He got me to my recliner and opened his arms. I stepped forward, leaned my hips against my walker and let him embrace me. *"Thank you for Date Night."* He kissed my head, waited for me to sit, tucked me in, kissed my head again and put his hand to my cheek. *"Call if you need me."*

"I will." I needed him for quite some time. While I waited for my Tramadol and Xanax to kick in, I listened to the recording I made. I laughed. I cried. And thanked God we had Date Night. A perfect Date Night.

A note from Tim O'Brien, my husband ...

Reading Sheryll's blogs will give you an understanding of what it was like living in our world. I am so proud that my wife welcomed you to be part of it.

Sheryll was a witness to my life and I to hers for more than three decades. There were more happy times than we could ever have hoped for. There were lots of challenges, too. This book is a compilation of the blog she wrote as she faced the most difficult time in her life, with humor, tenacity, courage, sensitivity, and love.

Sheryll had a pull on me like the moon has on the ocean's tides, powerful and constant. She was a source of comfort and love to us all, and I will miss her and love her for the rest of my days.

56. Turning the Corner ...

There is a point to this blog, but it's gonna take a while for us to get there. I used to own a Datsun 280Z sports car. I originally named her Zelda, but that was shortened to Z within a matter of weeks. I'm going to tell you more about Z, but first things first. I'm one of *those* people who names their cars. The practice began in 1976 when I bought my first car, a very used 1963, pale yellow Bel Air I named Bonnie Bell. The behemoth had a steering wheel the size of a Ferris wheel, a very long tail end, a black-soft-top, and supposedly power steering. She did not have power steering. After a year of driving Bonnie, there was a noticeable change to my shoulders and biceps. They'd broadened and toned way too much for my liking, think Bulgarian shot putter in training.

I only drove Bonnie to and from work because my friends had cool cars and my dates had cool cars and their cool cars didn't require two people to start them. Bonnie needed a start-crew of two: one person to hold a screwdriver to the battery while the other person turned the key. An annoyance for sure, but there was no shortage of guys who'd stop at the yellow Bel Air when its hood was in the upright position, and its owner was taking a hip to the bumper waiting patiently for an assist.

Bonnie and I parted ways when her exhaust fumes became unbearable and I just could not shake the constant fear that I'd be found passed out at a red light and slumped over the Ferris wheel. More to the point, and this is a very important point, it was nearly impossible finding a perfume strong enough, yet flirty enough, to cut the petrol smell that wafted from inside Bonnie Bell. I preferred wearing Charlie back then, but all things considered, White Shoulders was a much better spritz.

So, what's a girl to do? Out with the old, in with the brand spanking new. My first brand new car was a 1980 2-door, black Chevy Nova SS. Now we're talking! This sporty little number had a very nice interior: a simple dashboard with an appropriately sized steering wheel, black vinyl split-bench seats with a tiny bit of red piping along the edges, and a standard H-stick shift. For some reason, an oversized white ball was mounted at the top end of the shift. The functionality of the ball was clear, the person shifting the gears had something to grab onto. The design element left a lot to be desired and the color choice *very easily* could have been a dealbreaker. I mean, come on. A black and red sporty little number with a hideously sized white ball at the end of a long piece of steel. WTF?

Within days, I'd sanded the shiny object and painted the ball black. Easy-peasy. As for the exterior of my first major purchase, it was beautiful: shiny black with red detail striping that ran bumper to bumper, up and over the wheel wells that held really wide mag tires, and beautiful grill work in the front and dual exhaust in the rear.

I slapped the name Star on my Nova and learned really fast that I'd hit the driving stratosphere. Guys take an extra-long look at young women driving muscle cars. One could argue that my Nova SS didn't technically fall into the muscle car division, but it sure got a muscular response from the opposite sex.

Looking back at my earliest days of car ownership, I would have to give myself zero points on creativity in the car naming department. I kicked things up a notch or two over the next few decades. I'm putting my 280Z story on hold (there's a reason) and I'm jumping ahead a bit. As a married woman, I owned a Nissan Stanza named Stanley, a white RAV4 named Stella, and a black RAV 4 named Echo.

When Tim and I stuck as a dating couple, I started naming his cars, too. There was Babs and Mike, one was a Nissan something or other, and the other was so not worth remembering so I don't remember it. Tim purchased his cars using one metric — I need a car — I see a car — I can afford the car — I buy the car. He changed his tune when he saw Honey. The car who became the love of my husband's life.

Honey was a 1998 Hyundai Sonata GLS sedan, and she was absolutely beautiful, all black and sexy as hell. She had beautiful chrome work on the sides, and a very nice looking Hyundai logo in front. Her frame sat low to the ground, so you didn't get in the car — you got *into* the car. Her interior was gorgeous and loaded: tan leather heated seats, power everything, a dashboard that looked like wood grain with dials that lighted soft blue, a really cool sunroof, and a 'to die for' stereo system.

The *initial* problem for Tim when it came to purchasing the Sonata, she was a tad bit out of our price range. That was the *only* argument he had for not buying the car he wanted. That pesky pricing issue meant nothing to Sheryll Bodine. My counter-argument: "You fell in love with the car." The woman who's a bit of a motorhead could have stopped there, I should have been able to stop there, but Tim was practical, purposeful, and thoughtful, so he needed more work.

For the record, I've lived my life following the principles of practical, purposeful, and thoughtful, except when it comes to automobiles. In general terms, my purchasing practice comes down to this: you set a price range, you look at cars within that price range, you peek at cars that are slightly above your price range (strictly for shits and giggles). If you fall in love with a car, you wave the white flag of surrender and buy the car. Easy-peasy.

Mr. Wonderful always stayed in his lanes when it came to living his life, particularly when it came to big ticket purchases. Needless to say, when it came to buy Honey, Tim needed more of an incentive, so I gave him more "And you drive over an hour to and from work each way, where you put in long hours, and you should be comfortable on your drive, and you need a new set of wheels, and you never ask for anything, and you should have the car you want." *That* little push made

Tim O'Brien the proud owner of Honey — the 'new' woman in his life.

I had Stanley at the time and found no reason to become part of a lover's triangle, so I left Tim to his dalliance with Honey and spent my driving time with my Nissan Stanza, a really cool, raised, station wagon thingy with sliding rear doors and oodles of trunk space. The girls and I really loved Stanley, and when all four OBs were doing 'family time' we did it in the Stanza. Rarely did I drive Honey, but when I did, I knew why my man was more than a bit smitten. She had it all: beauty, warmth, and a sexy playfulness. On the rare occasion when I'd settle into Honey and pull off our driveway, the surround sound system went on blast, the sunroof slid back and tucked into the roof somewhere, and all four windows went down. Though she was an automatic, I watched and listened to her purrs and revs. I loved my infrequent times with Honey, so I treated her with the utmost respect.

And then this happened … I bolted upright in bed and read the alarm clock. It was just before 5 AM on a Saturday morning in early December. I padded softly to the bedroom window, moved the shade aside, and felt the bottom fall out of my innards. I quickly padded out of the room and down the stairs, grabbed my winter coat, stuffed my bare feet into my boots, grabbed a set of car keys we left hanging at the front door, and went flying out into the blizzard. I grabbed the shovel that's always left at the front stoop during winter months, quickly shoveled a path to Honey, key fobbed her open, and took several inches of snow to the front of me. I started to cry, then started **shoveling her out**. Yeup, I left the sunroof open the night before. There was at least 8" inside Tim's lover. No sexual innuendo intended. Really. I'm not sure why I didn't hear the approach of my growling husband, but he was on scene before I could make a run for it.

"Where are the keys?"

I handed them to him, even though I suspected this was it, he'd had enough and was planning his escape. Instead, he got into his lover, (okay, that just happened), turned her on, (okay, that was intended), touched her in that special way (forget it), and waited for her to respond. Slowly, ever so slowly, her sunroof slid forward which kept further snow from falling inside NO, it did not occur to me to do that. Tim got out, took the shovel from me, suggested I leave, then spent the better part of the morning shoveling Honey from the inside out.

I was banned from Honey. I totally understood his position, his obsession, because I nurtured it in him and because I loved Zelda once upon a time. Let me tell you about **her!** Zelda, my Datsun 280Z was gorgeous. She had a long, sleek front end and blunted rear, two prominent features of a 280Z. She was midnight blue with black leather interior, and had black rear window louvers. The dashboard was beautiful with large, circular, side-by-side speedometer and tachometer displays, and a low-slung cassette/radio all of which lighted to a soft melon color. The 5-speed stick was leather and chrome and was meant for business. The inside of my 280Z looked like a mini-cockpit, and I loved it.

When it comes to sports cars, beauty is in the eye of the beholder. Visual appearance is undoubtedly the most important thing, but there's so much more to 'the falling in love experience' and when it happens to you, you know it. If you've never heard yourself moan at the sight of something with four wheels, then you've never been in love with an automobile. I moaned when I first saw Z. In that instant, things I didn't even know existed became things that set the yearning and eventually sprung the trap. I'm sure for some, the falling in love might be inspired by the list of things found under the hood. I used to know stuff about horsepower and torque and redline rpms, huh, *that* blast from the past was fun. I knew all that stuff and enjoyed 'talking the talk' with other Z owners, but I did not buy Z based on what was under the hood, I bought her because of the way she made me feel.

Seeing her was one thing, but my love affair with her was about the sounds she made. The solid thump when the door closed, the awesome whoosh-click sound the blinker made, the gentle drag and slap of the windshield wipers, the sexy purr and guttural moan of the engine when she was up or down shifting. Mmmmm. Every single sound from Z was sexy as hell and I felt sexy as hell every time I slid into her low bucket seats. Mmmmm.

Driving was mundane before I met Z, it certainly wasn't an experience. My mother taught me how to drive on her Ford Granada. It was boxy, had an automatic transmission, and was a very popular 'family car' of the 1970s. My mother loved her car, and she should have, she worked hard to buy it, and she took great pride in owning it. And, she gets major props for teaching me how to drive it. When it came to learning how to drive a stick, well that came about in a very odd way. In the late 70s, I worked for an executive at Hanover Insurance company. He asked me to house-sit while he and his family were away on vacation. He left his wife's Pinto for me to use, unfortunately I didn't know how to use it, I didn't know that until after I'd been dropped off in Northborough by a friend. This was way back when cell phones didn't exist, at least they didn't in my world. I was stuck, and I would be for hours.

"A stick shift!" What's a girl to do? Teach herself how to drive a stick. It was a very ugly experience, one that eventually left me stranded on a track at a railroad crossing for way too long for my liking. There was a whole lot of bucking and stalling during that time on the tracks, and I'm quite sure the clutch needed replacing when the vacationers returned from their fun in the sun, but by then, I knew how to drive a manual transmission and I was hooked. That experience paved the way for me to purchase manual transmission cars and to date dudes who could drive manual transmission cars. It became a prerequisite, much like my dudes needed to love the Red Sox. I wasn't a hard ass about things. If a guy asked to buy me a drink, I didn't counter with questions about cars and baseball, but it didn't take long for me to suss out the pertinent info. Usually, all it took was a gentlemanly walk of this girl to her car, her 280Z. Broad smile and impressed nod of the dude's head = he knew how to shift a stick. No smile and no question = he wasn't long for my bucket seats.

I absolutely love being a part of the driving experience, the clutching and shifting and being one with the car. Driving a stick requires active participation, it involves anticipation about what gear you're in and what gear you'll need to be in when you get onto or off of a highway, for instance, if I was in fifth on an open stretch of road, and I needed to exit, I'd clutch and put Z into neutral, then figure things out as I needed to. There's a reason I'm telling you this — really there is.

Knowing how to drive a manual transmission doesn't mean you won't have a bumpy ride. Initially. It took no time at all for Z and me to find perfect harmony. No time before I didn't need to watch her RPMs to know when to clutch and shift. I could hear her subtle call. We were in perfect sync and we remained that way until Hannah was born and my two-seater went from sexy to impactable with one rev of the engine. I sold Z to Kevin Mullaney shortly after I gave birth to my firstborn. I remember meeting him on the driveway, telling him this and that about the object that had so perfectly objectified me for the 'footloose and fancy-free' fun years of my life. I said a silent goodbye to Z, handed off the keys, and went into the house. I just couldn't watch him drive away in my sexy little dream car.

I've been thinking a lot about Z lately. In fact, I had a dream about her not long ago. As soon as I steroided myself up, I started having dreams again. Almost all of them have been lovely. Almost all of them fit nicely into my theory that my life is passing before me in snippets. When I dreamt about Z, I sort of knew it wasn't just a dream, it held significance, a harbinger of things to come. A week or so ago, the meaning of Z became clear. I was readying for a downshift. I was readying to take a corner onto a new part of my journey.

A little backstep … On November 9, 2021, Tim took me to UMass hospital for the much dreaded bone scan. I met with a very understanding and very patient technician who helped prepare me physically and mentally for an IV push of radioactive material into my veins, and a terrifying trip into a partially enclosed machine. The results of that scan showed widespread cancer throughout my skeleton. I was put on high alert that the imminent cause of concern was a break of a major bone or the collapse of my spine which would lead to a rather quick demise. Barring that, it might take six months for the cancer to claim me. For months, I've been fearing a bone break, rightfully so. Every time I needed to leave the comfort of my power chair, I said a little prayer then held my breath until I was returned safely to my perch.

The months of October, November and December were a flurry of medical activity and talky-talk. There was so much information being thrown at me and way too many emotions to deal with to *really* deal with. Dr. Wonderful was with me every step of the way and gave the hard truth compassionately and suffered along with me at the reality of my situation. We have known one another for about fifteen years, so I know I am more than just a patient to him, not only because there's history with us, but because he is that kind of physician, a thinking and caring physician. It is beyond comforting knowing that my situation is more than professional for him. At the end of the day, Dr. Wonderful is my PCP, and as such, it was his job to answer my questions as often as I needed. He was a wealth of information, and if he thought he needed to check something out before doling out facts or plans, he said so. I trusted him then, I trust him now, and without his help, I would not have been able to handle this shit fest.

Anyway, the fear of a broken bone has been forefront in my mind since my diagnosis. My fear ratcheted up when I looked at my bone scan results a month or so ago and saw with my own eyes how much cancer is inside of me and how much deterioration has taken place. I've shared the scan images with a handful of people each of whom lost their breath when they first saw the ink black skeleton. Some uttered things like, "Whoa," or "Oh. My. God." or "How did you not know?" A couple echoed my sentiments upon seeing the devastation, "Fuck." I was sort of pissed with myself when I first looked at the images. It was one thing hearing Dr. Wonderful say I had bone cancer from my skull to my knees, but believe you me his words took on greater meaning when I saw it for myself.

Bottom line … I am so glad I've spent 24/7 on my ass. There have been only four instances when I rose to my feet for purposes other than peeing. 1) when my brother, Don, left my home on Christmas Day. We both knew it would be the last time we'd be together, and we both knew it needed to end with a hug. And it did. 2) when Kathy came to see me before she left for her winter trip to Florida. I needed her hug before she left just in case it was the last time we saw one another though we promised it wouldn't be. It won't be. 3) when Tim and I ended our Date Night. Enough said. 4) when I went to the door the other day to wave to guests who were leaving. The last two instances included a trip to the bathroom, so technically, they were a two-for.

Anyway, back to the downshifting taking place inside me. The physicality of it felt just like my dream of Z, coming off a long stretch of highway where I was coasting along pretty well, a step onto the clutch, a move of the shift into neutral, the steering onto an exit ramp, the pumping of the brakes, the slowing of the car, the slowing of the RPMs, the shifting into a lower gear, the release of the clutch and voilà — I'd taken a corner.

The physical manifestation of all of that ended with this realization: I could have a catastrophic break of a bone resulting in a sudden death OR the cancer that is so clearly spreading throughout my body could be the thing that kills me. It certainly has a death-grip on me. Based on the overall level of discomfort, I'm taking 12 Tramadol pills a day now, and the intensity of the stabbing and grabbing, nibbling and gnawing rodent on all parts of my body, and the overall fatigue, and the extra work it takes for me to sit upright and type a blog or read a book or chat with Tim, and the number of naps

I take now, is a constant reminder that I am dying of cancer. Slowly but surely, I am dying. You know that. I know that. And now, you and I know that I've turned the corner.

A note from Kevin Mullaney …

This is amazing. Period. Exclamation point.

Last October, when Sheryll learned that her cancer returned and metastasized with a vengeance, she went on a mission to provide an intimate portrait of her end-of-life journey.

Sheryll does not shy away from the heartache this devastating reality has on her and her family. She doesn't shy away from the disease's progression. The pain. But this is so much more than that. Sheryll talks about everything.

Part diary, part memoir, Sheryll is a master storyteller and an acute observer with an irreverent lean. There is so much sass. So much life.

57. Isn't It Ironic …

Sand and Surf. Last November, my 86-year-old mother learned I have terminal metastatic breast cancer of the bones. Like me, she thought the 2012 cancer scourge was behind me, after all, I'd jumped through whatever hoops my surgeon and oncologist set for me, and was deemed cancer-free in 2017. Like me, Mom was blindsided to learn my breast cancer had waged a stealth attack, taken a firm hold, and destroyed me from within without our knowing it. Like me, she's spent the past few months enduring long, lonely nights of prayerful thought and, like me, she gratefully welcomes morning's light, so we can hear one another's voice.

Last November, my soon-to-be 61-year-old sister learned my fate. She did a bit of falling apart, then pulled herself together and got on with business, the business of taking care of our mother. Like me, Marjorie wondered whether the aged woman, the one who has pushed through whatever life handed her without hand-wringing or hand-holding, could shoulder the fear, worry and grief about her dying daughter. Like me, my sister has spent hours in prayerful thought.

I am completely sure Marjorie has spent some of her time in a 'this for that' barter with God because who among us hasn't done that? With every fiber of my being, I suspect she has suffered through panic-shivers in the dead of night with this realization, the two women Marjorie has had by her side her whole life will, in all likelihood, predecease her. I can try, but I can't fathom the weight of carrying the loneliness she must already feel, and the fear she bears. Nor can I fathom how Mom is handling the newest shit fest to come her way. A couple of weeks ago, my mother took on a whole new set of worries. This time they are about my sister, the person I call, Marchrie. Before I get to the source of concern for Mom, you need a little background.

It was supposed to be a day trip … It is safe to say that Marjorie's longest and most steadfast friend is Helena Green McCarthy. The two met in grade school and have been buddies forever. They've circled in and out of one another's lives for very brief periods of time, but for decades — five+ decades — they've been a constant for one another. The women are very similar, blonde, light eyed, even-keeled and low key. Both women are very pretty. Marchrie with long lion-mane tresses, and Helena with a short and sassy pixie that very few women can pull off. She rocks it! When they were young they garnered their fair share of attention from guys, neither seemed to dither on about such things, at least from my vantage point.

Today's Helena McCarthy and Marjorie McCarthy are very successful women in their chosen professions. They are dependable, enjoyable to be around, and very nice people. Not only have they been friends for a lifetime, but they were also sisters-in-law for a brief period of time, each one marrying a McCarthy brother — Paul for Helena and Ken for Marjorie. My sister's marriage to Ken ended many years ago, but they immediately built a strong secondary relationship, a friendship based on respect and a singular purpose, the well-being of their daughter, Nicole. The adults put their bruised egos and disappointments aside and put their daughter first. They became the prototype of what divorced parents should be. In my humble opinion.

Anyway, back to the newest shit fest in our lives. First, I should introduce you to one more woman, a friend of Marjorie's and Helena's who I call Mary-Sue-Lou-Jo. When Mary Jo started palling around with M&M — McCarthy and McCarthy — I never quite hit the mark on Mary Jo's name. I'd say Mary Sue, Marjorie would say Mary Jo. I'd say Mary Lou, Marjorie would say Mary Jo. After a bit of this name-nonsense, I started calling the woman, Mary-Sue-Lou-Jo. It's a creative quirk — I suppose. For many years, the three women have gone places and done things. They make it a point to carve time out of their busy schedules to get together, for a weekend trip to the Cape, or a day trip to Rhode Island to park their asses in the sand and watch the surf roll in and out, or simply for a night out to have some good food, a few laughs, and some bonding time. They recently planned a secretive trip to Wells Beach, it turned into a shit fest. I imagine the hatching of this plan went something like this.

"Helena, I'd like to get up to Wells to get my sister some ocean water and sand."

"I'm in. I'll call Mary Jo."

Not exactly a NATO summit — but whatevs. Calendars were checked, a date was chosen, and a road trip was planned. This is how I learned about the trip. I hung up from my Sunday evening call with my brother, Don. My phone immediately rang and it was my mother, a bit odd since we don't often talk at night. We pushed through the hellos and some small talk.

And then this happened ... "I'm going to give the phone to Marjorie. She wants to talk to you."

"Okay."

Rustling noises and muffled talk. Then—

"Don't freak out – I'm okay."

Not sure how the rest of you would have responded to those words, but my blood pressure spiked and my hands produced a quick sweat. My sister continued.

"I slipped on some ice and shattered my right wrist, sprained my left wrist, might have cracked my tailbone, and may have torn a ligament in my left knee, and I twisted my ankle pretty badly."

"Jesus. Did you go to the hospital?

"Yeah, by ambulance."

"Oh, my God. Why didn't Mommy call us?"

"I didn't fall here, I fell in Maine. I went to Wells with Helena and Mary Jo to get you some ocean water and sand, and to just sort of hang at the beach for the day."

My heart sank. My mouth said. "Oh, Marchrie, I'm so sorry. Are you alright? What can I do?" Then I

Sheryll'd her. "Guess that'll teach you. No good deed goes unpunished."

She laughed BIG, then groaned, then moaned. *"No shit, right?"*

I asked a question about the how and wherefores of the slip and fall and she was off and running.

"We were enjoying the day, it was just what I needed, we were ending our time at the ocean and heading off for some food at Billy's Chowder House. Helena and Mary-Sue-Lou-Jo (she occasionally mocks me) *were at the car, I slipped on a patch of ice, both feet went skyward and I landed on my hands and my ass in a twisted, injured heap."*

She said she knew instantly that one wrist was broken, and feared the second might have had a similar injury. She said she was in agony as she waited for an ambulance and she guffawed uncontrollably when she said her friends were at her side in an instant, tending to her needs, and taking pictures of her supine-sprawled-self-served-over-ice. A Marjorie Martini.

"Save the pics. You might find one that'll make a nice Christmas card what with the ice and all."

"You're an ass."

She went into great detail about the very good care she received at the hospital in Maine, that she had some sort of temporary cast on one wrist and a wrap on the other, that she was in pretty bad pain, that she'd need surgery in a week or so, and that she was resting on a recliner in her living room.

I asked how the hell she planned on getting her ass off the recliner given her brokenness and all.

"I'll figure it out. You don't need to worry."

"I don't need to worry, but I do."

A little reminder here … My sister, upon hearing that I needed to live the remainder of my life sitting on my ass, took my husband to look for a recliner that would suit every need I ever had and then some. Then she forked over an obscene amount of money for a recliner that: raises and lowers the leg rest to several positions; raises and lowers the back section from an upright sitting position to various reclining positions; that raises and lowers a headrest section that nestles my head for rest or for television watching; that heats up different sections of my body; that slowly moves to a full upright standing position for an easy-peasy, non-jarring exit from the chair.

Within a nanosecond, my exceedingly comfortable perching upon my luxury leather lounger sent ripples of guilt throughout my body. I tried to diffuse my sudden discomfort by saying this to my battered and broken kid sister, "Too bad you don't have a really nice sister, the kind who'd buy you a super-de-duper recliner like mine."

She laughed.

"You know, Marchrie, before you bought my recliner, Tim found a medical supply rental place. He was going to rent a recliner for me; let us rent you a recliner. It could be in your home tomorrow."

"Let me see how things go tonight."

"Okay, but really think about it. You're in for a long-haul and you're going to need to be comfortable especially if you've done knee damage."

"We'll see how things go."

I could hear the fatigue in her voice, "You sound tired."

"I am."

"Do you need anything?"

"Nope, I'm good."

"If you need anything—"

"I'll call."

"How's Mommy?"

"Being strong for me."

"What the fuck? Seriously. Everyone's so fearful I'll break something, and now you're broken."

"A freak accident."

"Yeah."

"I'm gonna hang up and see if I can sleep."

"Okay." Before she could disconnect, I stopped her. "I've a question, an important question."

"What?"

"You still have my ocean water and sand, right?"

"Yeah." She laughed.

"You protected it, right?"

"You're an ass." She laughed harder.

"And you'll give them to me, right?"

"I know just where I'm gonna put them."

"Not possible what with the broken wrists and all."

She laughed until she cried.

When we hung up. I cried for a very long time.

It's a couple weeks out and Marchrie is on the mend. She had surgery on her fractured-in-several-places-wrist. It's been plated and screwed and casted. Her other wrist is feeling much better, as is her knee and ankle. She'll be going to a knee specialist to check things out, but she thinks it was a bad wrench and maybe not a tear or something. And so far, she's resisted our offer for a power recliner.

As for my mother. I called the other morning and she answered the phone, a bit out of breath, "Can I call you right back, Sheryll Anne? I'm putting Marjorie's socks on her feet."

Really? I'm mean, seriously? Is this necessary? I've changed my prayer. "God, please don't give my mother more than *she* can handle."

Tomorrow is Sunday and Marjorie and Mom will be chauffeured to my home by Mr. Wonderful to spend the afternoon. It's been over two weeks since I've seen them and I miss them more than words can express. Tonight, Tim and I will tag-team the making of a cheesecake — Marchrie's favorite of my desserts. I've given her one as a Christmas gift for more than 30 years. Seeing her again will feel like Christmas. As for Mom, as soon as she walks through my door I'm going to get onto my feet and give her a hug. Marjorie, too!

In Blog 25, Some Truth Telling, I wrote:

America's Favorite Pastime …

Christmas. ✓ Birthday. ✓ New Year's Eve and Day. ✓ ✓ Now, what? I've been so focused on living long enough to enjoy those lasts that I didn't put any thought into what comes next. That realization hit hard early New Year's Day. "What do I focus on now that the holiday milestones I set have come and gone? Do I choose Valentine's Day in February as my next wanna-see, or stretch beyond that to the first day of spring in March, or should I swing big and go for Opening Day of baseball in April? Or do I just sit back and wait for the telltale signs, the ones that announce my decline and then pick a day or week or month that seems doable — reachable?"

Thus began the snit about changes in Opening Day schedules and math equations based on calendar ditties and the beginnings of some bickering between Mr. and Mrs. Wonderful which led to this proclamation by the missus: "I've decided I'm swinging big. I'm going for Opening Day."

And then this happened ... Weeks later, my cell phone blew up with texts: MLB Opening Day canceled!!!!! — Did you hear? — No Opening Day!!!!! — Oh, Sheryll, did you hear the news? I heard and I felt gutted. I waited, my family and friends waited as contract negotiations pushed on and on and on. Then, everyone came to their senses. My cell phone blew up with texts: MLB Opening Day is rescheduled!!!!! — Did you hear? — Opening Day is happening!!!!! — Oh, Sheryll, did you hear? I heard and I felt elated for two reasons. My Opening Day goal was back on, AND, Opening Day was set for April as it should have been all along! Three plans are now set in stone. I'll be watching my beloved Red Sox on Opening Day. I'll be getting onto my feet during the 7th inning stretch. I'll be singing *Take me Out* and *Sweet Caroline.* AT. THE TOP. OF. MY. LUNGS. I'm swinging big, friends.

Where is Alanis Morissette when you need her ... I'm sooooo messing with her lyrics right now: It's a pill that can douse a flame ... It's a pill that can change a game ... It's a pill for another day ... It's a pill that takes teeth away ... Isn't it ironic? Don't you think?

Yeup! Tooth loss. Sort of. That's the new and exciting shit fest going on in my life. I thought long and hard about sharing this fabulous fuckery. Then my mind traveled back to a conversation I had with Tim when I started writing the blog. "If I write it, I write all of it. Right? Even the hard, ugly stuff. Right?"

"You write what you need to get out. The blog is supposed to be therapeutic. Right?"

"But, I suspect some of the stuff that's heading my way is going to be hard for people to read."

"If you can write it, they can read it or not."

So, I'm leaving it up to you. Read it. Or not. This is my very simplistic explanation of what's happening with my body. I had breast cancer. That is my primary cancer. I have bone cancer. That is my secondary cancer. My metastatic breast cancer is fueling my bone cancer. In December, I was put on a drug, Letrozole, to work against the fuel source. Theory: if the fuel source could be doused a bit, then the spread of my bone cancer might be slowed down a bit. That is how I connect the dots of information.

As with every drug I am currently taking, there can be positive and negative outcomes for the drug itself; in addition, all of the drugs need to play nice together. Needless to say, there is a lot of pharmaceutical jig-saw-puzzling being done by Dr. Wonderful and Nurse M. They are always monitoring and weighing benefits v risks, particularly when it comes to really powerful drugs. Letrozole is a powerful cancer drug. Tim needs to wear gloves when he's handling it. He's handling it because I'm taking it. The benefit of taking Letrozole: it can slow cancer spread. The risk of taking Letrozole: a whole bunch of scary stuff including tooth weakening or loss. Last weekend, I lost part of a back molar whilst eating a banana. Initially, I didn't know what the hard object surrounded by mushy fruit was. I spit the banana mush out, rooted around for the shard, cleaned it off, examined the fragmented piece from all angles, declared it was part of a tooth, saw how fragile it was, then crushed it between my thumb and forefinger as though it was a cookie crumb. I told no one. I wept myself to sleep with a whole lot of ugly crying going on.

I lost a piece of a different tooth on the same side of my mouth the next morning, and a third piece of tooth on the other side Monday afternoon. I called Dr. Wonderful's office and spoke to my contact person there; yes, I have a person who takes my calls, and she is beyond helpful and knowledgeable. I told Sharon what was going on, said it was absolutely **not** an emergency, and that I could wait for a return call that evening from the doctor. By the time I spoke with Dr. Wonderful I'd lost another piece of a different tooth. He took me off of the drug, the one that might have been slowing my cancer. I think the drug did some good, but that is no longer the case. I am familiar with my body in ways I have never known it before and I know the cancer gnawing rat is everywhere now. He still enjoys my thighs, but he's also nibbling away on my right shin, my left ankle, both shoulders and across my back in the thoracic area. Bottom line: the cancer isn't slowing down, it is ramping up and the pill that could have helped with that is a risk to me now.

Physically and emotionally … I cannot begin to tell you how upsetting — nope, how absolutely devastating it was to lose pieces of my teeth. I'm sure plenty of you have had dreams about losing your teeth. I've had them. They are very disturbing dreams, now imagine the dreams become a reality. I don't have to imagine. The reality of Banana Day made me profoundly sad. And it made me pissed as hell. My life has been on a downward spiral since November. I've sucked up every bit of emotionally crippling news that's been fired my way, I've tried to prepare my loved ones for my loss, I've worked very hard at dying with dignity and without the constant refrain of 'woe is me', but to fuck it all, this last bit of shit just isn't fair. In fact, it's been a bitter pill to swallow. Isn't it ironic?

58. Ocean …

I love to learn things. I've mentioned before that one of my favorite parts about the writing experience was the time I spent researching. Even as a kid, I liked learning stuff. When I did my weekly trip to the bookmobile to get my hands on the newest Nancy Drew, I'd also grab a book on whatever suited my fancy. Maybe I'd check out a book on flowers one week, and the next week follow up with a book on photosynthesis, which led me to something about horticulture, and then maybe to botany. I didn't read the entire books, I wasn't that much of a dweeb, but I followed my own system. First, I'd look at the pictures and read whatever was written beneath them. I learned lots of useful information that way. Then, if I wanted a more detailed understanding of the subject matter, I'd check the number of pages per chapter; let's say there were twelve, I'd read the first two pages and the last two pages of the chapter; they are the introduction and the conclusion of the pertinent information, then I'd move along. I was reading for fun, And this was my idea of fun.

Remember Donna Rosetti, my friend who knew everything about everything and kicked my ass in every game of Trivial Pursuit we ever played, well, she could do that because when she checked out a book from a library, you can bet your ass she read it cover to cover. Don't think for one second that made Donna a dweeb — Donna Rosetti was the coolest person I ever knew.

Anyway, as I was saying, after a trip to the Bookmobile, I would read long into the night; long after Marchrie did the whole untucking and retucking nighttime ritual and deemed her bed clear of spiders. I'd wait for her ass landing and scooching into place, then I'd push my pillows against the headboard, grab a little flashlight I kept next to my bed and do a bit of reading or playing dictionary until I fell asleep. Okay, I guess I wasn't a bookworm, I was a dweeb.

I've often described myself as a wealth of useless information; the 'wealth' being useful only when playing Trivial Pursuit. Let's face it, in the day-to-day chit-chat of life, it matters little that I know the crap that fills my head, but when I write my stories, the bits and bobs of information and push and pull of my desires find their way into my characters' lives.

Take Kitt Mahoney for instance; she is the central character in *Bullet Bungalow*, the one so connected to the ocean that she sees it as an essential part of her life. To her, it's as essential as the air she breathes. The ocean, the Atlantic ocean, the part that plays with the piece of shoreline she owns, owns her soul. Kitt gets that from me. There is nothing that I love more or need more than the sight, sound, and smell of the ocean.

As you know, Wells Beach is my most favorite place, my most favorite beach. The trip from Worcester to Maine takes about two hours. It's a straightforward highway romp: I-290 E, I-495 N, I-95 N, a trip across the Piscataqua Bridge and onto 'All Points Maine' highway system. It's when I read that sign that I begin feeling it. **The pull of the ocean.** As soon as we pull off the highway system, we power down the car windows and — wait for it — wait for it — wait for it. Ahhhhh, there it is, the smell of the ocean, off in the distance, but close enough to seep deep. Everything from that point on is intuitive. The OBs return to Wells is imprinted in our DNA, much like the migratory return of swallows from their winter home in Argentina to their summer home at the Mission of San Juan Capistrano, or the flit of North American hummingbirds between their southern wintering grounds and northern breeding grounds. Both are instinctive, natural, inborn.

Triumphant annual returns for the sparrows, the hummingbirds, and the OBs.

As soon as we turn onto Mile Road off the main drag through Wells, an internal happy dance begins. There's a sitting more upright in the seats, a lean forward into the trip, an uptick of excitement in our voices, and the release of the expectant, "Ahhhhh," when we pass through areas of marshland, the low-lying, transitional zone between land and water. There are lots of reasons to look at the marshland. It is a very pretty extension of ocean topography, but truth be told, there's only one thing said when the OBs see the marshes, "The tide is in — OR — the tide is out." No sooner is that declaration made than the Atlantic Ocean appears and captures my attention and owns my soul.

A little sidestep ... It is just past 2 AM. I woke from sleep with a headache, nothing to be concerned about, just a headache, but still, it needed an OTC. I grabbed one from my nightstand drawer at about the same time the rodent decided to do a bit of gnawing at my right shin. From somewhere in the recesses of my brain I remembered a rodent is also called a shrew (a small insectivorous mammal resembling a mouse, with a long, pointed snout and tiny eyes). I chuckled at a thought that skittered through my brain. So, here it is, my dear blogosphere friends, we are going a bit Shakespearean with something I'm calling, The Naming of the Shrew. Have fun naming the bane of my existence. The cancer nibbling and gnawing rodent. I look forward to reading your FB posts!

Back to the sidestep. I figured I may as well take a pain pill with the OTC. The pill popping and water slurping process woke me just enough that I knew it'd take a few minutes to settle in. I so did not want to check the happenings on the Hallmark Channel, so I opened a blank doc and typed the word ocean. Not sure why, but here we are. Why I chose that word is an interesting question. Why am I fascinated with, pulled helplessly to, and controlled by the ocean? Millions of people are drawn to it, and I'm sure countless of them feel the way I do — the ocean is a life source — their life force.

Time for some research. Because, why not. The ocean is a huge body of saltwater that covers about 71 percent of Earth's surface. The planet has one global ocean, though oceanographers have traditionally divided it into four distinct regions: the Pacific, Atlantic, Indian, and Arctic oceans.

An estimated 97 percent of the world's water is found in the ocean, and as such, it has considerable impact on weather, temperature, and the food supply of humans and other organisms. Despite its size and impact on every organism on Earth, the ocean remains a mystery. More than 80 percent of the ocean has never been mapped, explored, or even seen by humans. A far greater percentage of the surfaces of the moon and the planet Mars have been mapped and studied than has our own ocean floor, though oceanographers have made some amazing discoveries. For example, we know that the ocean contains towering mountain ranges and deep canyons known as trenches, just like those found on land. The peak of the world's tallest mountain, Mount Everest in the Himalaya, measuring 5.49 miles high would not even break the surface of the water if it was placed in the Pacific Ocean's Mariana Trench or Philippine Trench, two of the deepest parts of the ocean. On the other hand, the Atlantic Ocean is relatively shallow because large parts of its seafloor are made up of continental shelves, parts of which extend far out into the ocean, leaving the average depth of the Atlantic at 12,200 feet.

https://www.nationalgeographic.org/encyclopedia/ocean

Hmm. I knew some of that, but I learned some stuff. So, that was time well spent. Moving on. We know what the ocean is, so let's see why I and millions of others are controlled by the ocean's pull. On our way to finding that answer, let's take a look at ocean-related folklore. There are ample myths, traditions, and legends from every country whose shorelines meet the gentle lap or turbulent crash of sea water. There's plenty of folklore from the New England coastlines, so let's start there.

It's unlucky to begin a voyage on a Friday. (Didn't know that). Friday is considered an unlucky day on land as well as at sea. (Didn't know that). Friday is considered unlucky because it was the day of the crucifixion. (Huh, well, okay then). Seafaring people of long ago were a superstitious lot. They relied on a fair amount of luck, but they also worked overtime not to spit in the face of fate. (Believe you me, there were and are lots of things sailors and fishermen will and will not do).

Men boarding vessels emptied their pockets of pennies or else they prepared themselves for a small catch. Under no circumstances would men bring bananas onto their ship. (Huh, no explanation given on that one. Maybe a fear of slipping on a peel and falling overboard? Yeup, I'm going with that). Nothing could be eaten until the first fish of the day was caught. (Probably a strategy to get onto the ocean bright and early). The first caught fish of the day needed to be spit upon and thrown back into the ocean. (Haven't a clue). The location of a good haul was never spoken about, nor was a fishing boat taken to sea seven days straight. (According to this, the gods of the ocean looked down on greed, but apparently, they were perfectly fine with spitty-fish. I wonder why? I bet Donna Rosetti knew this shit).

Flowers weren't welcome aboard a ship because of their association with funerals. (Huh, if they were smuggled aboard and found, they were immediately tossed over the sides). Clergymen weren't welcome onboard for the same reason. (Huh, I wonder if they were tossed into the drink, too? I mumbled and chuckled). Sharks following a ship were thought to be harbingers of death. (Well, yeah, they're sharks. Duh). If someone died aboard a ship, over he went, but only after a bit of shroud affixing and needle-poking through the mate's nose to make sure there was no pain-sensory left. (Apparently, the nostrils are a sensitive area. I guess if no 'what the eff' spewed forth when a darning needle went in and out then a mighty old heave ho into the splash took place. Could have done without that bit of knowledge. Just sayin).

Sailors had a fatalistic view of drowning. (Well, duh! From a statistical standpoint, that stands to reason. I bet drowning was high on the Cause of Death list for sailors and fishermen. Even Sheryll Bodine gets that one). If a sailor fell overboard a rope might not be tossed to aid him because it was accepted by the crew that his death was preordained. (More like, premeditated murder, if you ask me. The 'no rope rule' probably explains the sailors' fatalistic view of drowning). A ship's bell was the only bell allowed on board and was used only to signal the changing of watch duties. If the bell rang of its own accord, it was feared someone was going to die. (My guess, the dude who rang it was the one slated for death).

Ebb tides were thought to hasten death, ebbing away the gravely ill or wounded. (Finally, something that makes sense). Men carrying the name Jonah were not allowed on ships nor were ships allowed to be named Jonah. Period. (Okay, got it). Birds were protected by the seafarers as it was thought they carried the souls of dead sailors back to land. Therefore, killing a bird was bad luck. (Probably why there are so many gulls around).

The folklore included a whole lot more of shit bad luck stuff for the sea-loving man: stepping aboard a ship with your left foot first, or losing a bucket overboard, or saying the words, 'drown' or 'pig' while at sea, or swearing while fishing. (Huh, I think I've heard, 'step right, maties'. I wonder if that referred to the leading foot, and who the hell hasn't lost a bucket at sea, hell I've lost them from the damned shoreline, and how else would you explain the missing dude doing the 'dead man's float' other than to say he drowned, and who the eff hasn't sworn while fishing)?

I scrolled up and read whatever this mess is about and was left with this: that's one hell of a long list of unluckies. Was anything allowed or, dare I ask, considered lucky? A bit more research. Yeup, in the good luck department. **Tattoos. Black cats onboard. Tossing a pair of old shoes overboard.** That's it. I wonder if extra 'lucky points' were given if the shoes being tossed into the drink belonged to the mate who slipped on a banana peel in his socken-feet and drowned because his mates wouldn't toss him a rope and his pockets were full of pennies that weighted him down? And, what the eff is up with tossing him his shoes, and not tossing him a rope? A bit harsh. Ah, 'tis the life of a sailor.

There are countless other things; like rain coming before seven will be ending by eleven, and clapping onboard causes thunder, and, and, and. I could go on, and on, and on, but who has the time? Not me, so I'll wrap this stuff up with the two most widely known sayings for the seafarer and the beachgoer alike.

Red sky in the morning, sailors take warning.
Red sky at night, sailors take delight.

So, off we go now to the point of this ramble ... Actually, sleep beckons, so I'm going to close my eyes and get back to this when the sun and I get up for the day.

Good morning! I've had my morning pills, I am sufficiently caffeinated, and I had a lovely apricot danish for breakfast. All's right with the world, my world, anyway. I'm going to ease back into this ramble about why I love the ocean. I know I'm in very good company, millions of people feel the way I do about the ocean, so the next part of the blog might interest a few of them.

Before I nodded off, I found this website: The Waters You're Drawn To Reveal Secrets About Your Personality. Right off, the author reminds or informs the reader that water makes up 60% of the human body, and therefore, it makes perfect sense that we are connected to and fascinated by the ever-changing element. Then the author, Cassandra Morris, jumps into the deep end with a personality test; you watch a somewhat hypnotic video of the ocean with the sounds of waves and piano music in the background. She suggests you clear your mind and just watch and listen for a bit. Then, for some unknown reason you are asked to look at a picture of sea shells laid out on sand and count the number of spiral ones and keep that number in your head. I did it, but I have no idea why I did it. Then, you are shown pictures of different bodies of water: ocean, lake, river, waterfall, pond, and others, from which you are to choose your favorite. And voilà

— your water personality floats to the top. There should be no surprise for any of you what body of water I chose.

The Calm Ocean ... By being drawn to the peaceful ocean, you reveal yourself to be a gentle, comforting, giving soul with a sensitive nature. You are very compassionate and warm, and you're eager to bring joy to those around you. You work hard and value responsibility, but you love nothing more than to let your hair down and have fun. You are very empathetic and compassionate, and you feel everything with your whole heart. You are something of a mystery to most people. One half of you is charismatic and bubbly, while the other half is introverted and quiet; sometimes you're adventuresome and eager to explore, while other times you're happy to stay home and enjoy the quiet. But one thing about you is for certain: you never make a promise you can't keep, and you always give everything your all.

By choosing the calm ocean, the symbol of distance, change, and cycles, this signifies that you will soon embark on a special trip. Whether it be physical or spiritual travel, you will be visited by the opportunity to expand your horizons and explore personally uncharted territory. If you embrace this chance, your life will be transformed in a very unexpected and rewarding way.

The Placid Lake ... Just for fun, I chose a second one. If you were drawn to the peaceful lake, this reveals that you have a calm, down-to-earth, and outgoing soul. Though you're not quite a social butterfly, you're happy to meet new people and expand your horizons. You always feel most at peace when surrounded by nature, and you have respect for all forms of life. You are genuine and warm, and you enjoy bringing happiness

to the people you love. Because you're so incredibly giving and compassionate, you'd happily give someone in need the shirt off your back. You're also the one people turn to when they need help, either spiritual or material. You are humble and hard-working. You are a salt of the earth person with a very kind heart.
Since you chose the calm lake, the symbol of strength, honor, and dependability, you will soon be entrusted with a big responsibility, one that will yield many wonderful things. You might not feel suited to the task at first, but just know that no one could do this job better than you. It will be so worth it.

https://littlethings.com/lifestyle/water-personality-test

There are lots of things that I identify with in both summaries. Some are spot on about who I am as an individual, but a couple of lines in each narrative are personally relevant: By choosing the calm ocean, the symbol of distance, change, and cycles, this signifies that you will soon embark on a special trip. Whether it be physical or spiritual travel, you will be visited by the opportunity to expand your horizons and explore personally uncharted territory. **I'm guessing this could mean my passing. Thoughts, anyone?** By choosing the calm lake, you will soon be entrusted with a big responsibility, one that will yield many wonderful things. You might not feel suited to the task at first, but just know that no one could do this job better than you. It will be so worth it. **I'm guessing this could mean my blog writing. Thoughts, anyone?**

You know and I know these little tests are for entertainment value only. This water test lived up to its end — it was entertaining. The thing that I find interesting, however, is this: I found the test because I woke at 2 AM and couldn't get back to sleep. I couldn't work on the blog I started writing yesterday because it's about the many wonderful cards and letters I've received, and the box I keep them in is across the room from me and I'm not allowed to meander to them. So, I opened a new document and without any thought at all, typed the word Ocean. One thing led to another and I ended up taking a water personality test because why not, right? Kinda feels like all of it was meant to be. And this next part is the only thing that I knew for sure would be included in this blog.

For months, friends and family have been sending me picture texts of the ocean. Guru Jessica has built a special place for them on my website (it's really quite lovely, and you might consider taking a look). Several people have taken the time to record and send to me videos of the rolling surf. Kathy sends frequent videos from Florida, and Helena sent one from the Cape, and Sheila sent one from somewhere in Maine, and Debbie sent one from Florida, and Guru sent one from Mexico, and Josephine, Marjorie, Nicole, Hannah and Jessica all sent videos from Wells. Each and every recording is very special to me and I've played them on more than one occasion. But the video that I play over and over and over again is the one that came attached to this text:

> Joyce: Taking you on a little walk on Wells Beach this morning. Hopefully this doesn't make you dizzy, if it does, look up.

For the next two minutes, Joyce McTigue and I walked the shoreline, together. The ocean rolled gently in, breaking at the end with a little froth. Swaths of wispy clouds cut the perfectly blue sky, and pebbles and shells littered here and there. The only sounds were the waves crashing and the gulls calling. It was the absolute perfect way to spend my time. With my friend. On my beach. At my ocean. Thank you, Joyce. It was a beautiful walk.

A note from Joyce McTigue ...

Sheryll Sneade caught the bouquet at my wedding. She was there with my husband's cousin, Tim O'Brien. My guess is that I was aiming for someone else (which bride doesn't), but I was pleased when she caught it and became part of our day. At the time, I remembered Sheryll as a beautiful girl who was a couple years older than me at our high school and that's about all I knew of her.

Several years later, we became neighbors when my husband and I purchased the McTigue home on Wildwood. At the time there were a dozen little kids running the yards including my kids and the O'Brien girls. During that time, I drove a bright red minivan (red...a surprise from my husband). When I traded my van in for a new car, Sheryll told me it was going to be harder for her kids to spot me when they played, "Where's Joyce."

As the kids got older, my daily commute to work got longer. I hardly saw our neighbors, but I would often see them as I backed my car in and saw house lights way up their driveway - that's how it gets sometimes when life is busy... checking in on each other from afar.

In the last few months I've learned more about Sheryll than I did in all the years living across the street from her. I always knew what a loving wife and mother Sheryll is, but I had no idea she was such a gifted writer or how incredibly strong she is. Anyone who has read her books or blog will agree. I am so grateful for the books she gave to me and our time reconnecting.

To be honest, when Sheryll called me to tell me about her terminal diagnosis my first instinct was to back away. I was angry. I've already lost way too many people before their time, so I was raising up my wall of protection.

Luckily, it only went up part way before I shook myself off and called her to chat.

I hope I've brought some sunshine into difficult days via the pictures I've shared with her.

Many years ago, Sheryll told me about a conversation her girls had when her mom was going to Florida. Jessica asked Hannah where Florida was. Hannah replied, "It's right next to Heaven only Florida has telephones." Never a funnier statement for a Snowbird to hear!

Sheryll may not get to be a Snowbird with me, but if her time comes before mine, according to Hannah, we'll be neighbors, again!

59. The Written Word

Guess what I did. I started reading *Bullet Bungalow,* my first published book. Debbie, Jennifer, and a new pal, Josephine Power, recently cracked the spines on the Pulling Threads series for the first time. They started talking about Kitt and Fred, and John and Joy, and Mayflower and Laurel Falls, and stalkers, and beachfront properties, and, and, and — so I decided to join the fun, fun, fun.

I mentioned in a recent blog that my body is slowing down, just a bit, nothing major, but enough to make a few differences in how I spend my 24/7. The takeaway is that I'm napping a lot more than I used to, and during the times when I'm awake, I don't always have the mindful energy to string sentences together, so it's a hard push to complete three blogs per week. So what's a girl to do? If the girl is an author, and she can't create, she can read one of her books. Or, she can read a book written by someone else. There's an itty-bitty problem in that for me, I do not want to start a book I may not finish. Imagine my getting halfway through the only Agatha Christie book I've yet to read, *The Murder of Roger Ackroyd*, and I drop dead before he does or before I learn who done him in. That would piss me off for all eternity. Seriously. It would piss me off.

At the very least, it would cause me to search for the long-dead mistress of mystery-writing upon my entrance through the Pearly Gates. Little known fact: the Bible is the best-selling book of all time; William Shakespeare and Agatha Christie are the top-selling authors of all time. I remembered that bit of useless info, then did an internet search to verify my memory. It's all good!

Okay, back to the horror of horrors, I've started reading a book, I've made some significant progress into the story, I drop dead before finishing it — no thank you, very much. Since I know the storyline of *Bullet Bungalow*, and the trials and tribulations of Ms. Mahoney, I feel safe starting it, and I've felt safe cracking the spine on a book called *Providence Noir*, a collection of short stories perfect for those who enjoy small doses of the darker side of humanity and really good storytelling.

Okay, putting that aside, one of my most favorite sounds in the world is the cracking of the spine on a hardcover book or journal when it's first opened. There's just something about a hardcover experience, holding a book with some heft, the sight of words filling pages, the first time opening the book to some random place, the stretching of the rigid spine, and the crack. I always repeat the process a few more times just because the crack of a book spine feels and sounds so good.

What does not sound good is the crack I'm hearing in certain parts of my spine when I move, particularly when I turn my head from side to side. The cracks don't happen every time I move, and they don't cause any pain, but they're happening with more and more frequency and they freak the hell out of me. It's hard to tell exactly what's happening inside of me, but I can make assumptions based on the munching that's been going on. The newest munch-area is my right wrist, and yes there is pain there and it has raised a concern for me, the person who relies on her hands to do the typing to keep her from going bonkers. And the increased cracking sounds along my spine make me wonder if they mean anything serious, or they simply cause a shudder, that has on occasion been accompanied with a crack. So, where are we? The crack of book spines – love it. The crack of body spines – not so much.

A shared love of music … I received a multi-page note, handwritten by my brother, Don. The very first thing you should know about the Ramblin' Man is that he is incapable of sitting down. When his feet hit the floor in the morning, he is upright on them all day long. The only time I've seen Don sit with any regularity or length is when we are at the beach. He does his fair share of lounging, but that bit of time is definitely offset with frequent long walks. For Don to sit his ass long enough to write anything is noteworthy, for him to take time to dig through his memory-bank and list the concerts he attended over the years is quite remarkable and therefore, I am remarking on it.

Don's trip down musical memory lane …

<u>The Ones That Got Away</u>:

The Rolling Stones. The best band of all time, bar none.
Beach Boys. My second favorite.
Allman Brothers. Song: Ramblin' Man.
David Bowie. Song: I love, love, Heroes.
Bob Seger. Songs: Main Street, and Sunspot Baby.
Linda Ronstadt. Very talented.
Bob Dylan. Probably the greatest solo artist and songwriter.
Jackson Browne. Great music.

There was a second list of several pages. *Been There Done That* were concerts he attended, listed by date, and in most cases, where the concerts took place. I'm telling you, this chronological endeavor was quite the ass-sitting commitment — not quite a 24/7 undertaking I'm doing, but still. I'm not going to run the list, but I am going to mention one concert because I discussed it briefly during a recent Sunday phone call with Don.

"I loved the list of concerts you sent."

"Yeah. That took some time."

"I bet. By the way, you and I were at the same concert."

"No shit. Which one?"

"I'm saving that bit of info for a blog."

Pause. *"I bet I know. I bet it was Aerosmith at the Brooks Concert Hall at Holy Cross."*

My brother was absolutely correct. I wish I'd known he was there. I would have loved being elbow to elbow watching Steven Tyler do his thing!

My favorite thing to do during the long, lonely nights … My postman Jose, has been working overtime with card deliveries to 183 Wildwood Avenue. I've received so many lovely cards, and I've enjoyed them all. In fact, I've become quite protective of them, enamored by them. Each folded gift, because let's face it that's what they are, has brought unexpected joy to me. Most cards have a printed saying on both the outside and the inside. All have come with a penned note by the sender. I make an effort to not read the return address before opening the card because I really enjoy being surprised. I've been keeping the cards in a pretty box, and on some nights, I ask Tim to set Hadley's rolling table near my chair and to put the box there so I can look through the cards again. It's become a lovely, peaceful practice.

One night, I was looking at a card from a woman who lived on Wildwood many years ago, and these words popped into my head, "Huh, that looks like a card Susie would send." Susie is a very sun-shiny woman, a fresh-faced beauty who spent as many daytime hours outside walking or gardening as she could. The card she sent held her personality. It had a pastel blue background and an old-fashioned bicycle drawing in the foreground. Resting in the handlebar basket was a bouquet of wildflowers. Long stems with gold and green foil leaves flopped over the sides, and a lone, oversized flower raised from the heavy cardstock. The card's message was simple and genuine: ***Thinking of you … and sending positive thoughts and feel-good wishes to brighten your world***. Those words hit the mark. Then, there was a beautiful note from Susie inside that most certainly brightened my world.

I pulled a random card from the box. This time it was white and had a scripted name across the top. That's it, no fanfare. It was from my sister-in-law, Helen. The card itself, and the handwritten message inside is *exactly* what I knew it'd be, simple, direct, and so perfectly Helen. ***There are no words to comfort you,***

but know that you are loved and always will be. And, just like that, I felt her love and I was comforted by her words.

I pulled another card from the box. It had a beautiful lavender envelope, and waiting inside was a beige parchment card with a single-stemmed, *"Wish flower,"* as Hadley calls the blow-away weeds. The flower had lavender swaths with dark, sparkly, already taken into flight blow-aways. The handwritten note inside was from the sister of my brother-in-law, Tommy, the man who shares his life with the She Devil. Patty is a nurse and she penned a few words about the scourge of metastatic breast cancer, then set about expressing her gratitude that I was blogging about this experience and the impact it's having on her, and she assumed on others, as well. ***This is not only a "thinking of you card," but a fan letter. I just learned about the blog and it is wonderful ... I've laughed out loud, and I've cried a lot. Keep the blogs coming! I am looking forward to hearing about Opening Day.***

A sidestep, of course there's a sidestep ... It would take an entire blog to tell you how many people have contacted me about the blog. I get feedback on Facebook, which is loads of fun, but the behind the scenes messages I've been receiving from people I know, and people I do not know and will never meet is quite something. There has been an outpouring of love and support, but there has also been the telling of tales and sharing of painful losses — from complete strangers. My book *Be, still* helped one woman a year after the passing of her father.

An email from a stranger ...

I think I understand why Dad pulled away during hospice. I assumed he would want to spend more time with his family. As the days went on, he wanted to spend them alone. After reading Be, still, I think he wanted more and more time for himself. If Dad was spending his time reflecting, like you've been, then I know he was enjoying his last months because he had a really full life. Thank you for a different perspective.

~ Monica

I pulled another random card from my box. This card was sent by a woman who has been besties with my sister-in-law, Kathy, forever. First a little about the card itself. It's a bold, colorful painting of an ocean making quite the impression on a rocky jetty. The abundant white froth and dark blue waters lets you know the seas are strong, but the horizon dares to butt against the rage with soft muted pinks and grayish-blues. It's a really beautiful card and it was most likely chosen because I love the ocean. That, in and of itself is thoughtful, the handwritten note inside, even more so. Paula said she was impressed ***...and inspired by your ability to express your feelings and tell your story in such an eloquent, interesting and emotional way***. She mentioned her heartfelt concerns for Tim and my girls, and then she ended with her thoughts and prayers, and this ... ***P.S. I hate the fucking WORDLE, too! – Love, Paula.*** Love Her, Just Sayin! Hellooooo, She Devil.

Other memorable cards and letters ... As a Christmas gift, I gave my mother, my sister and both of my daughters boxes of note cards. I chose cards that reflected their personalities. I knew there'd come a time when they'd want to send a note off to someone, you know, after my passing, and I wanted to help make the event easy-peasy for them. The cards I chose for Mom are very pretty: beige background with an array of thinly-stemmed wild flowers with a few tiny butterflies flitting about. The field of flowers are done in soft, muted blue and white tones. The bottom edge is scalloped cut, an attention to detail I knew my mother would appreciate, and the envelopes are a soft blue color, like her eyes.

Mom prefers sending correspondence the old-fashioned way, through snail-mail. Partly because her poor fingers just don't work as they once did, but mostly because she has a recessive gene when it comes to things with buttons and sequences. I take after her. I suck at technology but I've mastered texting, thank you very much. Not so much for Mom. God love her, she's tried, but let's face it, banging out a hello text should not take upwards of a half-hour. Her inability to text never bothered her, until I became sick. On more than one occasion she's said she wishes she could send a thinking of you text to me. So what's an old woman to do? If she's my mother, she makes do with what she has. I received these in the mail — the snail-mail. **My thoughts and prayers for you are constant. By the way, this is a text message.** And. **My darling daughter, Sheryll. I love you!!! Here's another text message. See how modern I'm becoming.** Is that the most adorable thing EVER! Yes. It is.

I sent a signed copy of *Be* to the woman who went with Marchrie and Helena to the beach that day, the third musketeer on that ill-fated trip, the woman who helped my sister in so many ways. I received a lovely beach-themed thank you note. The picture on the front of the card was of long-bladed, grass dunes, and weathered fencing along a pathway to a sandy beach. In the distance, beautiful blue waters played beneath a tranquil sky of soft pastel pinks, purples, and corals. The card was signed by Mary-Sue-Lou-Jo. What a hoot!

A little trip back in time. There were two handwritten notes I received at Christmas. The first note accompanied the beautiful painting Jennifer Lane Courville gave me. She quoted a children's book author from England.

> *Where do people go to when they die?*
> *Somewhere down below or in the sky?*
> *"I can't be sure," said Grandad, "but it seems"*
> *They simply set up home inside our dreams."*
>
> *~ Jeanne Willis*

I believe that is true.
I hope for my loved ones, it is.

And, now, a handwritten note of most significance. You'll remember, from a previous blog, that Don and Denise made the trek north from Georgia to spend Christmas with me. In Blog 22, Christmas, I wrote:

The thing I wanted most on my last Christmas was the gift of human contact. The embrace of family members, some who would drive a few miles to see me, and others who would travel the Eastern Seaboard to give and receive a hug. Had I not been diagnosed in November, my brother and sister-in-law would not have driven from Georgia to Massachusetts for Christmas. They always celebrate the holiday down south, choosing to make their annual trek north during summer months so we can all bask in the warmth of family love on the sandy beach in Wells, Maine. This year my 66-year-old brother did the 1,055 mile drive to ensure that I'd get the ultimate combo gift ever! Him.

When I heard that Don and Denise were making the trip north, my anticipation of milestone celebrations turned into sheer excitement at seeing them. I sort of missed the fact that after their visit, they would be leaving and I'd never be seeing them again. When my mother and sister made a hasty retreat from my home (on my birthday afternoon) supposedly because they didn't want to overstay their welcome. I knew **it** was coming.

It began when Denise got up and put on her coat. The room silenced. I stood from my recliner and waited for her goodbye hug. She said her *"I love you,"* and stepped away. We didn't look at one another when we parted. And I tried not to look at Don when he approached, but I couldn't help myself. By the time he reached me his eyes were full of tears.

My brother is a strong man, but he is a tender-hearted man, as well. There have been occasions when I've seen his tears form, but there have been very few times when I've seen his tears flow. He held them tight when he wrapped me in his arms and whispered how much he loved me. It took a good minute for us to end our embrace. I watched him exit my home and plopped onto my recliner without a single thought I might fracture my ass. Within seconds, he was back inside my house and I was once again in his arms. During that embrace, I whispered, "I'll see you on the flip side." I kissed his cheek and he left. A handful of days later I received an envelope with his handwriting on the front. Inside was a piece of paper that simply read. **Yes, see you on the flip side! Your loving brother.**

None of us knows for sure if there is a flip side. My faith ensures me that there is a Heaven, what it will be like is anyone's guess. During my long, lonely nights, I've come up with a few thoughts on the subject. I'll share them in an upcoming blog, but for now — Heaven Can Wait, please.

A note from Don Sneade, my brother ...

With trepidation, that's how I felt upon opening my sister Sheryll's first blog and how I've dealt with every subsequent one. Basically, I had to put my big boy pants on so to speak. I have read each and every one except #64 which I will not. If that makes me "one of them" so be it.

I have enjoyed each and every blog. Sheryll has been a master of expression. I now know who she is, how she feels about things, how she feels physically and emotionally. I now know the same of Timmy, Hannah, Jessica and Hadley.

I've learned that I can somewhat deal with Sheryll's day to day fight to live. I can see she fights this terrible disease for one thing and only one thing, her love of family! I have dealt with my own personal emotions while reading, however, I have on many, many occasions smiled, giggled and full belly laughed at some of the crazy shit that she (they) experienced and is now penned for all of us to enjoy.

My personal favorite line was in #73. I always knew that Timmy had a quick wit about him, and that was echoed when Sheryll requests a visit by Phil Gagnon, and Tim doesn't want Phil seeing the lawn and suggests the visit take place at night. During Sheryll and Tim's conversation, she says "the lights not broken", and here it is Tim says, "it will be", that line is poetic irony and just cracks me up!

Lastly, Sheryll's love of our mother, sister and myself is heartfelt and noted. Ditto!

Looking forward with trepidation, to further installments. Your brother Donnie.

60. Mashup ...

I'm going to start this blog with a Mashup Monday breakfast-tale. There are two components to breakfast at MammyGrams, one is eating, one is Hide 'N Seeking.

A little background ... Before Hadley bursts through our front door any given Monday-Friday, Tim has taken a little something, something from a stash of toys we keep in a kitchen drawer and has hidden it somewhere on the first floor of our home. This used to be part of my routine, but it's part of his now, his favorite part I might add.

At 5:15 AM, Mr. Wonderful comes downstairs, kisses the top of my head, shuffles to the kitchen, plugs in the percolator, takes a soon-to-be hidden treasure from our stash, and hides it. In the earliest days of this fun fest, when Hadley was about three years old, the hiding places fell into the category of 'hiding in plain sight' — like hanging some little thing from a lamp switch with just enough of the object easily seen below the shade, or sitting the object on top of a decorative tea pot or in a pretty bowl on my hutch. As time progressed, the hiding places became way more sophisticated, like inside the freezer, or inside the only coffee mug turned right side up in the cupboard, or tucked into a pair of shoes at the slider door, or in the pocket of someone's sweatshirt haphazardly tossed onto the back of a kitchen chair.

The practice of daily searches began back-in-the-day when Hannah and Hadley lived with Tim and me. Mr. Wonderful and I did the breakfast routine with our favorite little human while Hannah got ready for work. I'd venture to guess that in households around the world, mornings are the most fast-paced, amped-up, crazy time of day. There are lots of things that need to happen in a very short period of time and eating breakfast is inarguably the most important thing. It quickly became the pisser-part of my day with Hannah's daughter.

The first thing is this: Hadley doesn't wake with a need to eat. Left to her own druthers, she would probably wait until 9 AM before asking for anything to eat or drink. This is not helpful if the child needs to be up and out by 7:30. The second thing is this: Hadley wakes with a million things that need to be said — immediately! It's as though all of the previous day's events tumbled through her head all night and she just had to tell you all about them, right then before the essential caffeination process of the grandparents was complete. So, while her Rice Krispies were doing the snap, crackle, and pop, Hadley was yakking up a storm.

The constant refrain from me became, "Hadley, eat your breakfast, please." or, "When you stop for a breath, do some chomping before more talking." She'd laugh. She'd breathe. She'd chomp. She'd flap her jaws. One morning, while Mr. Chase and Mr. Sanborn were percolating, I found a little Hadley trinket she'd misplaced several days before. I knew she'd be thrilled that 'the most special thing ever' was headed back where it belonged, in Hadley's hand. I knew she'd want to bond with it as soon as possible.

And then this happened ... Lightbulb moment! When she came down for breakfast that morning, I told her I found her trinket, and that I'd hidden it, and that she could search for it, "Just as soon as you are done eating breakfast." That was that, folks. Hadley had an incentive to eat her food quickly.

MammyGram's technique may be a fail on the good/bad practices of Toddler Teaching, but it matters little to me. My thoughts on the subject: kids need to eat, that's the bottom-line. When it came to my Dawdling Diner, it was incumbent upon me to find a way to get food into the kid's mouth with as little stress as possible. If that meant I employed the 'eat and you shall find' methodology, so be it. And, before you start your judging, you should also know that I'm one of those parents/grandparents who doesn't stand on ceremony when it comes to breakfast offerings. If my daughters or granddaughter wanted leftover mac and cheese and orange juice, or a cookie-cutter, heart-shaped PB&J sandwich and milk, or a bowl of fruit salad and a granola bar for breakfast, then that is what they got for breakfast. It mattered not one bit what the fuel source for the day was — within reason, of course. This will come back to bite me in the ass before this blog is done. Count on it. Anyway, what did matter was that they ate their food, in a timely fashion and the meal time experience did not inflict lifelong battle scars.

I was a child of the 50s ... I carry a shrapnel wound or two from mealtime skirmishes. The rule in our house was this: food was put on the table at a precise time, and you ate it, whether you liked it or not. An equally important rule was this: you spoke if you were spoken to, whether you liked it or not. Generally speaking, I liked the guardrails of dinnertime: sit, eat, talk if need be. Without question, the best part of our dining experience was the food. My mother was a very good cook but she was on a very tight budget. The bottom-line of that was this: there were times when she needed to prepare inexpensive meals that would feed a family of six. Those meals did not always please the resident children at 10 Hobson Avenue. These REALLY didn't please the children. Donnie, green-bean casserole. Sheryll, corn chowder. Marjorie, salmon wiggle.

Just typing those words has brought a sweat to my upper lip and an uptick in my heart rate. I have one vivid memory of skipping gleefully into our home after having a wonderful day at school and stopping hard on the black and white tiled kitchen floor. The cold hand of dread grabbed hold of my spine and a cramping began in my innards when I saw a bag of potatoes and a couple cans of creamed corn resting on the counter. Within the blink of already filling eyes, I sent a pleading look my mother's way.

She whispered her preemptive apology. *"I'm sorry. It's all I have."* By the time dinnertime arrived, I was already ill from the tummy burning, turning, and churning. When dinner was over for everyone else, they fled the scene, sending, 'I'm sorry' looks my way. I stayed behind for the badgering and the uncomfortable stare from the man who insisted I eat the bowl of wretched creamed crap. When he finally tired of the Drill Down and retired for the evening, I remained perched at the pits of Hell.

Normally, I would stay at the table until such time as he took mercy on me and allowed me to go to bed — hungry. Most often, the table-sit punishment lasted just long enough to make me hate my life. One night, when I was about eleven or so, my mouth got the best of me. I drew a line in the sand that the two of us toed. The words that were said that evening would never be forgotten, by me, anyway.

"Eat your food."

"I don't like it."

"You would have liked it better when it was warm.

"Temperature doesn't matter. I hate corn chowder and I'm not going to eat it."

"Do you know how many kids there are in the world who are starving?"

"No. Do you?" That question began my downward slide.

"Those kids would do anything for a meal like that."

I pushed the bowl away, "Then send this to them." Slip-sliding away.

"They'd eat it. I can tell you that. They're starving."

"And they'll still be starving if I eat this crap." Hello, rock bottom. I fell asleep with my head on the table. It was still there when he got up for work. And as soon as he left, Mom rescued me with PB toast.

I much prefer the strategy I use with my granddaughter. Hadley bursts through the front door, heads directly to the table, concentrates on one thing only, eating. She then goes on a search for a little hidden treasure. We've done this for years, and as time went on, her taste in gadgets and gizmos changed. At the beginning of this school year, we began hiding Beanie Babies, the ones that were all the rage when Hannah and Jessica were young, the ones they collected and protected with their little lives. Each of my girls had a big-ass decorative basket in their bedroom full to the brim with the cute-as-can-be collectables; the ones that took over their souls and every square inch of my home when they escaped their baskets. The girls, and all of their friends, knew everything about the little critters, the names and dates on each hanging tag, how important it was to keep the tags affixed and in perfect condition, the rarity of certain Beanies, and the order in which they'd received them. Beanie Babies became my girls' version of baseball card collecting.

I thoroughly enjoyed the whole Ty experience, and did my fair share of helping them build their collection. I even had Tim visit Oak Brook, Illinois, the location of a Ty Warner manufacturing plant, during one of his trips to Chicago. Why, you may be asking yourself. I hoped he could purchase the rarified, 1st generation, 1993 Humphrey the camel. Apparently, I was obsessed, too.

A little something I learned doing research ... The first business to produce a direct-to-consumer website designed to engage a specific marketplace was Ty for their new Beanie Babies product line. When the Ty website was published in 1995, only 14% of Americans were using the internet. The marketing strategy of having a hangtag with the name and birthdate of the Beanies was brilliant. The inclusion of the Ty website URL on each tag was beyond brilliant. Consumers visited the website by the thousands to get information about the newest sensation which in turn, created the newest sensation.

Okay, back to the story. As soon as my girls headed off to college, the itty-bitty dust collectors were bagged and put into plastic storage bins in our basement where they've stayed for upwards of fifteen years. Recently, the Beanie Babies craze picked up again with a whole new set of critters being introduced to the new generation of collectors, children of the original collectors.

MammyGrams thought a little 'payback is a bitch' would be fun, so I had Mr. Wonderful haul the adorable Beanie Babies upstairs. On her first day of second grade, Hadley went in search of her after-breakfast-stash. It was the Peace Bear Beanie, one of her mother's favorites — until Hannah saw it in Hadley's hand.

"Tell me you're not going to hide all of them."

I laughed. She did not.

A few days after the 100th day of school celebration in February, we ran out of Beanie Babies. Hadley and I decided to have a celebratory half-sleepover with all of her critter friends in attendance. It took several trips back and forth between houses to carry the loot. When the last few were dropped onto the enormous pile I heard. *"Thank you, MammyGrams,"* from my granddaughter. And a *"Yeah, thanks,"* from my daughter. And I got a high-five from my husband. By the way, our high-fives have taken on the quality of the gentle flap of a butterfly wing so as to not break anything. Finally depleted of Beanies, I did a review of Hadley's newest interests and started hiding keychains and a new set of collectibles called Squishmallows. These adorable, very soft huggables come in a variety of sizes, and colors, and are fashioned as land, air, and sea animals.

Why am I telling you this … I honestly don't know. I think it's to establish a timeline for my mornings, but your guess is as good as mine, probably better. I need to scroll up. Okay, I'm back and I've brought with me the point of this blog. Hadley's Mashup Monday turned into Apple Day. She had a bowl of Apple Jacks cereal, half an apple cut into long strips she calls, *"Apple Fries,"* a dollop of apple sauce, and a small sip or two of apple juice and then she went searching for her hidden treasure. It was in a wooden fruit bowl on our kitchen table and it was a happy-faced apple-shaped Squishmallow, one of the newest line of fruit and veggie huggables. My girl got quite the kick out of Apple Day and headed off to school with a happy face of her own!

And then this happened … As soon as H&H get home each day, Hannah heads into her abode and Hadley comes to mine. She gives me a brief rundown of her day before she heads off to have a snack and to do her homework. Last Monday, there was no trip to MammyGrams. I watched H&H walk from the car. Hadley had her arms wrapped around Hannah's thigh and the mother had her hand resting on the child's shoulder. Hannah sent a look my way and headed inside. Within the hour, Hannah was stepping through my front door. *"I only have a minute. Hadley's doing ST Math. So, this happened, they were learning about philosophy and philosophers in class and at the end of the lecture they were told to take a few minutes to wonder about something and then write it down."*

I groaned. I grunted. I knew what was coming.

"Hadley said she got tears in her eyes because she wondered if the cancer boo-boo in MammyGrams

was getting bigger and how much time there was before."

My heart broke.

My daughter's heart, already heavy with sadness for her little girl, broke. Rarely seen tears found their way southward.

"What did you say?" I asked.

"That it was okay to feel sad and that I'm really glad she told me, and that you and she could have a heart-to-heart whenever she was ready."

I sighed, just a little bit. "You know, Hannah, you could have that heart-to-heart with her."

"Nope. Don't think I could." And off she went, out the door, with a guilty little wave sent my way.

I don't blame Hannah for passing the buck. That's the way I conditioned her, and Jessica, and Tim, and now Hadley. I am their touchstone. The one who isn't afraid of having difficult conversations, the one who takes information in, spins it a bit, then offers an opinion or an assessment or advice or whatever it is that is warranted. That is not to say my family blindly follows my spoken word — far from it. I'm basically the sounding board, I offer my opinion, they assess my position and either accept it or reject it outright, but I am always on the frontlines. The thing is: I won't always be on the frontlines. Until such time, I will push into the difficult discussions.

Hadley came for a half-sleepover on Saturday. It was a monkey themed fun fest. At 3 PM our guest arrived with every monkey thing she's already accumulated over the years. Her most treasured of all is a 'beyond adorable' 16" stuffed monkey that has a push-button activated voice recording of me saying, "Sleep well, Hadley. I love you, MammyGrams." She handed me her monkey and I handed her a list of scavenger hunt clues.

Backstory #1 ... A month or two ago, Hadley heard the word, 'fuck' for the first time. I know it's surprising that she didn't hear it at 183, but my house is a no-swear zone if Little Ones are in earshot. I think I mentioned in a previous blog that Hadley told us she heard the F-word at school, and that it sounded like 'buck' but the word was 'fuck' — I laughed like a 'bucking' fool inside when I heard my nerdy granddaughter say the F-word.

Conversations ensued between me and the kid, Hannah and the kid, Tim and the kid, Jessie and the kid, each of us explaining that kids shouldn't be using swear words. We further explained that in the world of swears, some were considered mildly-inappropriate, while others were absolutely not allowed and the F-word was one of those.

"How about freakin'? Is that word allowed?"

"That's between you and your mother," I said. See, I can pass the buck, too.

Out she went. In she came. *"Mom said I should try hard not to say it, and I could only say it at home or here."* Within days she said it here. *"The freakin internet is down," the 7-year-old bellyached.* I laughed.

Backstory #2 ... On Mashup Monday: Apple Day, Hadley complained to her teacher that she had a tummy ache. Off to the school nurse she went. Normal questions were asked.

"Do you feel like you might throw up?"

"No."

"Do you need to do Number 2?"

"What's that?"

"Do you need to poop?"

"No. Poop has a number?"

"You never heard Number 1 and Number 2?"

"No. What's Number 1?"

"Pee." The nurse continued. *"Did you eat anything different today?"*

"It was Apple Day at MammyGrams. I had Apple Jacks, a sliced apple, apple sauce, and apple juice."

"Okay. I think that's why your tummy is upset."

MammyGrams was thrown under the fucking bus! About Apple Day, and the entire O'Brien family neglected to teach the kid about Number 1 and Number 2. We suck!!!!!!!

When Hadley came over later that afternoon, I got a hand to the hip lecture about having too many 'like' foods for breakfast and a pissy-toned, *"Why didn't I know about Number 1 and Number 2?"*

I actually tried to defend myself to a 7-year-old. "Did you say it was Apple Day and it was a special occasion? And that your meals are usually varied and healthy? And you didn't know about Number 1 and Number 2 because we use actual descriptive words in our house? And did you tell the nurse she should cut me some slack because I am dying?" I didn't say that last sentence, but I came close. Thank God or Ron and anyone else who might be monitoring my flapping jaws. What I did instead was use some of Monday's events when I was making up scavenger hunt clues for our upcoming half-sleepover, then I parlayed the fun with monkey-themed keychains as prizes.

Here are the clues: This can open and it can close. And it can keep things very cold. It may not be right here. But it is very, very near. Refrigerator. This place you can sit a while. You do your thing, you get a smile. Do numbers 1 and 2. Then wash up when you're through. Bathroom Sink. The sun is for the light of day. The moon brightens the darkest way. But at night use one of these. Or else prepare for bumped up knees. Flashlight. This has a cute girl's name. But she can never play a game. Because she goes round and round. So what you seek can be found. Lazy Susan. This can hang from a hook. This can help you mix or cook. It can hold things deep inside. And makes a great place to hide. Measuring Cup. This can keep your hand from cold. Or hold things new or old. It's best to slide things really deep. Especially things you want to keep. Jacket Pocket. Each successful hunt ended with Hadley finding an adorable monkey keychain. The last clue brought her to a fit of laughter, a shiny silver keychain that says. **I just freakin' love monkeys. Ok.** Hadley freakin' loved that. Ok. MammyGrams freakin' loved that. Ok.

The other thing that happened on that Mashup Monday will stay with me forever. I recently wrote in a blog that I was expecting a visit from my mother and sister, and I had decided that I was going to get up from my recliner and hug them. Hadley and Hannah were here when I told of my plan, but they weren't here during the visit. First thing Hannah asked at supper that night was whether I got the chance to hug Grammy and Marjorie.

"Yes. When they got ready to leave, I got up and stepped into my walker. I asked each one to come as close as possible on the other side and then we hugged." I was choked with emotion when I finished telling her.

"Oh, Mom. I'm so glad."

On Monday mornings, my hospice nurse visits. I was heading into the bathroom to brush my teeth and I stopped in the doorway to wave to Hadley who was sitting at my kitchen table being poisoned by her Apple Day breakfast. When I came out of the bathroom and stopped to do another wave, Hadley was gone. I called out. "Is Hadley done with breakfast? Did Hadley leave?" When I rounded into the living room. Hadley was standing where I usually park my walker.

"Nope. I'm here, MammyGrams, waiting for a hug." She waited expectantly until I stepped into my walker. She stepped forward and wrapped her arms around me. Then she pressed her face to my chest and held on. It filled my heart with joy.

When she stepped back she had a huge smile on her face and a tear or two in her eyes. *"I can come over for a hug anytime you get up, MammyGrams. Just call."*

"You're right. You can."

And so, I call. And so, she comes. And then we hug. And, as for the philosopher-conversation, it went like this. "Your mother said you got upset at school the other day."

"Yeah."

"Do you feel like talking about it?"

She pulled her knees to her chest and wrapped her arms tightly around them. *"I don't want to talk."*

"Do you want me to talk?"

"Yes."

"Okay. I think the most important thing for you to know is that I've been feeling really good lately. And I'm taking really good care of myself. And although I am very sick, I don't feel sick today. And if things change and I start to feel sick, I'll tell you. So you should try not to worry. Okay?"

"Okay."

"And you can ask me anything at any time. Okay?"

"Okay."

"So, how about we enjoy our time together."

"Okay."

"What do you want to do?"
"Play Buckets. I freakin' love that game."
I freakin love that kid!!!!!!!

61. A Bit Untethered ...

The thing about not having a future — it leaves you feeling untethered. At least that's how I've been feeling. As soon as I learned I was dying, there was a heightened sense of urgency about some things — and an almost crippling sense of panic about everything else. Just the act of breathing became difficult, and the ordinariness of breath pulling in and breath pushing out seemed like victories rather than normal happenings.

Urgency and panic became tightly twisted with no discernable distinction between the two. I had no idea where one thread ended and the other began. Within days, the urgent things revealed themselves as being obligatory — devastatingly obligatory. I needed to tell my family about my impending death, and I needed to plan my funeral, and I needed to write letters to Tim and the girls, and I needed to get my financial things in order, and I needed to deal with my publishing responsibilities.

The things that caused panic — crippling panic — were way more difficult to identify and impossible to harness. That's because bouts of panic rolled in like waves — day and night. Some episodes hit with the fury of an ocean storm at high tide — others did a quick churn at the shoreline leaving no time to deal with the underlying cause because the undertow pulled whatever it was back to sea — only to return it again and again. I'm several months into the process now and I understand some of the underlying causes of the heart-pounding, tear-inducing, grief-fueled panic. At the forefront of my attacks was the question of when I will die. That question is still there, tumbling in the surf at the shoreline.

Last November, I was given an expiration date much in the same way perishable grocery items are given a 'sell by' or 'use by' date. The rather vague information for a dying woman — and for a carton of milk — is pitifully parallel and they are put into the universe with no real concern about specifics. Consider this recent go-around when Tim baked Marchrie her 'broken wrist' cheesecake. Before I get to that, consider for a minute how wonderful Mr. Wonderful is that he offered to or agreed to make my sister her favorite dessert. I can't remember how the conversation went, but I can remember that he shopped for the ingredients and planned some baking time into his busy schedule.

And then this happened … "Shit," he mumbled from the kitchen.

"What?"

"The 'sell by' date on the sour cream was five days ago. I just bought it yesterday. That pisses me off."

Silence from me because I knew where this conversation was heading.

A groan came from the kitchen. *"So is this still good?"*

"It's sour cream. I'm not sure we'd know one way or the other — unless it's blue or something. Is the date a 'sell by' date or a 'use by' date?"

"Sell by."

"So there's some after-the-sale consumption time factored in."

"How much consumption time?"

"No clue."

"We shouldn't have to be talking about this."

"No argument here." Pause. I have absolutely no insight as to why I started Round 2, but I did. "Everything should just have a 'use by date'. I think eggs have that."

"Nope. Eggs have a 'best if used by' date."

"Are you seriously reading labels right now?"

"Just on the stuff I'm using in the cheesecakes. So far, sour cream and cream cheese are 'sell by' products and eggs and graham cracker crusts are 'best if used by' products. That label is less ambiguous, but it still leaves room for guessing. This labeling system sucks. If it really matters that foods be eaten by a certain date, the labels should say 'eat this crap by 4:30 PM on March 12, 2022 or toss it into the garbage."

Pause. I started Round 3. Don't ask. "There's a way you can check if eggs are still fresh."

"How?"

"Put them in a bowl of cold water. If they sink, they're fresh." Just so you all know, I read that tidbit online the last time Tim and I were trekking across this 'sell by, use by' wasteland. I remembered the helpful hint. He did not. That's sort of the story of our lives together. My hubby vacillates between times when he participates in 'active listening' and times when he 'Just Isn't All That Interested' in my useless tidbits. We've been married almost 36 years folks, so I don't blame him one bit for zoning out!

The pissed-off-chef put a couple eggs into a bowl of cold water, watched them sink to the bottom, declared they were fresh to use, cracked them open and got on with things. The recipe yields two cheesecakes, so I can attest that the ingredients were perfectly fine and the finished product was absolutely delicious.

Okay, where were we … Right, I'm obsessing about the 'when' of things. I 'managed' the panic attacks of not knowing 'when' by choosing dates I hoped to see, Christmas Day, my 64th birthday, and New Year's Day; they were my first combo goal. After that, I hoped to navigate safely through a Minesweeper grid littered with important dates: Tim's birthday, February 26th; Jessica's birthday, March 5th; Hannah's birthday, April 4th, and Marjorie's birthday, May 1st. We are halfway through that set of hopefuls and smackdab in the middle of those really important dates is MLB Opening Day: April 7th. That was my new goal and I can't even begin to tell you how eager I am to see my guys take to the infield and outfield, it's something I always look forward to. This year, it's a bit more exciting, for sure. Having said that, I set a new goal. This day far exceeds any goal I have ever set in my entire life.

I need to live until Mother's Day. May 8th. I need to be here for my mother. I need to be here for my daughters. I need to be here for my granddaughter. Really, friends. I need to be here, for Mother's Day. It's my new goal. I would appreciate your positive energy. Thank you.

Some important information … There are some things you should know about the period of time that surrounds the writing and the posting of my blogs. When I begin a blog, I may stop halfway through, begin another one and post that one, and then circle back to the previous one. I'll be the first to admit that my writing habits aren't tight and my finished products don't always take the reader along a straight line. I've decided that that's a charming element of my newest form of writing. My swoopy-swoop-style is part and parcel of my not planning my blogs; a thought pops into my head, I type it and pull the thread. With very few exceptions, the end result is something I needed or wanted to get off my chest, or it's something reflective and appreciative in nature.

I try really hard to stay within chronological lanes so that you can follow along on the progression of things, but I may not always hit the mark, particularly when it comes to relaying information on Chewy Louie, the cancer munching rodent. Guru Jessica named the rat, thank you very much, and the name perfectly suits the little bastard. Anyway, by the time you get a blog to read, a week or more may have passed between the thinking, and the thread pulling, and the pain I was experiencing is under control, or a whole new round of pain has begun. So, keep that in mind if you think things don't quite match up in the day-to-day of my storytelling.

Women, Tough And Tender ...

Nurse M - This woman chose a very unique profession; one I would argue is more like a calling. She is a consummate professional, medically speaking, which is a really important thing for sure. She is not only part of my dying, but she is also part of my living. She provides excellent medical care and knowledge and she reads all of my blogs. Why? Because she knows how important my writing is, and she knows that my blog reveals things about my mental and physical health.

Kathy - My sister-in-law has been on the frontlines with me since Day One, with a sympathetic ear, and with words to inform and to encourage. Through it all, she has shared her heart, the one that frequently shows signs of breaking. She pushed-in with me and pulled-back with me when I thought hospice was the right choice; the first and the second time. An important thing to remember, Kathy and Tom are vacationing in Florida. When I need her, that fact matters little to either of them.

Out of the blue, I asked Kathy if she would look at my nuclear med body scan results, the ones I'd previously sworn I'd never look at, the ones I looked at, the ones I needed a witness to. The enormity of the event pulled me into a vortex of fear and panic, and I needed someone inside the swirl with me. I needed Kathy. I explained the situation. There was absolutely no Q&A about why I looked and there was no, *"Well, duh,"* when I told her I had a **very bad** reaction to the images. I asked if I could send them to her (I don't really remember why I needed her to have them, but I did). I said we didn't need to discuss them, and that I was going to delete the files as soon as I knew she'd received the email.

The next day she called to check in on me after my hospice visit. We chatted about my Stable Mabel status and then I said, in reference to the scan imagery, "It's bad, isn't it?"

There was an exhaled groan on her end and then the word, *"Yeah."* It felt to me as though she wanted to say something along the lines of, "Holy Shit, yeah it's bad!"

Maybe it was me who wanted to shout that.

Jessica - My younger daughter is my hospice buddy, the one who pushes into this shit fest with consistent physical and emotional support. She never passes by me without a tender touch and a loving word and pulls up a seat when I'm upset or when I need to talk with someone about anything.

Hannah - My older girl takes every one of my calls and patiently listens to dead air when I can't find the words to say or they just can't be said through my tears. She is doing the supportive lean-in with her child and preparing herself for the hard landing that Hadley and she will have together.

Donna - The rock I have always banged against when things scare me. The person to whom I can say anything without worrying about how the words come out of my mouth and who they're about. Donna will be the person saying a few words of her own at her friend's funeral gathering. I know how hard it will be for her to deliver my eulogy. I know how hard it will be for her to lose her friend.

Jennifer and Debbie - These two women brightened my doorstep with renewed friendship even though they know I'll be leaving and they'll be grieving more than they would have had they stayed on the protective sidelines. That tells you all you need to know about their character, it doesn't tell you how much I need and appreciate their love and support.

Mom - The slightly hunched woman with aged-blue eyes, and newly-etched lines of anguish on a face that resembles mine. Mom tries so hard to make this horrible ordeal as easy for her child as she can, just as a mother would.

Marjorie - The sister who currently sports a black cast on her right wrist. the sister who silently endures the pain of a breaking heart, the sister who does all she can to make sure I feel loved in every way possible. The loving and caring woman who shoulders the grief of our mother, just as a daughter would.

Denise - My sister-in-law who reaches across the states with calls and texts to tell me tales of this and that. She doesn't dig deep into the whole cancer thing with me because she's the one sharing the cancer thing with Don, the brother who spends an hour on the phone with his sister every Sunday night, the guy who most often ends the call on choked-back-tears.

Joyce - The woman who **never** misses an opportunity to take me away from this shit fest armed only with her cell phone. Her pictures and videos of the ocean come with regularity. Some are sent from her place in Maine and some are sent from her winter place in Florida. All of them are sent with a text that lets me know how much she cares.

And lastly, my Three Amigos: Andria, Nancy, and Jessica. These women have leaned-in with love and support, each in their own special way. I'm going to spend a few minutes discussing Andria. You all know that she sends me handwritten note cards with passages from my books on the outside, and editorial comments on the inside. Those Kraft brown cards and envelopes still come and I love them because they connect me to who I used to be (a novelist) and to what I used to do (write novels).

Please believe me when I say this … I am grateful for every minute I am able to write my blog. It has saved me. Literally saved me from the long 24/7 stretches of sitting and thinking. When this ordeal began, I'd just started the first book, *Treble Clef*, in a new series, Netti Investigations. That story is written in my head and I have begun the second and I know what would have happened in the third and fourth. The manuscripts will never be put to paper and that is okay because I am still writing them. In the normal course of things, I would have typed them at record speed, The Warden would have edited them, The Goddess would have published them, The Guru would have displayed them on my website and splashed them on social media. But, alas, the publishing team I built has disbanded. My favorite women of all time are off doing other things. Great things. Thoughtful things.

A little backstory … A while back, I wrote a blog. I'm not going to check how far back because I don't like to reread what I've written; more to the point, I'm not going to check because I don't need to. I received four greeting cards from Andria recently. The itty-bitty things are 3.5" x 4.5", and each has a picture of a happy tree on the front. It's the same tree, the only difference is the color of the leaves. They let you know right off that they represent the four seasons: spring green leaves, vibrant summer leaves, rich autumn leaves, icy winter leaves. Inside, each card is a handwritten quote of what I said to Hadley when I told her I was dying.

You may recall. "The newness of springtime is like the newness of a person's life." Or. "During summer, leaf buds turn to big leaves that fill the trees, and the flowers get really big and spread along the stonewall." Or, "Oh, fall is a really wonderful season, and it can be a really long season. In people's lives, it's when they kind of have everything they want in life.

"You're near winter. And that's when things die." Those were the words my sweet granddaughter said with big, tears forming on her beautiful blue eyes. Heartbreaking. Everytime I think about that interchange, it's heartbreaking.

As for the cards that keep coming, each one contains loving words from Andria, my wonderful friend in Texas. I treasure her sentiments, but I hold deep in my heart the realization that she knows exactly what I need and she takes the time to show me just how much she cares.

An important question … Debbie and I were deep in the weeds in conversation recently and she asked what the pain is really like for me. After some contemplation this is how I described the current state of things, to her — and then to Nurse M later that week.

I am in discomfort 24/7. Discomfort is not pain. Think of it this way, you spent the entire day outside raking leaves, and hauling them onto a tarp, and dragging them across the yard, and pushing them over a stonewall. When you finally sit after your daylong workout, you're left with a full-body-ache. There is an intensified ache whenever you move something that really hurts, like your lower back. On top of that, there's an overwhelming sensation of fatigue in your muscles, every muscle, and it pushes deep down to your bones. Now add this, if you touch any part of your body, it feels as though you've pressed against a bruise. The simplest contact between your hand and an arm or a leg or your face or your neck, it feels like you're pushing against a bruise.

The aches and pains you're experiencing might feel good, after all, you spent the day outside getting fresh air and exercise, and after a few OTCs and a couple days of relaxation, the aches and pains will lessen and then go away. That overall discomfort never fully goes away. It gets dulled by the pain meds and it is manageable. I have become very good at whisper touching now, like when I need to move my hair from my forehead, I do it softly and slowly. And Tim is the one who is in charge of putting a special lotion on my legs because: 1) I'm not supposed to bend because of the lumbar spine cancer, and 2) because rubbing the cream on by myself is just too painful. And when I have an itchy back, Tim needs to help with that because my entire torso hurts if I try to twist and reach behind. It just hurts too damned much.

Tramadol absolutely helps with the overall aches and pains, the raking the leaves kind of aches and pains, but the powerful pain pill does its real work on mitigating the Chewy Louie pain. That intense stuff is what I refer to as breakthrough pain. Those episodes can easily take my breath away and leave me in tears. Initially, when the pain was in my thigh and hip region, it felt as though the rodent was chomping hard and there was a rippling, traveling pain. The pain in those areas now feels like someone takes a baseball bat and smacks my leg, over and over and over. Without question, the thigh and hip pain is the absolute worst. When the pain is in my shin, or shoulder, or ankle, or wrist, it feels like someone is hitting me with a small hammer; that pain is swift and precise and tends to last a bit of time. When the pain is in my spine, it is mostly in the lumbar and thoracic area. Mostly it is a deep ache and it has been accompanied with an occasional smack.

I've gotten really good at describing pain. That's because I have to do it twice a week with Nurse M. In fact, I have to answer the same set of questions every time she visits. That way, she can track my answers, evaluate where I am, and watch for a decline.

Her questions ..."How are you feeling overall? Any pain right now? Any pain since I was last here? Where was it? When did you experience it? How long was the episode? Did the Tramadol help? Have you had any headaches? Were they the tension kind or were they like a vice grip? Did you use Tylenol? Did the headache go away? Have you had any nausea? Did you use Zofran? Did the nausea go away? Right away? Are you having trouble sleeping? Are you waking because you're in pain? Do you take a Tramadol if you wake? Does it help? How quickly? Are you having any trouble ambulating? Any pain when you're standing or walking? Any skin issues? How's your appetite? Are you eating? And you're drinking? How many fluid ounces? Any problems with your bowels? How about urination? How about with your breathing? Are you still able to care for yourself? Do you need to take a break between your sponge bath and getting dressed? Does it hurt when I touch here, and here, how about here?"

I almost kicked her even though her touch was whisper-soft.

"I'm sorry. I hate to cause you discomfort, but I need to gauge. You're experiencing more pain on the left side, today."

Uh, huh. That's when I wanted to kick her.

After the Q&A, Nurse M takes my vitals, smiles wide and agrees with my proclamation.

"So I'm Stable Mabel?"

"Yes you are."

The feeling I get when she agrees is similar to what I experienced when I got a Gold Star on a school paper in kindergarten. After the medical stuff has been taken care of, we usually delve into areas of concern. It is during these conversations that I've addressed some of the things that have caused panic — big and not so big.

I think you'd all agree that 'fear of the unknown' is difficult for most people. Whether you're in the dying process or not, humans fear losing their lives, ergo, death is at the top of the list of things that scare the crap out of us. Of course, the recent news reports about parachuting spiders have added a whole new thing to be afraid of; I mean seriously WTF. I'm going to steer clear of that incredibly terrifying discussion and stick close to far less terrifying topics — like my impending death — thank you very much.

Anyway, I have made peace with my very early demise, but that should in no way imply that I don't have anxiety over when exactly it will happen OR how it will happen OR if it will be sudden OR if it will be a long, slow, crawl. The unknowns surrounding all that have pushed me to say preemptive goodbyes to people in a variety of ways. There have been the 'just in case I have a catastrophic event' talks, and the 'just in case I am unconscious and lingering' chit-chats. I know it's going to be one or the other — fast or slow. The thing is this: I may never know which it is. And as hard as the waiting and wondering is, I wouldn't have it any other way. This time that I've been given is the greatest gift. Truly. I plan on delving into the many reasons I feel that way in an upcoming blog, but foremost, my mind has been opened to a new way of thinking. I shared my thoughts with Father Dude during a recent visit and I'll tell you about the conversation, and about The Stone he gave me; it's a really cool story.

And now, the point of this blog … It is a warning. As I noted, I don't normally plan out my blogs, but there is something in the works and I feel you need a heads up. Remember the whole 'When I'm 64' thing? I was hellbent on making my birthday milestone and I let everyone know. I received so much support beforehand and so many congratulations afterwards. It was wonderful and it gave me a tremendous boost. So thank you! Well here's something new: 'When It's 64' — the title in reference to Blog 64.

A blog you may not want any part of.

After much consideration and conversation with people who have seen my body scan images, and after many viewings by Yours Truly, I have decided to put a rendering of my scan up as a blog. For HIPAA reasons, I don't want to post my actual scan, so Tim is working on an exact rendering. There will be no words on Blog 64, so for those of you who do not want to see it, you don't need to.

Blog 63 will explain why I decided to post the images. Blog 65 will be my angry blog, the one that explains why I should not have been encouraged to get a bone biopsy or more pointedly why I should not have been subjected to a bone biopsy. Had I seen my scan images when I was being asked to make really important medical testing decisions I would have NEVER had a bone biopsy.

I believe Blog 64 will support my argument.

62. Special Moments.
They're all special now ...

Tim - The other night, in the wee hours when most everyone was silenced by sleep, I woke, not because I was in pain, but because I sensed I wasn't alone. I had a prickling of dread run my spine which caused me to clamp my eyes tight, just in case it was the Grim Reaper making an earlier than hoped for House Call. Within seconds, my fear passed because I knew I had guest. Tim had woken, snuck downstairs, and taken residence in his recliner. He hadn't intended to wake me, but having his energy nearby woke me. I didn't acknowledge him, I just watched him look longingly at me. It was really hard seeing him sitting alone in the dark. I knew what was working through his head — the loneliness that's already settling in. We didn't talk, we just shared the space. And then, just like that, he got up, touched my cheek, kissed the top of my head, and headed back upstairs. One night soon, he'll wake and come downstairs for a sit in his recliner and I won't be here to share the space with him. How sad.

Marjorie - A week or so after Marjorie's accident, a knock came upon her front door. Standing on the stoop was Sheila Lavallee Westerlind, the original Third Musketeer to Marchrie and Helena when they played together on the streets of Columbus Park. Sheila lives in New Jersey now. Her travels brought her to the Worcester area, and led her to Auburn, so she could stop in and see her friend, the one with a broken wrist, and a breaking heart.

Sheila is a mover and a shaker. She is always on the go as evidenced by her Facebook posts. The blonde, blue-eyed beauty is happily traveling here and there and everywhere, and she is doing it with a wide smile on her face, the one that is identical to that of her mother when she was Sheila's age.

The beautiful, Nordic-looking, Mrs. Lavallee raised her family of five children in the 60s and 70s in a sweeping Victorian home with a beautiful wrap-front-porch. She also spent long hours at work helping countless women bring new bundles of joy into the world. I was always awe-inspired by Mrs. Lavallee. There were other neighborhood moms who had jobs back then, my own included, but none of them had a career, certainly none that required a crisp, white, nurse's uniform, complete with a nurse's cap.

When Mrs. Lavallee had some 'free' time, she filled it by being a Camp Fire leader to a bunch of neighborhood girls. I don't recall what our leader wore in that capacity, though I think it was a white shirt and navy bottoms. I liked being part of the group and I looked forward to our weekly meetings in the Lavallee's big-ass old barn.

For those of you unfamiliar with the organization, Camp Fire Girls was the first nonsectarian, multicultural organization for girls in America. Its programs were designed as small group experiences and held after school. There were lessons about camping and stuff, but the focus was aimed at building confidence in young girls by introducing way-ahead-of-the-curve lessons about environmental protection, and more traditional classes on childcare skills, including CPR, and the importance of community service; the things Mrs. Lavallee was doing in her own life. Live by example, I guess.

I told Marchrie I was going to mention Mrs. Lavallee in a blog, and we both broke out into the Camp Fire Girl song. ***"Make new friends but keep the old. One is silver, and the other gold."*** I guess if you are a former Camp Fire Girl and you learn that an old friend has broken herself and your name happens to be Sheila Lavallee Westerlind, you show up on your friend's doorstep with an Irish bread and a beautiful plant. And if your name is Kathy Lavallee Budgell, you fire off text, after text, after text to Marjorie with countless offers of help: rides, meals, errand-running, whatever, whatever, whatever. You might remember it was Kathy's husband, Larry, who came to the OB rescue when Hannah's furnace crapped out one Saturday morning. I messaged Kathy way before it was respectable to do so, and within ten minutes of that text, Larry was onsite fixing our problem. I hadn't seen either of the Budgells for years before placing our S.O.S. — a fact that mattered not one bit.

Kathy - has let us know that she is standing at the ready to help, as are so many others. The instant my blog went up on my website about Marjorie's fall and subsequent injuries, I was flooded with text messages, emails, phone calls, and I'm quite sure I even saw a few Camp Fire Girl smoke-signals lifting skyward. Family and friends of mine, and even a few people I've never met were offering all kinds of help.

Ever since Marchrie's triple-klutz on ice, Helena McCarthy - has done the lion's share of schlepping her to surgical, and doctor and physical therapist appointments, and Mary-Sue-Lou-Jo is on the phone day and night with a sympathetic ear and a check-in on my sister and our elderly mom. And Sharon and Jackie, the women across Inwood Road, the lovely little cul-de-sac where Marchrie and Mom live, are running back and forth to grocery stores and pharmacies, and my Jessica, is helping with their laundry, garbage, and recycling. A slip on the ice landed my poor sister on her ass and in one fell swoop, it flipped the coin of concern and compassion from me to Marjorie. Just as it should have. People are absolutely wonderful. We may forget that in our day to day lives. I hope my blog reminds us of the kindness and willingness of so many to offer a helping hand, a shoulder upon which to cry, and a hug of comfort.

Mary and Linda - In my book, *Be, still* — I suggest that hospice patients be thoughtful, that they consider gifting a special trinket to someone while they are able to enjoy the experience. Since I'm on a roll about the thoughtfulness of others, I wanted to share something I did; I took my own advice. When I mentioned Fifi's chair in a previous blog, I heard from all three of Fifi's daughters. None of them knew their mom had a special seat at Mary O'Brien's table. I think this is a good time for a little backstory and it should begin with Tim's mother.

When I first met Mary McTigue O'Brien, she was already a grandmother to fifteen, give or take one or two. I think she was about the age I am now, give or take one or two. 'Nana' as she was called by just about everyone, was a tall, fit and trim, Irish-pretty woman with snow-white hair that was always done, but never looked done, if you know what I mean. Nana never looked like she just stepped out of Al's Golden Chateau, the place where women flocked to have their hair follicles permed, teased, and shellacked into an armored-halo. Every woman of a certain age, from one end of 01603 to the other, had helmet-hair, except for Mary O'Brien. Her hair looked casual, natural, soft, beautiful.

Fifteen Merchant Street was Mary O'Brien's home, her kitchen was the heartbeat of that home. I don't recall a single time when I entered that house when she wasn't in that room. I barely remember a time when she was sitting in that room upon my entrance. She was always upright doing something. As soon as she realized she had company, she was pouring a cup of coffee and slicing a piece of coffeecake, her specialty, and taking a seat with her guest. I felt like a guest in Mary's kitchen until I had Hannah, then I was a Bonafide OB. One who always tried to snag Fifi's chair.

As for The Chair, Tim remembers things this way: the two chairs at either end of the OB kitchen table were his parents' chairs. He said the one at the end nearest to the stove was his mother's and the one nearest to the back door entrance was his father's. The seats along the table sides, all ten of them, were for the kids. Tim's memory often puts his father in the chair at the end of the table closest to his mother, so they could sit near and talk around all the noise. So, technically, Fifi's chair was Papa's chair. I don't know when it was that she wriggled her ass onto it and claimed it, nor do I know exactly how Tim and I came to be in possession of it. I suppose, as it is with so many families, things get given to people upon the passing of loved ones. We ended up with the chair, a beautifully-carved mahogany seat which spent time in nearly every room of our house over the years. Proof of that statement is evidenced by the many layers of upholstery on the seat cushion.

My blogs about Fifi's chair piqued the interest of Fifi's daughter, Linda Bushee. She just loved that Fifi had her place at the OB's home, and that the chair became so special to me. A month or so ago, Linda, her husband John, and her sister Suzanne, traveled from Rhode Island for a visit with Tim and me. At the end of our time together, I gifted Linda with Fifi's chair. "I want it to go to a good home," I said with sincerity. She happily accepted.

Thunder - The other night, I was woken from a sound sleep by deep rolls of thunder. We'd had an unseasonably warm day in Worcester which banged against the ordinary cold of March in New England. The phenomenon led to the first thunderstorm of 2022. First off, you should know that I love thunder, and I like lightning. I do not, however, enjoy the wind that usually accompanies a real good storm. My mother, on the other hand, enjoys some wind and the thunder, but is terrified by the lightning. The first flash of light and accompanying crack of contact sends the poor woman toward shelter in her bathroom, or in the basement of her home.

If she is alone during a storm, she and I get onto our cell phones as she makes passage toward her haven of safety. I do a series of well-spaced check-ins with her, and then give her the 'All's Clear' when things become All Clear. When the thunder rolled and rolled and rolled the other night, and a few bolts of lightning lit the sky, I smiled because Mom was safe and sound with Marchrie — and then I cried because I knew Mom wouldn't have me to call when this year's summer storms fill the sky.

Brad - I actually had a Brad for chili. The woman who has been sustaining life by eating apricot danish had a hankering for chili. Go figure.

Joyce - The other night, out of nowhere, I had a memory, at least I thought I had a memory. The next day, I texted Joyce who was in Florida sitting poolside or perhaps on the beach with her husband, John.

Me: I think I had a memory. Did a Christmas tree fall in your living room?
Joyce: Yes. It was the last real tree we owned. It fell during the night, and we didn't hear a thing. Must have been a very slow fall ... you have a very good memory. John didn't remember that — nor do I recall telling anyone.
Me: I got a call from you in the morning because you wanted help driving the kids to school. You said, 'If a Christmas tree falls in your living room does it make a sound?' I said, "I don't know, Joyce, does it?" You said, 'Apparently, not.'

Score one for my memory.

Joyce: Wow. How do you do it? We don't recall yesterday! And the details you gave are amazing.
Me: I think it's part of my life passing ... I'm having really accurate memories ... I think I don't have cluttered thoughts about the future ... so my mind is really clear about the past – OR – I could be nuts.
Joyce: Whatever it is, it's amazing.

Spirit Animals - Hadley asked me the other day if I had a spirit animal.

"I sure do. It's a white-tailed deer. How about you?"

"A hummingbird. I don't know anybody who doesn't like seeing a hummingbird, they make people happy. I think a spirit animal should make people happy."

"Me, too."

Pause. Pause. Pause. *"You know MammyGrams, when you're a white-tailed deer, you need to make sure you find a place to hide as soon as it's Coyote O'Clock — that's when the coyote's come out, you know."*

"Good to know." Gotta love her. I'm head over heels in love with my spirited little hummingbird!

<u>Don</u> - During my most recent phone call with Don, he went off on a tangent about a piece of furniture he's refinishing. *"Denise and I have an old-fashioned, metal Hoosier cabinet that I've been restoring. I spent some time today screwing in a T-bolt to hold the marble top."*

I'm not sure what he actually said about the bolt because I'd already started zoning out. Ten effing minutes later I interrupted the snooze fest. "You do know I'm dying, right?"

Don cracked up laughing.

"And you just wasted ten effing minutes of my life, right?"

He kept on laughing. When he pulled himself together, he said, *"Yeah, sorry about that. Jesus, wait until Denise hears about this conversation. Every Sunday she asks if I let you get a word in edgewise."*

"Tell her the answer to that question is, nope."

"She already knows the answer." He cracked up again!

<u>She Devil</u> - I was over the moon happy when I learned that one of Kathy's best friends hated Wordle.

I felt I had an ally in the war against the wicked word game. But alas, Paula Dumas, the woman who ended her heartfelt card to me with these words: **P.S. I hate the fucking WORDLE, too! Love, Paula.** Apparently, she has had a change of heart. I heard about Paula's slide under the spell of Wordle from the She Devil, herself. The Gleeful One might have been brewing something in a kitchen cauldron when she cackled her victorious claim of another soul. Dratz!

<u>Mom</u> - I found myself alone with my mother, in my home, Sunday afternoon. I haven't been in my mother's company, by myself, since my diagnosis. We hadn't planned on spending alone-time, but there we were, without the distractions and interruptions of others, so our conversation went where it needed to go. I guess.

"I'm old. It should be me who's dying," she said through tear-filling eyes.

"It's not your time, Mom," I choked back.

"But you're only sixty-four and I'm in my eighties."

"I've had a really wonderful life." Pause. Pause. Then through a few tears, "I don't know why it's my time, I don't think I'm supposed to know why, but as much as I want to stay here, I'm okay with things. I've made peace with all of this." When I hear myself say those words, I can't believe I believe them, but I do.

My mother pulled herself together. I'm glad she did because she said this. *"I don't know how you are doing what you're doing. The blog, and planning a funeral, and taking care of everyone with all of the little things you're leaving behind to soothe Hadley. I can't believe how strong you are; what an incredible person you are. I've always been proud of you, Sheryll, but I can't believe that I am the mother of someone this amazing."* So, there's that. The most important words I'll ever hear.

When things go numb in the night ... Saturday evening. Telling you about my plans for Blog 64 was a big step. I wasn't sure how I'd feel after I went all-in, but overall, I was relieved. I committed to telling my whole story. I think it's best for me that I don't hide behind things. I think it's best to let you decide how you want to handle things. Look at the scan; don't look at the scan. Read the angry blog; don't read the angry blog. If there's anything I've learned from this whole mess it's this: I can't spend any time worrying about what others think of the stripped-down, vulnerable version of me; the person who is obliterating the shroud of privacy by telling the good, the bad, and the ugly about what is happening to me.

I've been awake since shortly after 3 AM staring at a blank page for nearly an hour. I had a physical incident earlier in the evening, one that left my right leg numb from my hip to my knee. The explanation of the incident might be TMI, but I spent a couple days backed up a bit, and when the time was right, I ended up spending too much time on the hopper. We've all been there, a long sit sometimes results in a numbing of the lower extremities. This was not *that* numbing. This numbing was, is, very concerning. As soon as I stood, I knew something was happening, or had happened, in my lumbar spine. There was a bit of pain on the left side, even though the numbness ran the length of the outer side of my right leg, most notably in the thigh region. I leaned against the bathroom wall for a minute or so, making sure I had strength in my legs, then waited for the tingling sensation, the kind that usually accompanies an awakening appendage to pass. There wasn't the expected 'pins and needles' feelings, so I called out to Tim to walk with me as I moved to my recliner.

I snuggled into the warm leather seat and waited for the feeling to return to my dead leg. Before any numbness abated, my nightly dose of Tramadol and Xanax pulled me under its spell. I'm awake now and I think it's safe to say I'll be awake for a while longer. So, while I wait for more of my leg to come back to life, I'll write. It's anyone's guess where these hours will lead us.

What fun … For the most part, writing the blog has been a therapeutic thing. It has allowed me to look at where I was when this all began and where I am now. It has given me a way to face my fears and loneliness, and the anger and resentment I sometimes feel. It has allowed me the freedom to ask the occasional Why Me? — Why This Soon? and it has left me with the questions of Why Not Me? — Why Not This Soon?

Haven't we all, at some point in our lives, asked those questions about someone else especially if a death was sudden and seemingly random? An accident, perhaps, when someone was in the wrong place at the wrong time or had taken an earlier flight because there was a seat available and then they were gone. Death happens when it happens. I keep trying to impress that fact upon me and those I love. With varying degrees of success.

You may think I spend most of my time perhaps an inordinate amount of time thinking about me, about this ache and pain, about that fear, about what's next. I suppose I'm guilty as charged. Let's face it, the circumstances of my life have isolated me, they've kept me from the natural order of things. They've positioned me in the spectator section of my life and everyone else's life. I was joking with Mr. Wonderful recently. I said that the long hours I used to spend at my desk or in my recliner writing was sort of like my Spring Training for the Big Leagues, the arduous 24/7 sitting requirement of my type of cancer. I asked Nurse M the other day if I'm a whiner; she laughed out loud.

"Far from it."

We went around a bit about the uniqueness of my situation as it relates to other types of terminal cancer and even other cases of bone cancer.

"Most hospice patients, even those with bone cancer, can get up and out of their homes, they can go sit on a park bench, or have a meal at a restaurant, or go to Sunday church services, or whatever."

She impressed upon me that I am living a very unusual life, and it's still an incredibly full life despite my being confined. She acknowledged the blog is at the center of it.

I agree. So, I thank you for taking time out of your busy lives to read along, and to comment from time to time. The blog was intended as my way of working things through. I've come to find that informing people about what's happening in my cancer-life and my hospice-life has been quite meaningful and purposeful. I can say with complete honesty that my mind is full of so many things. Lots of non-illness-related-things. Happy things. That's because I try to push all-in on the day-to-day happenings that I am smackdab in the center of, the whirlwind of 'comings and goings' of my little family unit. I may be on the sidelines, but I am still the one choosing Hide 'N Seekables. I am still distance-appropriate sitting with Hadley after school while she does homework or online math and language puzzles and games. I am still hanging out with 'our' dog, Piper, the beautiful rescue who used to live with Tim and me, but who lives next door with Hannah and Hadley now. I am still the one choosing, ordering, and prepping birthday gifts for my 3-year-old grandniece, Evelyn, the adorably precocious, ‘what goes around comes-around’ daughter of Nicole, my sister Marjorie’s adorably precocious daughter.

While I wait for the last ultimate answer to the only question that really remains, I’m looking toward the future. With a little creativity, I expect to be part of it. I’m making sure there are things in place to help Hadley and my daughters navigate through their period of loss and grief and I’ve prepared special things to remind them to have fun, full lives. I’ve stocked up on hideables so Tim can continue Hadley’s Hide ‘N Seek breakfasts. I think it’ll be really important that they keep steady with their Mashup Mondays, and Toast Tuesdays, and Wacky Wednesdays, and Eclectic Thursdays, and Cheesy-egg Fridays.

An important note … Friday breakfast day went through a name change. It is now referred to as Fantastical Fridays. Why, you might ask? Because Hadley has not wanted a cheesy-egg for the past couple of weeks. The horror of horrors. So, what’s a kid to do? Choose something else to eat and do some renaming. So far the Fantastical part of the renaming has focused on the accouterments rather than the food, although the food included sprinkles. More on that in a bit. One Fantastical meal was served on her princess plate, and one whilst she wore a princess tiara. I’ll keep you posted if things change beyond that.

Every Saturday, Tim makes a big batch of French Toast for breakfast. He packages up several pieces and tucks them into the freezer. They are up-for-grabs by anyone for any meal or snack. Hadley likes to microwave one afterschool or for an impromptu dinner at Gee’s and MammyGram’s.

When she put the kibosh on that Friday cheesy-egg morning, she checked the freezer, smiled wide, popped a cinnamon-square-yummy into the microwave, grabbed the rainbow sugar crystals we use for cookie decorating, and sprinkled a few onto her Fantastical Friday French Toast. She added a couple pieces of watermelon and a handful of blueberries to her sectioned-plate and brought it and a glass of milk into the living room, set it on her rolling table, and rolled it close enough for me to see the fruits of her labor.

"Not in the mood for eggs this morning?"

"Nope." She did a theatrical gagging. *"I did not want an egg. No seriously, MammyGrams, I would have puked if I had to eat one."*

I laughed. "Gagging sounds and puking references and it's only 7 AM. This day isn't getting off to a good start, I see."

She chomped a mouthful and countered with, *"It's getting off to a great start. This toast is awesome!"*

Looking toward the future ... I've signed Hadley up for summer camps. Last summer, during the height of Covid, she spent most of her time putzing around our house and yard. She spent one week at a horseback riding camp and had a little bit of outdoor fun at Broadmeadow Brook, the largest urban wildlife sanctuary in New England which just happens to be in Worcester. She's going to do another couple of weeks there, but she's decided to spend oodles of time at Giguere Gymnastics Center. She's all about learning to do a cartwheel and to do TikTok dancing and Carnival Week and Water Week and whatever else she wants to do this summer.

And then she can do this ... I bought a beautiful wooden box that has an old-fashioned brass key fixture. It's the kind of box that will make a lovely keepsake, one day. Until then, the box is wrapped as one of Hadley's birthday gifts and it will be given to her on June 28th. Inside she will find birthday cards from me, one for her upcoming 8th birthday and twenty-two others, one for each of her birthdays all the way through to her 30th. Each card has a few words from me that are relevant to whatever milestone she is celebrating.

And then ... I'll be leaving her the tape recordings of the time she and I are spending together. When I first began the tapings, she was aware and maybe a bit reserved, but as time went on, it didn't matter one bit to her that our words were being recorded, in fact, she flew into the house the other day and started telling Tim and me about the happenings at school. She'd spewed a couple sentences and then stopped cold. *"You should put the recorder on. You're gonna want this on tape!"* I want everything on tape. Her little voice keeps me company at night when I can't sleep. Like now.

What's next ... I'm not sure. I'll be putting Blog 63 up when 64 and 65 are completely written and reviewed. So, I might be off-the-grid for a bit. Muah!

63. Questioning God. Imagine that ...

John Lennon's, *Imagine*, was released in 1971. It was a hit record. In my humble opinion, it should have been. The lyrics are lovely, though to some, controversial. Musically speaking, the piano solo is beautiful, its simplicity is just brilliant. I was fourteen when the song was released, too young to really push into the controversy surrounding the lyrics. It wasn't until 1980 that I took another listen to *Imagine*. A good listen. Why? Apparently, John Lennon's words, his politics and his passions, put him in the crosshairs of an assassin.

I remember hearing about Lennon's murder during a Monday night Patriots game against the Miami Dolphins, a gridiron smackdown I never missed. So, when I settled in with some popcorn and a soda, that's what I expected for my Monday night, a football game. That's not what I got. If you were tuned into that night's game then you don't need to 'imagine' the action-call of Frank Gifford being interrupted by Howard Cosell with these words:

> "We have to say it. Remember, this is just a football game. No matter who wins or loses. An unspeakable tragedy confirmed to us by ABC News in New York City. John Lennon, outside of his apartment building on the West Side of New York City, the most famous, perhaps of all of the Beatles, shot twice in the back, rushed to Roosevelt Hospital, dead on arrival. Hard to go back to the game after that news flash, which in duty bound, we had to take."
>
> ~ Howard Cosell

Why am I telling you this? It's part of my history. I think it's interesting. It's a written segue. I've been having some weird dreams lately and in one of them, the events surrounding The Beatles breakup, and the Lennon/Ono coupling, and the politics and passions of that period in time tumbled freely in my semi-sedated mind.

The Lennon night — yeup, I've begun naming my weird dream nights. My world's become a bit small, and whatever needs to be done to make it interesting for me, is done. Anyway, I woke to find a few tears had started their trip down a well-established path on my cheeks, and the words from *Imagine* were being whispered from my lips. Certain lyrics pushed in and began digging a trench in my head and heart. *Nothing to kill or die for, And no religion, too, Imagine all the people, Livin' life in peace…*

I've figured out why those particular lyrics found me. The religion part, or the God part of my religion, is sort of the point of this blog, and I'll get to it, but I need to explain something. You know I don't reread my blogs once they've been posted, but in order to write Blogs 63 and 65, I needed to take a look back at my written words, and the thoughts and feelings I hoped they conveyed. Despite the emotional shit fest back then, I think I mostly hit the mark. For the purposes of these two blogs, the things I hoped to find there, were there and I'll be using them.

We've come to the point of this blog … We're doing some recap from. In Blog 3, Being Angry at God, I wrote:

> Someone asked me if I am mad at God. To be perfectly honest, the question caught me off guard. It never occurred to me that that was an option. For the record, I am not mad at God. I don't think He got up one day and said, "Hmmmmm, I'm gonna screw with Sheryll O'Brien and I'm gonna screw with her big time" … I believe He knows I am facing challenges and I pray that He hears my request — that I am given no more than I can handle. If that ends up being a handful of months, or perhaps a year, then so be it. I believe He supports my decision to not torture myself when I'm told there is no more hope, I know He does not want me to suffer. So, I guess what I'm saying is this, I will take the hand of God and trust that He will help me find my way through this mess, that He will hold me in his mercy because He accepts my faith in Him. And I believe my God is grateful that I chose to follow Him through my life and now toward my death.

I've had lots of time to think since then, some might say, *"Too much time."* No arguments from me, well some arguments because let's face it time is a pretty big commodity for someone like me. So I gratefully accept what I've been given. Anyway, I've had the time, so I've done the thinking. Central to my 'religious' thoughts was my strongly-held belief that God didn't **do** this to me. And then I read Blog 12, Firsts and Lasts, the part where I was mentioning to Father Dude a complaint I was having in the God department. I wrote:

> The only thing I have prayed for since the beginning of this ordeal, is that God won't give me more than I can handle. Sometimes, I think He might be missing my prayer … I've sort of been getting one blow after another: you have metastatic breast cancer; it's in your bones; it's full body bone cancer; it is terminal; your femur and L-1 are your biggest concerns; dying of bone cancer is excruciatingly painful; there may be a pill that can help with the amount of pain you have getting from here to hospice; you'll need to have a bone biopsy to see if you're eligible for the pill; the biopsy can be painful; you should meet with hospice in the near future; you should begin planning a funeral; and, and, and — all of this happening in the span of a few weeks. It's sort of been a lot, and it feels like it's more than I can handle, sometimes …
>
> But I guess I'm handling it because my friends and family tell me they can't believe how strong I am, or how important it is for me and for others that I'm blogging about this, or how in awe they are that I'm still enjoying life.

Apparently, I took another whack at trying to make sense of this mess I'm in. In Blog 15, Blessings Big and Small, I wrote:

Happily, I was put on notice that I am on my final journey. For those who know me well, you know that my receiving this little tidbit of information is for the best. After all, I am a planner, an organizer, a doer. I manage my life to the nanosecond, and to varying degrees, I manage the lives of those around me. I make lists for everything, even make lists reminding myself that I have lists. So, I imagine I would have been really pissed if I found myself dead one day leaving behind a basket of unfolded towels, or a half-written novel, or a half-eaten Ben & Jerry's in the freezer ... I'm quite sure God knows about my obsessive compulsive disorder, and I suspect it weighed heavily into His decision to give me fair warning about my impending demise ... and ... If I'd died suddenly, I wouldn't have had the opportunity to write a book for Hadley, to put a lifetime of grandmotherly advice between the covers of a 75 page book. Then again, I wouldn't have had gut-wrenching time to grieve the things that I won't be here to share with her. And to ache in places I didn't know existed.

It breaks my heart that she will be profoundly sad when she no longer finds her MammyGrams' wide open arms ready for the hug that she'll need, the hug only I can give, but won't be here to give ... My having time to really enjoy the things that could have slipped by without my appreciating them is a really big blessing. As for the small blessings, I guess there's really no such thing.

Okay. So, back then I didn't think God gave me terminal bone cancer **but** I did think He was torturing me with more than I could handle **and** I also thought he was blessing me with the gift of time. Head swirl. Maybe not for you, but for me. During the quiet and stillness of many nights I went back to the basics of my religious roots, not necessarily the best place to go when you're hopped up on drugs and your only companion is confusion, but it's now or never. Right?

Greendale People's Church

In Sunday School, from kindergarten through high school, the religious learning was all Bible based. Go figure. In the simplest of terms, Protestants don't have a church hierarchy to learn about or rules to follow beyond the Ten Commandments and the Golden Rule, so there's some drilling down on the words written on the pages of the Bible. Grade schoolers begin by learning the names of the books and then go through them one by one in age-appropriate fashion. The New Testament is left to high schoolers to continue their studies on their own. Why? Because high schoolers become part of the adult congregation and are welcomed at weekly church services in the chapel or the sanctuary.

I always chose the balcony in the sanctuary. Kinda felt cool looking down on the gatherers. My mother always sat in the pew at the base of a stained-glass window honoring Hannah and Esther. I found comfort whenever I saw her there. Except, on the somewhat rare occasion, when she fell into a fit of laughter with her bestie, Peggy Martin. I don't know what would happen with the two, but off they'd go on an uncontrollable, and unmistakable shaking fit of the giggles. They'd cover their mouths, and scooch away from one another, pretending it was the other one who was causing a scene. The ritualistic-remedy of pew-spacing had its successes, and the two Deaconesses would simmer down, until Round Two took over. FYI Mom, your laughing jigs were legendary. For shame. For shame.

Anyway, during long, lonely nights, I started searching my head for Biblical lessons about the things that were bothering me. A few times, I considered reading the Bible, something I admit I haven't done in a very long time. The idea felt so cliché. Dying woman + Biblical reading = brown-nose points with God. That didn't feel right, and besides, I still have that last unread Agatha breathing down my neck!

So, what's a girl to do … I cracked the spine of neither, but I did drill down into my religious memories a bit. I remembered some stuff; the most important thing, hands down, was that Luke the Evangelist is my guy. I made a promise to read some of the Gospel of Luke, and Acts before I leave the mortal plane, no matter what anyone thinks about it. With that plan behind me, I pushed into this question: does God have a hand in everything — even in my getting cancer? I remembered touching on some anger at God in one of my blogs. I went on a search, and there it was in Blog 29, I Am Dying. Here is some of what I wrote:

> I'm pissed that I won't be seeing Wells Beach again. I'm profoundly sad that I won't write another novel…I'm scared shitless by what's next and how it will play out…I can barely type through my tears remembering in great detail my need to call out to Tim, to have him come sit with me, and how overwhelming the urge was to rage at someone. So I chose God because I knew He was there with me. I've felt Him near me so often lately. Without my reaching out to Him in prayer, I have felt Him near…In that moment of darkness I was angry at God and I let him have it, not because I blame Him for this, but because there was no one else to be angry with. I know the things happening to me are no one's fault, certainly not His. My faith in Him assured me that He'd take and accept my rage and He'd keep me safe while I faced my truths…That's why I found the strength to call this out in the darkness that allowed such things. "I am

angry that I am dying!" And then I said the words that surprised me to my core. "WHY ME?"

And there it was, the ramble that clarified things. I demanded an answer from God: Why Me? That left me with a question: did I secretly blame God for this? Head Spin!

And then this happened … I looked at my body scan and in Blog 56, Turning the Corner, I wrote:

On November 9, 2021, Tim took me to UMass hospital for the much-dreaded bone scan. I met with a very understanding and very patient technician who helped prepare me physically and mentally for an IV push of radioactive material into my veins, and a terrifying trip into a partially enclosed machine…The results of that scan showed widespread cancer throughout my skeleton. I was put on high alert that the imminent cause of concern was a break of a major bone or the collapse of my spine which would lead to a rather quick demise. Barring that, it might take six months for the cancer to claim me.

The fear of a broken bone has been forefront in my mind since my diagnosis. My fear ratcheted up when I looked at my bone scan results a month or so ago and saw how much cancer is inside of me and how much deterioration has taken place. I was sort of pissed with myself when I first looked at the images. It was one thing hearing Dr. Wonderful tell me I had bone cancer from my skull to my knees, but believe you me, his words took on greater meaning when I saw the images for myself. You'll see it for yourself in Blog 64. If you so choose.

As for getting from back then to right here on thoughts about God's hand in all this, I've spent time with religious thoughts and memories and I've spent time riding the pendulum between Does It Really Matter and You Bet Your Ass It Does.

And then this happened … I flipped the coin and came up with this thought process: I was a very sick woman for a very long time and I had absolutely no idea **AND** I am a very sick woman who will die sooner rather than later **AND** I am a woman who probably should have died already. So, this is where I am: I don't know if His hand is in all of this. I do know it's a miracle that I'm still alive. I don't need to 'imagine' who is responsible for miracles. God is good. God is great. And I love Him.

64. Body Scan …

Body Scan: Sheryll O'Brien – November 2021

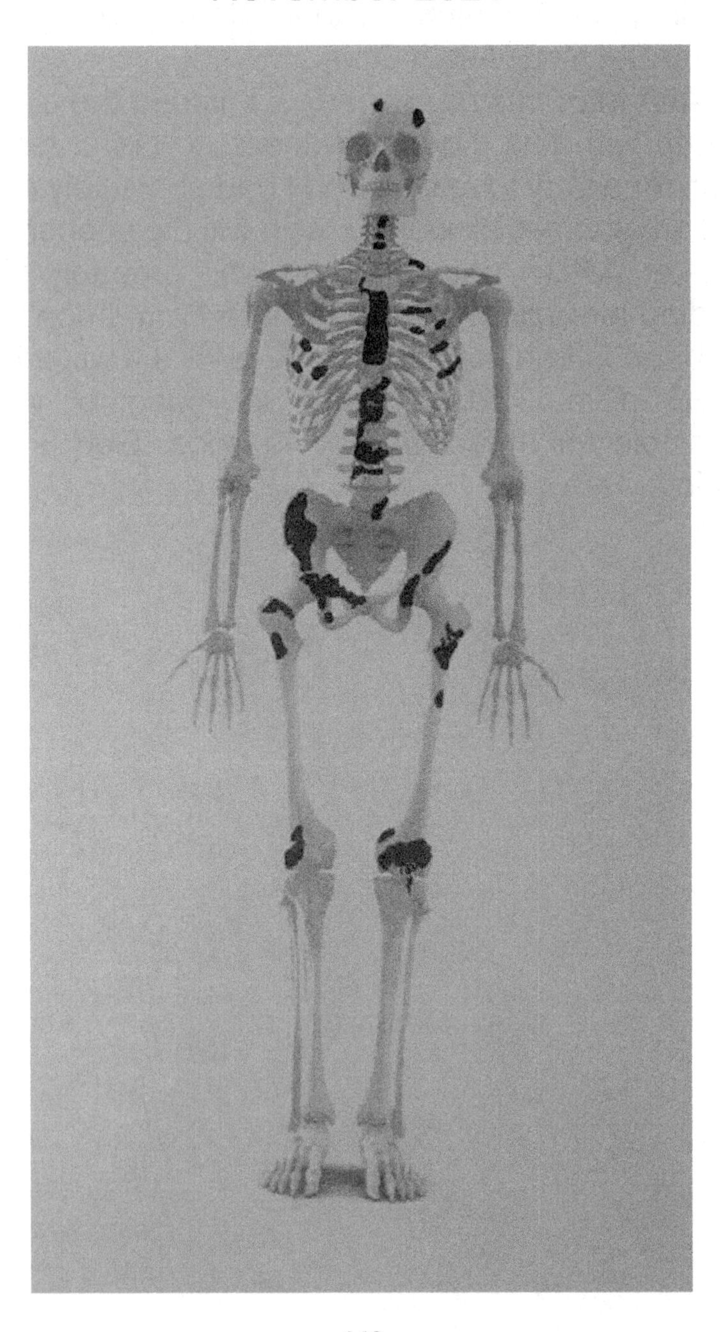

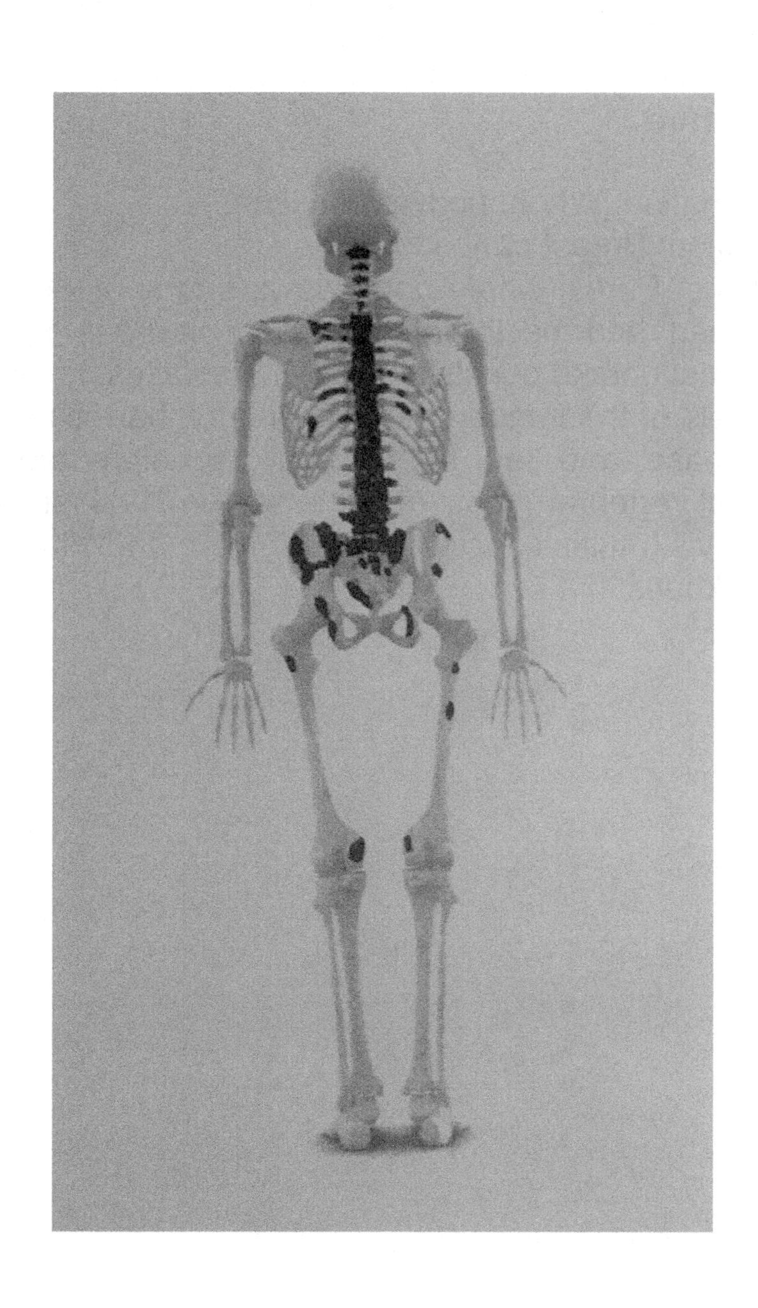

Narrative

Examination: Whole body bone scan.
Indication: Breast cancer.
Findings: Partial whole body views and spot views of the head and neck demonstrate numerous foci of abnormal uptake consistent with metastases, involving all levels of the imaged thoracic and lumbar spine, the skull base and left frontal skull, possibly multiple cervical vertebrae, most ribs, the sacrum, both sides of the pelvis (multiple foci) and both femora and bilaterally in the knees.

When I began writing my blog…

I feared I might not make it through the 2021 holiday season; I certainly had no reasonable expectation that I would live beyond the ‘possible six months’ I was given. As I write this, I am just shy of marking my ninth month.

I remember when I opened a word document and typed the number 14. I wondered at that time how many blogs I would get to write. I just finished Blog 97. That is amazing to me. Back around the 30 blog mark, there came a steady request from readers that I publish the blogs as a book. As the number of blogs grew and grew, it caused me to consider the best way to present my final writings. Ultimately, it seemed wise to have a Book One and Book Two.

It is rather odd to say, “I hope you enjoyed Book One.” After all, this is an end of life story — my end of life story. As I said in the beginning, the pages of Muah! Would hold wonderful and wacky childhood memories, and tidbits that turned into treasured traditions, and tales that reminded me of the full, rich life I’ve lived — a life that is ending far too soon for my liking — a life that I am honored to share with you.

We all know what the ultimate ending of Book Two will be, but there is so mush more living, laughing, and loving to present to you. I hope you will join me and my family and friends as we finish Muah! The Sound of a Kiss Goodbye.

~ Sheryll

Made in United States
North Haven, CT
24 September 2022